BRIT
ELECT
& PARTIES
REVIEW
VOLUME 14

EDITORS

Roger Scully • Justin Fisher
Paul Webb • David Broughton

First published in 2004 in Great Britain by
TAYLOR & FRANCIS LTD.
4 Park Square, Milton Park, Abingdon, Oxfordshire OX14 4RN

and in the United States of America by
TAYLOR & FRANCIS GROUP JOURNALS
325 Chestnut Street, Suite 800, Philadelphia,
PA 19106, USA

Website www.tandf.co.uk/journals

British Library Cataloguing in Publication Data

A catalog record of this
book has been requested.

ISBN 0 4153 6266 0
ISSN 1368 9886

Printed in Great Britain by
Antony Rowe, Ltd., Chippenham, Wilts.

CONTENTS

Devolution

Parties and Political Elites

PREFACE

This is the fourteenth annual volume published under the auspices of the Elections, Public Opinion and Parties (EPOP) specialist group of the Political Studies Association (PSA) of the United Kingdom. EPOP continues to thrive as a PSA specialist group, and the success of these volumes reflects the extraordinary vigour both of the group and of UK-based research in the areas of political science that EPOP covers.

Earlier versions of the contributions to this volume were presented at EPOP-sponsored panels at the PSA's annual conference in Leicester in April 2003, or at EPOP's annual conference in Cardiff in September 2003. As with all previous volumes of the *Review*, the articles here have been subject to rigorous peer-review and have been extensively revised before publication. We are grateful to all the authors for producing this excellent collection of papers and for responding to referee comments in a timely manner.

The 2003 Cardiff conference was distinguished by excellent weather and a welcome from the First Minister for Wales, Rt Hon. Rhodri Morgan AM. The conference was also notable for excellent contributions from many overseas speakers and an unprecedented number of graduate students; for enabling many of these two groups to attend, we are very grateful for financial support from the ESRC, two of the ESRC's Research Programmes (*Democracy and Participation* and *Future Governance*), the British Academy Conference Fund, the School of European Studies at Cardiff University, the PSA Conference Fund, the Electoral Commission and the McDougall Trust.

We are grateful to the Thistle Hotel, Cardiff, and to local organiser David Broughton and his conference team for the smooth running of the Cardiff conference. And we would also like to thank Cathy Jennings of Frank Cass and Daniel Och of Taylor & Francis, for ensuring that corporate takeovers did not disrupt the smooth production of the *Review*.

For further information on EPOP membership, and on the annual conference, please see the group's website: http://www.psa.ac.uk/spgrp/epop/epop.htm.

Roger Scully   David Broughton   Justin Fisher   Paul Webb

NOTES ON CONTRIBUTORS

Robert Andersen is Assistant Professor in Sociology at McMaster University and a Research Fellow with the Centre for Research into Elections and Social Trends, Department of Sociology, University of Oxford. His research and teaching interests are in political sociology, social inequality and social statistics.

David Broughton is a Senior Lecturer in Politics in the School of European Studies at Cardiff University. He co-edited the first six volumes of *British Elections & Parties Review* between 1991 and 1996. He has written two recent articles on public opinion under the current Labour government since 1997 for *Developments in Politics*, chapters on Participation and Voting for *Developments in West European Politics 2* (Palgrave, 2002), and on the 2001 British General Election for *The Conservatives in Crisis* (Manchester University Press, 2003) as well as two articles for *Representation* on the Welsh Assembly elections in 1999 and 2003.

Sarah Butt is a graduate student at Nuffield College, University of Oxford. Her doctoral research examines the capacity of opposition parties to influence voter choices and election outcomes in Britain.

Harold Clarke is Ashbel Smith Professor, School of Social Sciences, University of Texas at Dallas, and Adjunct Professor of Government, University of Essex. He is Editor-in-Chief of *Electoral Studies* and Joint Editor of *Political Research Quarterly*.

Philip Cowley is Reader in Parliamentary Government at the University of Nottingham. His previous publications include *Revolts and Rebellions: Parliamentary Voting Under Blair* (Politico's, 2002) and *Conscience and Parliament* (Frank Cass, 1998).

Geoffrey Evans is Official Fellow in Politics and Professor of the Sociology of Politics at Nuffield College, University of Oxford. He is co-editor of *Electoral Studies*, and has published widely on electoral change, social class and political behaviour.

Justin Fisher is Senior Lecturer in Political Science at Brunel University and convenor of EPOP. He is the editor of *Central Debates in British Politics*

(Longman, 2002) and numerous articles and chapters on parties, elections and campaigning. He has recently edited a special issue of *Party Politics* on comparative party finance (forthcoming 2004).

Peter Fitzgerald is currently completing a PhD on political leadership at Dublin City University, having completed a Masters on organizational change in the Irish Labour Party. He has contributed to the forthcoming fourth edition of *Politics in the Republic of Ireland*. His research interests include political parties, political leadership and political marketing.

Oliver Heath is a PhD student in the Department of Government at the University of Essex. His current research interests include political participation, social capital and political culture in Britain.

Peter John is Professor of Politics in the School of Politics and Sociology, Birkbeck College, University of London. He teaches and researches into public policy and urban politics and is author of *Analysing Public Policy* (Pinter, 1998) and *Local Governance in Western Europe* (Sage, 2001).

Ron Johnston is Professor in the School of Geographical Sciences at the University of Bristol. His research covers various aspects of electoral geography, and he is currently involved in a large ESRC project exploring neighbourhood effects in British voting patterns.

Fiachra Kennedy is a member of the Irish National Election Study research team as well as a researcher for the Environmental Values, Attitudes and Behaviours Research Programme and an Associate Editor for *Irish Political Studies*. He is completing a PhD thesis in comparative politics at Trinity College Dublin.

Pat Lyons is a member of a research network examining the Dynamics and Obstacles to EU Governance at the Department of West European Studies, Charles University, Prague. Previously, he was a research fellow at the Public Opinion and Political Behaviour Research Programme at the Institute for the Study of Social Change, University College Dublin. He is completing a PhD thesis on Irish public opinion at the Department of Political Science, Trinity College Dublin.

Nicola McEwen is Lecturer in Politics at the University of Edinburgh and Associate Director of the University's Institute of Governance. She obtained her PhD from the University of Sheffield in 2001, after completing a doctoral thesis on the territorial impact of welfare state development in Scotland and

BRITISH ELECTIONS & PARTIES REVIEW

Quebec. Her main research interests include comparative nationalism and territorial politics, the politics of devolution in the UK, and Scottish politics, and she is currently working on a monograph and an edited collection on nationalism and the welfare state.

Michael Marsh is Associate Professor of Political Science at Trinity College Dublin. He was a principal investigator for the first Irish election study (2002) and is currently writing a book on that study. He recently co-authored with Michael Gallagher *Days of Blue Loyalty*, a study of the Fine Gael party (2002) and co-edited two books on the 2002 general election: *The Sunday Tribune Guide to Irish Politics* (2002) and *How Ireland Voted 2002* (2003).

Zoë Morris is Nuffield Fellow in Health Policy at the Judge Institute of Management, University of Cambridge. Before that she was a research associate at the Faculty of Social and Political Sciences, University of Cambridge. Her research interests relate to public policy, mainly education and health.

Charles Pattie is Professor of Geography at the University of Sheffield. He has published widely with Ron Johnston on electoral geography and recently completed (with Patrick Seyd and Paul Whiteley) *Citizenship in Britain: Values, Participation and Democracy,* drawing on the ESRC-funded Citizen Audit (Cambridge University Press, 2004). He is currently working with Ron Johnston on *Putting Voters in Their Place* (Oxford University Press), an introduction to the electoral geography of the United Kingdom.

David Sanders is Professor of Government at the University of Essex and co-editor of the *British Journal of Political Science.* Along with Harold Clarke and Paul Whiteley, he directed the 2001 British Election Study. Clarke, Whiteley, Sanders and Marianne Stewart are co-authors of *Political Choice in Britain* (Oxford University Press, 2004).

Roger Scully is Senior Lecturer in the Department of International Politics and Director of the Jean Monnet Centre for European Studies at the University of Wales, Aberystwyth.

Patrick Seyd is Professor of Politics at the University of Sheffield. He has written extensively on party politics and party membership, including (with Paul Whiteley) *High Intensity Participation* (Michigan University Press, 2002). He recently completed (with Charles Pattie and Paul Whiteley) *Citizenship in Britain: Values, Participation and Democracy,* drawing on the ESRC-funded Citizen Audit (Cambridge University Press, 2004).

Marianne Stewart is Professor, Government, Politics and Political Economy, University of Texas at Dallas. From 1998 to 2000, she was Political Science Program Director and Visiting Scientist, Division of Social and Economic Sciences, Directorate for Social, Behavioral and Economic Research, National Science Foundation.

Mark Stuart is a research assistant at the University of Nottingham and a Research Fellow in the Centre for Legislative Studies at the University of Hull. He is writing the authorized biography of John Smith.

Paul Webb is Professor of Politics at the University of Sussex. His research interests focus on representative democracy, particularly party and electoral politics. He is co-editor of *Party Politics*, and his recent books include *The Modern British Party System* (Sage, 2000) and *Political Parties in Advanced Industrial Democracies* (Oxford University Press, 2002).

Paul Whiteley is Professor of Government at the University of Essex. He was Director of the ESRC's Democracy and Participation Programme, Economic and Social Research Council from 1998 to 2003. He recently completed (with Patrick Seyd and Charles Pattie) *Citizenship in Britain: Values, Participation and Democracy*, drawing on the ESRC-funded Citizen Audit (Cambridge University Press, 2004). He has also conducted research (with Patrick Seyd) into party membership, including *High Intensity Participation* (Michigan University Press, 2002).

Richard Wyn Jones is Senior Lecturer in the Department of International Politics at University of Wales, Aberystwyth, and Director of the Institute of Welsh Politics.

ABSTRACTS

Political Knowledge and Routes to Party Choice in the British General Election of 2001

Sarah Butt

This article explores the role of political knowledge in determining voter choices in Britain. The importance of knowledge depends on what is assumed about the basis upon which choices are made; not all routes to party choice need be equally dependent on knowledge. Using data from the general election of 2001 this article confirms the importance of political knowledge for successful issue voting. It then goes on to consider the effectiveness of retrospective voting as a heuristic for party choice. The evidence suggests that all voters can and do make use of retrospective evaluations of government performance in deciding how to vote. However, political knowledge influences the type of retrospective evaluations relied upon and the extent to which these evaluations are an accurate reflection of government performance.

Do Issues Decide? Partisan Conditioning and Perceptions of Party Issue Positions across the Electoral Cycle

Geoffrey Evans and Robert Andersen

In this article we examine the impact of long-term partisan loyalties on perceptions of party positions on major issue dimensions. In contrast to the assumptions of issue voting theories, we argue that partisanship is a pervasive force shaping citizens' perceptions of party positions and the proximity between those positions and their own issue preferences. The analysis employs a five-wave inter-election panel study to demonstrate the impact of Labour partisanship on perceptions of where the parties stand. We then model the reciprocal influences between Labour Party support and issue perceptions over the electoral cycle, revealing contemporaneous and lagged effects of partisanship on perceptions of issue proximity that far outweigh the contemporaneous effect of proximity on party choice. We conclude that partisan bias in political perceptions plays a crucial role in conditioning perceptions of party issue positions and that conventional rational choice interpretations of the associations between issue perceptions and vote choice are flawed.

Switching and Splitting: Local Contexts and Campaigns from Intentions to the Ballot Box – New Zealand 1999

Ron Johnston and Charles Pattie

Under New Zealand's multi-member proportional (MMP) electoral system, electors have two votes, one for a national party list and the other for a constituency MP. The results of the list vote determine the composition of the House of Representatives, so that electors may vote a split-ticket. When the election campaign starts, most voters have decided which party they will vote for in each contest, but many change their minds during the campaign. Using the 1999 New Zealand Election Study pre- and post-election surveys, this article reports on successful tests of hypotheses regarding the nature of those changes in voter decisions.

Modelling the Components of Political Action in Britain: The Impact of Civic Skills, Social Capital and Political Support
Oliver Heath

This article analyses the individual-level determinants of voting, campaign activity and participation in social movements. It shows that alternative types of political action are similar in some respects and different in others. These similarities and differences are related to the components of action, such as whether it is individual or collective, electoral or non-electoral. The article shows that whereas civic skills and political engagement are associated with all three types of activity, political costs and social capital are only associated with collective types of action. Moreover, whereas political support has a positive association with electoral participation it has a negative association with non-electoral participation.

What are the Origins of Social Capital? Results from a Panel Survey of Young People
Peter John and Zoë Morris

The literature on social capital is dominated by a debate about its beneficial consequences for societies and localities, but there is much less research about its origins. The conventional wisdom indicates that levels of social capital, such as volunteering and trust, transfer through families, so reflect variations in social-economic status (SES). Given this powerful driver, the impact of schools and citizenship education is often thought to be limited. But these results are not conclusive, leaving the research agenda open. To test the impact of school context on social capital, this research uses multi-level models to analyse a panel survey of 15–17-year-olds in Hertfordshire in 2000 and 2001. In wave one we find that television watching depresses trust and volunteering; civic education predicts volunteering and trust. Across the panel we find that television watching depresses trust and civic education predicts volunteering. These findings add to a growing body of knowledge about the beneficial effects of citizenship education, even if the traditional and powerful mechanisms of socialization remain intact.

The Dynamics of Citizenship: The Effects of the General Election on Citizenship

Charles Pattie, Patrick Seyd and Paul Whiteley

One of the side-effects of the 2001 British General Election was a focus of attention on politics. While turnout fell compared to 1997, other forms of political activism seem to have been more common after the election than before it, suggesting some mobilization. This article investigates panel data drawn from the Citizen Audit survey to understand the factors that influence the dynamics of citizenship in the UK. On the whole, the more interested people were in politics to start with, the more they felt they got out of their lives, the greater the resources they had to draw on, and the better integrated they were into informal networks of friends and acquaintances, the more active they became over time, and the more positive they felt in their civic attitudes. But the more television a respondent reported watching on average in 2000, the less likely they were to increase their political engagement a year later.

Public Attitudes towards Political Protest in Britain, 2000–2002

David Sanders, Harold Clarke, Marianne Stewart and Paul Whiteley

The article examines the explanatory power of six different, though in some respects complimentary, theoretical accounts of the sources of protest activity. The rival models – Relative Deprivation, Cognitive Engagement, Civic Voluntarism, Social Capital, Rational Actor and General Incentives – are tested using data from a series of monthly representative sample surveys, conducted between July 2000 and December 2002. The empirical results show that people turn to protest for three main reasons: because they make rational calculations about its costs and benefits; because they believe that it can rectify the sense of dissatisfaction or deprivation that they feel; and because they are mobilized into action by personal social contacts. Successful protests by a minority also act as a spur for the majority to increase its 'protest potential'.

Opinion Polling in Scotland: An Analysis of the 2003 Scottish Parliament Election

Nicola McEwen

In contrast to election polling at the UK level, opinion polling in Scotland has never faced sustained scrutiny. This article aims to take a small step towards bridging the 'scrutiny gap'. It focuses upon opinion polls conducted in advance of the 2003 Scottish Parliament election, revealing substantial inaccuracies in polling results. It argues that techniques employed in conducting Scottish polls require revision to address problems evident in polling across Britain. It is further argued that pollsters must devise techniques appropriate to meet the challenges of polling in an additional member electoral system and a distinctive, multi-party political system.

Minor Tremor but Several Casualties: The 2003 Welsh Election
Richard Wyn Jones and Roger Scully

The inaugural election to the devolved National Assembly for Wales in May 1999 produced a sensational result, often described since as a 'quiet earth-quake' in Welsh politics. Four years on, the second election saw a less dramatic, but still important outcome. In this article we review the background to the May 2003 election, analyse the results and examine detailed survey evidence about how 2003 differed from 1999 in terms of the factors shaping voting patterns and the overall outcome in Wales' second devolved election.

When Sheep Bark: The Parliamentary Labour Party since 2001
Philip Cowley and Mark Stuart

This article examines the voting behaviour of Labour MPs in the first two sessions of the 2001 Parliament. It details the rebellions that have taken place so far, placing them in their historical context, and shows that the government whips face a parliamentary party in which Labour MPs are now rebelling more often than government MPs in any post-war Parliament. It lists the most rebellious Labour MP and explains how far the habit of rebel-lion has now spread within the PLP. It examines the behaviour of the 2001 intake in detail – to determine the effect of changes in Labour's selection procedures – as well as examining the factional nature of the voting behav-iour. Although there are many MPs who are willing to rebel against it, the government does not yet face any large-scale factional opposition on the backbenches of the PLP.

The Irish Labour Party Leadership Election, 2002: A Survey of Party Members
Peter Fitzgerald, Fiachra Kennedy and Pat Lyons

Political parties are seen within liberal democracies to be essential organiza-tions for the selection of candidates and leaders. While voters have some choice over the candidates elected they have much less choice over the selec-tion of prime minister and ministers following the process of government formation. This makes leadership elections within political parties an impor-tant issue. Until recently all leadership elections within Irish political parties were restricted to members of parliament, with ordinary party members having no direct role to play in this process, but in October 2002, the Irish Labour Party chose its new leader using a postal ballot with an Alternative Vote (AV) electoral rule. In this article we provide a brief discussion and analysis of this unique election and the opportunities which leadership election surveys offer scholars of political parties, electoral behaviour, political participation and representation.

None of that Post-modern Stuff around Here: Grassroots Campaigning in the 2002 Irish General Election

Michael Marsh

This article explores grassroots campaigning in Ireland using evidence from the 2002 Irish election study. It describes a very extensive system of door-to-door campaigning carried out both by the candidates themselves and by teams of party workers with around four-fifths of voters reporting that contact was made with their home. This is very unusual in modern democracies. There remains some doubt, however, about whether such campaigning matters in the modern era. This article demonstrates strong links between vote choice and contact, with association evident between lower preferences and contact as well as first preferences and contact. Significant associations remain even when controls are introduced for political predispositions, and it is suggested that this provides good evidence for the argument that personal campaigning, and in particular campaigning by the candidates themselves, matters in Irish general elections.

PUBLIC ATTITUDES AND VOTING

Political Knowledge and Routes to Party Choice in the British General Election of 2001

Sarah Butt

Political knowledge has been described as the 'currency of citizenship' and a necessary resource for effective political participation (Delli Carpini and Keeter, 1996: 8). However, like many resources, political knowledge is not equally distributed across the population. This raises the possibility that less knowledgeable individuals are disadvantaged by their lack of knowledge when it comes to participating effectively in the electoral process. Research has shown that political knowledge affects the nature of people's political opinions with more highly knowledgeable individuals holding sets of opinions that tend to be both more internally consistent and more stable over time (Zaller, 1992; Bartle, 2000). Knowledge may also affect actual vote choice and the ability of voters to translate their opinions into effective party choices (Bartels, 1996).

Whether or not this is the case depends on how voters make their choices and decide how to vote. There are a number of possible routes to party choice – not all of which are equally dependent on political knowledge. Research in both the US and Britain has demonstrated the importance of political knowledge for successful issue voting. Less knowledgeable voters are more likely to make mistakes in matching their own policy positions to party platforms, and so are less likely to vote for a party supportive of their policy interests (Delli Carpini and Keeter, 1996; Andersen et al., 2002). However, the extensive literature on decision heuristics highlights a range of different informational shortcuts that voters can use to make approximately rational choices even on the basis of very little knowledge (Popkin, 1991; Sniderman et al., 1991). One such heuristic is the so-called 'incumbency' heuristic, with voters deciding to vote for or against the incumbent party depending on its record in office.

This article compares the effects of knowledge on issue-based versus retrospective voting, and consider the usefulness of retrospective voting as a heuristic for vote choice. At first glance, voting retrospectively to reward or punish the incumbent party for its performance in office appears to be an effective route to party choice for all voters, regardless of political knowledge. The fact that the governing party stands to be 'punished' if the electorate is dissatisfied with its performance means that retrospective voting is effective

British Elections & Parties Review, Vol. 14, 2004, pp. 3–17
ISSN 1368-9886 print
DOI: 10.1080/1368988042000258754   © 2004 Taylor & Francis Ltd.

in ensuring that governments remain accountable and act in voters' interests (Key, 1964; Fiorina, 1981). However, compared to issue voting it places far fewer demands on voters. Voters need not have a detailed knowledge of party platforms or a range of issues; they need only have an opinion on whether they are happy with the job the current government is doing, something they can establish from their everyday experiences.

However, political knowledge may make a difference to the nature of the judgements that voters form about the government's performance and the extent to which these judgements are accurate. Less knowledgeable voters may rely more heavily on evaluations of their own personal experiences when judging government performance because this information is particularly low cost and easily obtainable (Delli Carpini and Keeter, 1996). More knowledgeable voters should take greater account of objective economic indicators such as the unemployment rate and consult external sources of information such as television news in forming their subjective evaluations (Mutz, 1993). Knowledge may also make a difference to the way in which voters attribute responsibility for economic outcomes to the government, with more knowledgeable voters having greater awareness of the fact that a wide range of actors besides the government may influence economic outcomes (Abramowitz et al., 1988; Gomez and Wilson, 2001). Such differences could have potentially important consequences for the effectiveness of retrospective voting as a means of holding the government to account.

Whilst the effect of knowledge on retrospective voting has been much researched in the United States it has received less attention in the British context. This article goes some way to redressing this balance by examining the effects of knowledge on both issue based and retrospective performance voting in the 2001 general election. Using data from the British Election Panel Study (BEPS) 1997–2001, it tests the proposition that all voters, regardless of knowledge levels, make use of retrospective evaluations in deciding how to vote.[1] It also considers how the nature of these evaluations differs with knowledge and compares the relative importance of personal versus national economic evaluations for the vote choices of high and low knowledge voters.

Measuring Political Knowledge

Before investigating the effects of political knowledge on vote choice, the concept of political knowledge must be defined. Downs argues that there are three broad requirements for voters to make rational, informed decisions: *reason* or *cognitive capacity*, *contextual knowledge* (i.e. the background knowledge relevant to understanding a given field such as politics), and *information* (i.e. data about current developments in the relevant field such as party issue positions) (Downs, 1957: 79). Within the existing literature, political knowledge has, at various times, been defined according to each of these three criteria. This article follows the example of several authors including Delli Carpini and Keeter (1996) and Gomez and Wilson (2001) by focusing on contextual or civics knowledge. Contextual knowledge is a key aspect of political knowledge, with a basic understanding of the political process being an important pre-requisite for the accumulation and interpretation of other, more specific, knowledge.

The 1997–2001 British Election Panel Study included a political knowledge quiz that provides us with a measure of respondents' civics knowledge. Respondents were asked six true or false questions testing their knowledge of the number of MPs in the House of Commons, the maximum time between elections, the type of electoral system used in Britain, the type of MP who sits on parliamentary committees, whether European elections were held separately from general elections and whether MPs have to pay a deposit to stand for election. They were then assigned a score from 0 to 6 depending on the number of correct answers given. In line with previous work those responding 'don't know' were treated as having given an incorrect answer.[2] The knowledge quiz has some advantageous features as a measure of knowledge. It is completely objective, relying neither on interviewers' assessments of respondents' knowledge nor respondents' self-reported knowledge, the latter likely to be biased as respondents try to appear 'good citizens' (Zaller, 1992: 335). Second, there is evidence that civics knowledge is measuring relevant knowledge; it is positively correlated with other aspects of more specific knowledge such as that concerning party issue positions which are of direct importance for voter choices (Andersen et al., 2002).

Table 1 shows the distribution of correct responses to the knowledge quiz. The distribution is skewed with, for example, nearly a third of respondents giving correct answers to all six questions. However, a significant proportion of respondents (17%) answered fewer than half of the questions correctly, confirming that levels of knowledge do vary across the electorate. In the analysis below, the importance of knowledge for party choice is tested by comparing the behaviour of high, medium and low knowledge voters. Respondents giving three or fewer correct answers are considered as low knowledge, those answering all six correctly are considered as high knowledge with the remainder classified as medium knowledge.[3]

The effect of political knowledge on both issue-based and retrospective voting will be considered. Successful issue voting is measured according to people's tendency to cast their vote for the party whose policy position is closest to their own on three major issues: taxation and spending, Europe, and privatization. The positions of both voters and parties on each issue are identified along 11-point scales with lower scores indicating attitudes in favour of

TABLE 1
DISTRIBUTION OF RESPONSES TO POLITICAL KNOWLEDGE QUIZ

No. correct	% respondents
0	2
1	6
2	9
3	12
4	17
5	21
6	32

Note: N=2323.
Source: BEPS, 1997–2001.

increased spending, more nationalization and further integration with Europe. Higher scores indicate a preference for tax cuts, greater privatization and a reduction in ties with Europe. On the basis of their election manifestos, the Conservatives are taken to be furthest to the right (i.e. score highest) on all three issues in 2001. The Liberal Democrats are furthest to the left (score lowest) on taxation and Europe, whilst Labour are furthest to the left on privatization. If people did vote in line with their policy interests in 2001, voters' position on the issue scales should be positively correlated with support for the Conservatives over either of the other two parties.

Retrospective voting will be measured according to people's tendency to vote in line with their evaluations of economic performance. Respondents' evaluations of what happened to both their personal financial situation and the national economy over the 12 months preceding the election will be considered. This allows us to test whether knowledge affects the type of retrospective evaluations relied upon. Responses are coded on a five-point scale ranging from 1 (= 'got a lot worse') to 5 (= 'got a lot better'). If retrospective voting is taking place we would therefore expect to observe a negative relationship between economic evaluations and support for the incumbent Labour Party.

Political Knowledge and Voter Opinions

The first step in investigating how civics knowledge affects vote choice is to consider whether voters' evaluations of the key variables hypothesized to influence vote choice, namely party issue positions and economic performance, differ with knowledge. The evidence from looking at respondents' placements of the parties along the various issue scales suggests that there are

TABLE 2
EVALUATIONS OF PARTY POSITIONS ON TAX BY KNOWLEDGE

	Con	Lab	Lib Dem	N
High	7.2	4.3	3.1	737
Medium	6.1	4.1	3.1	893
Low	5.3	4.1	4.4	693

Note: Figures are means of perceived position on 11-point scale.
Source: BEPS, 1997–2001.

important differences in the extent to which voters are aware of party issue positions. For example, less than 40% of low knowledge voters correctly identified the Conservatives as being the party furthest to the right on taxation and privatization compared with over 75% of high knowledge voters. Low knowledge voters prove less likely to differentiate between parties' issue positions, whereas high knowledge voters observed the greatest differences between the parties and were more likely to clearly identify parties as being to the left or right. Low knowledge voters, on the other hand, tended a tendency to place all three parties close together in the centre of the scale. Table 2, which shows the mean placement of the parties on taxation by the different knowledge groups, illustrates this pattern. The behaviour of low knowledge voters is consistent with them not having well-formed opinions on party issue positions and merely expressing 'top of the head' opinions or 'non-attitudes' in response to the interview questions (Converse, 1964; Neumann, 1987). This leads us to expect that there will be differences, on the basis of knowledge, in the extent to which party choices are consistent with issue preferences.

There may also be knowledge-based differences in voters' evaluations of economic performance and the extent to which these evaluations are an accurate reflection of economic reality. Given that the effectiveness of retrospective voting as a route to party choices relies on the incumbent party being correctly held accountable for its performance, this is particularly important. Figure 1 shows how the percentage of respondents believing the national economy to have improved over the previous 12 months varied depending on knowledge. Making use of the panel element of the data we can compare not just evaluations at one point in time but also how these evaluations changed over time between 1997 and 2001. The data show that evaluations did differ with knowledge; high knowledge voters were always more optimistic about the economy than less knowledgeable voters. However, it is reassuring to note that the evaluations of each group appear to vary in similar ways over time, suggesting that all voters responded in similar ways to the experience of living under the Labour government.

FIGURE 1
EVALUATION OF NATIONAL ECONOMY BY KNOWLEDGE 1997–2001

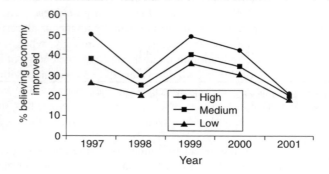

We should also consider how voters' evaluations of particular economic outcomes such as unemployment or inflation varied over time, to compare these evaluations with objective indicators to see whether how closely voters' subjective evaluations reflects reality. Unfortunately, questions on specific economic policies were not asked consistently throughout the 1997–2001 panel. However, we can get some idea by looking at data from the 1992–97 panel, which includes not only questions asking for respondents' evaluations of economic outcomes but also the same political knowledge quiz as for 1997–2001, allowing us to group respondents by knowledge in a comparable way. Figure 2 shows the percentage of high, medium and low knowledge

FIGURE 2
EVALUATIONS OF CHANGES IN UNEMPLOYMENT 1993–97 BY KNOWLEDGE

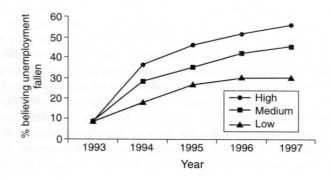

respondents believing unemployment to have fallen 1993–97, a period over which the seasonally adjusted claimant count rate did in fact fall steadily year by year from 9.7% in 1993 to 5.4% in 1997.[4] The figure suggests that whilst each group did pick up on falling unemployment, by no means all respondents did so, particularly in the low knowledge group. Similarly, when it came to correctly identifying the reduction in interest rates over the course of the 1997 parliament, only 23% of low knowledge voters did so compared with 59% of high knowledge voters. Voters' awareness of the economy and economic performance would appear to vary with political knowledge; this should be borne in mind when judging the effectiveness of economic voting as a heuristic for party choice.

Political Knowledge and Voter Choices

Whether political knowledge makes a difference to the basis upon which voters cast their votes is examined by dividing the sample into three groups based on knowledge (high, medium and low as defined above) and comparing the effects of both issue positions and retrospective evaluations on vote choice across the groups.[5] A multinomial logit model of vote choice is employed to take account of the several different party choices facing voters. Respondents who voted for each of the three main parties – Labour, Conservative and Liberal Democrats – are considered; non-voters and tactical voters (i.e. those deliberately choosing not to vote for their first party on the basis of either issue positions or retrospective evaluations) are excluded. Given that the primary focus of this article is the incidence of retrospective voting and the extent to which people's evaluations of government performance influence their vote choices, the results presented below take Labour, i.e. the governing party, as the reference category. The results demonstrate the effects of the explanatory variables on voting Conservative over Labour and voting Liberal Democrat over Labour. As well as the main explanatory variables, the model includes controls for demographic characteristics such as age, sex, occupational class and education. Whether or not the respondent voted Labour in 1997, as recorded in wave 1 of the panel, is also controlled for.

Table 3 presents the logit coefficients obtained from modelling the vote choices of high, medium and low knowledge voters in turn. Notable differences emerge between the groups in terms of whether issue positions and/or economic evaluations serve as significant predictors of vote choice. Looking at the Conservative/Labour contrast it is clear that knowledge makes a difference in the extent to which issue positions predict vote choice. Whereas all three issue positions are significant for high knowledge voters (and in the expected direction, with more right-wing issue positions having a positive effect on voting for the Conservatives over Labour), Europe is the only issue

TABLE 3A
DETERMINANTS OF PARTY CHOICE BY KNOWLEDGE (CON/LAB)

	High	Medium	Low
Taxation	0.26***	0.06	0.11
	(0.11)	(0.09)	(0.09)
Europe	0.36***	0.32***	0.29***
	(0.07)	(0.05)	(0.06)
Privatization	0.24**	0.21**	−0.01
	(0.08)	(0.07)	(0.07)
General economy	0.78***	0.71***	0.65**
	(0.24)	(0.21)	(0.21)
Household finances	0.56**	0.55**	0.02
	(0.22)	(0.20)	(0.19)
Age	0.01	0.01	0.04
	(0.32)	(0.26)	(0.26)
Male	−0.27	−0.64*	0.07
	(0.39)	(0.34)	(0.38)
Degree	0.03	−0.74	−0.25
	(0.06)	(0.40)	(0.50)
Salariat	1.74**	0.21	0.42
	(0.61)	(0.41)	(0.37)
Voted Labour '97	−3.79***	−5.22***	3.53***
	(0.45)	(0.55)	(0.49)
Constant	0.80	2.10*	−0.32
	(1.38)	(1.10)	(1.10)
N	477	533	358
Chi2 (20)	469.5	440.0	191.0

Notes: Figures are logit coefficients with standard errors in parentheses.
            *** $p<0.001$ ** $p<0.01$ * $p<0.05$.
Source: BEPS, 1997–2001.

significant for the low knowledge group. Voting on the basis of retrospective evaluations appears less affected by knowledge with evaluations of the general economy having a highly significant effect on the choice between the Conservatives and Labour for all knowledge groups. However, evaluations of personal finances, though significant for high and medium knowledge voters, are not significant for low knowledge voters.

The results from looking at the Liberal Democrat/Labour vote contrast are less straightforward. Issue positions are not significant for any of the three groups – perhaps because the positions of the two parties in 2001 were fairly similar, making it hard for all voters to distinguish between parties on this basis. However, both sets of economic evaluations are significant predictors

TABLE 3B
DETERMINANTS OF PARTY CHOICE BY KNOWLEDGE (LIB DEM/LAB)

	High	Medium	Low
Taxation	−0.06	0.03	−0.12
	(0.10)	(0.08)	(0.10)
Europe	0.09	0.04	0.12
	(0.06)	(0.05)	(0.06)
Privatization	0.04	0.10	−0.01
	(0.08)	(0.06)	(0.07)
General economy	0.51**	0.39*	0.25
	(0.22)	(0.18)	(0.22)
Household finances	0.46**	0.44**	0.02
	(0.20)	(0.17)	(0.19)
Age	0.01	0.01	0.01
	(0.28)	(0.23)	(0.27)
Male	−0.07	−0.35	−0.40
	(0.36)	(0.30)	(0.41)
Degree	0.50	0.27	0.73*
	(0.36)	(0.34)	(0.43)
Salariat	0.41	0.03	0.46
	(0.40)	(0.36)	(0.39)
Voted Labour '97	−3.29***	−2.52***	2.16***
	(0.34)	(0.31)	(0.38)
Constant	4.02**	2.31*	0.94
	(1.2)	(1.01)	(1.14)
N	477	533	358
Chi2 (20)	469.5	440.0	191.0

Notes: Figures are logit coefficients with standard errors in parentheses
*** $p<0.001$ ** $p<0.01$ * $p<0.05$.
Source: BEPS, 1997–2001.

of vote choice, at least for high and medium knowledge voters, with worsening evaluations having a positive effect on voting for the Liberal Democrats over the incumbent Labour Party. This highlights the importance of considering retrospective evaluations as a route to party choice alongside issue voting. The fact that economic evaluations fail to show up as having a significant effect on the choices of low knowledge voters may be because less knowledgeable voters are generally less aware of the Liberal Democrats (being a third party) with very few respondents in this group actually casting their vote for the party.

The differing effects of variables across knowledge groups can be seen more clearly if results are presented in terms of predicted probabilities. By

TABLE 4
EFFECT OF ISSUE POSITIONS AND RETROSPECTIVE EVALUATIONS ON PARTY
CHOICE – COMPARING HIGH AND LOW KNOWLEDGE VOTERS

	Conservative		Labour		Lib Dem	
	High	Low	High	Low	High	Low
Taxation	0.63	0.26	−0.30	−0.23	−0.34	−0.03
Europe	0.53	0.36	−0.50	−0.40	−0.03	0.05
Privatization	0.53	0.04	−0.52	−0.05	−0.01	0.00
General economy	−0.54	−0.62	0.67	0.61	−0.13	0.01
Household finances	−0.26	−0.07	0.39	0.11	−0.13	−0.04

Notes: Figures are predicted probabilities calculated for a hypothetical voter who is male,
working class, without a degree and of average age. Figures in table represent change in
probabilities of this hypothetical individual voting for each party after changing the
value of the variable of interest from one extreme on scale (left/got a lot worse) to the
other (right/got a lot better) whilst holding all other variables constant.
Source: BEPS, 1997–2001.

making use of 'first differences' we can calculate the predicted probability of
a hypothetical voter supporting each of the three parties and then examine
how these probabilities change in response to changes in the values of certain
variables. The figures in Table 4 show the marginal effects of respondents'
issue positions/economic evaluations on the probability of voting for a particular party. Comparing the results for high and low knowledge voters, we see
that the overall effect of changing issue positions on party choice is, as
expected, greater for high knowledge voters especially in the cases of privatization and taxation. It is however worth noting that changing position on
Europe had a sizeable effect on the probability of voting for Labour or the
Conservatives even among low knowledge voters. Table 4 also reinforces the
idea that retrospective voting is an important route to party choice for all
voters with evaluations of the general economy having a large and similar
sized effect for both high and low knowledge voters. However, changing evaluations of personal finances had only a negligible effect on the choices of low
knowledge voters.

Discussion

These results provide us with a number of insights into the effect of knowledge on party choice that are worthy of further discussion. First, it appears
that the effect of knowledge on retrospective voting varies depending on the
type of retrospective evaluation considered. The finding that retrospective

evaluations of personal finances were an important factor in the party choices of more knowledgeable voters, but not those with low knowledge, is at first glance surprising. We might have expected it to be less knowledgeable voters who relied most heavily on the shortcut provided by personal experience. One explanation for these findings may be that knowledge makes a difference to the way in which voters attribute responsibility for economic outcomes. In the US context, Gomez and Wilson (2001) show that less knowledgeable voters are less likely to appreciate the connection between their own financial situation and the wider economic picture and to attribute responsibility for their personal financial situation to government action. Hence, they make less use of personal evaluations when deciding how to vote.

However, the evidence from Britain in 2001 does not entirely support Gomez and Wilson's argument. They also predict that more knowledgeable voters will rely less on sociotropic evaluations of the national economy than less knowledgeable voters. This is because knowledgeable voters can better appreciate that the national government is not the only actor who may have influenced the state of the economy and so are less likely to attribute responsibility to the incumbent party. The results presented here suggest that, in fact, knowledgeable voters rely just as much on evaluations of national economic conditions when deciding how to vote as do low knowledge voters. Furthermore, a preliminary look at how voters assigned the credit and blame for economic outcomes in 2001 does not suggest any significant differences on the basis of knowledge. BEPS respondents were asked whether they considered changes in both their own standard of living and the general standard of living to be mainly the result of government policies or for some other reason. There was little difference in the extent to which high and low knowledge voters blamed the government in either case, although both sets of voters were significantly more likely to hold the government responsible for changes in the general standard of living than their own standard of living.[6]

It may, of course, be that personal economic evaluations do have an effect on the vote choices of less knowledgeable voters, but that these effects operate indirectly and so fail to show up as significant in the model tested above. Mutz (1993) argues that, in the absence of more objective information about the economy, less knowledgeable voters base their evaluations of the national economic situation primarily on their own personal experiences. The variable measuring evaluations of the general economy may therefore be capturing the effect of pocketbook evaluations. For more knowledgeable voters, evaluations of the national economy are less likely to be a simple reflection of their own experiences, leaving scope for pocketbook evaluations to make an independent contribution to party choice as demonstrated above. There is clearly a need for further research into how knowledge affects the relationship between

different types of retrospective evaluations and the precise nature of the association between these evaluations and vote choice.

Second, there is a need to consider how the effects of knowledge on issue
voting differ depending on the particular issue under consideration. Whilst
knowledge was important for voting on the issues of privatization and taxation, low knowledge voters were able to vote in line with their issue preferences on Europe. In the context of the 2001 election this is perhaps not
surprising; the Conservatives placed particular emphasis on Europe in their
campaign and the issue was widely reported in the media. Analysis of this
election has shown that Europe was an important issue for the electorate in
general, more so than traditional left–right issues such as taxation or privatization, and that voters perceived greater ideological distance between the parties
on Europe than other issues (Evans, 2002). It may be that even less knowledgeable voters are able to match their own issue preferences to party platforms in situations where party platforms on an issue, or at least the
differences between them, are well publicized and easily identifiable.

Finally, the results suggest the importance of political knowledge for the
success of the Liberal Democrats. It appears that the ability of the Liberal
Democrats to attract support as a result of changes in issue positions or
economic evaluations varies with knowledge. Table 4 shows that among high
knowledge voters, changes in position on taxation had a sizeable effect on
the probability of voting Liberal Democrat, whilst the party also made gains
as the probability of voting for the incumbent party decreased with the
assumption of worsening economic evaluations. Among low knowledge
voters, however, the effect of any changes in issue position or economic
evaluations on the probability of supporting the Liberal Democrats was
negligible; voters simply switched between the two main parties. We would
expect more knowledgeable voters to be more aware of the presence of the
Liberal Democrats as a third party, and consequently be more willing to vote
for them when appropriate rather than simply switching between the two
main parties.

Conclusions

From the results presented above it is clear that voters' political knowledge
did influence the basis upon which party choices were made in 2001.
However, the extent to which knowledge was important varied, depending on
which route to choice was being considered. On the one hand, the evidence
supports the hypothesis that retrospective voting is an important heuristic for
all voters, with the effects of evaluations of the national economy on vote
choice being comparable across knowledge groups. This is in contrast to
voting on the basis of issues, where successfully matching one's own position

on taxation or privatization to party choice was a function of increased knowledge. However, the importance of knowledge does not differ simply between issue voting and economic voting. The evidence also suggests that knowledge may affect voting on the basis of some issues, e.g. Europe, less than others. Furthermore, several important differences between high and low knowledge voters emerged with regards to the pattern of retrospective voting. Pocketbook evaluations were a significant predictor of party choice only amongst high knowledge voters, whilst knowledge was also an important factor in enabling the Liberal Democrats to attract the support of those dissatisfied with the incumbent's economic performance.

This article has highlighted both the importance of retrospective economic voting as a heuristic for party choice and the potential complexity of the relationship between retrospective evaluations and knowledge. In particular, whilst it is fairly easy to demonstrate that the choices of all voters, including the less knowledgeable, depend on retrospective evaluations, it is less straightforward to determine the nature of these evaluations or how they are arrived at. There may be important, knowledge-based differences in the nature of the retrospective judgements held by voters. Further research is necessary into how voters' perceptions of government performance differ with knowledge, including the extent to which voters are aware of changes in objective performance indicators such as the unemployment rate, their tendency to attribute responsibility for policy outcomes to the government and the sources of information upon which their evaluations are based. The answers to these questions will determine whether we can claim not just that retrospective voting is a route to party choice used by all voters but that it is an effective route to party choice which all voters, including the less knowledgeable, can use to successfully hold the government to account for its performance.

ACKNOWLEDGEMENTS

I would like to thank Anthony Heath and Geoff Evans for helpful comments and advice on earlier drafts of this article. I am also grateful to the ESRC for funding award number PTA-030-2002-00978.

NOTES

1. The panel consists of a baseline survey of 3165 respondents interviewed for the British Election Study 1997 along with seven further waves, each involving re-interviews with the original respondents, conducted between autumn 1997 and June 2001. The analysis that follows focuses primarily on the final wave of the panel conducted shortly after the 2001 election. The final sample size was 2323.

2. There is some discussion in the literature as to how to deal with 'don't know' responses to knowledge items. Mondak (2001) suggests that 'don't know' responses to open-ended questions may be a function of respondents' 'propensity to guess' as much as their knowledge, with shy respondents, even if they have partial knowledge, discouraged from answering. Treating these responses as wrong answers may therefore underestimate knowledge. However, this is unlikely to be a serious problem in this context where questions take on a true/false format and the proportion of 'don't know' responses is very small.
3. Various different categorizations of respondents by knowledge were considered to test the robustness of the findings. The key divide in terms of the effect of issues/retrospective evaluations on vote choice appears to be between those respondents giving three or fewer correct answers (classified here as low knowledge) and the rest.
4. Source: *Economic Trends* (Office for National Statistics).
5. The effects of knowledge on party choice were also tested by running a model of vote choice that included interaction terms between the various explanatory variables and knowledge as defined over the full seven-point scale. The results obtained are consistent with the findings described in the text. However, given that several key findings centre on the absence of significant coefficients it was considered more informative to present results in terms of group comparisons as done here.
6. Knowledge continues to have no effect on the assignment of credit/blame even after controlling for partisanship and the nature of the evaluation (whether it is positive or negative), both factors that have been shown to affect the attribution of responsibility.

REFERENCES

Abramowitz, Alan I., David J. Lanoue and Subha Ramesh (1988) 'Economic Conditions, Causal Attributions and Political Evaluations in the 1984 Presidential Election', *Journal of Politics* 50: 848–63.

Andersen, Robert, Anthony Heath and Richard Sinnott (2002) 'Political Knowledge and Electoral Choices' in Lynn Bennie, Colin Rallings, Jonathan Tonge and Paul Webb (eds) *British Elections and Parties Review Vol. 12*, pp. 11–27.

Bartels, Larry (1996) 'Uninformed Votes: Information Effects in Presidential Elections', *American Journal of Political Science* 40: 194–230.

Bartle, John (2000) 'Political Awareness, Opinion Constraint and the Stability of Ideological Positions', *Political Studies* 48: 467–84.

Converse, Philip (1964) 'The Nature of Belief Systems in Mass Publics' in David Apter (ed.) *Ideology and Discontent*. New York: Free Press, pp. 206–61.

Delli Carpini, Michael and Scott Keeter (1996) *What Americans Know About Politics and Why it Matters*. New Haven, CT: Yale University Press.

Downs, Anthony (1957) *An Economic Theory of Democracy*. New York: Harper & Row.

Evans, Geoffrey (2002) 'European Integration, Party Politics and Voters in the 2001 General Election' in Lynn Bennie, Colin Rallings, Jonathan Tonge and Paul Webb (eds) *British Elections and Parties Review Vol. 12*, pp. 95–110.

Fiorina, Maurice P. (1981) *Retrospective Voting in American National Elections*. New Haven, CT: Yale University Press.

Gomez, Brad T. and J. Matthew Wilson (2001) 'Political Sophistication and Economic Voting in the American Electorate: A Theory of Heterogeneous Attribution', *American Journal of Political Science* 45: 899–914.

Key, V.O. Jr (1966) *The Responsible Electorate: Rationality in Presidential Voting 1936–1960*. Cambridge, MA: Harvard University Press.

Mondak, Jeffery J. (2001) 'Developing Valid Knowledge Scales', *American Journal of Political Science* 45: 224–38.

Mutz, Diana A. (1993) 'Direct and Indirect Routes to Politicizing Personal Experience – Does Knowledge Make a Difference?', *Public Opinion Quarterly* 57: 483–502.

Neuman. W. Russell (1986) *The Paradox of Mass Politics: Knowledge and Opinion in the American Electorate.* Cambridge, MA: Harvard University Press.

Popkin, Samuel L. (1991) *The Reasoning Voter.* Chicago: University of Chicago Press.

Sniderman, Paul, Richard Brody and Philip Tetlock (1991) *Reasoning and Choice.* New York: Cambridge University Press.

Zaller, John (1992) *The Nature and Origin of Mass Opinions.* New York: Cambridge University Press.

Do Issues Decide? Partisan Conditioning and Perceptions of Party Issue Positions across the Electoral Cycle

Geoffrey Evans and Robert Andersen

Are the stances parties take on important political issues crucial to winning or losing elections? Common sense, and influential rational choice theories of voting, would presume so. The assumption is that voters have independently formulated issue positions and perceptions of where the parties stand on these issues. These assumptions inform a wide range of approaches to both party competition and voting behaviour. However, an alternative 'partisan contamination' approach would predict that voters' positions on issues, and their perceptions of where the parties stand, are influenced by their partisanship. It is argued that voters often lack well-formulated issue positions and clear understandings of where the parties stand, and thus their placement of self and the parties on issues is likely to be an expression of how close they feel to a particular party, rather than an independent basis for deciding whether to vote for that party. But to what degree are voters' own positions on issues, and their perceptions of the issue positions held by parties, influenced by pre-existing partisan orientations? If the answer to either question is 'to a large extent', issues cannot be taken to provide an independent basis for deciding between parties when voting. Instead, the role of partisan influence would need to be given more weight when assessing how voters decide to vote, and the role of issues downplayed, with subsequent implications for the plausibility of issue-voting theories and our understanding of processes of political change.

Determining the extent to which the effects of issue perceptions on vote are spurious requires calculation of the degree to which they are initially influenced by partisan attitudes. In this article we employ data from a five-year, inter-election panel study to estimate this influence with respect to perceptions of the Labour Party along four important dimensions of political issues: redistribution, taxation, jobs and European integration. We show that issue perceptions are indeed heavily contaminated by other aspects of political belief systems. One's political orientation influences how one perceives the locations of parties on issue dimensions, and in turn explains the relationship between personal issue preference and perceived party positions on those

British Elections & Parties Review, Vol. 14, 2004, pp. 18–39
ISSN 1368-9886 print
DOI: 10.1080/1368988042000258763   © 2004 Taylor & Francis Ltd.

issues. In other words, the causal arrow between issue perceptions and party support is reversed.

Comparing Two Approaches to the Nature and Role of Issue Perceptions

The Rise of Issue Voting

Many commentators have assumed that social change is shifting the basis of electoral choice by transforming the skills and resources of contemporary electorates. With increasing access to further and higher education far more citizens now have sufficient levels of cognitive complexity and mobilization to follow the complexities of politics, and thus have the potential to act as issue voters, than was the case as recently as the 1960s (Dalton, 1996). For observers of British electoral behaviour such as Rose and McAllister (1986), voters have now begun to choose rather than voting on the basis of long-held allegiances. Franklin (1985: 176) similarly argues that the consequence of a decline in social structural sources of voting has been to open the way to choice between parties based on issue preferences rather than class loyalty (see also Franklin et al. 1992: 400). Himmelweit et al. (1985) have explicitly formulated an issue-voting model that treats voters as consumers who select parties on the basis of their espousal of policies that enhance personal utility. Consistent with these changes, Sniderman and his colleagues (1991) find that the better educated and the politically sophisticated place more weight on issues as a basis of their electoral decision-making; less sophisticated voters rely more on partisanship and social cues. This aptitude is facilitated by a far greater information stream through the broadcast media.

In the most well known of the issue-based rational choice models, voters' perceptions of their own and the parties' positions on issue (or ideological) scales are used to estimate issue distance. Voters are assumed to have independent issue preferences, to perceive party issue positions neutrally, and to vote for the party that is closest to their own position: 'The theory assumes that the voter recognises his own self-interest, evaluates alternative candidates on the basis of which will best serve this self-interest, and casts his vote for the candidate most favourably evaluated' (Enelow and Hinich, 1984: 3). This 'issue distance' from voters' own positions can be calculated using the individual's perception of the parties' positions, or alternatively, by using the mean/median perception of the parties' positions. Various types of spatial proximity (Enelow and Hinich, 1984) or directional (Rabinowitz and Macdonald, 1989) theories have used this model of voter rationality to generate predictions about party competition and electoral outcomes. Proponents of issue voting are attracted by its use as a way of understanding party competition and political change, as it provides a characterization of the electoral context which enables estimation of the costs and benefits of shifts in party position along issue dimensions for electoral support (Alvarez et al., 2000), or provides grounds for deducing theoretically-derived predictions about changes in party fortunes and the structure of the party system (Kitschelt, 1994, 1995).

Partisan Perceptual Bias

Research into perceptual biases has a long history in political science, going back at least to Berelson et al. (1954: 220), who encountered evidence that voters' perceptions of candidate stances appeared to be affected by their own policy preferences: 'In almost every instance, respondents perceive their candidate's stand on the issues as similar to their own and the opponent's stand as dissimilar – whatever their own position... Overlaying the base of objective observation is the distortion effect – distortion in harmony with political predispositions'. The authors of *The American Voter* likewise based their model of electoral behaviour to a large degree on 'the role of enduring partisan commitments in shaping attitudes toward political objects' (Campbell et al., 1960: 135). This emphasis continued with Stokes' (1966: 127) observations on the 'capacity of party identification to colour perceptions', while Converse's (1964) seminal work emphasized the centrality of partisan attachments to voters' political belief systems compared to the peripheral nature of issues. More recently, studies by authors such as Markus (1982) and Zaller (1992: 241) have concluded that: 'people tend to accept what is congenial to their partisan values and to reject what is not', while various studies have demonstrated the role of partisan cues in political information-processing (for example, Conover and Feldman, 1989; Jacoby, 1988; Lodge and Hamill, 1986; Rahn, 1993).

The key question from the partisan contamination perspective is how 'observers with different preconceptions interpret the same piece of evidence in ways that conform to their initial views' (Gerber and Green, 1999: 197). The mechanisms through which consistency between personal and party perceptions occurs can involve various processes: an expression of partisan loyalty, the role of the party as a source of trusted information, cognitive consistency biases which assimilate personal preferences and party positions, or simply a desire to maintain the appearance of consistency in the interview context. Accordingly, researchers have drawn on psychological models of attitude change and persistence which either emphasize the cognitive costs of holding inconsistent views (Abelson, 1968), or cognitive biases in information processing (Nisbett and Ross, 1980). Regardless of the exact process, however, the significance of such partisan contamination for issue-voting models is apparent: should issue perceptions be found to be influenced by the type of phenomena they are assumed to influence – party preference – their impact will be over-estimated by models that fail to control for this reciprocal relationship. Moreover – and in contrast to the implications of the cognitive mobilization literature, with its emphasis on the role of political knowledge in facilitating issue voting – work by Zaller (1992: 241) argues that it is the most politically aware segment of the public that are most likely to engage in 'partisan resistance' by filtering out information that does not conform to their existing political predispositions.

Despite these concerns, and a substantial body of survey-based findings, research into the influence of political orientations on issue perceptions has had little impact on the literature on issue voting (for an exception, see Bartels, 2002). This article develops and presents a series of tests that evaluate the extent to which partisan biases undermine issue-based explanations of party preference.

Testing the Partisan Contamination of Issue Perceptions and Issue Voting: Hypotheses

Both partisan contamination and issue-voting models predict that a person's own issue position will be closer to their preferred party than to less preferred parties. In order to assess the validity of the competing interpretations of this commonly observed finding, other predictions therefore need to be derived concerning the consequences that would follow if partisan beliefs influenced issue perceptions rather than vice versa. The main methodological problem we face is of estimating the relative extent of 'causal influence' rather than simple 'association'. The latter can be observed from cross-sectional data but the former is notoriously difficult to infer on such a basis. This is the advantage of using a multi-wave panel design. By measuring partisan affiliations at time-points prior to those used to examine issue perceptions and concurrent party preference, we can have greater confidence that at least the temporal condition for inferring causality has been met. Our hypotheses therefore make use of this methodological asset to specify expected outcomes from processes specific to the partisan contamination model but not to models that use issue distance as the explanation of party preference.

If the partisan contamination model is valid, we should find evidence that partisan identification systematically influences judgements of where self and parties are placed on issue scales designed to measure opinions along major dimensions of party competition and public policy domains. This can occur because, once an issue position becomes associated with a party, voters may change their own positions to coincide with their party's policy, or they may bias their perceptions of party policies so as to bring their own party closer to their own preference – and/or perceive a disliked party to be further away from their own issue preference. Or there may be a combination of these tendencies. We therefore can derive the following hypotheses.

If issue perceptions are contaminated to a substantial degree by partisan orientations:

H1. Partisans will perceive their party as close to them regardless of where they place themselves on the issue scales.[1]

H2. Controlling for measures of partisanship over the electoral cycle will substantially reduce the association between issue distance and vote preference.

If partisanship is more central than issues to voters' orientation towards politics then:

H3. The effects of prior partisanship on issue proximity will be stronger than *vice versa*.

As issues vary in the degree to which they are linked to partisan alignments, then we would predict that:

H4. Conditioning effects will be more pronounced for issues that are more closely integrated into the main party cleavage. Prior partisanship should have more pronounced effects on: (a) the distance between self and party positions and (b) the association between issue distance and vote preference for established left–right issues such as *redistribution* than for less-established partisan issues such as *European integration* (Evans, 1999, 2001).

Data, Measurement and Analysis

We use the five face-to-face waves of the 1997–2001 British Election Panel Study (BEPS). BEPS re-interviewed respondents to the 1997 British Election cross-section survey at regular intervals through the 1997 to 2001 electoral cycle. Interviews for the particular waves used in the analysis took place in the spring of each year of the study: 1997 (the 1997 British Election Study served as the baseline sample for BEPS), 1998, 1999, 2000 and 2001 (during the 2001 election campaign). The analyses reported here are based on respondents who participated in all five of the waves. Most panel studies have a fair degree of attrition, and the 1997–2001 BEPS is no exception. The initial sample size for BEPS was 3615 respondents in 1997. After removing missing cases, our final analytical sample size was 2039. An available case analysis – i.e., one in which cases were included even if they participated even in only one wave – yielded similar substantive results as those reported here.[2]

Variables

Our variables of primary interest are the strength of Labour Party identification and measures of issue proximity. These variables are measured for all waves of the study. The control variables are measured only during the first wave of the study (1997). Details of the measures are given below.

Labour Party Identification

Our measure of Labour Party identification taps the strength of party identification on a 4-point scale. Three items were used to construct this measure. The first of these asked respondents 'Generally speaking, do you think of yourself as Conservative, Labour, Liberal Democrat (Nationalist/Plaid Cymru) or what?' Those who reported 'none' to this question were asked the follow-up question: 'Do you generally think of yourself as a little closer to one of the parties than the others?' Respondents whose response to either of these first two questions was not the Labour Party were given a score of 0, indicating no identification with the Labour Party. Those who did report having a Labour Party identification were further assessed as to how strongly they identified with the party using the question: 'Would you call yourself very strong Labour (coded 3), fairly strong (coded 2) or not very strong (coded 1)?

Issue Proximity Variables

We explore the relationship between party identification and perceptions of proximity to the Labour Party on four issues: (1) jobs, (2) taxation and spending, (3) Europe and (4) income distribution. For each question, respondents were initially asked to place their own position on an 11-point scale, with left-wing responses receiving low scores and right-wing responses receiving high scores. Respondents were then asked for their perceptions of the Labour Party's position on the same issues. Issue proximity was then determined for each issue by the absolute distance between the respondent's own position and their perception of where the Labour Party stood. Such variables are derived for each year under observation. The specific question wordings are below:

Jobs

Some people feel that getting people back to work should be the government's top priority. These people would put themselves in Box A. Other people feel that keeping prices down should be the government's top priority. These people would put themselves in Box K. And other people have views somewhere in-between...

Taxes

Some people feel that the government should put up taxes a lot and spend much more on health and social services. These people would put themselves in Box A. Other people feel that the government should cut taxes a lot and spend much less on health and social services. These people would put themselves in Box K.

Europe

Some people feel that Britain should do all it can to unite fully with the European Union. These people would put themselves in Box A. Other people feel that Britain should do all it can to protect its independence from the European Union. These people would put themselves in Box K.

Income

Some people feel that government should make much greater efforts to make people's incomes more equal. These people would put themselves in Box A. Other people feel that government should be much less concerned about how equal people's incomes are. These people would put themselves in Box K.

Control Variables

All analyses presented here control for age, gender, education and social class. Our measure of education is operationalized as a set of four dummy regressors coded (1) degree, (2) some post-secondary education, (3) A-level, (4) O-level/ CSE, and 'other' (the reference category). Social class is a modification of the Goldthorpe class schema, operationalized as a set of four dummy regressors: (1) salariat, (2) self-employed, (3) routine non-manual, (4) manual working class. Respondents whose class was unclassified are the reference category.

Our preliminary models include further control variables. First, two measures of economic perceptions are employed: (1) retrospective egocentric perceptions, and (2) retrospective sociotropic perceptions. Sociotropic perceptions are measured by a question asking respondents how well they thought the British economy was performing. The egocentric perception items asked respondents how they felt their own personal household income had been affected in the past year. Both variables are measured with four-point scales coded so that high values indicate positive perceptions (i.e., the perception that the economic situation had improved). Finally, opinions of Tony Blair's leadership qualities are tapped with a five-point Likert item that asks, 'How good a job do you think Tony Blair is doing as Prime Minister?' Responses range from 'not at all good' (coded 0) to 'very good' (coded 4). Economic perceptions and appraisals of Blair's leadership are not included in the graphical chain models.

Statistical Models

Our primary analysis involves graphical chain models to assess the relationship between perceptions of issue proximity and strength of Labour Party identification (see Cox and Wermuth, 1996: 31). Graphical chains are particularly helpful for modelling temporal relationships in panel data. The graphs are used both to guide the analysis and to display the results from that analysis. The basic strategy of graphical chain modelling is straightforward. We start by arranging the variables in a graphical chain that reflects chronological (or potential causal) order. We then regress each variable on the variables that come before it in the graphical chain. The standard practice in graphical chain modelling is to remove any predictors for which the studentized regression coefficient is less than 2.0. Nonetheless, we keep these predictors in the model as controls so that direct over-time comparisons can be made. We do remove their paths from the depiction of the final graphical chain models, however, implying that the conditional independency is weak enough not to be of substantive interest.

We fit two graphical chain models. Model A measures the contemporaneous relationship between issue proximities and Labour Party identification. The part of the model that predicts Labour Party identification takes the following form:

$$\text{LabID}_t = \alpha + \beta_1 \text{gender} + \beta_2 \text{age} + \sum_{q=1}^{4} \gamma_q \text{class}_{qi} + \sum_{h=1}^{4} \lambda_h \text{education}_{hi} + \beta_3 \text{Job}$$
$$+ \beta_4 \text{Taxes}_t + \beta_5 \text{Europe}_t + \beta_6 \text{Income}_t + \beta_7 \text{LabID}_{t-1} \tag{1}$$

Where LabID_t represents strength of Labour Party identification at the time of interest; LabID_{t-1} represents strength of Labour Party identification measured in the previous year; Jobs_t, Taxes_t, Europe_t and Income_t represent the issue proximity variables measured at the same time as Labour Party identification.

The general equation predicting issue proximities is:

$$\text{Issue}_{jt} = \alpha + \beta_1 \text{gender} + \beta_2 \text{age} + \sum_{q=1}^{4} \gamma_q \text{class}_{qi} + \sum_{h=1}^{4} \lambda_h \text{education}_{hi}$$
$$+ \beta_3 \text{Issue}_{kt} + \beta_4 \text{Issue}_{lt} + \beta_5 \text{Issue}_{mt} + \beta_6 \text{LabID}_t \tag{2}$$

Here Issue_{jt} represents the issue proximity variable for the issue of interest; Issue_{kt}, Issue_{lt}, and Issue_{mt} are the other proximity variables, all measured at the same time as the issue proximity being predicted. Notice that for this model the issue proximity variables are predicted by strength of Labour Party identification also measured at the same point in time. The complete model – i.e., both the Labour Party identification and the issue proximity portions – is fitted for each year of the study.

Model B differs from Model A only in that it assesses the lagged effects of Labour Party identification on the issue proximity variables. In other words, the portion of the model predicting strength of Labour Party identification remains the same as for Model A. The issue proximity portion, however, now takes the following form:

$$
\begin{aligned}
\text{Issue}_{jt} = \alpha + \beta_1 \text{gender} + \beta_2 \text{age} + \sum_{q=1}^{4} \gamma_q \text{class}_{qi} + \sum_{h=1}^{4} \lambda_h \text{education}_{hi} \\
+ \beta_3 \text{Issue}_{kt} + \beta_4 \text{Issue}_{lt} + \beta_5 \text{Issue}_{mt} + \beta_6 \text{LabID}_{t-1}
\end{aligned}
\tag{3}
$$

We see from equation (3) that the LabID_{t-1} (i.e., Labour identification measured in the previous year of the issue questions) replaces the LabID_t term in equation (2).

Results

The Effect of Partisan Conditioning on Perceptions of Party Issue Positions

We begin with some preliminary analyses. The bivariate relationships between a respondent's position on the four issues and their perception of the Labour Party's stance on the issues in 2001 can be seen in Figure 1, which plots a local polynomial regression curve ('Loess smooth', see Fox 1997) for each issue. The upper charts compare the pattern of association between self and party positions for Labour identifiers and non-identifiers in 2001. The lower charts repeat this comparison, but using Labour Party identification/non identification in 2000 to condition the 2001 positions.

This evidence establishes a *prima facie* case for the extent to which prior partisan attachments influence current perceptions of party issue positions. For both contemporaneous and lagged party identification we can see the expected pattern: Labour voters are much more likely to see the Labour Party's stance on issues as similar to theirs – regardless of how far to the left or right they place themselves – than are non-identifiers. The general pattern of association for non-identifiers is flat or curvilinear.[3]

The lagged effect of 2000 identification versus non-identification on the pattern of association between self and party placement is weakest for the jobs issue (indicated by solid line), which displays an element of curvilinearity for both groups. The pattern for the European integration issue among 2000 iden-tifiers also flattens as we move to the right end of the scale, but there is still a far closer positive relationship than is found among non-identifiers. Thus the main finding is that, consistent with Hypothesis 1, respondents are more likely

FIGURE 1
LOESS SMOOTHS OF RESPONDENTS' PERCEPTIONS OF THE LABOUR PARTY'S
POSITIONS ON ISSUES IN 2001 BY THEIR OWN PERSONAL POSITIONS IN 2001,
LABOUR AND NON-LABOUR IDENTIFIERS IN 2001 AND 2000

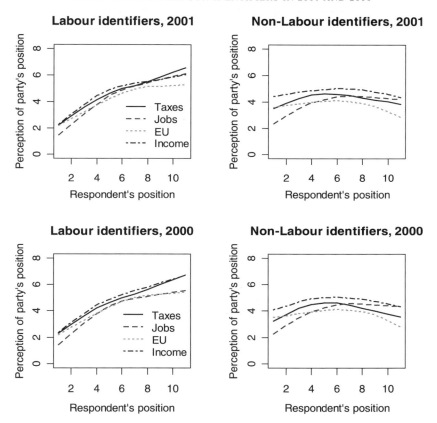

to see the Labour Party as having a similar stance to their own if they identify with the party – whether at an earlier time point or concurrently. This suggests, then, that respondents' perceptions of party positions on issues are influenced by their political orientations. Further analyses demonstrate similar effects when using vote at the previous 1997 election as the conditioning variable.

Modelling the Effects of Partisan Conditioning on Issue Voting

We now estimate issue-distance models predicting the strength of Labour Party identification in 2001 that will form the basis of our dynamic modelling of the reciprocal association between party identification and issue proximities over the electoral cycle. These models provide evidence of three things (see Table 1): The relationship between perceived party proximity and Labour Party identification (Model 1); this relationship weakens once we control for previous party identification (Model 2); and the removal of the extra control

TABLE 1

PRELIMINARY REGRESSION MODELS PREDICTING STRENGTH OF LABOUR PARTY IDENTIFICATION IN 2001

	Mod 1	Mod 2	Mod 3	Mod 4
Constant	−.164	.504**	.008	.002
	(.158)	(.158)	(.080)	(.081)
Men	.065	.027	.028	.041
	(.047)	(.045)	(.027)	(.027)
Age	.0002	.0004	.008	.008
	(.0006)	(.0006)	(.013)	(.013)
Education				
O/CSE level	−.110	−.093	−.078*	−.085*
	(.058)	(.056)	(.034)	(.034)
A level	−.108	−.012	−.078	−.090*
	(.076)	(.073)	(.044)	(.044)
Some post-sec.	−.235**	−.246***	−.084	−.086
	(.076)	(.072)	(.044)	(.044)
University degree	−.069	−.111	−.103*	−.122*
	(.086)	(.083)	(.050)	(.051)
No qualifications	–	–	–	–
Social Class				
Working class	.362**	.361**	.115	.121
	(.141)	(.133)	(.081)	(.082)
Self employed	−.190	−.094	−.033	−.034
	(.154)	(.148)	(.089)	(.091)
Routine nonmanual	.943	.072	.034	.042
	(.142)	(.135)	(.082)	(.082)
Salariat	−.018	.018	−.023	−.012
	(.140)	(.134)	(.081)	(.082)
Unclassified	–	–	–	–
Blair Rating	−.00007	−.00006	.001	
	(.0001)	(.0001)	(.012)	
Economic Perceptions				
Past Sociotropic	.333***	.254***	.086***	
	(.027)	(.268)	(.014)	
Past Egocentric	.122***	.097***	.022	
	(.026)	(.024)	(.013)	

TABLE 1
CONTINUED

	Mod 1	Mod 2	Mod 3	Mod 4
Proximity Measures				
Jobs		−.031**	−.0057	−.014
		(.011)	(.013)	(.013)
Taxes		−.026*	−.027*	−.034*
		(.012)	(.013)	(.014)
Europe		−.067***	−.047***	−.056***
		(.007)	(.014)	(.014)
Taxes		−.026*	−.027*	−.034*
		(.012)	(.013)	(.014)
Europe		−.067***	−.047***	−.056***
		(.007)	(.014)	(.014)
Income		−.053***	−.044**	−.047**
		(.010)	(.014)	(.014)
Labour Identification in 2000			.732***	.753***
			(.014)	(.014)
Residual standard error	.998	.951	.576	.584
Multiple R-Squared	.154	.232	.670	.662
N	2039	2039	2039	2039

Notes: Coefficients for quantitative variables have been standardized. Standard errors are in parentheses. *** p-value<.001; ** p-value<.01; *p-value<.05.

variables does not substantially alter the coefficients for the issue proximity variables (Model 4).

We start with Model 2. Not surprisingly, the addition of the issue proximity variables improves the fit of the model – explained variation in the Labour identification variable increases from 15 per cent to 23 per cent, and the average prediction error declines from .998 to .951. Moreover, all four proximity variables have a strong negative effect on Labour Party identification. In other words, the further away from their own positions that respondents perceived the Labour Party to be, the less likely the respondents were to vote for the party.

Model 3 adds Labour Party identification in 2000 as a predictor. A few findings from this model are noteworthy. First, the model fits much better than Model 2, now explaining 67 per cent of the variation in Labour identification with an average prediction error of only .576. Second, the extra control variables – economic perceptions and Blair's leadership rating – have very little effect. In fact, only sociotropic perceptions remain statistically significant, though its coefficient has diminished to .086 from .254 in Model 2.[4] Finally, although the issue proximity variables remain important, their coefficients are of far smaller magnitude than in Model 2. In fact, the jobs issue no longer has a significant effect.

In Model 4 we remove the leadership and economic perceptions variables from the model. This does not substantially affect the coefficients for the proximity measures, and our earlier research on the endogeneity of economic perceptions indicates that their 'effects' on party identification are to a large degree spurious (Evans and Andersen, 2001), while the questions required to construct the leadership variable do not exist for all waves of the study. Nonetheless, as we see from Model 4, omitting these extra control variables has very little effect on the coefficients for the proximity measures, increasing them only slightly. Based on these findings, we can be confident that the graphical chain models which follow, based on Model 4, are not biased towards our arguments.

Graphical Chain Models of the Dynamics of Party Identification and Issue Proximity

We now turn to the graphical chain models. Recall that our main goal here is to assess the relative impact of perceptions of issue proximity on party identification versus party identification on perceptions of issue proximity. We start with Figure 2, which reports the findings from Model A,[5] the contemporaneous model that includes reciprocal paths between variables measured at the same point in time.

The findings here provide strong support that issue proximity is affected by party identification rather than the other way around. These findings are noticeable for all issues examined, but are most noteworthy for European integration. Here we see that the standardized coefficients for the effect of party identification on the European integration proximity measure are consistently more than twice as large as the coefficients for the reciprocal paths. In fact, according to this model, during the election year of 2001, party identification had more than three times the effect on perceptions of the Europe issue than the reverse effect (0.22 vs 0.066). The coefficients for the over-time stability of party identification also indicate high levels of stability and, by comparison, relative immunity to the impact of the issue proximity measures.

Although its findings are consistent with our arguments, this analysis makes strong assumptions about causal impacts on the basis of contemporaneously measured attributes. This is at best a weak test of relative causal impact. Our next step is therefore to impose a more demanding test of our model of partisan conditioning by including only lagged effects of party support in our model and comparing these effects to those of contemporaneously measured issue proximity. Should the effects of party remain dominant, this would

FIGURE 2
GRAPHICAL CHAIN MODEL OF THE CONTEMPORANEOUS RELATIONSHIP
BETWEEN ISSUE PROXIMITY AND LABOUR PARTY IDENTIFICATION, 1997–2001
(MODEL A)

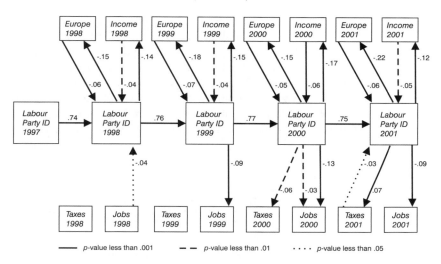

indeed remove any doubt about the powerful impact of partisanship in conditioning issue proximity. The results of this analysis are shown in Model B, Figure 3 (for estimates predicting issue proximities in 2001, see Table 3). Recall that in this model we do not include measures of party identification in the same year as issue proximities when trying to predict issue proximities. The results are no less striking that those from Model A, however, indicating that our general finding that perceptions of issue proximities are more strongly influenced by party identification than the other way around is robust.

Conclusions

The uniquely valuable data provided by the British Election Panel Study has enabled us to investigate the temporal dynamics of the partisan conditioning of issue perceptions more thoroughly than has hitherto been attempted. On this basis we have established that pre-existing partisan orientations strongly bias the perception of proximity between self and party issue positions. Consistent with this bias we have shown that the dynamic reciprocal association between party identification and issue proximity is heavily weighted in favour of the former influencing the latter. Partisan effects are simply much more powerful than those of issue proximity. Moreover, these effects are

FIGURE 3
GRAPHICAL CHAIN MODEL OF THE RELATIONSHIP BETWEEN ISSUE PROXIMITY
AND LAGGED LABOUR PARTY IDENTIFICATION, 1997–2001 (MODEL B)

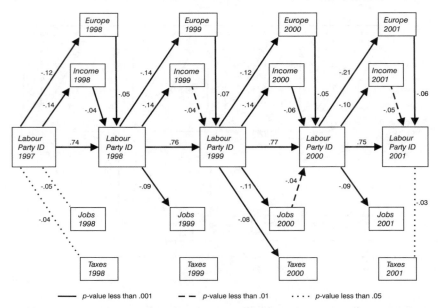

found using only a simple, single-item measure of partisanship compared with four complex measures of issue proximity.[6] Even when we compare the one-year lagged effects with contemporaneous measures it is party that impacts on issue proximity rather than vice versa. Our findings thus accord closely with claims originally advanced in *The American Voter* that 'the influence of party identification on attitudes toward the perceived elements of politics has been far more important than the influence of these attitudes on party identification itself' (Campbell et al., 1960: 135). Indeed, our arguments concerning partisan bias can be taken to be especially persuasive given that the perceptions under examination are relatively anodyne perceptions of position rather than explicitly evaluative judgements of party performance.

   Not all of the hypotheses survived the empirical tests. Both the preliminary comparison of Loess-smoothed associations between self and party-issue positions, and the dynamic analysis indicated that issue perceptions of European integration were no less likely to be conditioned over time by party identity. This suggests that the effects are more general than was predicted by Hypothesis 4, which therefore confirms rather than undermines arguments concerning the pervasiveness partisan conditioning.

TABLE 2
FINAL REGRESSION MODELS PREDICTING STRENGTH OF LABOUR PARTY
IDENTIFICATION THROUGH THE 1997–2001 ELECTORAL CYCLE

	1998	1999	2000	2001
Constant	−.121	−.078	−.016	.002
	(.086)	(.082)	(.081)	(.081)
Men	.025	.032	−.008	.041
	(.030)	(.028)	(.027)	(.027)
Age	−.018	.015	.0009	.008
	(.014)	(.013)	(.013)	(.013)
Education				
O/CSE level	.013	−.013	.009	−.085*
	(.037)	(.034)	(.034)	(.034)
A level	.080	−.009	−.059	−.090*
	(.048)	(.045)	(.045)	(.044)
Some post-sec.	−.038	−.044	−.045	−.086
	(.047)	(.044)	(.044)	(.044)
University degree	.036	−.032	−.002	−.122*
	(.054)	(.051)	(.050)	(.051)
No qualifications	–	–	–	–
Social Class				
Working class	.161	.125	.031	.121
	(.087)	(.082)	(.080)	(.082)
Self employed	−.024	.022	−.004	−.034
	(.097)	(.092)	(.090)	(.091)
Routine nonmanual	.144	−.008	.048	.042
	(.088)	(.084)	(.083)	(.082)
Salariat	.038	.110	.034	−.012
	(.087)	(.083)	(.082)	(.082)
Unclassified	–	–	–	–
Proximity Measures				
Jobs	−.008	−.017	−.039**	−.014
	(.014)	(.014)	(.013)	(.013)
Taxes	−.008	−.012	.009	−.034*
	(.015)	(.014)	(.014)	(.014)
Europe	−.055***	−.067***	−.052***	−.056***
	(.014)	(.014)	(.013)	(.014)
Income	−.040**	−.044**	−.065***	−.047**
	(.015)	(.015)	(.014)	(.014)
Lagged Labour Identification	.744***	.763***	.770***	.753***
	(.015)	(.014)	(.014)	(.014)
Residual standard error	.622	.590	.585	.584
Multiple R-Squared	.616	.655	.660	.662
N	2039	2039	2039	2039

Notes: Coefficients for quantitative variables have been standardized. Standard errors are in parentheses. *** p-value<.001; ** p-value<.01; *p-value<.05.

TABLE 3
REGRESSION MODELS PREDICTING ISSUE PROXIMITIES IN 2001

	Jobs	Taxes	Europe	Income
Constant	.112	.146	.074	−.218
	(.129)	(.129)	(.124)	(.121)
Men	−.025	−.049	−.138**	.030
	(.044)	(.044)	(.041)	(.041)
Age	−.002	.008	.059**	−.041*
	(.021)	(.021)	(.020)	(.019)
Education				
O/CSE level	−.024	−.056	.030	.083
	(.055)	(.054)	(.053)	(.052)
A level	−.044	.025	−.087	.064
	(.071)	(.071)	(.068)	(.067)
Some post-sec.	−.061	.058	−.159*	.074
	(.070)	(.070)	(.068)	(.066)
University degree	.027	.201*	−.321***	.120
	(.081)	(.081)	(.078)	(.076)
No qualifications	–	–	–	–
Social Class				
Working class	−.025	−.164	.089	.098
	(.130)	(.129)	(.125)	(.122)
Self employed	.026	−.115	.203	.159
	(.144)	(.144)	(.139)	(.135)
Routine nonmanual	−.105	−.180	−.021	.099
	(.132)	(.132)	(.127)	(.124)
Salariat	−.157	−.119	.040	.236
	(.131)	(.131)	(.127)	(.123)
Unclassified	–	–	–	–
Proximity Measures				
Jobs	–	.140***	.071***	.191***
		(.021)	(.021)	(.020)
Taxes	.140***	–	.074***	.210***
	(.023)		(.021)	(.020)
Europe	.076***	.079***	–	.234***
	(.023)	(.023)		(.021)
Income	.217**	.236***	.247***	–
	(.023)	(.023)	(.074)	
Lagged Labour Identification	−.094***	−.041	−.210***	−.095***
	(.022)	(.022)	(.021)	(.020)
Residual standard error	.931	.930	.900	.875
Multiple R-Squared	.137	.142	.196	.239
N	2039	2039	2039	2039

Notes: Coefficients for quantitative variables have been standardized. Standard errors are in parentheses. *** p-value<.001; ** p-value<.01; *p-value<.05.

This partisan conditioning has implications for political change in that it serves to retard changes in preferences or in behavioural responses to party-voter issue dealignments such as vote switching, thus providing continuity in cleavages and other aspects of political structure. This consequence was signalled many years ago by Stokes (1966: 127), who observed that the 'capacity of party identification to colour perceptions holds the key to understanding why the unfolding of new events, the emergence of new issues, the appearance of new political figures fails to produce wider swings of party fortune. To a remarkable extent these swings are damped by processes of selective perception.' Thus, issue voting models such as those exemplified by Kitschelt's (1994, 1995) or Alvarez et al.'s (2000) cross-sectional analyses of the implications of parties' issue shifts are unlikely to predict actual political change with accuracy, because they take perceptions of issues and issue preferences as exogenous, and fail to estimate the effects of partisanship on voters' responses.

The mechanisms through which this process works cannot be identified with any precision in this study. Partisans may attach more importance to information about their party that is consistent with their partisan predispositions than to that which is discordant. Or we might expect processes of consistency and projection to be present. Party identification is also clearly much more stable over time than issue positions. It may simply be the case that many voters do not have positions on the issues examined nor any view about where the parties stand, which suggests that, as in *The American Voter* model, party identification is central to a voter's political belief systems and issue preferences are towards the periphery. Whatever the mechanisms may be, the result is that perceptions of these political phenomena are strongly coloured by pre-existing partisan loyalties.

Of course, perceptions of party issue positions are not the only variables typically employed in models of voting behaviour that might be 'contaminated' by prior influences – economic perceptions, party images, and perceptions of leaders are all potentially strongly influenced by previous partisanship. In this respect our finding that the impact of economic evaluations was dramatically reduced by controlling for prior partisanship confirms Evans and Andersen's (2001) study of the 1992–97 election cycle. Only socio-demographic factors such as age, sex, religion, education and social class are exempted from this concern. Thus, our analyses indicate that although they are only *indirect* influences on vote, in that their effects are usually removed once subjective perceptions are included in our models, social-structural influences – such as social class (at least in the British context) or religion, ethnicity and region – continue to be important for understanding the main parameters of party competition and political change. Clearly, a structural basis for vote is not vulnerable to criticisms concerning the effects of framing or cognitive consistency in the way that perceptions of issue positions are, and would thus justify more attention than has sometimes been advocated by political scientists working in this area (for example, Achen 1992).

Our conclusions might need to be qualified by limitations of the panel data at our disposal. Respondent attrition, for example, can be an important issue for generalizations from panel studies. *Ceteris paribus*, the later waves of any panel study of political attitudes and behaviour will tend to contain a greater proportion of politically informed and motivated respondents than are present in the population from which it was sampled – not only through attrition but possibly also because of the conditioning effects of panel responding. From the perspective of the cognitive complexity argument (Sniderman et al., 1991) this serves only to strengthen the implications of our findings, as these are exactly the types of voters who should possess independently formulated issue positions, perceive the parties more accurately and engage in issue voting. However, Zaller's (1992) partisan resistance theory would predict that there should be more partisan conditioning among our informed sample. We therefore tested for the presence of differences in the extent of partisan conditioning among high information/knowledge and low information/knowledge categories of respondent by specifying interaction terms in our models (details available). There were no significant effects. Estimates of partisan bias were not significantly different for high and low knowledge groups of respondents. Thus, neither the cognitive complexity argument nor the partisan resistance argument is confirmed. This suggests that partisan bias is widespread and that its effects are not significantly mitigated or enhanced by access to political information.

It might be suggested that party loyalties in Britain are more fixed and the British party system is more ideologically polarized than in other countries. If so, this would provide an unusually favourable context for the expression of political influences on voters' beliefs and would inhibit generalization of the findings. Again, however, all of the evidence indicates that by the time of the 1997–2001 panel study, British politics was in many ways less polarized, and British party supporters less partisan, than at any previous time for which measures can be obtained (Bara and Budge, 2001; Crewe and Thomson, 1999; Sanders, 1999b; Webb and Farrell, 1999).

We can thus conclude that our findings challenge not only assumptions about the role of issues in party preference, and by extension voting, in the British context but the more general assumptions underlying issue voting theories. They point instead to the important role of political conditioning as an explanation of party preference and vote. If these findings are generalizable, cross-sectional models using issue perceptions and proximity measures as independent variables, without examining the conditioning of such responses by party attachment, can be assumed to overestimate their effects on voting. By demonstrating 'the role of enduring partisan commitments in shaping attitudes toward political objects' (Campbell et al., 1960: 135), these findings signal the importance of augmenting the large number of individual-level issue voting studies using cross-sectional data with more extensive panel-based analysis. On this basis we can obtain a fuller understanding of the endogeneity of factors relating to party preference that have been too readily assumed to be exogenous.

NOTES

1. It also follows that over time there should be an increasing convergence between perceptions of voters' own positions and their preferred parties' positions, and divergence between their own positions and the positions of parties they dislike: this can occur because own position moves closer to preferred party position (party influence); because perceptions of preferred party position will move closer to their own position (projection); or because their own and preferred party's positions converge (both of above). Further work is currently being conducted to examine these predictions.
2. The British Election Panel Study data used in this analysis were collected under the auspices of the Centre for Research into Elections and Social Trends (CREST). CREST is an Economic & Social Research Council designated research centre linking the Department of Sociology, Oxford and the National Centre for Social Research and co-funded by the Sainsbury Charitable Trusts.
3. The extent of the positive linear association between self and party positioning is even more dramatic with respect to perceptions of issue stances for the Conservative party (details available).
4. Analyses which include ratings of Hague's leadership in addition to those for Blair produce significant effects for perceptions of both leaders (see Andersen and Evans 2003), but their inclusion does not change the other findings in the models presented here.
5. For estimates of models of Labour Party identification for models A and B see Table 2.
6. Analyses which use vote in 2001 as the dependent variable, rather than party identity, produce substantively equivalent findings to those presented here (details available).

REFERENCES

Abelson, Robert P. (1968) *Theories of Cognitive Consistency: A Sourcebook.* Chicago: Rand McNally.

Achen, Christopher H. (1992) 'Social Psychology, Demographic Variables, and Linear Regression: Breaking the Iron Triangle in Voting Research', *Political Behavior* 14: 195–211.

Alvarez, R. Michael, Jonathan Nagler and Shaun Bowler (2000) 'Issues, Economics, and the Dynamics of Multiparty Elections: The British 1987 General Election,' *American Political Science Review* 94: 131–49.

Andersen, R. and G. Evans (2003) 'Who Blairs Wins? Leadership and Voting in the 2001 Election.' *British Elections & Parties Review,* 13: 229–47.

Bara, Judith and Ian Budge (2001) 'Party Policy and Ideology: Still New Labour?', in P. Norris (ed.) *Parliamentary Affairs,* 54: 590–606.

Bartels, L.M. (2002) 'Beyond the Running Tally: Partisan Bias in Political Perceptions', *Political Behavior,* 24: 117–50.

Berelson, R., P.F. Lazarsfeld and W.N. McPhee (1954) *Voting: A Study of Opinion Formation in a Presidential Campaign*. Chicago: University of Chicago Press.
Butler, David and Dennis Kavanagh (2002) *The British General Election of 2001*. New York: Palgrave.
Campbell, Angus, Philip Converse, Warren Miller and Donald Stokes (1960) *The American Voter*. New York: Wiley.
Conover, Pamela J., and Stanley Feldman (1989) 'Candidate Perceptions in an Ambiguous World: Campaigns, Cues, and Inference Processes' *American Journal of Political Science* 33: 917–40.
Converse, P. (1964) 'The Structure of Belief Systems in Mass Publics', in D. Apter (ed.) *Ideology and Discontent*. New York: Free Press.
Cox, David R. and Nanny Wermuth (1996) *Multivariate Dependencies: Models, Analysis and Interpretation*. London: Chapman & Hill.
Crewe, Ivor and Katarina Thomson (1999) 'Party Loyalties: Dealignment or Realignment?', in Geoffrey Evans and Pippa Norris (eds) *Critical Elections: British Parties and Voters in Long-Term Perspective*. London: Sage.
Dalton, R.J. (1996) *Citizen Politics: Public Opinion and Political Parties in Advanced Western Democracies*. Chatham, NJ.: Chatham House.
Enelow, J. and M. Hinich (1984) *The Spatial Theory of Voting*. Cambridge: Cambridge University Press.
Evans, Geoffrey (1999) 'Europe: A New Electoral Cleavage?' in Geoffrey Evans and Pippa Norris (eds) *Critical Elections: British Parties and Voters in Long-Term Perspective*. London: Sage.
Evans, G. (2001) 'European Integration, Party Politics and Voting in the 2001 Election'. *British Elections & Parties Review*, 12: 95–110.
Evans, Geoffrey and Robert Andersen (2001) 'Endogenizing the Economy: Political Preferences and Economic Perceptions across the Electoral Cycle', *CREST Working Paper Series, Number 88*, accessed at http://www.crest.ox.ac.uk/papers.htm.
Fox, John Fox (1997) *Applied Regression Analysis, Linear Models, and Related Methods*. Sage.
Franklin, M. (1985) *The Decline in Class Voting in Britain: Changes in the Basis of Electoral Choice, 1964–1983*. Oxford: Oxford University Press.
Franklin, M.N., T. Mackie and H. Valen et al. (1992) *Electoral Change: Responses to Evolving Social and Attitudinal Structures in Western Countries*. Cambridge: Cambridge University Press.
Gerber, Alan, and Donald Green (1999) 'Misperceptions about Perceptual Bias', *Annual Review of Political Science* 2: 189–210.
Himmelweit, H., P. Humphreys and M. Jaeger (1985) *How Voters Decide*. Milton Keynes: Open University Press.
Jacoby, William G. (1988) 'The Impact of Party Identification on Issue Attitudes', *American Journal of Political Science* 32: 643–61.
Kitschelt, H. (1994) *The Transformation of European Social Democracy*. Cambridge: Cambridge University Press.
Kitschelt, H. (in collaboration with Anthony J. McGann) (1995) *The Radical Right in Western Europe: A Comparative Analysis*. Ann Arbor: Michigan University Press.
Lodge, Milton G. and Ruth Hamill (1986) 'A Partisan Schema for Political Information Processing', *American Political Science Review* 82: 737–61.
Markus, Gregory B. (1982) 'Political Attitudes during an Election Year: A Report on the 1980 NES Panel Study', *American Political Science Review* 76: 538–60.
Nisbett, R. and L. Ross (1980) *Human Inference: Strategies and Shortcomings of Human Judgment*. Engelwood Cliffs, NJ: Prentice Hall.
Rabinowizt, G. and S.E. Macdonald (1989) 'A Directional Theory of Issue Voting', *American Political Science Review*, 83: 93–121.
Rahn, Wendy M. (1993) 'The Role of Partisan Stereotypes in Information Processing about Political Candidates', *American Journal of Political Science* 37: 472–96.
Rose, R., and I. McAllister (1986) *Voters Begin to Choose: From Closed-Class to Open Elections in Britain*. London: Sage.

Sanders, David (1999) 'The Impact of Left-Right Ideology,' in Geoffrey Evans and Pippa Norris (eds) *Critical Elections: British Parties and Voters in Long-Term Perspective.* London: Sage.

Sniderman, P.M., R.A. Brody and P.E. Tetlock (1991) *Reasoning and Choice: Explorations in Political Psychology.* Cambridge: Cambridge University Press.

Stokes D.E. (1966) 'Party Loyalty and the Likelihood of Deviating Elections', in A. Campbell, P.E. Converse, W.E. Miller and D.E. Stokes (eds) *Elections and the Political Order.* New York: Wiley.

Webb, Paul, and David M. Farrell (1999) 'Party Members and Ideological Change', in Geoffrey Evans and Pippa Norris (eds) *Critical Elections: British Parties and Voters in Long-Term Perspective.* London: Sage.

Zaller, J.R. (1992) *The Nature and Origins of Mass Opinion.* New York: Cambridge. University Press.

Switching and Splitting: Local Contexts and Campaigns from Intentions to the Ballot Box – New Zealand 1999

Ron Johnston and Charles Pattie

Election campaigns have two main purposes – to win support for a party and to mobilize those who intend to vote for them. Increasingly, the two elements involve separate activities. National election campaigns are aimed at winning support, focused on the party's policies and leadership, and are promoted through the mass media, whereas local campaigns pay much more attention to identifying a party's existing supporters and ensuring that they turn out to vote. The latter campaigns are especially important in constituency-based electoral systems, with parties focusing on the marginal seats in which elections are won and lost. Numerous studies over the last two decades have shown that a party's performance in each constituency is related to the intensity of its campaign there: parties perform best where they put in most effort at 'turning out the vote' (see, for example, Green et al., 2003, on canvassing experiments, Denver and Hands on constituency campaigning, and Johnston and Pattie, 2003, on the impact of campaign spending).

Less attention has been paid to the degree to which such local campaigns are important in sustaining voters' initial intentions or even winning them over. Recent work on the 2001 UK general election, using data on voting intentions prior to the campaign as well as actual behaviour, has shown clear evidence that local campaigning did influence some individuals (Johnston and Pattie, 2003b). This article extends that work by looking at a recent New Zealand general election in which, under the multi-member proportional (MMP) system, the constituency and list contests can be de-coupled: electors can indicate which party they prefer to be in government – their 'sincere preferences' – in the list contest but vote for another in their local electorate contest without significantly diluting the impact of the former vote on the overall outcome. In such situations, local campaigns may be very effective in changing people's minds regarding how to vote in the electorate contest. Does local context and campaigning influence vote-switching in such a potential split-ticket situation?

British Elections & Parties Review, Vol. 14, 2004, pp. 40–71
ISSN 1368-9886 print
DOI: 10.1080/1368988042000258772   © 2004 Taylor & Francis Ltd.

MMP in New Zealand

The MMP electoral system, deployed in Germany for the last 50 years and recently introduced to a number of other countries, allows for split-ticket voting. (On the recent international expansion in the system's use, see Shugart and Wattenberg, 2001.) Electors can support a different party in the list section of the contest from the one that they choose for the separate constituency electorate contests. In New Zealand, which has used the system for three general elections (1996, 1999, 2002), the volume of split-ticket voting has been substantial: 37 per cent of those who voted in 1996 cast a split-ticket, for example, as did 35 per cent in 1999. Appreciating the reasons for, the volume and direction of, and the location of this split-ticket voting has attracted academic interest recently, although it gets relatively little coverage in general discussions of the system.

New Zealand's MMP system has two components. Each elector has two votes, one for a party list (referred to here as the list contest),[1] and one for their local constituency (referred to as the electorate contest). The latter uses the first-past-the-post system, the candidate having most votes being declared elected. In 1999, 67 of the 120 seats in the House of Representatives (New Zealand's unicameral Parliament) were determined in this way.[2]

The remaining seats are allocated to ensure proportional representation in the House according to each party's percentage of the votes cast in the list contest. To qualify for seats, a party must win either more than five per cent of the valid votes cast in the list election or at least one electorate contest. Whichever threshold is crossed, the party is then allocated a percentage of the total number of seats commensurate with its share of the votes cast in the list contest. Thus the composition of the House, and the relative strength of the parties there, is a function of the list votes.

One consequence of the introduction of MMP in New Zealand has been an increase in the number of political parties represented in the House of Representatives. New Zealand was formerly a predominantly two-party system, with parties from the left (Labour) and right (National) gaining a majority of the votes at every general election and an even greater majority of the seats (as illustrated in Johnston, 1976, 1992). Parties of the left (the Greens and the Alliance), the centre (Christian Heritage and New Zealand First), and the right (Association of Consumers and Taxpayers – ACT) all won seats at the 1999 general election, for example, and several were involved in the post-election coalition negotiations after each of the three MMP elections (1996, 1999 and 2002). In addition, other parties campaigned for votes in the list contest at each election but did not win sufficient support to cross the five per cent threshold and gain seats in Parliament.

Strategic and Split-Ticket Voting under MMP

At all elections in New Zealand, a substantial proportion of the electorate determine their voting intentions before the campaign begins – some with greater certainty than others. In MMP elections, many will thus identify which party to support in the list contest and also which party/candidate to vote for in their constituency contest, prior to the onset of campaigning. Some may then be influenced by the campaigns, and change their minds on one or both of the contests; others may sustain their original choices; while a third group – who had no prior intentions – make their selections during the campaign period.

What proportion of the electorate does have a clear set of intentions prior to the campaign which they then carry through to election day, and who are they? Following on from that, which electors change their minds during the campaign period, who are they, and what aspects of the campaign influence their decisions with regard to both components of the election? Those two questions are the core of the analysis of the 1999 New Zealand general election presented here, using data collected by the New Zealand Election Study.[3] In particular, we focus on geographical variations in the volume of split-ticket voting, which was considerable in 1999 – from 28 to 73 per cent of those who voted across the 67 constituencies (Johnston and Pattie, 2003a). Analyses of election results – at both aggregate and individual voter scales – have related that variation to aspects of the geography of the election campaign (Johnston and Pattie, 2003a, 2003c). The analyses here extend those studies by investigating the vote-switching that took place during the official (six-week) campaign period preceding election day.

For individual voters, the list vote is crucial for influencing the composition of the House, and thus the nature of the government formed. The electorate vote has no influence on this, unless the winning candidate's party fails to cross the five per cent threshold in the list contest, in which case an electorate victory is necessary to gain representation. The general understanding of first-past-the-post systems formulated by Duverger – that they favour two parties – has been carried forward into MMP systems. In New Zealand, whose politics were dominated by two parties throughout the twentieth century (first-past-the-post was deployed there until 1996), the two predominant parties of the pre-reform period (Labour and National) would be expected to prevail in the MMP electorate contests, but the list contest could produce a multi-party outcome (Vowles, 2002a). Electors should identify their list contest vote as the one that will influence the overall election outcome, with that choice reflecting their 'sincere preference' – i.e. the party that they most want to see in government. But they should also realize that their electorate vote can be allocated to another party, without in any major way (save in exceptional circumstances) affecting the overall outcome.[4] That realization may come about during the campaign period, when parties and others may convince electors to switch from their original intentions for their local constituency, whilst sustaining their original voting intention in the party list.

Why should people allocate their electorate votes to a party other than that which they supported in the list contest? In the most detailed analysis to date of split-ticket voting in New Zealand at the level of the individual voter, Karp et al. (2002: see also Banducci et al., 1998; Denemark, 1998; Vowles, 2002a) have deployed ideas derived from theories developed by Duverger (1954), Cox (1997) and others regarding strategic voting, of which split-ticket voting is one example. Their analysis of New Zealand's first MMP election in 1996 suggested four reasons, to which a fifth has been added here (Karp et al., 2002: 7):

1. That electors take seriously the possibility of an overhang (a party getting more seats than entitled under the proportional allocation because of its large number of constituency victories), and wish to support the party that would benefit from it, even though it is not their preferred choice in the list contest;
2. That electors take into account the personal characteristics and/or past behaviour (including representing their constituency) of individual candidates and decide to vote for them to represent their personal and/or local interests, irrespective of party affiliation;
3. That electors value the ideology (or policy orientation) of a party and vote for its candidate because they are the most viable alternative in the local context;
4. That electors unfamiliar with the system may believe that the electorate contest influences the overall outcome (which they imply was particularly likely in the first of the elections using the system); and
5. That electors wish to ensure that a party not expected to cross the threshold for representation in the list contest gains a constituency success and so is allocated a number of seats in the House.

Of these, the first will occur only rarely – and electors would be unlikely to evaluate its likelihood for themselves without suggestions from either or both of the media and the party(ies) involved; the same is true of the fifth. The second and third are the most likely influences at the second election in a sequence using MMP, on the assumption that over time more of the electorate gains an accurate appreciation of the system's operation.[5]

We focus here on the second and third factors, therefore, looking – to the extent possible with available survey data – at switches in 'candidate-specific voting' in the electorate contests and spatial variations in party-oriented electorate voting which reflect both political awareness and attitudes among electors and the local context in which they operate. In some constituencies a party voted for in the list contest may have little or no chance of victory there: to support its local candidate would thus mean, in effect, wasting one's vote. Far better, perhaps, for such a voter to switch support to the candidate of another party whose position is relatively close to that of their preferred party supported in the list contest – if such a party existed. In that way, it may be possible to ensure that a relatively sympathetic member from an allied party (perhaps one that could potentially join the most preferred party in a coalition government) is elected from the constituency, rather than voting for the party supported in the list contest and thereby possibly assist the victory of a candidate for a party whose policy positions are far from one's own.

Such strategic switch-voting depends on two factors. First, the elector has to be aware of the potential for such action, which implies an appreciation of the MMP system. Second, the elector has to be aware of the situation in their own constituency – both the electoral chances of the candidates for the various parties and the attractiveness of candidates of other parties to that voted for in the list contest on the salient policy positions. Some electors may be well informed regarding the various candidates' chances, although as New Zealand's constituency boundaries change every five years (including between the 1996 and 1999 general elections) it may be difficult for them to develop an accurate evaluation; they may also have a clear evaluation of the policy positions of the candidates from various parties. Other electors (probably a majority?) may not be so well informed, and may lack the motivation to devote the time and effort necessary to obtain the needed information: as Downs (1957) pointed out, it is rarely rational to do so. And so they will only be aware of the local potentials if they are provided with relevant information, either through their local context (including others living there and the local media) or from a party seeking their support. Parties use election campaigns to provide that information in a variety of ways: the more effort they put into persuading electors of the desirability of supporting their candidate in the electorate contest, the more they are likely to win over voters.

This argument suggests that split-ticket voting resulting from switches during the election campaign is most likely to occur in particular situations. The first is where the elector is predisposed to vote in that way, which suggests somebody who is aware of the nuances of the MMP system and its potential: this is the behavioural model of split-ticket voting derived from Duverger. The second is the strategic model, where electors are persuaded of the value of voting for a party in the electorate contest by its campaign there. Karp et al.'s (2002) findings for the 1996 contest are consistent with both of those expectations with regard to split-ticket voting, but they undertook no analyses of switches in voting intentions. At the aggregate level they found that the more a party spent on the campaign in a constituency (especially one of the smaller parties) the lower its 'net vote wastage' (defined as the difference between its list and electorate contest vote shares). And at the individual level they found greater levels of split-ticket voting among the more politically-knowledgeable and the better educated, but lower levels of such voting as the partisan identification with a particular party increased. They also found that those with low political knowledge were more likely to cast a split-ticket the greater the local spending by the party in their constituency. The implication is that certain types of voter in particular contexts were more likely to switch their vote in the electorate contest during the campaign than were others, elsewhere: that implication is tested formally here.

Prior Intentions and Final Vote

Karp et al. (2002) have provided substantial insights into the split-ticket voting decision. However, they assume (at least implicitly) that the decision is taken during the campaign period: until then, most electors will have but a single partisan preference and – unless they are going to vote for an electorate candidate on the basis of personal qualities and qualifications irrespective of party – intend to vote for the same party in both contests. This is unlikely, however. Some electors will be well informed about both the system (given that MMP had been used at the previous general election) and the local situation and will have determined to vote a split-ticket prior to the campaign. The goal of the parties during the election campaign, then, is twofold:

1. At the national level, assisted by local campaigning where possible, to win or sustain the support of those committed to them in the list contest; and similarly
2. At the constituency level to sustain and/or win over their support.

This may mean changing electors' minds on one of their intentions: it may mean changing them on both.

How Minds are Changed During Campaigns

The literature on local effects in voting patterns identifies a number of potential influences on voters' decision-making, of which two are relevant to the current issue and can be tested using the available data.

The first is *friends-and-neighbours voting*, an argument developed by Key (1949) from studies of intra-party contests in the American south, and developed by others in a variety of contexts – such as the at-large elections for Christchurch City Council (Johnston, 1972, 1973). According to this argument, individuals may be prepared to desert their normal partisan preferences

to vote for a local candidate: either because the candidate is known personally
to them; because they know somebody who knows, and speaks well of, them;
or because they believe that person will best represent local interests whatever
their party. In first-past-the-post elections, such friends-and-neighbours voting
is likely to be small in most cases because it may involve harming the chances
of the party which electors favour: only their 'sincere preferences' can be
expressed. It is feasible to vote for a local candidate on grounds other than
party under MMP, however, because to do so will almost certainly not affect
the overall election outcome and the composition of the government.

Second, there are *campaign effects*. Parties have two main goals during an
election campaign: to ensure that their committed supporters both remain
loyal to them and go out and vote; and to convince as many others as possible
to switch from their original intentions. A range of strategies is used to
achieve these goals. Many are nationally oriented through mass media, with
campaigns focused on party leaders, policy positions and, where relevant,
records in government.[6] Others are locally conducted, involving parties –
through their candidates, agents and activists – contacting members of the
electorate, personally, impersonally or indirectly (through advertising
campaigns, for example), and seeking their support. In an MMP election, for
the electorate contests, this may involve encouraging strategic voting, urging
people to vote for a party's candidate in the constituency because they have a
better chance of victory than the party an elector may be supporting for the list
contest (and showing that not to do so may enhance the chances of the candidate of a less desirable party).

Switching and Splitting: Intentions and Outcomes

Over one-third of those who voted in New Zealand's 1999 general election
used a split-ticket strategy. But how many changed their strategy during, and
presumably as a consequence of, the campaign? The 1999 New Zealand Election Study surveys had a before-and-after component. Respondents were
asked in a pre-campaign (telephone) interview which party they intended to
vote for in each section of the election and then, in a post-election survey by
postal questionnaire, which party they actually voted for. These data provide
the dependent variables for our analyses here. We only analyse data for those
respondents who were on what is known as the 'general roll' in New Zealand,
thereby omitting the six constituencies reserved for Maori voters in 1999,
where there was a slightly different pattern of party competition.[7] Furthermore, since our focus is on those who change from their original vote intentions, we also omit those who had not decided how to vote in either contest
when interviewed during the pre-election phase of the survey. (These
comprised 21 per cent of the total sample.[8])

Although a large number of parties contested the 1999 election – in the list contest if not in a majority of the constituency electorate contests – the competition was in effect between seven parties. Of these, two predominated: Labour and National had been hegemonic in New Zealand politics between the 1930s and 1996, providing a single-party majority government after every election up until the final years before the first MMP contest. They remained the dominant political forces thereafter, with National winning 44 of the 125 seats in the 1996 election, and Labour 37. National formed a coalition government with New Zealand First following several weeks of post-election negotiations. Of the other five parties, the Alliance was a grouping of left-of-centre parties whose leader was a former Labour Cabinet Minister. The Green Party was a member of the Alliance in the 1996 campaign and Parliament, but contested the majority of constituencies in 1999 as a separate party.[9] On the right of the political spectrum was the Association of Citizens and Taxpayers (ACT), and in the centre were Christian Heritage and New Zealand First. The latter had been in a coalition government with National between 1996 and 1998 (although general expectations in 1996 had been that it would form a coalition with Labour), but the coalition, and the party, collapsed a year before the 1999 election.

The analyses here use the 60 general roll constituencies as their spatial template. Of those, 41 were identified as 'safe' for one of the parties in 1999, based on estimates of the results of the 1996 election if the new constituencies had been used then. A safe constituency was defined as one in which the leading party had over 10 percentage points more of the 1996 votes than its nearest rival: 21 of those constituencies were held by National, 18 by Labour, and just one each by the Alliance and New Zealand First. A further 12 were marginal – with the leading party having a margin over the second-placed of 5–10 percentage points: seven of these were held by Labour with National in second place, and four by National with Labour second: there was one constituency with three parties (Labour, National and the Alliance) within 5–10 points of each other. Finally there were seven very marginal constituencies (a gap of less than five points between the leading parties): only four involved parties other than Labour or National.[10] Thus in the great majority of constituencies the contest was between the two largest parties, with candidates of the other five having little chance of victory.

The overall pattern of intended and actual voting in 1999 suggests both consistency across the two contests and relatively little net change between electors' initial intentions and final decisions (Table 1).[11] In the list contest, for example, there are no shifts between the intended and actual outcome for any one party of more than three percentage points of the total. The main changes (in absolute terms) were the decrease in support for National, which was largely compensated – in net terms at least – by those who either voted for another party

TABLE 1
INTENDED AND ACTUAL VOTES IN THE TWO CONTESTS

	List		Electorate	
	I	A	I	A
Alliance	8.1	6.6	6.7	5.9
Labour	37.5	37.6	42.7	42.4
National	34.7	30.1	34.3	29.1
NZ First	4.6	3.3	4.0	2.5
ACT	8.1	7.9	5.1	4.8
Christian	2.3	2.6	1.2	1.7
Green	3.0	4.4	2.7	3.4
Other/DNV	1.8	7.7	3.2	10.2

Notes:
I – Intended vote as indicated in the pre-election survey; A – Actual vote as reported in the post-election survey.

or did not vote at all (Table 1). The electorate contests display a similar very limited amount of net change between intended and actual. Across contests, too, the overall indication is of stability, with the smaller parties (i.e. those other than Labour and National) having a lesser share of both the intended and actual electorate than list votes – presumably reflecting their generally poor chances of winning all but a few of the first-past-the-post electorate contests.

The Pattern of Splitting: Intended and Actual

The data in Table 1 are net figures only: the gross patterns indicate much greater variation. The matrices in Table 2 show the patterns of intended and actual votes across the two contests as the percentages of those intending to vote for a party in the list contest who also intended to vote for its candidate in the electorate contest. Among the intended votes (the first block), only Labour and National had more than half of their list contest supporters also intending to vote for them in the electorate contest and in three cases – the Alliance, ACT and the Greens – a plurality of list contest supporters intended to vote for another party in the electorate contest. In each case those who intended to vote a split-ticket from the smaller parties predominantly allocated their electorate contest support to either Labour (Alliance, New Zealand First and Green list voters) or National (ACT and Christian Heritage list voters). These patterns are entirely in line with the hypothesis of ideological similarity – supporters of small parties on the right switched their constituency support to National whereas those whose 'sincere preferences' were for parties of the left and centre switched to Labour.

TABLE 2
STRAIGHT- AND SPLIT-TICKET VOTING: INTENDED AND ACTUAL (% OF ROW
TOTALS)

Intended Electorate List	A	L	N	NZF	ACT	C	G
Alliance	34.5	51.4	5.6	2.1	1.4	0.7	2.8
Labour	8.5	81.0	4.4	1.7	0.5	0.2	2.6
National	0.7	12.0	74.9	1.0	7.4	0.3	1.2
NZ First	2.5	33.3	9.9	49.4	1.2	0.0	0.0
ACT	1.4	8.5	56.7	0.0	27.0	1.4	0.7
Christian	5.1	10.3	23.1	23.1	0.0	35.9	0.0
Green	3.7	38.9	11.1	1.9	0.0	0.0	35.2
Actual Electorate List	A	L	N	NZF	ACT	C	G
Alliance	26.7	57.8	3.4	2.6	0.0	0.9	4.3
Labour	8.5	77.7	2.9	1.7	0.6	0.2	4.0
National	1.3	9.9	73.2	0.8	7.8	0.4	1.3
NZ First	1.7	43.1	8.6	41.4	0.0	0.0	0.0
ACT	1.5	12.4	50.4	0.0	27.0	0.7	1.5
Christian	2.2	23.9	8.7	4.3	0.0	43.5	0.0
Green	7.9	42.1	13.2	1.3	1.3	0.0	23.7

Note: Figures do not sum to 100 because of those who either voted for a party in the contest
other than the seven listed or did not vote having intended to do so.
Key to parties:
A – Alliance; L – Labour; N – National; NZF – New Zealand First; ACT – Association of Citizens
and Taxpayers; C – Christian Heritage; G – Green.

Very similar patterns are shown in the matrix for the actual votes in Table
2. Again only Labour and National had more than half of their list contest
supporters also voting for their party's candidate in the electorate contests.
Well over half of the Alliance's list voters cast an electorate ballot for their
constituency's Labour candidate, as did over 40 per cent of both NZ First's
and the Greens'; just over half of the ACT's list supporters shifted to voting
for a National candidate.

Shifts in Straight- and Split-Ticket Intentions

There was a great deal of split-ticket voting, both intended and actual, therefore. Furthermore, the pattern was not stable between voters' initial intentions
and what they actually did at the ballot box. There was a great deal of switching during the campaign. Table 3 shows the amount (again the figures are
percentages of the row totals so that, for example, of those intending to
support the Alliance in the list contest, only 56.7 per cent actually did so). In
the list contest, in each case the majority of those intending to vote for each

TABLE 3
SWITCHES BETWEEN INTENDED AND ACTUAL VOTING

List vote Intended	Actual (%)						
	A	L	N	NZF	ACT	C	G
Alliance	56.7	26.2	2.8	0.7	2.8	5.0	2.8
Labour	4.6	81.7	3.1	0.9	0.2	0.3	2.7
National	0.3	8.4	74.7	0.7	4.9	1.3	1.8
NZ First	0.0	18.5	9.9	55.6	1.2	2.5	2.5
ACT	0.7	3.5	23.4	0.7	69.5	0.7	0.7
Christian	2.4	7.3	4.9	0.0	0.0	63.4	0.0
Green	1.9	11.1	7.4	0.0	3.7	0.0	66.7

Electorate vote Intended	Actual (%)						
	A	L	N	NZF	ACT	C	G
Alliance	49.6	31.6	6.8	0.9	0.0	1.7	4.3
Labour	3.6	80.7	4.4	1.2	0.7	0.7	2.5
National	1.0	10.7	71.0	0.5	4.8	0.7	1.0
NZ First	2.9	21.7	13.0	40.6	0.0	4.3	0.0
ACT	4.5	7.9	25.8	3.4	52.8	1.1	1.1
Christian	5.0	0.0	15.0	0.0	0.0	65.0	0.0
Green	4.3	17.0	2.1	0.0	2.1	0.0	55.3

Note: Figures do not sum to 100 because of those who either voted for another party in the electorate contest or, in the lower matrix, did not vote having intended to do so.
Key to parties:
A – Alliance; L – Labour; N – National; NZF – New Zealand First; ACT – Association of Citizens
and Taxpayers; C – Christian Heritage; G – Green.

party actually did so, although there was considerable leakage from some –
notably the Alliance and NZ First – and even Labour and National lost around
one-fifth/one-quarter of their original supporters. In the electorate contests,
shown in the second matrix, the amount of switching was even greater, especially from those initially intending to vote for one of the smaller parties. New
Zealand First retained the support of only 40.6 per cent of those who intended
to vote for its constituency candidates, for example, and the Alliance also lost
about half of its intended voters.

Two conclusions stand out from these first three tables:

1. Despite the apparent overall similarity in the pattern of party choice across
    the two contests – whether for intended or actual votes – this net situation

(Table 1) concealed a great deal of gross split-ticket voting, with a substantial proportion of voters either intending or actually voting for a different party in the two contests; and

2. Despite the apparent similarity in the pattern of voting at each contest between the intended and actual outcome, this net pattern also conceals a great deal of 'campaign period churning', with a substantial proportion of voters switching their preference in at least one of the contests during the short period before polling day.

Table 4 summarizes the shifts. The top two rows show the percentage of respondents who did not change their minds over the campaign period: some 73 per cent remained loyal to the party they intended to vote for in the list contest, and 69 per cent were loyal in the electorate contest. The second block of data show that only 57 per cent remained loyal at both contests, however: 43 per cent of the respondents changed their minds on at least one of the contests during the campaign period, with fully 15 per cent changing their minds on both. (The small number who either voted for a candidate representing a party other than the seven main ones listed here or, having stated in the campaign survey that they intended to vote in the electorate contest and then did not, are excluded from this table.)

Our analyses of this switching will involve three stages. In the first, we test whether voters differed in the degree to which their overall political preferences (regarding party, policy and potential Prime Minister) influenced their original voting intentions in the two contests. Our expectation was that, given the relative unimportance of the results of the electorate contests to the overall outcome, these preferences would be much more important influences on the list than electorate contest intentions. If that were validated, this would indicate that other influences – such as the nature of the local campaign – would be more significant on the electorate than the list contests, perhaps stimulating vote-switching. The second stage looks at switching during the campaign

TABLE 4
THE DEGREE OF CHANGE BETWEEN INTENDED AND ACTUAL VOTES
(% OF THOSE SURVEYED)

Voted for intended party in party contest	72.9
Voted for intended party in electorate contest	68.7
Voted for intended party in both contests	56.8
Voted for intended party in party but not electorate contest	16.0
Voted for intended party in electorate but not party contest	11.9
Voted for intended party in neither contest	15.3

Note: The intended party is the one that the respondent said they would vote for in the pre-election survey.

period, analysing the influences on whether voters changed their minds regarding either the list or both contests; this anticipates that vote switching will be more likely among some groups of voters, in some contexts than others. Finally, in the third stage we will investigate vote-switching away from original intentions for the electorate contest, which we anticipated would be most influenced by the local context and the intensity of party campaigns.

Who Preferred Which Party at the Outset of the Campaign? The Behavioural Model

The List Contest

We assume that the party which electors intended to vote for in the list contest at the outset of the campaign was the one that they wanted to see in government because they identified with it and/or felt it offered the best policies and leadership. List contest choice at the outset of the campaign should be a function of attachment to that party as indexed by a party identification measure plus, for example, beliefs that it offers the best policies on the issues most important to the voter and that its leader is the preferred candidate for Prime Minister.

Data were collected during the campaign survey (before respondents were asked their vote intentions) on which party, if any, they identified with, which candidate they preferred as Prime Minister, which issue was most important to them during the election, and which party was closest to their position on that issue. On the first of these – party identification – a large majority of those who identified with a party also intended to vote for it in the list contest. There was some switching within the 'left' and 'right'-wing blocks, however, with over one-fifth of Alliance identifiers intending to vote Labour and nearly the same percentage of ACT identifiers intending to vote National. Regarding potential Prime Minister (for which data were collected on five party leaders), in four of the five cases a majority intended to vote for their most favoured PM's party. Finally, respondents were asked the most important issue for them in the election and which party was closest to them on that issue. (Some 21 per cent said health, 15 per cent education and 10 per cent the economy.) In each case, the majority of those saying that a particular party was closest to their position on their most salient issue intended to vote for it in the party contest.

The Electorate Contests

Intended voting in the party contest sustains the general arguments advanced here from the behavioural model. What of the intended vote in the electorate contests? In these, as discussed above, many of the candidates of respondents' preferred parties had little chance of victory, and in the majority of cases it was likely that either Labour or National would provide the constituency MP. So were people as likely to vote in the same way in those contests? With regard to party identification, smaller percentages intended to vote for the party they identified with in the electorate than in the party contest: for Labour and National the differences were small (as Duverger's hypothesis suggests), but for the Alliance, NZ First and ACT they were substantial. In each case, considerable numbers intended to vote for another party of the 'left' or 'right': there was substantial switching from the Alliance and NZ First to Labour and from ACT and Christian Heritage to National.

The same patterns emerge regarding preferred candidate for Prime Minister. Most of those who preferred either Clark or Shipley intended to vote Labour or National respectively in the electorate as well as the list contest, but many more who thought the ACT leader would make the best PM intended to support that party in the list than in the electorate contest. In general, those who preferred the leaders of the three smaller parties were less likely to intend voting for their parties in the electorate than in the party contests. Finally, smaller percentages were also intending to vote for the party closest to their salient issue position in the list than in the electorate contests.

These data provide substantial support for the behavioural model with regard to the pattern of list contest voting intentions, but much less so for the electorate contests. In the list contest, electors intended to vote for the party they identified with, which had the best policies on the issues they thought salient, and had the perceived best potential Prime Minister. In the electorate contests, on the other hand, more were intending to vote for a party other than that preferred on the three criteria. In terms of government-formation – the list vote – electors voted for their preferred party. In terms of local representation, many apparently voted on other criteria, suggesting that to appreciate the outcome at the constituency contests it is necessary to explore the strategic and campaign effects model as well as the behavioural model – especially since, as already demonstrated, there was so much change between intentions and actual voting. Was vote-switching in the constituency contests linked to the context and campaigning there?

Adding the Structural and Campaign Effects Model

There was therefore a great deal of intended and actual split-ticket voting and also of campaign 'churning' at the 1999 New Zealand general election. To appreciate the nature of those patterns, we report on tests of models constructed to account for people's intentions, actual votes and, in particular, their shifts during the campaign, in the context of the behavioural and strategic models of split-ticket voting discussed earlier. In each case, the models reported are selected from a number experimented with because they gave the clearest pictures of the correlates of the observed patterns.

For the behavioural model, a range of variables was explored covering individuals' partisan identification and its strength, as derived from the 'standard' questions on party identification,[12] their interest in politics, their decision-making: when they decided how to vote in each contest, and whether they considered changing their vote. Others – such as preferences for Prime Minister – were discarded since they overlapped strongly with the party identification question.

Within the strategic model, the best available data for the friends-and-neighbours effect come from a post-election survey question as to which party's candidate in the relevant constituency was personally most liked. Substantial numbers of those intending to vote for a party in the electorate contests also found that party's candidate the one that they 'personally most liked' by the end of the campaign (Table 5). With Labour, for example, of those who intended to vote for the party in the electorate contest only 66 per cent of those who intended to vote Labour in that contest when interviewed before the election found its candidate the most attractive in their constituency at the time of the contest, and for three of the smaller parties only 36–39 per cent identified the candidate of their chosen party as the most attractive on offer.

If people acted on such beliefs, therefore, their vote intentions should have been changed, with larger percentages actually voting for the candidate they found most attractive. The second column of Table 5 shows that this was so, with substantial increases in most cases in the percentages reporting having voted for the party of their most-liked candidate. (The exceptions were Labour, for which there was only a small increase from a large base, and Christian Heritage, most of whose intended supporters deemed its candidate

TABLE 5
LIKING AND VOTING FOR A CANDIDATE IN THE ELECTORATE CONTESTS

Party supported	Intended	Actual
Alliance	44.0	60.2
Labour	66.1	71.6
National	50.5	60.1
New Zealand First	36.4	53.5
ACT	36.9	51.3
Christian Heritage	57.9	57.7
Green	38.6	53.7

Note: The figures are the percentage of respondents saying that the candidate of the party they intended to and actually voted for in the electorate contest was also the candidate they 'personally most liked' in the relevant constituency.

the most likable.) The circumstantial evidence of friends-and-neighbours voting is considerable, therefore, with substantial numbers switching their constituency preference during the campaign to their 'most-liked' candidate – with the identification of that person presumably a function of the local campaign for their election.

To investigate campaign effects we used two types of variables. The first was 'objective' variables taken from sources other than the survey: the estimated result for each party in the 1996 electorate contest in the respondent's constituency, and the amount that each party spent on its campaign there (the maximum allowed was NZ$20,000); previous aggregate-level studies have shown close links between local spending and election outcome (Johnston and Pattie, 2002). The more a party spent on the constituency campaign, the better its candidate's expected performance there in the electorate contest, by winning over 'switchers' from other parties and mobilizing its own supporters so that they did not defect from their original intentions.

The 'subjective' data included two items from the pre-election survey: which parties' candidates the respondent thought would win and come second in the constituency. Others were taken from the post-election survey: whether the respondent had been contacted by a party or not. (Four possible types of contact were listed: telephone, visit, letter and pamphlet. Very few had more than two contacts, and after experimentation we reduced the variable to a single number: whether or not the respondent was contacted by that party.) With each of these variables, we expected that electors' choices for the constituency contests would be influenced by their evaluations of their preferred party's chances of victory there. For example, of those who intended to vote for the Alliance in the list contest, we anticipated that more would also intend voting for it in the electorate contest if they believed it had a good chance of victory there. This was the case: of those who expected the Alliance candidate to come either first or second, 65 per cent intended to vote for its candidate in the constituency contest, whereas of those who thought the Alliance candidate would come third or worse, only 29 per cent intended to vote for them. (The comparable figures for other parties were 84 and 71 per cent for Labour, 78 and 62 per cent for National, 81 and 38 per cent for New Zealand First, and 50 and 22 per cent for ACT.) Intended split-tickets were most likely where the voter's preferred party had little chance of victory in the electorate contest.

Testing the Models: I – Who Intended a Split-Ticket Vote?

The implication of the data cited above is that whereas most respondents were intending at the onset of the campaign to vote for their preferred party in the list contest (i.e. it was their 'sincere vote'), significantly fewer – especially among supporters of parties other than Labour and National – intended to vote for that party in the electorate contest too. This suggests a sophisticated electorate (or, at least, that a substantial proportion of it was sophisticated), whose members acted strategically, realizing that a vote for their preferred party of government was not necessarily the best option in the electorate contest. For those voters, as their candidate had little chance of victory there, they would be better advised to vote for a better-placed candidate from a party that was relatively close to their own preference who, if elected, might help ensure that their preferred party was involved in a coalition government.

Such split-ticket voting should be less likely among those strongly committed to a particular party and those with little interest in politics: the latter would be less aware of either the complexities of the system or the situation in their local constituency.[13] Respondents were asked both the strength of their party identification and how interested they were in politics. A strong commitment to a party should generate a greater likelihood of supporting it in both contests. Intending to vote a split-ticket, we argue, would be most likely in constituencies where the respondents' preferred party in the list contest had little chance of victory in the electorate contest. As shown by the variables introduced above: the greater a voter's preferred party's chances of victory locally, whether it was the favoured party or was in second place, the greater the expectation of a straight-ticket vote.

These hypotheses were tested by a logistic regression, in which the dependent variable was whether the respondent intended to vote a straight ticket (coded 1) or not (coded 0). The independent variables were: interest in politics; strength of party identification; the 1996 electorate vote for the party the respondent intended voting for in the party contest;[14] whether the respondent expected that party to win the electorate contest (coded 1 if yes; 0 otherwise); and whether that party was expected to come second (coded 1 if yes; 0 otherwise).

Table 6 shows a clear relationship between party identification and vote intention: the weaker the level of party identification the smaller the chances of a straight-ticket vote. (Those with no party identification were only 0.42 as likely – the exponent of the regression coefficient of −0.87 – to intend voting a straight ticket as those who identified very strongly with a party.) On the other hand, once party identification is held constant, there is little relationship with interest in politics.

Turning to the local context variables, the better the respondents' preferred list party performed in the electorate contest in the relevant constituency in 1996, the more likely they were to intend voting for it in the 1999 electorate contest (i.e. vote a straight ticket). The other variables suggest that this was because they expected their preferred party either to win or to come second in the constituency: those who thought their preferred party would win were

TABLE 6
LOGISTIC REGRESSION OF SPLIT-TICKET VOTING INTENTIONS

Interest in politics	List party expected to win in constituency		
(Comparator: very interested)	(Comparator: not first or second)		
Fairly	0.24		
Slightly	0.37**	Come first	2.36**
Not at all	0.36		
Strength of party identification	List party expected to be second in constituency		
(Comparator: very strong)	(Comparator: not first or second)		
Fairly strong	−0.58**		
Not very strong	−0.91**	Come second	1.12**
None	−0.81**		
1996 electorate vote	0.01*		
% correct			
all		72.6	
straight-ticket		78.4	
chi square		339.26	
−2 log likelihood		1743.1	

Notes: The dependent variable is coded 1 if the respondent intended to vote a straight-ticket and 0 otherwise. **coefficient statistically significant at the 0.05 level or better; *coefficient statistically significant at the 0.05–0.10 level.

10.6 times more likely to vote a straight-ticket than those who thought it would come third or worse (the exponent of the coefficient of 2.36), whereas those who thought it would come second were 3.1 times more likely. Where preferred parties in the list contest had a good (either real or perceived) chance of victory in the electorate contest, respondents intended to vote for them in both contests. Intended straight-ticket voting was rational with regard to the geography of the constituency contests.

Testing the Models: II – Switching from Pre-Campaign Vote Intentions

The List Contest

Why should respondents change from their intended voting choices? In the list contest, this would presumably be because aspects of the campaign convinced them that another party was better placed to bring their desired benefits. Such changes should be produced by the campaign itself, and be greatest among those with least initial commitment to any one party: those strongly identifying with a party when the campaign started would be less likely to change their minds than those who had at best only a weak partisan identification.[15] To evaluate whether this was so, models were fitted to predict whether respondents changed their choice of party for the list contest during the campaign.

Two sets of variables are included in these models. The first – *political attachment* – represent the behavioural model, with six variables. The second – *party campaigning and the local electorate* – comprised seven variables related to the campaign effects component. (The friends-and-neighbours model regarding preferred candidate was not relevant to the list contest.) The full list of variables involved is in the Appendix.

The logistic regression model was fitted twice. In the first, the dependent variable was all those who voted for the party that they reported intending to support in the list vote, irrespective of whether they changed their electorate vote. (These were coded 1 if the respondent intended to vote and actually voted for the same party in the list contest, and 0 otherwise.) In the second, the dependent variable was those who voted for their intended party in both contests (coded 1 if they voted in the actual contest for the party that they intended to vote for in both the list and the electorate contest, and 0 otherwise).

The results (Table 7) indicate that, as hypothesized, those with the strongest degree of commitment to a party were least likely to change their mind regarding their list vote during the campaign: those who identified with that party

TABLE 7
LOGISTIC REGRESSIONS OF LIST VOTES – INTENDED AND ACTUAL

	Voted for intended party in	
	List contest	Both contests
Political attachment:		
Identified with party intended to vote for in list contest (comparator: no)		
Yes	0.44**	0.29*
Changed party identification (comparator: yes)		
No	0.32*	0.29*
When decided list vote (comparator: during campaign)		
Before campaign	0.99**	0.50**
When decided electorate vote (comparator: during campaign)		
Before campaign	−0.10	0.51**
Interested in politics (comparator: very)		
Fairly	−0.09	−0.26
Slightly	−0.36	−0.31
Not at all	−1.41**	−1.38**

TABLE 7
CONTINUED

	Voted for intended party in	
	List contest	*Both contests*
Considered voting differently during campaign (comparator: yes)		
No	0.57**	0.40**
Thought of not voting	−0.18	−0.26
Don't know	−0.75*·	−0.99**
Party campaigning and the local electorate:		
Any contacts with party intended to vote for in party contest (comparator: no)		
Yes	0.39**	0.15
Number of contacts with other parties (comparator: 0)		
1	−0.24	0.11
2	0.21	0.30
3	0.26	0.17
4	−0.43*	−0.12
Spending by intended party in party contest	−0.002	0.011
1996 electorate vote	0.01	0.02**
Party vote party expected to win in electorate (comparator: not expected)		
Yes	0.43**	0.41**
Party vote party expected to come second in electorate (comparator: not expected)		
Yes	0.65**	0.36**
Spending by other parties	−0.008	0.006
When interviewed (comparator: first 8 days)		
Days 9-16	0.15	0.35*
Days 17-24	0.32	0.17
Days 25-32	0.49**	0.55**
Days 33-40	0.91**	0.74**
% correct		
all	76.7	71.2
dependent	92.8	82.2
chi square	248.2	286.9
−2 log likelihood	1316.0	1592.2

Notes: ** coefficient statistically significant at the 0.05 level or better;
* coefficient statistically significant at the 0.05-0.10 level.

were 1.6 times (the exponent of 0.44) more likely to vote for it than those who did not. In addition, those who had determined how to vote in the contest before the campaign started were 2.7 times (the exponent of 0.99) more likely to vote for that intended party than those who had not so determined how to vote: longer-term commitments were more likely to be sustained. On the other hand, and as expected, those who changed their party identification during the campaign were 1.4 times more likely to change the party they would vote for than those who did not. Finally, and also as expected, those not interested in politics were only 0.24 times (the exponent of −1.41) as likely to remain consistent by voting for the party they originally intended to support than those who were very interested in politics. The latter were more steadfast in their decisions, as were those who never considered changing their vote during the campaign. In terms of the behavioural model, therefore, those committed to a party, those who had determined how to vote before the campaign, and those who did not consider other options during the campaign, were most likely to sustain their intentions when the election was held.

Turning to the impact of party campaigning, contact with their intended parties sustained their intentions. If the party respondents intended to vote for contacted them, they were 1.5 times more likely to vote for it than if it did not, but contacts with other parties were not linked to changing their minds. Spending by the parties in their local constituency had no impact on whether they changed people's list vote intentions, but their chosen party's chances of victory in the electorate contest there did, however. If a party was expected to win or come second in the constituency, respondents were more likely to remain loyal to it in the list contest than if it was not a strong runner there.

Finally, the coefficients for the timing of the interview show, as anticipated, that the closer the interview came to the election itself, the greater the probability that respondents voted for the party that they intended to support. This does not mean that those interviewed late in the campaign did not change their mind during it, only that the change had occurred before they were interviewed.

The second regression in Table 7 focuses on those who changed neither their list nor their electorate vote: they remained steadfast in their original intentions. All of the coefficients significant in the first model are also significant in the second. In addition, those who had determined their electorate vote before the campaign were, like those who had so determined their list vote, less likely to change.

In sum, therefore, those who changed their chosen party for the list vote during the campaign were those less committed to any party and those who thought their party had a good chance of victory in the parallel electorate contest in their constituency. The national campaign had some impact on them (if they changed the party they identified with they probably changed the party they voted for), but there was little evidence that local party campaigning and contact with them had much influence.

Overall, these two regression models provided good fits to the data. They correctly classified 77 and 71 per cent of the respondents respectively, and were even more successful at identifying the loyalists whose final vote was for their intended party: they accounted for 93 per cent of those who voted for their intended party in the list contest and 82 per cent of those who were loyal in both contests.

The Electorate Contest

What of change in the electorate votes, which should have been more open to the impact of local campaigns? For this we look at: (1) those who remained consistent – i.e. voted for the party they intended to vote for; and (2) those who shifted their electorate vote from their original intention to either Labour or National. (There were insufficient cases to allow study of other shifts; as Table 3 shows, shifts to the two largest parties dominated.)

Tests for expected relationships from the behavioural and structural models included a variable relevant to the friends-and-neighbours model. Respondents were asked a number of questions in the post-election survey, including which of the candidates standing in their constituency for the electorate contest they 'personally most liked'. While some of the respondents may have interpreted this in party terms, others may have seen it as referring to the individuals' personal qualities alone, hence its relevance to that model. Table 5 shows the percentage of those who both intended to and actually voted for each party in the electorate contests who said that party's candidate was the one they 'personally most liked'. The percentages are relatively low, especially for parties other than Labour, suggesting a clear distinction in many electors' minds between party considerations and personal characteristics.

After several experimental runs, 16 variables (listed in the Appendix) were included in a final logistic regression for those who *voted for their intended party in the electorate contest* (i.e. coded 1 if they voted for the intended party and 0 otherwise).[16] The results are in the first column of Table 8.

Looking first at political attachment, there is a clear difference between list and electorate voting behaviour: in the former (Table 7), those who identified with a party were very likely to fulfil their intention to support it; for the electorate contest, there was no such relationship (Table 8). Those who had determined their electorate vote before the campaign started were more likely to sustain that intention than those who made their minds up later, however, and those who were uninterested in politics were more likely to change their minds than those who were very interested. Compared to those who intended voting for Labour (the party that retained the largest proportion of its intended support: Table 3), those who intended to vote either National or NZ First were

TABLE 8
LOGISTIC REGRESSIONS OF ELECTORATE CONTEST VOTE-SWITCHING

| | Shifted to | | |
	Loyal	Labour	National
Political attachment			
Identified with party intended to vote for in electorate contest (comparator: no)			
Yes	0.28	−0.13	−1.98**
Changed party identification (comparator: no)			
Yes	0.01	−0.64*	1.47**
When decided list vote (comparator: before campaign)			
During campaign	−0.37*	−0.25	0.42
When decided electorate vote (comparator: before campaign)			
During campaign	1.01**	−0.50	−1.08**
Interested in politics (comparator: very)			
Fairly	−0.29	−0.26	1.05**
Slightly	0.13	−0.38	0.33
Not at all	−1.34**	0.88	−4.77
Considered voting differently during campaign (comparator: yes)			
No	−0.04	0.08	−0.39
Thought of not voting	−0.85*	−0.06	0.46
Don't know	−1.01**	0.52	0.28
Intended electorate vote (comparator: Labour National Labour)			
Alliance	−0.64**	1.38**	−0.59
National	−0.34*	–	–
NZ First	−0.76**	0.19	−0.52
ACT	0.03	−1.64**	1.47**
Christian	1.30*	−7.19	1.80
Green	1.68**	0.28	−8.53
Straight-ticket vote intended (comparator: no)			
Yes	0.99**	−0.99**	−0.68*
Voted for intended party in party contest (comparator: no)			
Yes	1.44**	−0.80**	−0.80**
Party campaigning and the local electorate			
Candidate of party intended to vote there personally most liked (comparator: no)			
Yes	1.87**	−2.17**	−1.59**
Party intended to vote for in electorate most likely to win there (comparator: no)			
Yes	0.28	−0.06	0.04
Party intended to vote for in electorate likely to come second there (comparator: no)			
Yes	0.33	0.20	−1.29**
Contacts with party intended to vote for in electorate (comparator: no)			
Yes	0.53**	−0.32	−0.09
1996 electorate vote for party intended to vote for in electorate vote			
	0.02**	−0.04**	−0.03*

TABLE 8
CONTINUED

| | Shifted to | | |
	Loyal	Labour	National
Spending by party intended to vote for in electorate contest			
	0.02*	0.02	−0.03
Candidate of party voted for in electorate personally most liked (comparator: no)			
Yes	–	0.89**	−0.24
Party actually voted for in electorate most likely to win there (comparator: no)			
Yes	–	0.52	0.03
Party actually voted for in electorate likely to come second there (comparator: no)			
Yes	–	0.62*	2.45**
Contacts with party actually voted for in electorate (comparator: no)			
Yes	–	0.60*	0.06
1996 electorate vote for party actually voted for in electorate vote			
	–	0.06**	0.08**
Spending by party actually voted for in electorate contest			
	–	−0.18	0.10**
When interviewed (comparator: first 8 days)			
Days 9–16	0.57**	0.07	−1.05
Days 17–24	0.33	0.13	0.37
Days 25–32	0.79**	−0.51	−0.02
Days 33–40	0.71**	−0.68	−0.17
% correct			
all	83.1	90.2	94.9
dependent	92.2	49.1	43.1
chi square	633.1	241.6	221.2
−2 log likelihood	1089.9	409.6	290.7
N total	1409	782	952
N loyal/shift	986	114	73

Notes: ** coefficient statistically significant at the 0.05 level or better; * coefficient statistically significant at the 0.05-0.10 level.

less likely to sustain that intention whereas those who intended to vote either Christian Heritage or Green were more likely to. The small numbers intending to vote for the parties with least chances of electorate contest success were most likely to keep to their intentions.

The implication is that for many respondents at least, the electorate vote decision was independent of that for the list contest. Contrary to that, however, those who intended to vote a straight-ticket were more likely to remain loyal to their original choice for the electorate contest than were those who intended a split-ticket, as were those who fulfilled their intention in the list contest: loyalty in one part of the contest was linked to loyalty in the other.

Many aspects of the local campaign and electorate also influenced the volume of voter loyalty to their original intentions. The friends-and-neighbours hypothesis was clearly validated: those who said that the candidate of their chosen party was also the one they personally liked best were 6.46 times more likely (the exponent of 1.87) than those who preferred another candidate to confirm their intention and vote for that party's candidate. They were not more likely to vote for the party that they originally intended to support in the electorate contest if they believed it would come third or worse there, however, although they were much more likely to sustain their original support if their intended party contacted them. They were also more likely to remain committed to the party the better its performance in the constituency at the previous contest and the more that the party spent there. Campaigning by the intended party and its chances of victory were clearly very influential on whether voters remained loyal to their original intentions in the electorate contest.

Finally, two regressions were run to investigate those *who switched their electorate vote to either Labour or National* (i.e. the sample analysed excluded those whose initial intention was to vote for Labour or National, respectively). In addition to the variables used in the analysis of loyalty, five others were included so that the local context of both the party the respondents originally intended to support and the one they finally voted for were included.

For those whose original intention was not to vote Labour in the electorate contest but who actually did so, few elements of their party attachment were related to that decision to switch (the second column of Table 8). Those who originally intended to vote for the Alliance were more likely to switch to Labour than those who originally intended to vote National, whereas those who intended to vote ACT were less likely: this is entirely consistent with the parties' relative ideological positions. Similarly, those who intended to vote a straight-ticket that excluded Labour were less likely to shift their electorate support to Labour; and those who voted for the party that they intended to support in the list contest were less likely to switch their support to Labour in the electorate contest.

There was a strong friends-and-neighbours effect. Those for whom the candidate of the party they originally intended to vote for was also personally best liked were only 0.11 times as likely (the exponent of −1.27) to switch their electorate vote to Labour as those for whom their initially preferred party did not also provide their preferred candidate. They were 2.42 times more likely (exponent of 0.89) to switch their vote to Labour if that party's candidate was their most liked by voting day.

With regard to campaign intensity, those contacted by the party they originally intended to vote for were less likely to switch to Labour (the counterpart of the positive relationship for those retaining their intended vote shown in the first regression), as were those who lived in constituencies where their intended party performed well in 1996. Others were more likely to switch to Labour if they thought it was in second place, though not in first place, suggesting strategic shifts to bolster Labour's chances – especially if they were contacted by Labour during the campaign and Labour had performed well there in 1996. This suggests clear strategic voting – people switching their support to Labour to enhance its chances of overtaking the leading party when encouraged to do so during the local campaign.

Regarding switches to National (the final column of Table 8), those who identified with the party they originally intended to vote for were less likely to switch than those who did not; those who intended to vote Alliance were less likely to shift their support to National than those who originally intended to vote Labour; those who originally intended to vote ACT were more likely to; and those who continued to support their intended party in the list contest were also less likely to switch their electorate vote to National. As with Labour, there was also a strong personal effect, at least with regard to deserting a party. If the candidate of the party the elector originally intended to vote for was also their most liked candidate personally, they were only 0.20 times as likely to switch to National as those whose personal preference was for the candidate of another party. There was no positive relationship with the personal characteristics of the National candidate, however.

Regarding the campaign, contacts with the party they originally intended to vote for were not related to respondents' decisions to switch to National, but spending by those parties was. As with Labour, if respondents thought that National was likely to come second they were much more likely to switch to it – again, presumably, to boost its chances of victory, especially if National had performed well there in 1996 and spent heavily on its local campaign.

All three of the models reported in Table 8 are reasonably successful, not only at predicting the outcome for the entire population of respondents in the relevant equation (83, 90 and 95 per cent respectively) but also at predicting those who were coded 1 in the dependent variable – the loyalists in the first equation, those who switched to Labour in the second and those switching to National in the third. Over 92 per cent of those who fulfilled their original vote intention were correctly predicted, as were 49 per cent of those who switched to Labour and 43 per cent of the relatively small number who switched to National.

Conclusions

The voting decision in New Zealand's MMP system presents electors with two choices during campaigns that may be pushing them to vote for different parties in the two parts of the election. In 1999, most voters approached the election with clear intentions regarding which party to support in both the list and the electorate contest, but many changed their minds during the election campaign, switching away from their original intentions in at least one if not both of the contests.

In this article, survey data – combined with aggregate data about aspects of the constituencies in which the electorate contests occurred – have been deployed to test hypotheses derived from the behavioural and strategic models of straight- and split-ticket voting in such circumstances. Both have been validated to a considerable extent.

The behavioural model suggests that those strongly committed to a party are likely to support it at the election, to have determined that would be the case before the campaign started, and to be largely resistant to the campaign (so that at no stage do they consider changing from their original intentions, unless their party identification changes too). This was the case with the 1999 list contest: the committed remained committed. It was also to some extent the case with the electorate contests, but many respondents entered the campaign intending to vote for a party other than that they identified with, presumably for strategic reasons: again, the stronger their commitment overall (if not to a particular party), the less likely they were to change their mind.

Many voters are not strongly committed to a party, however, and are open to influence during the campaign period by party activities and by their perceived prospects in the constituencies. This was of only marginal relevance in the list contest, with electors more likely to remain with their original choice for that contest if the party's candidate also had a strong chance of victory in their constituency. In the electorate contests, however, the local context was much more important. There was very strong evidence of a friends-and-neighbours effect, with electors apparently more prepared to desert their chosen party if they preferred the characteristics of another party's candidate but less prepared to do so if their preferred candidate was standing for their originally favoured party. They were also influenced by the local electoral context and local campaigns, being much more likely to switch from their originally intended vote to either Labour or National if that party needed their votes (i.e. was perceived to be in second place), and if it contacted them.

Local election campaigning matters. Many voters were persuaded to switch from their original intentions at New Zealand's 1999 general election, in both the list and the electorate components of that MMP contest. In the list contest, behavioural factors were crucial in determining whether people shifted their party preferences; in the electorate contests the local context was crucial too. In understanding how people decided to vote in those two contests, and why many of them changed their minds during the month of the campaign, we need to look at the geography of the election as well as the characteristics of the electors involved.

APPENDIX
VARIABLES USED IN THE LOGISTIC REGRESSIONS

For the List Contest

Political Attachment
1. *Whether the respondent identified with the party that they intended to vote for*: those who did should be less likely to change from their original vote intention than those who had no party identification or who intended to vote for another party than that they identified with.
2. *Whether the respondent changed party identification during the campaign* (the question was asked in both waves of the survey): those who did change would be more likely to change their vote.
3. *When respondents decided their list vote*: either during or before the campaign – those who had determined how to vote before the campaign should be less likely to change their mind.[17]
4. *When respondents decided their electorate vote*: either during or before the campaign – again, those who had determined how to vote before the campaign should be less likely to change their mind.
5. *Interest in politics*: those with little interest in politics may, following Denemark's findings, be more likely to change their mind as a consequence of the campaign.
6. *Whether the respondent considered voting differently during the campaign*: those prepared to consider changing would be more likely to do it.

Party Campaigning and the Local Electorate
7. *Whether the respondent had any contact with the party that they intended to vote for during the campaign*: those who were contacted by the party should be less likely to change from their original voting intention.
8. *Whether the respondent had any contact with other parties during the campaign.* (Contact with each party was counted as 1, and as data on contacts were not collected for two of the parties – Christian Heritage and Green – the total possible score was 4.): the more contacts a respondent had with other parties, the more likely they were to change list vote from that initially intended.
9. *The 1996 electorate vote of the party that the respondent intended to vote for*: the larger this was, the greater the probability of not changing their mind because of the party's strength there.
10. *Whether the party the respondent intended to vote for in the list contest was also expected to win in the electorate contest*: if it was, then the respondent should be less likely to change their mind.
11. *Whether the party the respondent intended to vote for in the list contest was expected to come second in the electorate contest*: if it was, then the respondent should be less likely to change their mind.
12. *Spending on the constituency campaign by the party intended to vote for*: the more that it spent the greater the probability that the respondent would vote for that party as a result of the impact of that campaigning.
13. *Spending on the constituency campaign by the other parties*: the more that they spent the greater the probability that the respondent would vote for another party than that intended.

In addition, because the campaign survey was conducted on a rolling basis, with a set number of interviews each day over the 40-day period, it was likely that the closer the interview was to the election, the less likely those respondents would change from their vote intention.

14. *When the campaign interview was conducted* (with the 40-day period divided into five eight-day periods).

For the Electorate Contest

Political Attachment

1. *Whether the respondent identified with the party that they intended to vote for in the electorate contest.*
2. *Whether the respondent changed party identification during the campaign.*
3. *When respondents decided their list vote.*
4. *When respondents decided their electorate vote.5.*
5. *Interest in politics.*
6. *Whether the respondent considered voting differently during the campaign.*
7. *Intended electorate vote.* Those who intended to vote for a party other than the largest two (Labour and National) may have been more likely to switch from their intended vote.
8. *Intended straight-ticket vote*: those who intended a straight-ticket vote should be less likely to change their mind on one component than those who intended a split-ticket.
9. *Whether the respondent voted for their intended party in the list contest*: those who did not change their mind in the list contest should have been less likely to in the electorate contest also:

Party Campaigning and the Local Electorate

10. *Whether the candidate of the party the respondent intended to vote for was also 'personally most liked' among the candidates in the local constituency*: if the candidate was the most liked, the respondent should be less likely to change their mind.
11. *Whether the party the respondent intended to vote for in the electorate contest was expected to win in that contest*: if it was, then the respondent should be less likely to change their mind.
12. *Whether the party the respondent intended to vote for in the electorate contest was expected to come second in that contest*: if it was, then the respondent should be less likely to change their mind.
13. *Whether the respondent had any contact with the party that they intended to vote for in the electorate contest for during the campaign.*
14. *The 1996 electorate vote of the party that the respondent intended to vote for.*
15. *Spending on the constituency campaign by the party intended to vote for.*
    and
16. *When the campaign interview was conducted.*
b) The regressions for those who shifted from their original intention to either Labour or National.
    The above plus:
17. *Whether the party the respondent actually voted for was expected to win that constituency contest.*
18. *Whether the party the respondent actually voted for was expected to come second in that constituency contest.*
19. *Whether the respondent had any contacts with the party actually voted for in the electorate.*
20. *The 1996 electorate of the party that the respondent actually voted for.*
21. *Spending on the constituency campaign by the party that the respondent actually voted for.*

NOTES

1. This is generally known as the party vote: our preferred term of 'list vote' is simply to avoid confusion when talking of parties and party votes!

2. Full details of New Zealand's transition to MMP and of the system there can be found in Jackson and McRobie (1998), Baker et al. (2001), Denemark (2001).

3. The data from the surveys are deposited in the Australian Social Sciences Data Archive, study number D1044. We are grateful to Prof Jack Vowles of the University of Auckland for assistance in using these data.

4. One such exceptional circumstance would be what is technically termed an 'overhang', in which a party wins more electorate seats than its list percentage entitles it to – in which case it is allowed to retain those 'extra' seats and the size of the House is enlarged until the next election, so as not to penalize any other party. Such 'overhangs' have occurred in Germany, especially in the 1990s: in New Zealand, with just 125 Seats in the House, they are unlikely to involve more than 1–2 seats at the most.

5. A considerable amount was spent on public education when the system was introduced. Banducci et al., 1998, showed that at the first MMP election in 1996 a majority of New Zealanders knew that the list vote was the most influential and that less than 1-in-12 thought the electorate vote the most important. Furthermore, they also showed that the aggregate pattern of ticket-splitting was consistent with that understanding.

6. The mass media may be involved indirectly in the process of changing voter intentions, through the publication of opinion poll data: Vowles (2000, 2002b) found no significant evidence for any impact of the polls on support for Labour, National or NZ First.

7. On Maori voting see Sullivan and Margaritis (2000, 2002). Several of the Maori constituencies are also very large in terms of area, making the conduct of election campaigns – in which spending is limited to $NZ20,000 per candidate – difficult.

8. Of those undecided voters at the pre-election stage, only 48 per cent voted a straight-ticket.

9. As a new party, therefore, it was not possible to obtain estimates of its 1996 performance in the constituencies.

10. The 60th constituency – Ohariu-Belmont – was a special case because of the absence of a National candidate in 1996.

11. In all of these tables the respondents who had not determined which party they intended to vote for at one or both of the contests were excluded.

12. There is much debate in the British voting literature on the best way to measure party identification: the questions deployed in the New Zealand Election Study use the 'traditional' procedure derived from the 'Michigan school' (Scarbrough, 2003).

13. Denemark (2002) has shown that level of interest in politics was inter-related with campaign effects in Australian voting: those with low interest were much more likely to be influenced by media campaigns.

14. Because the constituencies were altered between the two elections, all of the analyses here use estimates of the 1996 result in the new constituencies, as calculated by Alan McRobie from the polling booth data. We are grateful to him for making these data available.

15. As already noted, preferred Prime Minister and policy position were removed because of collinearity with party identification.

16. Many of these variables are the same as those included in the previous sections, so details of expectations are not given again.

17. The analyses, as already noted, omit those respondents who reported that they had not determined which party to support in both contests in the pre-election survey. This did not therefore exclude all those who had not made up their mind before the campaign commenced, because most were interviewed after the campaign had started and so could have started the campaign undecided but come to a decision during the campaign before they were interviewed. Some 52 per cent of respondents said that they had determined their list vote before the campaign, of whom 15 per cent (i.e. 8 per cent of the total) changed their mind.

REFERENCES

Banducci, S.A., J.A. Karp and J. Vowles (1998) 'Vote Splitting under MMP', in J. Vowles, P. Aimer, S.A. Banducci and J.A. Karp (eds) *Voters' Victory? New Zealand's First Election under Proportional Representation.* Auckland: Auckland University Press, pp. 101–19.

Barker, F., J. Boston, S. Levine, E. McLeay and N.S. Roberts (2001) 'An Initial Assessment of the Consequences of MMP in New Zealand', in M.S. Shugart and M.P. Wattenberg (eds.) *Mixed-Member Electoral Systems: The Best of Both Worlds?* New York: Oxford University Press, pp. 297–322.

Cox, G.W. (1997) *Making Votes Count: Strategic Coordination in the World's Electoral Systems.* Cambridge: Cambridge University Press.

Cox, K.R. (1969) 'The Voting Decision in Spatial Context', *Progress in Geography Volume 1.* London: Edward Arnold, pp. 81–118.

Denemark, D. (1998) 'Campaign Activities and Marginality: The Transition to MMP Campaigns', in J. Vowles, P. Aimer, S.A. Banducci and J.A. Karp (eds) *Voters' Victory? New Zealand's First Election under Proportional Representation.* Auckland: Auckland University Press, pp. 81–100.

Denemark, D. (2001) 'Choosing MMP in New Zealand: Explaining the 1993 Electoral Reform', in M.S. Shugart and M.P. Wattenberg (eds.), *Mixed-Member Electoral Systems: The Best of Both Worlds?* New York: Oxford University Press, pp. 70–95.

Denemark, D. (2002) 'Television Effects and Voter Decision Making in Australia: a Re-Examination of the Converse Model', *British Journal of Political Science* 32: 663–90.

Denver, D. and G. Hands (1997) *Modern Constituency Electioneering.* London: Frank Cass.

Downs, A. (1957) *An Economic Theory of Democracy.* New York: Harper & Row.

Duverger, M. (1954) *Political Parties: Their Organization and Activity in the Modern State.* New York: John Wiley.

Green, D.P., A.S. Gerber and D.W. Nickerson (2003) 'Getting Out the Vote in Local Elections: Results from Six Door-to-Door Canvassing Experiments', *American Journal of Politics* 65: 1083–96.

Huckfeldt, R. and J. Sprague (1995) *Citizens, Politics and Social Communication: Information and Influence in an Election Campaign.* Cambridge: Cambridge University Press.

Jackson, K. and A.D. McRobie (1998) *New Zealand Adopts Proportional Representation.* Aldershot: Ashgate.

Johnston, R.J. (1972) 'Spatial Elements in Voting Patterns at the 1968 Christchurch City Council Elections', *Political Science* 24: 49–61.

Johnston, R.J. (1973) 'Spatial Patterns and Influences on Voting in Multi-Candidate Elections: the Christchurch City Council Election, 1968', *Urban Studies* 10: 69–82.

Johnston, R.J. (1976) 'Spatial Structure, Plurality Systems, and Electoral Bias', *The Canadian Geographer* 20: 310–328.

Johnston, R.J. (1992) 'Electoral Geography'. in M. Holland (ed.), *Electoral Behaviour in New Zealand.* Auckland: Oxford University Press, pp. 25–50.

Johnston, R.J. and C.J. Pattie (2002) 'Campaigning and Split-ticket Voting in New Electoral Systems: The First MMP Elections in New Zealand, Scotland and Wales', *Electoral Studies* 21: 583–600.

Johnston, R.J. and C.J. Pattie. (2003a) 'Spatial Variations in Straight- and Split-Ticket Voting and the Role of Constituency Campaigning: New Zealand's First Two MMP Elections', *Geographical Analysis* 35: 1–23.

Johnston, R.J. and C.J. Pattie (2003b) 'Do Campaigning and Canvassing Work? Evidence from the 2001 General Election in England', in C. Rallings, R. Scully, J. Tonge and P. Webb (eds.), *British Elections and Parties Review,* 12, pp. 248–73, London: Frank Cass,

Johnston, R.J. and C.J. Pattie (2003c) Spatial Variations in Straight- and Split-Ticket Voting and the Role of Constituency Campaigning at New Zealand's First Two MMP Elections: Individual-Level Tests', *Australian Journal of Political Science,* 38: 535–47.

Karp, J.A., J. Vowles, S.A. Banducci and T. Donovan (2002) 'Strategic Voting, Party Activity, and Candidate Effects: Testing Explanations for Split Voting in New Zealand's New Mixed System', *Electoral Studies* 21: 1–22.

Key, V.O. Jr. (1949) *Southern Politics in State and Nation.* New York: Alfred A Knopf.

Pattie, C.J. and R.J. Johnston (2000) '"People Who Talk Together Vote Together": An Exploration of Contextual Effects in Great Britain', *Annals of the Association of American Geographers* 90: 41–66.

Scarbrough, E. (2003) 'On the Shoulders of Giants: A Tribute to Warren E. Miller', *Electoral Studies* 22: 197–216.

Shugart, M.S. and M.P. Wattenberg (eds) (2001) *Mixed-Member Electoral Systems: The Best of Both Worlds?* New York: Oxford University Press.

Sullivan, A. and D. Margaritis (2000) 'Maori Voting Patterns in 1999 Campaign', in J. Boston, S. Church, S. Levine, E. McLeay and N.S. Roberts (eds) *Left Turn: The New Zealand General Election of 1999.* Wellington: Victoria University Press, pp. 175–83.

Sullivan, A. and D. Margaritis (2002) 'Coming Home: Maori Voting in 1999', in J. Vowles, P. Aimer, J. Karp, S.A. Banducci, R. Miller and A. Sullivan, *Proportional Representation on Trial: The 1999 New Zealand General Election and the Fate of MMP.* Auckland: Auckland University Press, pp. 66–82.

Vowles, J. (2002a) 'What Happened at the 1999 Election?' in J. Vowles, P. Aimer, J. Kerp, S. Banducci, R. Miller and A. Sullivan, *Proportional Representation on Trial: the 1999 New Zealand General Election and the Fate of MMP.* Auckland: Auckland University Press pp. 83–98.

Vowles, J.A. (2002b) 'Did the Polls Influence the Vote? A Case Study of the 1999 New Zealand General Election', *Political Science* 54: 67–78.

CITIZENSHIP AND SOCIAL CAPITAL

Modelling the Components of Political Action in Britain: The Impact of Civic Skills, Social Capital and Political Support

Oliver Heath

It is generally believed that different factors influence political participation in different ways. Some factors act as a spur, or a motivation, and others act as a resource. However, when just one type of political activity is examined it is difficult to judge the nature of the impact. Whereas many studies of political participation focus on why some people participate while others do not, in this article I examine why some people participate in one type of political activity while others are relatively more likely to participate in another. Alternative types of political activity are similar in some respects and different in other respects. By modelling these similarities and differences, I build a picture of the different components of political action and the factors that are associated with each.

There are two rather different traditions in political science that study political participation. One focuses on sociological and attitudinal variables and seeks to explain participation in terms of the resources which people have such as their education and income (see Verba et al., 1995). The other focuses on the instrumental costs and benefits of participation (see Olson, 1965). In order to examine how different components of action are influenced by different factors I draw upon these concepts. In particular I focus on the perceived costs and benefits of participation: civic skills, such as education and political knowledge, and political engagement, such as political awareness and efficacy (Verba et al., 1995); social capital, meaning social networks and trust (Coleman 1990, and Putnam 1993, 2000); and political support, meaning attitudes towards various levels of the political system (Easton, 1977 and more recently Norris, 1999).

The first part of the article explores the theoretical and measurement issues surrounding the different concepts and the second part analyses their impact on different types of political action. I show that whereas civic skills and political engagement are important factors for predicting all types of political action, social capital and the costs of participation are important for predicting collective modes of action as opposed to individual modes, and political

British Elections & Parties Review, Vol. 14, 2004, pp. 75–93
ISSN 1368-9886 print
DOI: 10.1080/1368988042000258781   © 2004 Taylor & Francis Ltd.

support is important for predicting electoral forms of participation rather than non-electoral forms of participation.

Theoretical and Measurement Issues

The Costs and Benefits of Participation

The classic rational choice account of political behaviour states that individuals will only participate if their actions are effective in producing the desired outcome net of the associated costs. The general formulation therefore is that individuals will only participate when $p*b>c$, where p=probability that individual's participation will bring about desired benefit, b=the desired benefit in question, and c=the costs to the individual of participation. Since p is often very small the right hand side of the equation is usually very much larger than the left hand side, suggesting that the rational individual will not participate. Although this appears to present something of a paradox, since we know that in fact many people do participate, it is possible to extend the model so that it more realistically reflects the calculations that individuals make when they decide whether or not to participate. For example, following Olson's (1965) extended selective incentives model, Whiteley et al. (1994) introduce terms for selective outcome incentives, selective process incentives and ideological incentives for political activity. Fisher (1999) adopts a similar framework and shows how these differ for different types of activity.

For the sake of simplicity this article only examines a reduced rational choice model and primarily focuses on the perceived costs and benefits of participation. Using the 2001 British Election Study,[1] it looks at whether political activity is considered to be a good way to get personal benefits and group benefits on the one hand, and whether it is considered to take too much time and effort and difficult to understand on the other.[2] This approach is adopted in order to examine two main possibilities. First, to test whether some types of activity are perceived to be more efficacious than others for delivering results and hence more driven by the perceived benefits that they might bring about; and whether, on the other hand, some types of activity are considered more difficult than others and hence more driven by the perceived costs of participation. Second, to examine whether the other factors, such as civic skills, social capital and civic engagement influence the impact of the costs and benefits and whether they have a differential impact for different types of activity.

Civic Skills and Political Engagement

The civic voluntarism model, developed by Verba et al. (1995), is one of the most prominent theoretical models in political science and seeks to explain political participation mainly in terms of factors that facilitate participation, such as resources and mobilization, and reduce the associated costs. In addition it also includes psychological engagement with politics. The model tries to make theoretical sense out of a whole host of socio-demographic and attitudinal variables, such as income, age, free-time, education and social class, that are repeatedly found to be important in predicting different types of political participation. As a whole, the model is rather generally specified and includes factors that are of little, if any, theoretical interest, such as the notion that an individual's amount of free time constitutes a resource for participation. However, certain aspects of the model are more robust than others. In particular, the idea of resources such as civic skills and political engagement give a plausible (if partial) account of why some people participate and others do not.

The civic skills components of this model argues that the better educated and more knowledgeable are more likely to participate in a wide range of activities than the lower educated because they possess the relevant skills that reduce the costs of participation and make it more manageable. Verba et al. (1995: 15–16) postulate that people fail to participate because they lack skills and knowledge about the political process, and lack political engagement, such as interest in politics and the belief that activity will make a difference. I measure civic skills in terms of education and political knowledge, and political engagement in terms of political awareness and political efficacy.[3]

Social Capital

Civic skills are not the only resource that facilitates participation. There are potentially many different types of resource, and each type has slightly different behavioural consequences. Whereas some resources, such as civic skills, can be thought to facilitate political activity in general and influence whether or not people participate at all, other resources can be thought to facilitate some types of activity and not others. For example, according to Fisher (1999) the costs of making donations to political parties are very different to the costs of other types of party activism, and rely almost entirely on financial resources. In this respect I examine the extent to which social capital facilitates some types of political activity as opposed to others, with a particular emphasis on collective against individual modes of participation.

Although there is a fair amount of controversy surrounding the concept of social capital, it is generally agreed that it is essentially a resource that makes possible the achievement of certain ends that in its absence would not be possible, or would only be possible at a higher cost (Coleman, 1990: 304). All different forms of social capital integrate two common characteristics: 'they all consist of some aspect of social structure, and they facilitate certain actions of individuals who are within the structure' (1990: 302).[4]

Social capital has attracted a great deal of criticism for a perceived lack of clarity in terms of specifying causal mechanisms. On the one hand, Levi (1996: 47) questions the mechanism by which membership in a bird-watching group generates the kind of generalized reciprocity and trust that Putnam commonly refers to. And on the other hand, she questions the mechanism by which social capital is able to influence government performance in the way that Putnam says it does. Although many of these criticisms are sound enough, they stem, in part, from an overly general conception of what social capital is and what it does. Social capital is often used to explain so many different phenomena in so many different ways it is hard to keep track of exactly what it is. In some ways, it has come to be thought of as a panacea for many of society's ills, and has been used to 'explain' crime, economic growth and health. However, as Putnam (2000: 22) states, it can equally be used for antisocial purposes. Thus, rather than being preoccupied with what, if anything, social capital generates, it is more fruitful to return to Levi's initial criticism and examine the potential mechanisms through which social capital can operate.

Both Coleman (1990: 311) and Putnam (1993: 167) suggest that under some circumstances social capital can ease the problem of free-riding and facilitate collective action, although in neither case is a particularly well-developed argument put forward. Coleman (1990: 311) simply states that 'a prescriptive norm that constitutes an especially important form of social capital within a collectivity is the norm that one should forgo self-interests to act in the interests of the collectivity.' However, drawing upon the work of Axelrod (1984) a more straightforward account can be developed of how social capital can maintain a cooperative equilibrium. Using the format of a computer tournament, Axelrod compared the success of 'nice' and 'mean' strategies, where nice strategies were based on cooperation and mean strategies on defection. Axelrod showed that by introducing multiple iterations of the prisoners' dilemma game the strategy of defection was severely undermined. Nice strategies did significantly better in the long run even though they never beat the mean strategies in face-to-face competition. In a way social capital represents the social equivalent of this process. The social network provides the setting for on-going interactions, and social trust lubricates cooperation in the same way as 'nice' strategies. In this sense, social capital can facilitate collective modes of political activity because it helps to alleviate some of the problems associated with free riding. Its core components are thus social networks on the one hand and social trust on the other.

Social capital is somewhat difficult to operationalize. Although its core operational components are generally considered to be membership in a social network and social trust, previous research has tended to analyse these terms separately. However, it is the presence of both together that provides the resource. Trust without a network and a network without trust does not meaningfully refer to social capital. This can be illustrated by the example Coleman (1990: 109) cites of diamond traders in London.[5] If a trader loses the trust of his associates then his business is essentially ruined. There is no social capital in a network without trust. Rather than treating social capital as *either* trust *or* networks it is better to treat it as trust *and* networks. For this reason to measure social capital in this article I use a multiplicative index of two social trust indicators (combined range 0–10) and willingness to volunteer (0–10 scale).[6] The social capital index is rescaled so it has a range 0–10.

Political Support

Studies on political participation have tended to stress the factors that enable participation, such as resources, at the expense of factors which are concerned more with substantive aspects of participation. In recent years, the concept of political support has attracted a lot of attention in this respect. People are now less likely to trust politicians than they were 20 years ago (Jowell and Curtice, 1995), and less likely to trust the state apparatus, such as the local council, the courts and the police. This detachment from the political system is both a sign of cynicism and realism, and Norris et al. (1999) have interpreted it as signalling a growth in critical citizens. Although at this stage the majority of research on political support has concentrated on examining its determinants, it is clear that its behavioural consequences are also potentially very important.

According to Easton (1975: 436) political support refers to the 'way in which a person evaluatively orients himself to a [political] object through either his attitude or behavior'. It is multidimensional, and can be distinguished according to the object of support, such as the community, the regime, and the authority. Easton (1975: 444) also differentiates political support in terms of whether it is diffuse or specific. Diffuse political support refers to evaluations of what an object is or represents – to the general meaning it has for a person – not what it does. It is thus independent of outputs and performance in the long run and is usually durable. This has also been interpreted as measuring the legitimacy of a political system or political institutions (Muller and Jukam, 1977). On the other hand, specific support relates to the 'satisfactions that members of a system feel they obtain from the perceived outputs and performance of the political authorities' (Easton, 1975: 437). This distinction is broadly similar to what Almond and Verba (1963) refer to as affective and evaluative beliefs. However, Fuchs et al. (1995: 330) argue that discussions about whether a particular indicator measures diffuse or specific support is not particularly fruitful. The distinction is somewhat ambiguous, particularly in empirical terms. It is difficult to separate the extent to which attitudes towards a political object are influenced by feelings towards the incumbent government. For example, levels of political trust and democratic satisfaction are generally higher among supporters of the ruling party than supporters of the opposition. Specific evaluations can therefore often colour what may be thought of as diffuse orientations. This has led to uncertainty over what objects are diffuse or specific. For example, whereas Muller et al. (1982) consider political trust to be a measure of diffuse support, Dalton (1999: 58) considers it to be specific. Similarly, 'satisfaction with democratic performance' has been treated as both an indicator of specific support (see Schmitt, 1983: 365 and Merkl, 1988: 29) and diffuse support (see Weil, 1989: 690 and Widmaier, 1990: 23).

For the purposes of this article, political support is measured at three different levels. As shown in Figure 1, the different objects of political support can be placed on a continuum ranging from the most diffuse support at the top to the most specific support at the bottom (see Norris, 1999: 10). The first level concerns evaluations of regime performance, meaning satisfaction with the democratic system.[7] The second level focuses on support for political institutions. Attitudes towards political institutions have received a great deal of attention and have been analysed in terms of trust, respect and confidence. Political-institutional support is measured by a series of questions relating to how much citizens respect political institutions and authorities.[8] This relates to what Rose (1997) terms a 'realistic' view of democracy. Lastly, the third level focuses on support for key political actors. Strength of party identification is used to measure this.[9] The responses are recoded so that those who do

FIGURE 1
LEVELS OF POLITICAL SUPPORT

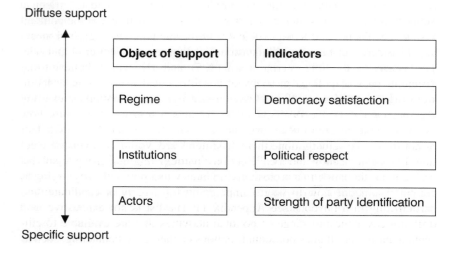

Diffuse support

Object of support	Indicators
Regime	Democracy satisfaction
Institutions	Political respect
Actors	Strength of party identification

Specific support

not identify with any particular party score 0, and those who have a very strong identification score 3.

In studies on political action, with particular emphasis on voting, some aspects of political support – such as political trust and party identification – have received more attention than others. However, they have rarely been analysed within the theoretical framework of political support and have tended to be viewed in isolation. Drawing upon this conception of political support, a number of rival hypotheses can be formulated. First, low levels of political support depress political behaviour in general, with political cynicism associated with apathy. In this instance, the expected relationship between the objects of support and the different types of political action would be positive for each instance. If the pattern is the same across the different levels of the system, then it suggests that what is observed is a system-level effect rather than a particular effect. Alternatively, rather than depressing all types of political participation, low political support depresses institutional (or conventional) forms of participation, but encourages non-institutional participation. In addition, different objects within the political system may be associated with different forms of participation in different ways. For example, partisan activities, such as voting, may be driven more by attitudes towards what is the political, narrowly defined, than by attitudes towards democracy in general.

Different Types of Political Action

In order to examine the impact of these concepts on different types of political action, this article uses data from the 2001 BES. Political action commonly refers to all voluntary activities by individual citizens intended to influence either directly or indirectly political decisions at various levels of the political system (see Barnes and Kaase, 1979: 42; Verba and Nie, 1972: 2). It is generally considered to be a multidimensional phenomenon (see Verba and Nie, 1972, Parry et al., 1992, Verba et al., 1995), and it is widely believed that different types of political activity influence political decisions in different ways, and are differentially effective in conveying information or exerting pressure (Verba et al., 1995: 37). The political action items measure how likely respondents are to undertake various political acts, rather than whether or not they have actually done them. The items are: voting in a general election, European election and local elections; participating in a group to solve a problem; participating in a protest; giving money to a political party; trying to convince someone how to vote; campaigning for a party or candidate; and participating in a boycott (see Appendix 1). The list is not exhaustive, and does not cover the full range of political activities that are available to citizens. In particular, it does not include actions connected to contacting, such as

TABLE 1
WILLINGNESS TO PARTICIPATE IN POLITICAL ACTS: PRINCIPAL COMPONENTS
ANALYSIS (VARIMAX ROTATION)

	Component		
	1	2	3
	Vote	Campaign	Social movements
Vote- European election	0.68		
Vote- Local election	0.88		
Vote- General election	0.86		
Give money to political party		0.78	
Convince someone how to vote		0.75	
Work for party or candidate		0.77	
Work with group to solve problem			0.74
Participate in protest/ demonstration			0.82
Boycott goods or services			0.69
Eigenvalue	2.82	1.77	1.11
% variance explained	31.40	19.70	12.30

Notes: Values under 0.4 suppressed. Minimum Eigenvalue 1.
          N=2146.
Source: 2001 British Election Study.

writing letters to MPs or civil servants or contacting the local council (see Parry et al., 1992: 51).[10]

In order to establish the different types of political action, factor analysis is used, which is the appropriate data reduction technique for ordinal level data of this type. The factor analysis identifies three broad factors, or types, of political action (see Table 1). The different types can be given meaning by their relationship with the indicator variables. Thus, from the pattern of the loadings, it can be inferred that factor 1 refers to voting, factor 2 to campaign activity, and factor 3 to social movements. These types or action closely correspond to those identified in previous research on political participation (see Parry et al., 1992: 50-61). The factor scores are saved in standardized form with a mean of 0 and a standard deviation of 1.

Modelling the Components of Political Action

Table 2 shows separate OLS regression estimates for each of the different types of political action. The regression model contains five blocks of variables. The

TABLE 2
MODELLING DIFFERENT TYPES OF POLITICAL ACTION: OLS REGRESSION
UNSTANDARDIZED BETA COEFFICIENTS

	Vote		Campaign		Social movements	
	b	*S.E*	*b*	*S.E*	*b*	*S.E.*
(Constant)	−2.39	0.18	−0.56	0.21	−0.28	0.19
Age (*10)	0.29***	0.07	−0.18*	0.07	0.16*	0.01
Age squared (*100)	−0.02***	0.01	0.02*	0.01	−0.02***	0.01
SEX	−0.12**	0.04	0.02	0.04	−0.10*	0.04
ETHNIC	−0.25**	0.09	0.41***	0.10	0.33***	0.10
COSTS	0.01	0.02	−0.09***	0.02	−0.07**	0.02
BENEFITS	0.03	0.02	0.03	0.02	0.04*	0.02
UNI	0.14*	0.07	0.06	0.07	0.12	0.07
ALEVEL	0.10*	0.05	−0.04	0.06	0.08	0.05
GCSE	0.03	0.06	−0.14	0.07	0.14*	0.07
Knowledge	0.09***	0.02	0.01	0.02	0.03	0.02
SOCCAP	0.01	0.01	0.05***	0.01	0.12***	0.01
Attention	0.07***	0.01	0.02**	0.01	0.05***	0.01
Influence	0.00	0.01	0.07***	0.01	0.02*	0.01
Party id	0.15***	0.03	0.29***	0.03	0.02	0.03
Political trust	0.09***	0.01	0.03*	0.01	−0.06***	0.01
Dem satisfaction	0.03	0.03	0.01	0.03	−0.11***	0.03

Notes: N=1882
***p < 0.001; **p < 0.01; *p < 0.05.
Source: 2001 British Election Study.

first block contains demographic variables such as sex, ethnicity and age. An age-squared term is also included because age generally has a quadratic rather than linear relationship to social and political activity. These act as controls. The second block contains the simple cost-benefit variables. The third contains resources – civic skills and social capital. The fourth block contains the political support variables, and is measured for three different levels of the political system, and the fifth block contains political engagement variables.

Looking first at the demographics, men are less likely than women to vote and participate in social movements, although there is no difference in terms of campaign activity. For voting and social movements there is a curvilinear age effect – with the very young and the very old the least likely to partici-pate. This is shown by the significant and negative effect of the age-squared coefficient: the likelihood of voting increases with age until 64 and then

begins to tail off (minimum or maximum $= B_1/B_2$ where B_1 is the age coefficient and B_2 is the age-squared coefficient). Participation in social movements has a much younger social base. The likelihood of participating
increases with age until 33 and then tails off, with people in their late 40s and
early 50s less likely to participate than people in their late teens and early
20s. However, for campaigning there is evidence that it is the young and the
very old who are most likely to participate. The likelihood of campaigning
decreases with age until 58 and then increases again with those in their late
teens and early twenties the most likely to be active in this way. Minority
ethnic groups are less likely than white British to vote, but more likely to
participate in campaign activity and social movements. There is thus
evidence that the demographic base is slightly different for each of the types
of political action.

Turning to the costs and benefits of political action, we can see that costs
are not associated with voting. However, somewhat greater costs seem to be
associated with participation in collective modes of participation such as
campaigning and social movements. The coefficients are significant and
negative, indicating that participation is less likely when the costs are
greater. Moreover the magnitude of the effect is very similar for campaigning (b= −0.09) and social movements (b= −0.07). However, the benefit side
of the equation performs less well. Benefits as operationalized here do not
have a significant impact on voting or campaigning. They do have a borderline impact on social movements (p=0.04) but the magnitude of the effect is
small. Overall, there is not much difference between the magnitude of the
benefit term for voting (0.03), campaigning (0.03) and social movements
(0.04).

Interestingly, we can see that the impact of the cost term for the different
types of activity is substantially reduced when we control for the other variables
(see Table 3). The cost term for voting decreases from a significant −0.10 to a
non-significant −0.01; the cost term for campaigning decreases from −0.19 to
−0.09; and the cost term for social movements decreases from −0.17 to −0.07.
In particular the costs of voting are substantially reduced by resources − such
as education, political knowledge and social capital. The magnitude of the
effect is halved when these resources are controlled for and the costs term
decreases from a highly significant −0.10 to a borderline significant −0.05 (see
Table 3). Similarly, the magnitude of the cost term for participation in social
movements decreases from −0.17 to −0.10 when resources are controlled for,
although a slightly weaker pattern is observed for campaigning, which
witnesses only a marginal decrease from −0.19 to −0.15. These findings support
the SES interpretation that high status individuals tend to participate more
because they possess the relevant civic skills, such as education and political
knowledge that reduce the costs of participation.

TABLE 3
THE IMPACT OF POLITICAL COSTS AND BENEFITS CONTROLLING FOR
DEMOGRAPHICS, RESOURCES, POLITICAL SUPPORT AND POLITICAL
ENGAGEMENT: BLOC-WISE OLS REGRESSION UNSTANDARDIZED BETA
COEFFICIENTS

	Demogs	Resources	Support	Engagement
Political Costs				
Voting	−0.10***	−0.05*	−0.02	0.01
Campaigning	−0.19***	−0.15***	−0.12***	−0.09***
Social movements	−0.17***	−0.10***	−0.10***	−0.07**
Political Benefits				
Voting	0.07***	0.08***	0.04	0.03
Campaigning	0.08***	0.09***	0.04	0.03
Social movements	0.04	0.05*	0.05*	0.04*

Notes: N=1882
\qquad ***$p < 0.001$; **$p < 0.01$; *$p < 0.05$.
Source: 2001 British Election Study.

The political engagement indicators also reduce the magnitude of the different costs terms and so do the political support indicators, although not by as
much, and in the case of social movements not at all. This suggests that political engagement perhaps acts as a selective incentive for participation that
reduces the perceived costs (rather than increasing the perceived benefits).
People who have an interest in politics may treat participation as something of
a hobby and derive pleasure from taking part rather than treating it as a bit of a
chore.

Turning to civic skills, from Table 2 it can be seen that there is a modest
education effect.[11] Those with a university degree are significantly more
likely to vote, although the magnitude of the effect is not great. Overall, the
magnitude of the coefficient is relatively similar for all three types of participation. Although it is significantly different from zero for voting, it seems
plausible that none of the terms are significantly different from each other.
Surprisingly, political knowledge is a significant predictor only for voting.
This could reflect the partisan nature of the questions that were asked. Other,
more general measures of political knowledge, possibly derived from 'don't
know' responses, also need to be examined to see whether this is the case or
not. Also, it could suggest that in some respects voting represents a more
considered type of activity than the other two types of participation, and one
in which it pays to know both sides of the argument.

Turning to political engagement, attention to politics has a significant and
positive impact on each of the types of political action, and there is not much

difference in terms of the size of the effect either. The pattern for political efficacy is not quite so clear-cut. It has a highly significant and relatively strong
positive impact on campaigning and social movements, as expected, but does
not have a significant impact on voting. Overall, the impact of civic skills and
political engagement does not vary much by type of political action. In particular, education and political awareness have a fairly uniform impact on type
of activity. Civic skills and political engagement help to explain why some
people participate and others do not, but they do not help to explain why some
people participate in one type of activity while others participate in another.
There is thus evidence to suggest that they constitute a general political
resource. This finding should, however, be treated with a certain degree of
caution. Political knowledge and political efficacy do not have a uniform
impact on the different types of political action. They are thus not quite as
general as the other variables. More research needs to be carried out on these
items in order to examine whether these discrepancies are substantial or not.

Turning next to social capital, it has a significant and strong positive impact
on campaign activity and social movements, but no significant impact on
voting. The unstandardized beta coefficient is slightly larger for social movements (0.12) than it is for campaign activity (0.05), although overall it is relatively strong for both modes. This is consistent with the hypothesis that social
capital facilitates collective modes of action but not individual modes of
action. This finding is given further credence by the fact that social capital
does not distinguish between other potential dimensions of action, such as
electoral and non-electoral forms of participation. In this sense it is morally
neutral. It does not distinguish between the substance, or purpose, of participation – only its mode. There is no reason to suspect that this would be any
different if more extreme types of behaviour were examined. Controlling for
social capital also reduces the size of the education beta coefficients for
campaign activity and social movements. This suggests that social capital may
also reduce some of the individual costs associated with participation.

Finally, considering political support, there is evidence that evaluations of
the political process in general have a positive relationship with electoral
forms of participation and a negative relationship with non-electoral forms of
participation. Political respect and democratic satisfaction have a significant
negative relationship with social movements. High levels of support for these
objects are associated with low levels of participation. This supports, to some
extent, the finding that political cynicism fuels protest politics (Norris, 1999:
261) and low 'system affect' (legitimacy) is a spur for aggressive political
behaviour (Muller and Jukam, 1977: 1563). However, it should be noted that
social movements, as measured here, are not an extreme type of political
behaviour. Thus, rather than over-stating the destabilizing potential of political cynicism, the results seem to support Dalton's assertion that dissatisfaction

with the institutions and processes of representative democracy lead to a move towards participatory democracy (Dalton, 1999: 76). This hints at the existence of alternative participatory systems. On the other hand, party identification and political respect both have a significant strong positive impact on voting and campaigning. The relationship runs contrary to some previous findings. For example, Dalton (1999: 59) suggests that citizens often become dissatisfied with political office-holders and act on these feelings to select new leaders at the next election. Thus, if people are stimulated to express their dissatisfaction, alienation with institutions of representative democracy could mobilize citizens to throw out office-holders, and seek institutional redress (Citrin and Green, 1986). However, this kind of dynamic is probably dependent on a more specific version of political support. When the attitude in question refers to a generalized perception of an object in the political process, the results presented here show that people need to have faith in the political system in order to participate in electoral forms of action. If they do not have that faith, they voice their political concerns in ways that are less closely connected with it – in non-electoral forms of participation such as social movements.

There is also evidence of a slightly different pattern. Objects at different levels of the political system are more important for some types of political activity than others. Party identification is associated with voting and campaigning but not social movements, whereas democratic satisfaction is associated with social movements but not voting and campaigning. Political objects at the specific end of the continuum influence electoral forms of participation whereas political objects at the diffuse end of the continuum influence non-electoral forms of participation. This shows that people not only distinguish between different objects of the political system, but that these distinctions also have behavioural consequences. In particular, it shows that electoral forms of participation are driven much more by the political than by wider attitudes towards democracy. Turnout is unlikely to be driven by attitudes towards the regime. Thus, concern about low turnout signalling a 'democratic crisis' is somewhat misleading.

Conclusion

Alternative types of political action are similar in some respects and different in other respects. For example, voting and campaign activity are similar in that they are both electoral forms of participation; they are both partisan; and they are both relatively episodic. However, whereas voting is a fairly low-cost activity, campaign activity requires more time and effort. In addition, whereas voting is an individual mode of political action campaigning is collective. The theoretical distinctions between the different types of political activity are important in a number of respects. By modelling these similarities and differences it is possible to examine the impact of different concepts on different components of action. Figures 2–4 provide a summary. A connecting line

FIGURE 2
VOTING: THE IMPACT OF COSTS, BENEFITS, CIVIC SKILLS, SOCIAL CAPITAL,
POLITICAL ENGAGEMENT AND POLITICAL SUPPORT

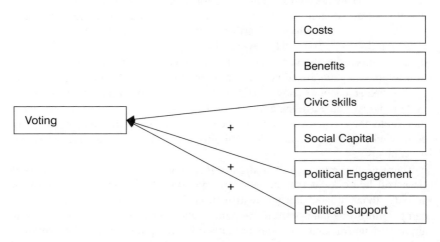

FIGURE 3
CAMPAIGNING: THE IMPACT OF COSTS, BENEFITS, CIVIC SKILLS, SOCIAL
CAPITAL, POLITICAL ENGAGEMENT AND POLITICAL SUPPORT

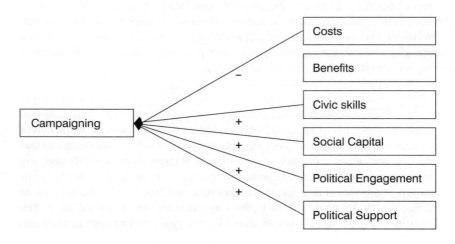

FIGURE 4
SOCIAL MOVEMENTS: THE IMPACT OF COSTS, BENEFITS, CIVIC SKILLS, SOCIAL
CAPITAL, POLITICAL ENGAGEMENT AND POLITICAL SUPPORT

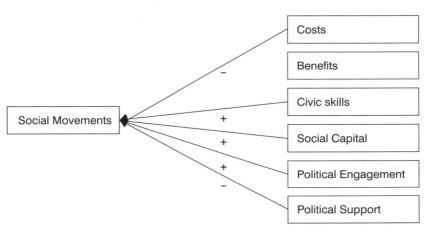

depicts a relationship between the concept and the dependent variable and a '+' or '–' symbol shows whether the relationship is positive or negative.

In this article I have shown that there are some factors that are general and that facilitate all three types of political action. In this respect the story is a familiar one. Those who are endowed with high levels of education, political knowledge and political awareness are more likely than those who are not to participate in a range of political activities. From Figures 2–4 we can see that civic skills and political engagement have a positive impact on all three measures of political activity. Variables of this type can be thought of as general political resources and are positively associated with all different types of political action. They are thus able to discriminate between those who participate and those who do not, but they do not distinguish between who participates in what.

On the one hand, the difference between individual and collective modes of action is more mechanical. Collective action is influenced by the problems of free-riding and is often considered much more 'difficult' to sustain than individual action. This is borne out by the finding that the impact of the perceived costs of participation is much stronger on collective modes of participation than it is on the individual mode of participation. The driving force behind this component of action is related to resources. Whereas some resources facilitate all types of political activity, other resources, such as social capital, facilitate collective modes of action as opposed to individual modes of action. It thus constitutes a more specific resource, and helps ease the problems associated with

free riding. From Figures 2–4 we can see that costs and social capital have a positive impact on campaigning and social movements but no impact on voting.

On the other hand, the difference between electoral and non-electoral forms
of action is more a question of substance. These forms of participation have
also been referred to as conventional and unconventional participation, and
Barnes and Kaase (1979: 45) argue that they can be distinguished on the basis
of legality and legitimacy – that is, their conformity to positive legal norms
relevant for a given type of behaviour and the extent to which a given population at a given point in time approves or disapproves of them. The driving
force behind these different forms of action is related to how people perceive
the political system in general, as well as their attitudes towards different
aspects of it. First, on a general level, from Figures 2–4 we can see that political support has a positive impact on electoral political behaviour such as
voting or campaign activity, but a negative impact on non-electoral action
such as social movements. Second, whereas campaign activity and voting are
strongly influenced by the most specific level of political support – party identification, involvement in social movements is strongly influenced by the most
diffuse kind of political support – democratic satisfaction. Electoral forms of
political activity are not driven by such deep-seated democratic values. This
suggests that electoral forms of political activity are not particularly useful
barometers for the health of democracy. Although a low turnout may signal a
'crisis of democratic politics' (Whiteley et al., 2001: 222) it does not follow
that it also signals the more serious scenario of a crisis of democracy.

Different types of participation are distinct in a number of ways. Failing to
take into account these differences (by treating participation as a whole) is
misleading. It is likely to exaggerate the impact of the predictors for activity in
general, such as civic skills and political engagement, and to underestimate the
impact of predictors for specific components of action, such as social capital
and political support. The fact that participation is often measured either as a
whole (see Parry et al., 1992) or in terms of levels of general involvement (see
Topf 1995) has emphasized this problem and contributed to the pre-eminence
of the so-called 'usual suspects' as explanations for political participation. In
this article, I have shown that approaches of this type maybe unsatisfactory. In
order to adequately describe why people participate or not, or why some people
are relatively more likely to participate in one type of activity rather than
another, it is necessary to clearly specify the different types of participation,
and theoretically derive the factors associated with each of their components.

This article has concentrated on individual-level accounts of participation.
This is only part of the story however, and to gain a deeper understanding into
the factors that lead people to participate or not it is necessary to take in to
account the context that influences their behaviour, both over time and across
space.

APPENDIX
POLITICAL PARTICIPATION INDICATORS

Question number	*Question*
Pre Q6.	Please think of a scale that runs from 0 to 10, where 0 means **very unlikely** and 10 means **very likely**, how likely is it that you will vote in the general election?
Post Q41	Now, a few questions about how active you are in politics and community affairs. Let's think about the next few years. Using a scale from 0 – 10, where 0 means very unlikely and 10 means very likely, how likely is it that you will:
a)	Vote in the next election for the European Parliament.
b)	Vote in the next local election
c)	Work actively with a group of people to address a public issue or solve a problem **[INTERVIEWER NOTE: If respondent needs clarification, read: for example, like getting involved in a neighbourhood watch]**
d)	Participate in a protest, like a rally or a demonstration, to show your concern about a public issue or problem.
f)	Give money to a political party.
g)	Try to convince someone else how to vote.
h)	Work for a party or a candidate in an election campaign.
j)	Join a boycott, that is, refuse to buy a particular product or to shop at a particular store.

Source: 2001 British Election Study.

ACKNOWLEDGEMENTS

Thanks to David Sanders, Justin Fisher, Anthony Heath and participants at the Democracy and Participation panel at the PSA Annual Conference for helpful comments and suggestions.

NOTES

1. The 2001 BES was conducted by Harold D. Clarke, David Sanders, Marianne C. Stewart and Paul F. Whitely. It was funded by the Economic and Social Research Council. Data and related information are available at www.essex.ac.uk/bes.
2. Political benefits are measured by Q17d and Q17f and political costs are measured by Q17e and Q65b. Q17 (post). Now, let's talk for a few moments about politics and government generally. Please tell me whether you agree or disagree with each of the following statements. d) Being active in politics is a good way to get benefits for me and my family; e) It takes too much time and effort to be active in politics and public affairs; f) Being active in politics is a good way to get benefits for groups that people care about like pensioners or the disabled. Q65 (post). Please tell me if you agree or disagree with each one of the following statements. b) It often is difficult for me to understand what is going on in government and politics.

3. Political awareness is measured by Q57 (post): On a scale from 0 to 10, how much attention do you pay to politics and public affairs? The political knowledge index ranges from 0 to 6 and is based on the number of correct responses to the following questions: Q68 (post). Please tell me if you think that the following statements are true or false. If you don't know, just say so and we will skip to the next one. Remember- true, false, or don't know. 1) Polling stations close at 10: 00 p.m. on election day. 2) It is official Conservative Party policy that Britain should never join the single European currency. 3) The Liberal Democrats favour a system of proportional representation for Westminster elections. 4) The minimum voting age is 16. 5) Unemployment has fallen since Labour was elected in 1997. 6) Only taxpayers are allowed to vote in a general election. Political efficacy is measured by Q36 in the pre-election survey: On a scale from 0 to 10 where 10 means a great deal of influence and 0 means no influence, how much influence do you have on politics and public affairs?
4. On the one hand it has been suggested that social capital can be a collective resource, and as such constitutes a public good (Putnam 1993). On the other hand, this claim has been disputed (see Portes 1998), and it has been argued that the good is not public at all, but is only a good for the individuals participating in the network. For the purposes of this article social capital is treated as having only an individual level impact rather than an aggregate impact.
5. 'Men walk around Hatton Garden with a hundred thousand pounds worth of diamonds that were handed over to them in trust. In a dingy office a man shows another man a number of stones that cost him a fortune, and then goes away while the buyer inspects them carefully. No contracts are made. Nothing is written down. All deals are settled verbally.'
6. Q41. Now, a few questions about how active you are in politics and community affairs. Let's think about the next few years. Using a scale from 0–10, where 0 means very unlikely and 10 means very likely, how likely is it that you will: e) Be active in a voluntary organization, like a community association, a charity group, or a sports club. Q48. Generally speaking, would you say that most people can be trusted, or that you can't be too careful dealing with people? Please use the 0–10 scale to indicate your view, where 0 means can't be too careful and 10 means most people can be trusted. Q49. Do you think that most people you come into contact with would try to take advantage of you if they got the chance or would they try to be fair? Please use the 0–10 scale again where 0 means would try to take advantage and 10 means would try to be fair.
7. This is measured by Q32 in the pre-election survey: On the whole, are you satisfied or dissatisfied with the way that democracy works in this country?
8. Political respect is measured by Q13 in the pre-election survey: Now, thinking about political institutions like Parliament, please use the 0–10 scale to indicate how much respect you have for each of the following, where 0 means **no respect** and 10 means **a great deal of respect**. a) The Parliament at Westminster d) Local Government in your area f) Politicians generally.
9. This is measured by the pre-election question: Q5d. [PARTY GIVEN IN Q.5a OR Q.5c] Would you call yourself very strong [PARTY GIVEN IN Q5a OR Q5c], fairly strong or not very strong?
10. Political activity such as political violence is relatively infrequent. Its omission from the analysis does not distort the overall picture of participation.
11. If political knowledge and political awareness are not controlled for, education is significant and has a strong impact on all types of political activity. Thus, education in some sense re-describes political knowledge and political awareness.

REFERENCES

Almond, G., and S. Verba (1963) *The Civic Culture: Political Attitudes and Democracy in Five Nations*. Sage.
Axelrod, R. (1984) *The Evolution of Cooperation*. Basic Books.
Barnes, S. and M. Kaase (1979) *Political Action: Mass Participation in Five Western Democracies*. Sage.

Citrin, J., and D. Green (1986) 'Presidential Leadership and the Resurgence of Trust in Government', *British Journal of Political Science* 16: 431–53.

Coleman, J. 1990. *Foundations of Social Theory.* Belknap Press.

Curtice, J. and R. Jowell (1995) 'The Sceptical Electorate', in R. Jowell, J. Curtice, A. Park, L. Brook and D. Ahrendt, *British Social Attitudes: The 12th Report.* Dartmouth.

Dalton, Russell J. (2002) *Citizen Politics: Public Opinion and Political Parties in Advanced Industrial Democracies.* Chatham House.

Easton, D. (1965) *A Systems Analysis of Political Life.* John Wiley.

Easton, D. (1975) 'A Re-assessment of the Concept of Political Support', *British Journal of Political Science* 5: 435–57.

Fisher, J. (1999) 'Modelling the Decision to Donate by Individual Party Members: the Case of British Parties', *Party Politics* 5(1) 19–38.

Fuchs, D. (1993) 'Trends of Political Support in the Federal Republic of Germany', in D. Berg-Schlosser and R. Rytlewski (eds), *Political Culture in Germany.* Macmillan.

Fuchs, D., G. Guidorossi and P. Svensson (1995) 'Support for the Democratic System', in H.-D. Klingemann and D. Fuchs (eds.) *Citizens and the State.* Oxford University Press.

Lane, R.E. (1959) *Political Life: How and Why Do People Get Involved in Politics.* Free Press.

Merkl, P.H. (1988) 'Comparing Legitimacy and Values among Advanced Democratic Countries', in M. Dogan (ed.), *Comparing Pluralist Democracies: Strains on Legitimacy.* Westview.

Muller, E. and T. Jukam (1977) 'On the Meaning of Political Support', *The American Political Science Review* 71(4) 1561–95.

Muller, E., T. Jukam and M. Seligson (1982) 'Diffuse Support and Anti-system Political Behaviour: A Comparative Analysis', *American Journal of Political Science* 26: 240–63.

Norris, P. (ed.) (1999) *Critical Citizens: Global Support for Democratic Government* Oxford University Press.

Olson, M. (1965) *The Logic of Collective Action.* Harvard University Press.

Parry, G., G. Moyser and N. Day (1992) *Political Participation and Democracy in Britain.* Cambridge University Press.

Putnam, R. (1993) *Making Democracy Work: Civic Traditions in Modern Italy.* Princeton University Press.

Putnam, R. (2000) *Bowling Alone: The Collapse and Revival of American Community.* Simon & Schuster.

Schmitt, H. (1983) 'Party Government in Public Opinion: A European Cross-National Comparison', *European Journal of Political Research* 11: 353–76.

Topf, R. (1995) 'Beyond Electoral Participation' in H.D. Klingemann and D. Fuchs (eds.) *Citizens and the State.* Oxford University Press

Verba, S., N. Nie and J. Kim (1971) *The Modes of Democratic Participation: A Cross-national Comparison.* Sage.

Verba, S. and N. Nie (1972) *Participation in America.* Harper & Row.

Verba, S., K.L. Schlozman, H. Brady and N. Nie (1993) 'Race, Ethnicity and Political Resources: Participation in the United States', *British Journal of Political Science* 23: 453–97.

Verba, S., K. Schlozman and H. Brady (1995) *Voice and Equality: Civic Voluntarism in American Politics.* Harvard University Press.

Weil, F. (1989) 'The Sources and Structure of Democratic Legitimation in Western Democracies: A Consolidated Model Tested with Time-Series Data in Six Countries Since World War II', *American Sociological Review* 54: 682–706.

Whiteley, P., H. Clarke, D. Sanders and M. Stewart (2001) 'Turnout' in P. Norris (ed.) *Britain Votes 2001.* Oxford University Press.

Whiteley, P., P. Seyd, J. Richardson and P. Bissell (1994) 'Explaining Party Activism: The Case of the British Conservative Party', *British Journal of Political Science* 24(1) 79–94.

Widmaier, U. (1990) 'Political Stability in OECD Nations', *International Political Science Review* 11: 219–42.

What are the Origins of Social Capital?
Results from a Panel Survey of Young People

Peter John and Zoë Morris

The current interest in social capital has led to a profusion of research and commentary on its desirable political and social effects. The earlier emphasis on group membership, which shows that the variations in associational life have little connection to public policy outcomes (Knack and Keefer, 1997; Whiteley, 2000), has given way to a broader conceptualization, one that emphasizes the networks involved, the unique contribution of 'bridging social capital', the positive experiences that result from group membership, and the willingness to engage with the wider public sphere, including politics. Policy-makers and researchers have increasingly realized that enhancing a society's overall level of social capital has desirable effects, relating to the efficiency of democracy, a more buoyant economy, better health and lower crime, to name a few. But what causes social capital to emerge in the first place? We know that political orientation, levels of trust and voluntary activities transfer across generations (Nie et al., 1996). We also know that the provision of social capital is tied to socio-economic status (Verba et al., 1995), which changes very slowly over time and would suggest that each society and locality has a pre-determined level of social capital. But do context and other influences have an impact in addition to socio-economic status? And does government have a lever through its control of one of the key sites for the generation of values, the school? Such a question is particularly topical, as the UK government has introduced citizenship education as part of the National Curriculum in England, with civic ideas at its core. But do schools and 'civics' have an impact on social capital in addition to political knowledge and awareness? This article seeks to answer these questions by an analysis of a panel survey of 15–17 year olds, focusing on the determinants of volunteering and social trust.

Literature Review

The long-standing literature on political socialization places parents at the centre of values and behaviour formation (Beck and Jennings, 1982; Rosen-han, 1970; Colten and Gore, 1994; Prancer and Pratt, 1999). Socio-economic status (SES) is an important determinant of attitudes of both adults and young

British Elections & Parties Review, Vol. 14, 2004, pp. 94–112
ISSN 1368-9886 print
DOI: 10.1080/1368988042000258790   © 2004 Taylor & Francis Ltd.

people (Milbraith and Goel, 1977; Verba et al., 1995), which is expressed as intergenerational SES – SES transmitted from parents to children (Beck and Jennings, 1982). Parental civic orientations and actions, in the context of the family, transfer across generations, such as positive attitudes to democracy and histories of participation (Dowse and Hughes, 1971; Verba et al., 1995).

Longitudinal research suggests that socialization is a gradual process, which is not fixed at an early point in adolescence but continues to change up until the mid-20s and beyond (Jennings and Niemi, 1981). There may be critical junctures in the socialization process, points where volunteering and positive attitudes to democracy may take an upward or downward turn. Some studies show the weakness of the parental transmission of values (Jennings and Niemi, 1968; Jennings and Niemi, 1974). Some survey evidence, correlating the attitudes of parents and children, shows the amount of transfer across generations of interpersonal trust and membership of associations is relatively small, which leaves room for other influences (Jennings and Stoker, 2001a and b). Such ideas have as their apogee the developmental approach to political socialization that assumes 'lifelong plasticity' (Flanagan and Sherrod, 1998) or 'lifelong openness' (Sears, 1990). Whilst the extremity of such views has been questioned by recent research that shows the stability of attitudes (Riedel and Smith, 2001), it is possible to infer that SES and intergenerational mechanisms that transfer behaviour and values are not as strong as a previous generation of researchers considered them to be. There are many 'pathways' to political socialization, such as the media and peers, as well as social and family background (Beck and Jennings, 1982).

Whilst acknowledging the powerful impacts of the socio-economic and family environment, the complexity of the relationships allows researchers to hypothesize that school and curricula may, in certain conditions, influence attitudes and reported behaviour. For example, Beck and Jennings (1982) suggest that extra-curricular activities are better predictors of adult political participation than the experience of civics classes. These findings have been supported in most recent work, often because they generate psychological benefits such as improved well-being and self-esteem (e.g. Paulsen, 1991; Smith, 1999), but not all (Lawson, 2001). Social attitudes may be directly affected as research has consistently demonstrated that education is an important contributor to adult social and political behaviour (e.g. Nie et al., 1996), though it is less clear *what* it is about education that matters. School climate is important to the development of attitudes and behaviours favourable to democracy and participation (Finkel and Ernst, 2002). Factors include the extent to which pupils are active participants in their classrooms and schools (e.g. Ashworth, 1994; Torney et al., 1975).

Just as social capital is distributed differently across space, so schools vary in the extent to which they influence the level of social capital. Coleman's

(1988) research shows that varying levels of social capital surround the school, which are transferred from parents and students and maintain themselves over time. Whilst much of the effect is social in character, such as the family social capital that encourages child achievement (Teachman et al., 1996), the regime of the school also influences attitudes and behaviour through school classes and cultures. US research suggests that, once established by these powerful socialization mechanisms, these forms of behaviour transfer into adulthood (Verba et al., 1995; Janoski et al., 1998).

Schools contribute to associational life and volunteering, as well as to political activities more generally (e.g. Nie et al., 1996). Yet it is less clear what are the causal mechanisms: whether it is the culture and regime of the school, what may be called school climate, that is important to the development of attitudes and behaviours favourable to democracy and participation (Finkel and Ernst, 2002), such as whether pupils are active participants in their classrooms and schools (e.g. Ashworth, 1994; and Torney et al., 1975); perhaps the availability of voluntary activities that form a pathway to participation (Beck and Jennings, 1982); or whether civic education is the key?

The English citizenship curriculum model is based on a specific interpretation of citizenship, which reflects current fears of increased apathy, cynicism, social disintegration and alienation. Citizenship education is intended to halt this trend by developing particular knowledge, values and attitudes, and the norm of participation. According to the 1988 report of the Advisory Group on Education for Citizenship and Teaching Democracy in Schools, which laid down the recommendations for citizenship education, it 'aims at nothing less than a change in the political culture of England' by making young people knowledgeable, responsible, and ultimately participative (Crick, 1988). But much of the early work, mainly undertaken in the US, suggests that such expectations might be misplaced; that teaching civics does not develop 'good' citizens (e.g. Conley, 1991; Langton and Jennings, 1968; Patrick, 1977; and Slomczynski and Shabad, 1998). Recent evidence has questioned the inevitability of this conclusion, however (Delli Carpini and Keeter, 1996; Denver and Hands, 1990; Ehman 1980; Maitles, 2000; Nieimi and Junn, 1998). Increasingly, the message seems to be one of uneven effects across domains. Curricular content can encourage students to volunteer and influence their wider set of social attitudes.

Research Methods and Analysis

Our project first surveyed 15–16 year olds (school year 11) at the start of their final year before a key examination, GCSEs in the late part of 2000.[1] This age group is important because it is when young people start to develop more sophisticated political views of their own. The research site was one county – a large local government area from which the research team drew a range of schools. Hertfordshire was chosen because it offered a range of neighbourhoods – from scattered villages to urban outer-London – and a range of social environments, including some of the most deprived areas in Britain.

Our aim was to recruit 24 schools according to a stratified sample based on social intake, quality (examination performance) and the extent of provision of 'citizenship-type' activities, as well as how much 'citizenship' schools taught.[2] We sorted schools into eight groups on each of the criteria and we chose the schools from the top, bottom and middle. The study also included three fee-paying schools, which we selected by the same process, except that fees were one of the selection criteria.

Approximately one year after the first wave, we re-surveyed the young people by a postal questionnaire sent to their home addresses that we had gathered in the first phase. We carried out three follow-up mailings – two to their home address, and once through their schools. We achieved a 56 per cent response rate, approximately what we anticipated.

The analysis seeks to explore what predicts the social capital measures, participation in voluntary activities and social trust: first for year one of the study, and then for change across the panels. Because there are two levels of analysis – schools and students – multilevel modelling is appropriate to generate the estimates (Goldstein, 1995; Hox, 2002), a procedure that is common in education research (e.g. Smith et al., 1989). This technique avoids underestimates of the standard errors and incorrectly specified models; it also allows the exploration of the unit of interest in this study, the school. In this case, and for simplicity, we estimate models with explanatory variables that define the fixed part of the model with coefficients that represent the average relationship rather than those which vary across units at one or more levels. We use the *gllamm* set of commands in Stata's software (Rabe-Hesketh et al., 2001) to estimate the models. This command uses Stata's maximum likelihood procedure with a modified Newton Raphson algorithm and an adaptive quadrature that the authors find to be superior to the Gaussian quadrature.

Group Activities

To represent group activities we created a variable that adds ten specific questions about voluntary activity, which has values from 0 to 8.[3] The components of the variable scale well, with an alpha of .57 for year 1, and .53 for year 2. The scale has an average of 2.08 for year 1 and .79 for year 2. The two observations thus show a considerable drop in voluntary activity between the years, though a high correlation between them (Pearson=.437; sig=00). The striking change over a short period of time prompts an initial hypothesis: does moving to leave school or the take-up of A-levels or further education mark a new direction for young people, when they tend to shake off parental-led voluntary activities? In part our panel analysis seeks to answer whether the availability of television watching and part-time work decreases voluntary activity at this crucial point of development, and whether citizenship education has the potential to limit the decrease.

In building our analytic model, we draw on the literature that shows that voluntary activities are predicted by social-economic status (Verba et al., 1995; Colten and Gore, 1994). Second, parental voluntary activity transmits across generations as with other forms of behaviour and orientations. It has been found that parents influence their children by the extent to which they participate in civic life themselves. Beck and Jennings' (1982) analysis of a US panel survey, for example, reveals that parent's civic participation strongly predicts that of their children, although SES remains the strongest predictor overall.

Religious activity also encourages voluntary activity (Pattie, Seyd and Whiteley, 2002; Verba et al., 1995). More generally, social awareness may predispose students to volunteer. These values emerge because of the environment in which the individual develops (Eisenberg, 1992), perhaps encouraged by the institutions of religious participation, which may include the school. In addition, some studies show that there are gender differences in volunteering, with girls being more willing to volunteer than boys (Eisenberg, 1992; Eagly and Crowley, 1986), especially non-political volunteering. Furthermore, it is likely that race affects voluntary activity since conventional voluntary activity may be dominated by the white majority, and non-whites may not identify or be socialized into voluntary activities. Roker et al. (1999) also find differential levels of participation amongst young people based on their ethnicity, which is explained largely by specific cultural norms.

There is also a psychological aspect to volunteering. It involves liking being with others rather than being alone. There may be some psychological predisposition to participate in voluntary organizations deriving from life satisfaction and feelings of happiness (Lane, 2000). In contrast, stress may cause the young adult to withdraw from associational activity. Whereas it is hard to disentangle the causes and effects of adult volunteering, which may help individuals enjoy being with others, it is possible to assume that that effect has not yet taken place with students. Those who are lacking in self-esteem or are unhappy, unwell, or anxious tend to turn inwards and withdraw from society; low self-esteem is correlated with fewer personal interactions, lower confidence and more passivity (Sniderman, 1975). Self-esteem is also associated with a desire for group approval and for conformity and, perhaps more importantly, a strong desire to avoid disapproval, which reinforces inaction and withdrawal. Educational achievement is another factor that causes students to be more confident and hence more willing to engage in formal group activity (Steinberg, 1996).

We also measure whether respondents work part-time. We hypothesize, following Putnam (2000), that volunteering may depend on the amount of free time an individual has, so if respondents have part-time jobs, this may reduce the time they have available for voluntary work. Nonetheless, Putnam (2000) finds that people who work are more active, so we argue that the sign on part-time work may be positive or negative. We also follow Putnam (2000) by arguing that watching television is civically damaging because it substitutes for something else, that is, 'joining'.

Finally, schools may generate social capital, here concentrating on voluntary engagement. This activity is central to citizenship education, which aims to make pupils more self-confident and responsible both in and beyond the classroom, to encourage pupils to play a helpful part in the life of their schools, neighbourhoods, communities and the wider world. The school climate, which is the way in which schools are responsive to their students, may encourage volunteering.

For the analysis of the first year's data, we create a baseline model, using the SES variables of the number of cars or vans in the household and a dichotomous variable that indicates whether the students' home is owned by their family. We represent SES by a summary score, which adds together the item scores. We do not have a direct measure of parental volunteering, but an indication of their voluntary activities in relationship to the school, which is a measure of parental involvement based on students recollection that their parents coming to parents' evenings and to fundraising activities, which is the sum of the individual item scores (alpha=.47).

A religion variable measures whether the student is Protestant, Jewish, Catholic etc. or not. We also use a social awareness variable, which indicates whether the respondents agree or disagree with the statement 'More should be done to help the poor'. In addition, we enter gender and race as dichotomous terms. Because of small numbers of non-white respondents, we adopt a simple dichotomous definition of the variable by adding together different ethnic groups into the definition of non-white. We deploy a psychological variable to indicate sociability, which shows whether the respondents agree or disagree with the statement 'I enjoy being with other people'. Academic proficiency is self-reported on a five-point scale from low to high. Table 1 reports descriptive statistics for these and other variables.

Table 2 sets out models to predict volunteering at the first time point. The baseline model 1 includes all the variables bar television watching, social capital and school culture. All have the hypothesized signs and, with the exception of gender and ethnicity, are significant. The effect for part-time work is positive and significant, suggesting that the busy do more or that

TABLE 1
DESCRIPTIVE STATISTICS OF THE MAIN VARIABLES

Variable	N	Mean	St Dev	Min	Max
Wave 1					
Volunteer	1248	1.817	1.657	0	8
SES	1249	1.179	.4167	0	2
Parental involvement	1240	2.202	.9495	0	4
Religion	1236	.6019	.4897	0	1
Social conscience	1187	.8804	.8716	0	4
Gender	1247	.4627	.4988	0	1
Ethnicity	1226	.1378	.3448	0	1
Enjoyment	1245	3.482	.6421	0	4
Proficiency	1220	3.311	.9288	1	5
Part-time	1249	.6525	.4763	0	1
TV hours	1242	2.674	.9771	1	4
Citizenship education	1101	9.468	4.589	0	18
Citizenship education (student perception)	1188	6.304	3.267	0	18
School climate	1247	2.238	.6801	0	4
Trust	1235	.4194	.4937	0	1
Lying justified	1157	.9041	.5521	0	2
Panel variables (stacked)					
Volunteer	1379	1.712	1.569	0	8
Social conscience	1319	.9719	.8684	0	4
Enjoyment	1389	3.483	.6513	0	4
Proficiency	1253	5.79e-09	.9996	−2.528	2.627
Part-time	2072	.5294	.4992	0	1
Television watching	1348	2.428	.9981	1	4
Citizenship education (student perception)	1329	−6.62e-09	.9996	−1.965	3.513

doing work increases self-confidence and thus volunteering. It may be the case that work increases a sense of social responsibility, which thus affects joining. There appears to be a very modest school effect in this model as shown by the σ^2 for between the schools.

To explore Putnam's view that television watching should reduce volunteering, we add into model 2 how many hours of television and videos students say they have watched in a day. We find that the sign on television watching is negative, as hypothesized, and within conventional levels of statistical significance; thus, it is possible to conclude that watching TV decreases voluntary activity. It may be that Putnam is right, or that young people who do volunteer are less inclined to or have less time to watch television.

TABLE 2
FACTORS THAT PREDICT VOLUNTARY ACTIVITY – WAVE 1

	Model 1	Model 2	Model 3	Model 4	Model 5
Socio-economic status	.3867*	.4063*	.3426*	.4051*	.4103*
	(.1183)	(.1211)	(.1280)	(.1238)	(.1240)
Parental involvement	2713*	.2950*	.2944*	.2885*	.2878*
	(.0520)	(.0528)	(.0558)	(.0543)	(.0545)
Religion	.3211*	.2997*	.3450*	.2714*	.2727*
	(.0995)	(.1011)	(.1064)	(.1035)	(.1034)
Social conscience	−.1547*	−.1450*	−.1598*	−.1410*	−.1399*
	(.0546)	(.0565)	(.0587)	.0580*	(.0581)
Gender	−.1171	−.1114	−.0437	−.1166	−.1157
	.0984	(.1003)	(.1048)	(.1034)	(.1032)
Ethnicity	−.1313	−.1351	−.1299	−.0986	−.0978
	(.1390)	(.1421)	(.1534)	(.1471)	(.1470)
Enjoyment	.2071*	.1866*	.1980*	.1835*	.1837*
	(.0731)	.0747	(.0812)	(.0766)	(.0768)
Proficiency	.3282*	.3154*	.3465*	.3024*	.3039*
	(.0552)	(.0563)	(.0598)	(.0578)	(.0578)
Part-time work	.2017*	.2266*	.3057*	.2052*	.2063*
	(.0971)	(.0990)	(.1041)	(.1013)	(.1013)
Television hours	−.1177*	−.1674*	−.1036*	−.1022*	
	(.0487)	(.0514)	(.0497)	(.0497)	
Citizenship education	–	–	−.0060	–	–
			(.0159)		
Citizenship education (student perception)	–	–	–	.0359*	.0347*
				(.0151)	(.0157)
School climate	–	–	–	–	.0251
					(.0778)
Constant	−1.1396	−.8028	−.7516	−.9764	−1.044
	(.3530)	(.4004)	(.4539)	(.4152)	(.4381)
σ^2(students)	2.2845	2.2719	2.199	2.263	2.264
	(.0973)	(.0985)	(.1017)	(.100)	(.100)
σ^2 (schools)	.0560	.0521	.0562	.0636	.0599
	(.0317)	(.0308)	(.0342)	(.0348)	(.0337)
log-likelihood	−2077.4	−2000.6	−1744.7	−1919.1	−1919.1
N	1129	1089	958	1045	1045

Note: * – significant at p < .05

    The citizenship education variable adds together responses from our practice survey, a questionnaire to school heads carried out before the main survey, which asked schools how much teaching they provide on rights, justice system, diversity, government, parliament, elections, voluntary organizations, conflict resolution and the media. There is another variable, what students perceive they have been taught, which we analyse separately. This variable adds together their positive responses to questions about their citizenship course content: how laws are made; different races and ethnicities; the courts and the judicial system; political parties and voting; local government; principles of democratic government; rights and responsibilities of citizens; community based and voluntary organizations; and the media in society. This term does not correlate strongly with the formal record of civic education (Kendall's Tau-b=.013, p=.557), which probably reflects the particular experiences of Year 11 students in addition to the formal provision. As the variables measure different things, we use the formal record in model 3 and the student recollection in model 4. But it is only the student recollection variable that is significant. Model 5 includes the school climate variable, but it is not significant, making model 4 our final regression.

Thus, from wave 1 there are only some tentative suggestions that the UK experiment at attempting to translate the ideal of the model citizen into practice is starting to occur. But it may be the case, as Lawson (2001) writes, that inculcating values of 'shared obligation' in schools though participation in community activities may not be strong because most students who engage in voluntary activity do so for a specific time-bound purpose – for the sake of their school record or achieving awards, and were encouraged to do so for the same reasons. Hence we need to see what happens to volunteering after GCSEs.

We repeat the analysis with the count of voluntary activities in the second year, reported in Table 3. It might be possible to explain the difference in voluntary activities by using voluntary activities from the first wave as an independent term, a static score or conditional change model (Finkel 1995: 6–12). However, statisticians caution against the use of the first year measure as a control. It is better to have a model that includes the changes in dependent and independent terms, what may be called a change-score model, which itself resembles an analysis of covariance or ANCOVA-like model where those at the starting point do not share a similar score as they do in the ANCOVA model. With such an analysis, we are in a strong position to unpack some of the causal effects because we have two observations of volunteering, and also of civic education, television watching, enjoyment, social conscience, which are measured in the same way in both years. In year 2 we were able to ask about actual proficiency scores rather than grades. We use the GCSE passes as the response variable. It correlates fairly highly with the self-reported grades, with a coefficient of .69. As academic proficiency measure is measured differently in each wave, we standardize both variables to create the change score.

Table 3, model 1 presents the variables from the final model from Table 2, which predict volunteering, adding a time variable that is conventional in

TABLE 3
FACTORS THAT PREDICT VOLUNTARY ACTIVITY – CHANGE MODEL

	Model 1	Model 2	Model 3
Socio-economic status	.1117	.1066	.1257
	(.1198)	(.1197)	(.1203)
Parental involvement	.2417*	.2369*	.2367
	(.0501)	(.0500)	(.0502)
Religion	.0550*	.0557*	.0550
	(.0191)	(.0191)	(.0191)
Social conscience	−.1309*	.1332*	−.1290*
	(.0505)	(.0504)	(.0505)
Gender	.0380	.0486	.0383
	(.0939)	(.0939)	(.0936)
Ethnicity	−.3334*	−.3265*	−.3390*
	(.1319)	(.1319)	(.1320)
Enjoyment	.1279	.1366*	.1216
	(.0659)	(.0659)	(.0661)
Proficiency	.2550*	.2557*	.2590*
	(.0507)	(.0506)	(.0507)
Part-time	−.0509	−.0478	.0581
	(.0874)	(.0973)	(.0876)
Television hours	−.1178*	−.0477	−.1164*
	(.0446)	(.0733)	(.0446)
Time	−.7439*	−.4671*	−.7433*
	(.0875)	(.2361)	(.0876)
Citizenship education (student perception)	.1117*	.2280*	.0989*
	(.0427)	(.0708)	(.0442)
Citizenship*time		−.1798*	
		(.0872)	
Television hours*time		−.1101	
		(.0892)	
School climate			.0798
			(.0694)
Constant	1.2803	1.0766	1.114
	(.3197)	(.3514)	(.3518)
Variance at level 1 equation for log	.4435	.4421	.4446
standard deviation: σ^2 (con)	(.0323)	(.0322)	(.0323)
σ^2 (time)	−.2559	−.2556	−.2565
	(.0445)	(.0443)	(.0445)
Variance at level 2 σ^2 (schools)	.0490	.0485	.0447
	(.0285)	(.0285)	(.0277)
log-likelihood	−1870.0	−1867.4	−1869.3
N	1077	1077	1077

panel analysis to indicate a growth function – or in this case a decay – across the panels. This term is negative and significant as expected, reflecting the drop in volunteering we observe from the descriptive statistics. The rest of the variables perform much as expected – the change in observations over the panel is partly determined by the change in observations over the year as well as by the constant variables. We find that parental involvement and religion continue to predict as non-time-varying variables, though part-time work and socio-economic status do not reach conventional levels of significance. Ethnicity starts to predict in this model, indicating a drop in the inclination to volunteer among non-white groups. Social conscience and enjoyment continue to predict as time-varying variables. Gender remains unimportant. But television watching remains a powerful and significant variable, indicating that it is not an effect of low interest in volunteering but a likely cause.

Model 2 explores the interaction terms, controlling for other predictors. The two that are of interest are television watching and civic education interacted with time, which can explore the growth or decay effects. Here we find that there appears to be an interaction effect not with television watching, but only with civic education, which means that having controlled for the amount of civic education they receive in years 1 and 2, the interaction of education in year 2 and civic education is negative and significant. Does this mean that part of the decline in volunteering may be due to civic education itself? Or could it be that there is an undetected school effect: that there is less academic achievement in schools that provide more civic education, which in turn have less volunteering (Lawson, 2001)? Model 3 reintroduces the school climate variable, dropping the time-interaction terms, but this is not significant, making model 1 the preferred model. In a separate model not reported here, we introduce a dummy variable that indicates whether the student has left school or not, which may predict a decline in volunteering, though this too does not have an effect. But the results of this part of the research are clear – television watching predicts the decrease in volunteering, particularly in wave 1; but civic education increases it.

Trust

Trust is at the core of social capital. There are different sorts, but it is social trust that is central to social capital, which is ascertained by asking by the classic and much used question: 'Generally speaking do you think that most people can be trusted, or that you can't be too careful in dealing with people?' The measure has its problems – not least the lack of a scale – but it is at the core of much research of the last 20 years. Unlike the previous dependent variable, it is a discrete response, which can be estimated as a multilevel model with a binomial distribution, in this case a logit function, with the value 1 as the trust value and 0 as the lack of trust.

The analysis proceeds, as before, by creating a baseline model from the background terms (ethnicity, gender and SES) and student orientations, such as religion. As with some of the other models, we introduce variables that reflect cognitive styles. It is possible that students who are happy are more likely to trust (Lane, 2000), so we use the enjoyment variable. As with voluntary behaviour, trust may emerge from religious orientation and moral outlook. For the latter, we use belief in telling the truth rather than belief in helping the poor as the predictor variable, as trust is not so much a social action in itself, but an assessment in response to others' behaviours. We test this baseline set of variables in model 1 in Table 4, which shows expected signs for all the variables. The performance of the SES variable is weak. The psychological variables all have the hypothesized signs and significant standard errors. There is a small 'school effect' shown by the coefficient in the school term and its variance.

As with the other social capital variables, we test the possible negative effects of television watching (Putnam 2000). As before, we add the variable of the number of hours watched in model 2, but this term does not prove to be significant. Models 3 and 4 test for the citizenship education effects as before. Here we find that the student recollection variable has the hypothesized sign, is within conventional levels of significance and wipes out the effect of the other school variables. Citizenship education, when directly experienced by the student, affects social trust. Next we hypothesize that a range of school factors help generate trust, one in the form of imitation – from the student perception of whether teachers work well together (i.e. trust each other); the other is the classroom practices that assist trust, which is about students working together. We use again the aggregate score of school climate. In model 5 we find that the school variables are of the right sign and have impressive levels of efficiency, which corresponds to the literature that suggests that classroom climate has a positive effect on civic orientation (Torney-Purta et al., 2001; Finkel and Ernst, 2001).

As before, we test for the trust levels in the second year (Table 5). Unlike with voluntary activities we find that trust does not change much between years 1 and 2, rising from an average of .4576 to .4647, and which correlates highly at .352 (Kendall's Tau-b, sig=.00). As with voluntary activity, we run a change model where the dependent term varies from 0 to 1 within each year, but can vary again at these values in year 2. As before, we run the 'full' set of independent terms from wave 1 as model. Unsurprisingly, they work much as in wave 1. Socio-economic status predicts trust over the panel; not believing lying to be justified is a predictor; and enjoying being with people assists trust as well. White people trust more. Television hours watched is not significant,

TABLE 4
FACTORS THAT PREDICT TRUST – WAVE 1

	Model 1	Model 2	Model 3	Model 4	Model 5
Socio-economic status	.4332*	.4241*	.2932*	.4361*	.4550
	(.1640)	(.1691)	(.1725)	(.1702)	(.1707)
Religion	.1153	.0978	.2005	.0495	.0422
	(.1353)	(.1384)	(.1441)	(.1403)	(.1405)
Lying justified	−.3508*	−.3808*	−.3772*	−.3610*	−.3422
	(.1172)	(.1230)	(.1236)	(.1231)	(.1244)
Enjoyment	.3939*	.3681*	.3838*	.3651*	.3374*
	(.1063)	(.1102)	(.1152)	(.1091)	(.1097)
Gender	.2230	.2086	.2723	.1593	.1584
	(.1353)	(.1386)	(.1446)	(.1399)	(.1397)
Ethnicity	−.3114*	−.3822*	−.6612*	−.4029*	−.4224*
	(.1965)	(.2053)	(.2329)	(.2100)	(.2117)
Television hours		−.0085	–		–
		(.0660)			
Citizenship education			−.0183	–	
			(.0204)		
Citizenship education (student perception)				.0641*	.0507*
				(.0208)	(.0215)
School climate					.2365*
					(.1063)
constant	−2.059	−1.900	−1.741	−2.289	−2.672
	(.4629)	(.5225)	(.5285)	(.4845)	(.5182)
σ^2 (between students)	.2302	.2296	.2286	.2273	.2263
	(.0099)	(.0100)	(.0104)	(.0010)	(.0099)
σ^2 (between schools)	.0979	.1025	.0818	.1117	.1101
	(.0638)	(.0673)	(.0598)	(.0711)	(.0709)
Log-likelihood	−772.8	−744.7	−675.5	−732.2	−729.6
N	1116	1077	982	1066	1066

though the sign is negative. The time variable is not significant; nor is school climate. Religion has a massive standard error, suggesting it is better to drop this variable in future regressions.

Model 2 drops religion, runs the rest of the terms and adds the two interactions of time with civic education and with television watching. Here we find that civic education drops out of the range of significance; the time variable becomes positive and significant and the television interaction term is negative and significant. Overall, it suggests that television watching has a time-varying negative effect on trust that is not balanced by exposure to civic

TABLE 5
FACTORS THAT PREDICT TRUST – CHANGE MODEL

	Model 1	Model 2	Model 3	Model 4
Socio-economic status	.6972*	.6765*	.7292*	.6775*
	(.2870)	(.2910)	(.2952)	(.2911)
Religion	−.0024			
	(.2169)			
Lying justified	−.4747*	−.4855*	−.4962*	−.4858*
	(.1981)	(.2018)	(.2018)	(.2019)
Enjoyment	.5792*	.5895*	.5797*	.5881*
	(.1512)	(.1527)	(.1529)	(.1526)
Gender	.0610	.0612	.0759	.0596
	(.2183)	(.2207)	(.2218)	(.2206)
Ethnicity	−.8625*	−.8893*	−.8567*	−.8907*
	(.3175)	(.3216)	(.3248)	(.3216)
Television hours	−.1735	.0926	.0617	.0909
	(.0976)	(.1279)	(.1284)	(.1275)
Time	.0180	1.421*	1.277*	1.340*
	(.1526)	(.5737)	(.4360)	(.4346)
Citizenship education	.0534*	.0573	.0560	.0515
(student perception)	(.0294)	(.0398)	(.0300)	(.0299)
School climate	.0617	.0794	.0528	.0819
	(.1619)	(.1653)	(.1650)	(.1650)
Television hours*time	–	−.5454*	−.5178*	−.5416*
		(.1685)	(.1677)	(.1673)
Citizenship education*time		−.0112		
		(.0507)		
Left education			.0769	
			(.2300)	
constant	−2.723	−3.487	−3.397	−3.447
	(.8257)	(.0507)	(.8658)	(.8610)
σ^2 (between students)	2.5367	2.6704	2.6400	2.6761
	(.6383)	(.6680)	(.6629)	(.6688)
σ^2 (between schools)	.1832	.1940	.2043	.1939
	(.1308)	(.1367)	(.1406)	(.1366)
Log-likelihood	−735.5	−732.8	−726.4	−732.9
N	1163	1168	1159	1168

education. Model 3 tests for a further wave 2 effect on trust – whether leaving the school environment may cause a decline in trust. But the coefficient does not indicate any effect. Model 4, which is the final model, shows similar results to model 2, but without the education and time interaction terms.

Conclusions

This article has explored the determinants of social capital through the results of a panel survey. We argue that the creation of social capital is a continuous process, at which different periods and events in adolescence trigger and influence behaviour. With voluntary action we find that the age of 16 is a crucial time when changes in lifestyle influence the willingness to volunteer. It seems the path of early adolescence is one where joining groups, perhaps with parental support, and school encouragement, gives way to less joining. Of interest for the Putnam thesis is that media-related variables affect voluntary activity in wave 1, though they do not do so in the panel. We hypothesize that the change in voluntary activity across the waves is partly explained by changing student choices as they are given greater freedom by their families. It is, however, hard to find evidence for this conclusion. Television watching should affect the change in volunteering as adolescents gain more freedom, but the panel does not show strong support for the hypothesis. But as both television watching and volunteering drop across the panel,[4] it may be the case that adolescents trade-off television watching in wave 1, but not in wave 2. The contrast is trust where the panel shows the strong effect of television watching in depressing it.

But we do not present an overly pessimistic picture. The findings in this article extend what scholars know about the positive impact of citizenship education. Whereas most studies concentrate on its effects on political knowledge, here we find that it has an impact on voluntary action and trust. Whilst the effects are not strong and consistent across all the waves of the panel, there is a positive and significant influence of citizenship education programmes even when controlling for SES, parental and background variables – as well as a range of other school-based factors. We also add to knowledge through our conceptualization of civic education: what is important is the individual student experience rather than the formal record of tuition in the school. There is variation in what students receive from citizenship education which reflects both school differences and variation between pupils. Such a finding is confirmed by the weak school effects but strong individual effects in most of our multilevel models.

Our final addition to knowledge is to affirm the importance of cognitive styles for volunteering and trust, where the psychological variables show strong coefficients and highly significant results. In line with our theoretical approach, we downplay the importance of socio-economic status and background variables. The research also shows that student values and reported behaviour derive from a small range of demographic variables, though not always the SES ones. Nonetheless, there remain important factors that families transmit to their children, particularly patterns of voluntary activity; so some of our findings also confirm long-held social science wisdom. Overall, we show some encouraging results of civic education, and policy-makers may draw comfort from these findings.

APPENDIX
CODING OF THE VARIABLES

Cars – 0=none, 1=1, 2=2+ (v3)
Charity – 1= taken part in community organizations and charities, 0=not (v10i)
Citizenship education – adds variables 62–70 – questions from practice survey which ask schools how much they provide on rights (v62), justice system (v63), diversity (v64), government (v65), parliament (v66), elections (v67), voluntary organizations (v68), conflict resolution (v69) and the media (v70).
Demo – 1= Joining a demonstration; 0=not (v10j)
Electcam – 1=participated in election campaigns, 0=not (v10f)
Enjoyment – 'I enjoy being with other people' – 0=disagree strongly, −1= disagree, 2=neither, 3=agree, 4=agree strongly (v17a)
Envproj – 1= taken part in environmental projects, 0=not (v10h)
Ethnic – 0= white, 1=non-white (v41)
Fundrais – 1=engage in fund raising activities, 0=not (v10b)
Gender – 0=girl, 1=boy (v1)
Groupwk – groupwork in class – 0=never, 1=very occasionally, 2=not very often, 3=often, 4=very often (v29)
Helpeld – 1= Helping the elderly, 0=not (v10g)
Helppoor – More should be done to help the poor – 0=agree strongly, −1= agree, 2=neither, 3=disagree, 4=disagree strongly (v27c)
Lying – 0=never justified, 1=sometimes justified, 2=always justified, dk=missing (v20c)
Owner – 1=own own home, 0=if not (v2)
Fundraise – parents come to school for fundraising activities – 0=never, 1=very occasionally, 2=not very often, 3=often; 4=very often, dk=0 (v37b)
Part-time – 1=in part time employment, 0=not (v10a)
Petition – 1=sign a petition, 0=not (v10c)
Proficiency – 1=Es or below, 2=Ds, 3=Cs, 4=Bs 5=As, too varied to say=3 (v4)
Ranger – 1=participated in Ranger Guides / Venture Scouts, 0=not (v10d)
Religion – 1=religious, 0=none (v5)
Relproj – 1=participated in religion-based projects, 0=not (v10e)
Socio economic status – summary variable from *cars* and *owner*
Civic education – student recollection – amount of citizen education topics covered as perceived by students – adds together v32a-i.
Teachers – teachers work well or badly – 0=very badly, 1=badly, 2=neither, 3=well, 4=very well (v34)
Tvhours – 1=0–1 hours, 2=1–2 hours, 3=2–3 hours, 4=more than 3 hours a day (v8)
Tvnews – 1= less than once a week, 2=once or twice a week, 3=3 or 4 times a week, 4=everyday, 2.9=don't know (average) (v9)
Trust – 0=no trust, 1=trust (v14)
Volunteer – adds *fundrais, petition, ranger, relproj, electcam, helpeld, envproj, charity, demo, volother*
Volother – 1=other, 0=not other (v10k)

NOTES

1. The project, 'Social capital, participation and the causal role of socialization', L215252009, is part of the ESRC's Democracy and Participation programme. The datasets are logged with the Essex Data Archive.
2. Proportion of pupils in receipt of free school meal, ranked. The LEA would only provide schools by rank and not the actual proportions for reasons of school confidentiality. Ranked free school meal data was provided by the education authority. Examination (GCSE) data was gathered from Secondary School Performance Tables for 1999. Citizenship practice data was gathered from all schools (that is secondary, special, pupil referral units and independent schools) by means of a two-sided A4 questionnaire, which we sent to head teachers in the summer term of 2000.
3. This variable is skewed because of the concentration of values at the lower levels and a long tail. In models not reported here we re-estimate the model with Box-Cox power transforms of volunteer implemented by the Stata programme to create zero skewness, which reveals much the same results. We also re-estimate the models with a logit function, recoding the variable into 0 and 1 categories, which again does not alter the results substantively.
4. The mean is 2.6 on our scale for wave 1 and 2.25 for wave 2.

REFERENCES

Ashworth, Laura (1995) *Children's Voices in School Matters: A report of an ACE survey into school democracy.* London: Advisory Centre for Education.
Beck, Paul and M. Kent Jennings (1982) 'Pathways to Participation', *American Political Science Review* 76: 94–108.
Coleman, James (1988) 'Social Capital in the Creation of Human Capital', *American Journal of Sociology* 94: 95–120.
Colten, Mary and Gore, Susan (1994) *Quality of Adolescent Relationships and Caring Behaviours,* Chicago: University of Chicago Press.
Conley, Frank (ed.) (1991) *Political Understanding Across the Curriculum.* The Politics Association.
Crick, Bernard (1998) *Education for Citizenship and the Teaching of Democracy in Schools, Final Report of the Advisory Group on Citizenship (The Crick Report),* London, Qualifications and Curriculum Authority.
Delli Carpini, Michael and Scott Keeter (1996) *What Americans Know About Politics and Why It Matters.* New Haven: Yale University Press.
Denver, David and Gordon Hands (1990) 'Does Studying Politics Make a Difference? The Political Knowledge, Attitudes and Perceptions of School Students', *British Journal of Political Science* 20: 263–88.
Dowse, Robert and John Hughes (1971) 'The Family, the School and the Political Socialisation Process', *Sociology* 5: 21–45.
Eagly, A. and M. Crowley (1986) 'Gender and Helping Behaviour: a Meta Analysis of the Social Psychological Literature', *Psychological Bulletin* 100: 283–308.
Ehman, L.H. (1980) 'The American School in the Political Socialization Process', *Review of Educational Research* 50: 99–199.
Finkel, Steven (1995) *Causal Analysis With Panel Data.* London: Sage.
Finkel, Steven (1985) 'Reciprocal Effects of Participation and Political Efficacy: A Panel Analysis', *American Journal of Political Science* 29: 891–913.
Finkel, Steven and Howard Ernst (2001) 'Civic Education and the Development of Political Knowledge and Democratic Orientations in Post-Apartheid South Africa', paper to APSA meeting, San Francisco.
Flanagan, Constance and Lonnie Sherrod (1998) 'Youth Political Development: an Introduction', *Journal of Social Issues* 54(3): 447–56.
Goldstein, Harvey (1995) *Multilevel Statistical Models.* London: Edward Arnold.

Hox, Joop (2002) *Multilevel Analysis.* London: Lawrence Erbaum Associates.

Janoski, Thomas, March Musick and John Wilson (1998) 'Being Volunteered? The Impact of Social Participation and Pro-social Attitudes on Volunteering', *Sociological Forum* 13(3): 495–519.

Jennings, M. Kent and Robert Niemi (1968) 'The Transmission of Political Values from Parent to Child', *American Political Science Review* 62: 169–84.

Jennings, M. Kent and Robert Niemi (1974) *The Political Character of Adolescence.* Princeton, NJ: Princeton University Press.

Jennings, M. Kent and Robert Niemi (1981) *Generations and Politics.* Princeton, NJ: Princeton University Press.

Jennings, M. Kent and Laura Stoker (2001a) 'The Persistence of the Past: The Class of 1965 Turns Fifty' (1 Jan. 2001), Institute of Governmental Studies. Working Paper WP2001-16, accessed at http://repositories.cdlib.org/igs/WP2001-16.

Jennings, M. Kent and Laura Stoker (2001b) 'Generations and Civic Engagement: A Longitudinal Multiple-Generation Analysis', paper to APSA annual conference, San Francisco.

Knack, Steven and Philip Keefer (1997) 'Does Social Capital Have an Economic Payoff? A Cross Country Comparison', *Quarterly Journal of Economics* 112(4): 1251–88.

Lane, Robert (2000) *The Loss of Happiness in Market Democracies.* New Haven: Yale University Press.

Langton, Kenneth and M. Kent Jennings (1968) 'Political Socialisation and the High School Civics Curriculum in the United States', *American Political Science Review* 62(3): 852–67.

Lawson, H. (2001) 'Active Citizenship in Schools and the Community', *The Curriculum Journal* 12(2): 163–78.

Maitles, H. (2000) 'Political Literacy: the Challenge for Democratic Citizenship', *The School Field,* XI: 125–34.

Milbraith, Lester and M. Goel (1977) *Political Participation.* Chicago: Rand McNally.

Nie, Norman, Jane Junn and Kenneth Stehlik-Barry (1996) *Education and Democratic Citizenship in America.* Chicago: University of Chicago Press.

Niemi, Robert and Jane Junn (1998) *What Makes Students Learn.* New Haven: Yale University Press.

Patrick, J.J. (1977) 'Political Socialisation and Political Education in Schools', in S.A Renshon, *Handbook of Political Socialization.* New York: Free Press.

Pattie, Charles, Patrick Seyd and Paul Whiteley (2002) 'Citizenship and Civic Engagement: Attitudes and Behaviour', Paper presented to the Political Studies Association Annual Conference, University of Aberdeen, 5–7 April 2002.

Paulsen, Ronnelle (1991) 'Education, Social Class, and Participation in Collective Action', *Sociology of Education,* 64(2), 96–110.

Prancer, Michael and Mark Pratt (1999) 'Social and Family Determinants of Community Service Involvement in Canadian Youth', in M. Yates and J. Youniss (eds.) *Roots of Civic Identity: International Perspectives on Community Service and Activism in Youth.* Cambridge: Cambridge University Press.

Putnam, Robert (2000) *Bowling Alone.* New York: Simon & Schuster.

Rabe-Hesketh, Sopia, Andrew Pickles and A. Skrondal (2001) *GLLAMM Manual,* Institute of Psychiarity. London: King's College:.

Riedel, Eric and Elizabeth Smith (2001) 'Persistence of Political Attitudes: Symbolic Versus Nonsymbolic Attitude Stability', paper to Annual Meeting of the APSA, San Francisco, September.

Roker, Debbi, Katie Player and John Coleman (1999) *Challenging the Image: Young People as Volunteers and Campaigners.* Brighton: Youth Work Press.

Rosenhan, D. (1970) 'The Natural Socialization of Altruistic Autonomy', in J. Macauley and L. Berkowitz (eds.) *Altruism and Helping Behaviours.* Orlando: Academic Press.

Sears, David (1990) 'Whither Political Socialization Research?', in O. Ichilov (ed.), *Political Socialization, Education and Democracy.* New York: Teachers College Press.

Slomczynski, Kazimiez and Goldie Shaband (1998) 'Can Support for Democracy and the Market be Learned at School? A Natural Experiment in Post-Communist Poland', *Political Psychology* 19(4): 749–79.

Smith, Elizabeth (1999) 'The Effects of Investment in the Social Capital of Youth on Political and Civic Behaviour in Young Adulthood: a Longitudinal Analysis', *Political Psychology* 19(4): 749–79.

Smith, David J., Sally Tomlinson, Terrence Hogarth and Hilary Thomes (1989) *The School Effect PSI report number 688 A Study of Multi-Racial Comprehensives.* London: Policy Studies Institute.

Sniderman, Paul (1975) *Personality and Democratic Politics.* London: University of California Press.

Steinberg, Lawrence (1996) *Beyond the Classroom: Why School Reform Has Failed and What Parents Need to Do.* New York: Simon & Schuster.

Teachman, Jay, Kathleen Paasch and Karen Carver (1996) 'Social Capital and Dropping Out of School Early', *Journal of Marriage and the Family,* 58: 773–83

Torney, Judith, A.N. Oppenheim and Russell Farnem (1975) *Civic Education in Ten Countries.* Stockholm: Almquist & Wiksell.

Torney-Purta, Judith, Rainer Lehmann, Hans Oswald and Woldfram Schultz (2001) *Citizenship and Education in Twenty-Eight Countries: Civic Knowledge and Engagement at Age Fourteen.* Amsterdam: International Association for the Evaluation in Educational Achievement.

Verba, Sidney, Kay Schlozman and Henry Brady (1995) *Voice and Equality.* Cambridge, Mass: Harvard University Press.

Whiteley, Paul (2000) 'Economic Growth and Social Capital', *Political Studies* 48(3): 443–66.

The Dynamics of Citizenship: The Effects of the General Election on Citizenship

Charles Pattie, Patrick Seyd and Paul Whiteley

A frequent, if controversial, claim in recent academic and popular discussions of civic life in the western democracies has been that public involvement in politics is on the decline, and democracy is, in some sense, in crisis (see, for instance, the chapters in Norris, 1999a, and Pharr and Putnam, 2000). The relative absence of time-series data makes it difficult to generalize accurately about trends in many aspects of civic engagement. Nevertheless, where we can measure change over time, indicators are not always encouraging (though see Norris, 2002). For instance, United Kingdom general election turnout data reveals a trendless fluctuation in the 13 post-war elections between 1945 and 1992, but then in the most recent two elections, a significant decline (e.g. Pattie and Johnston, 2001a). In addition, there is evidence of declining participation in political parties (Seyd and Whiteley, 2002a; Whiteley and Seyd, 2002), and declining trust in political leaders and institutions (Mortimore, 1995; Norris, 1999b). Similar patterns of declining civic engagement are apparent in other advanced industrialized countries (Norris, 1999a). Explanations of the reduction in civic engagement vary, but most commonly include a discussion of dwindling social capital (Putnam, 2000), weakening networks of civic engagement (Verba, Schlozman and Brady, 1995), and declining cognitive engagement (Huckfeldt and Sprague, 1995).

The apparent evidence of malaise in the western body politic also extends to worries about public attitudes towards the political system. Scandals and government failure are felt to have eroded popular trust in politicians and state institutions. Where once societies like the United Kingdom and the United States had a rich civic culture, typified by both a willingness to get involved in society and a sense of trust in government (Almond and Verba, 1963) there is now, it seems, widespread cynicism and distrust (e.g. Kavanagh, 1980; Jowell and Topf, 1988; Mortimore, 1995; Dalton, 1999; Pattie and Johnston, 2001b). That said, there is some debate over how inexorable these trends are (see e.g. Norris, 2002) and over whether they really indicate a collapse of support for democracy *per se*. Some would argue that while respect for and trust in government has declined in the advanced societies, support for democracy (particularly in the sense of direct involvement) has increased (e.g. Inglehart,

British Elections & Parties Review, Vol. 14, 2004, pp. 113–146
ISSN 1368-9886 print
DOI: 10.1080/1368988042000258808   © 2004 Taylor & Francis Ltd.

1999). Clearly, therefore, trends in civic engagement – and in attitudes towards civic life – are important.

One factor, however, which has tended to be neglected in these discussions is the role of electoral participation itself as a trigger for encouraging wider political engagement. Elections are most commonly seen as dependent variables in these discussions, the outcomes of which need to be explained by other factors. But elections can be regarded as independent political factors, which mobilize or demobilize individuals to participate more widely beyond the electoral arena. There has been some limited work on the mobilizing effect of elections (Finkel, 1985; Clarke and Kornberg, 1992; Rahn, Brehm and Carlson, 1999), but this issue has rarely been examined in Britain (see, however, Banducci and Karp, 2003).

The aim of this article is to model the extent to which citizenship in Britain is renewed or reinvigorated by electoral participation. The broad question is, to what extent does electoral participation sustain or diminish wider citizen engagement and the norms and values that support the democratic polity? This question will be investigated by using the Citizen Audit panel survey, a unique dataset that examines all aspects of citizen participation in Britain over the period of a year between 2000 and 2001. Conducting the Citizen Audit panel involved re-interviewing a group of respondents to the original 2000 survey 12 months after their original interviews. We can therefore look not only at net change, but also at how particular individuals' views and actions change. And because we know what they said in 2000, we know that the results of the 2001 panel reflect real change, not just sampling error (a potential problem if we had relied on two distinct cross-section surveys with completely different respondents in each).

A well-known feature of panel surveys is that it is easier to re-interview those who are relatively interested in the topic being investigated than those who are not interested. And that is what has happened here. Panel respondents were indeed more civically-minded on most measures than were all respondents to the 2000 survey (many of whom did not take part in the panel). However, our main interest here is not in who does what, but in explaining change. And as we will see, even among our relatively active group of panel respondents, there was significant change between 2000 and 2001.

We acknowledge that the general election of 2001 was only one of a number of significant political events that occurred between waves 1 and 2 of the panel survey. In September 2000, Britain experienced severe disruption to oil and food supplies for a short period of time arising from farmers' and hauliers' demonstrations and blockades in protest at the level of fuel taxes. Then in September 2001, the World Trade Centre and the Pentagon were attacked by terrorists. So there were a number of major events, of which the general election was only one, which might impact upon democratic norms and political participation. Nevertheless, during a short period of between four and six weeks in April and May 2001, political debate and controversy intensified. General election campaigns are multifaceted and multidirectional as parties attempt to ensure popular support at national, regional and local levels (Seyd and Whiteley, 2002b). All forms of media – television, radio and newspapers – increase their coverage of politics. For example, television news broadcasts were dominated by the election campaign during the four weeks prior to the 1997 general election (Norris et al., 1999). In addition, limited though it remains, there is a greater likelihood of direct personal contact with politicians during an election campaign. It is, therefore, reasonable to assume that this major domestic political event might affect civic engagement.

Turnout in the 2001 general election was the lowest in any general election in contemporary British history. This raises the possibility that electoral participation, or lack of it, demobilized individuals and contributed to a decline in civic engagement rather than the opposite. There may therefore be a spiral of demobilization at work in which declining electoral participation triggers declining citizen engagement which, in turn, suppresses electoral participation further.

This article will first examine the shifts in citizen attitudes and behaviour that occurred between waves 1 and 2 of the Citizen Audit, during which a general election intervened, and then will model the relationships between campaign exposure, electoral participation and civic engagement.

The Dynamics of Citizen Attitudes

Over this period of 12 months the public's satisfaction with a wide range of local services decreased. Nevertheless, the percentage of people satisfied with 'the way democracy works' increased. Figure 1 reveals that an overall rise of eight per cent occurred in the number of people satisfied.[1] Whereas people had been fairly evenly divided into three groups of satisfied, dissatisfied and no strong opinion, by 2001 a plurality of satisfied democrats now existed.

People regard their vote as important in determining the outcome of an election and, furthermore, they believe it matters which party is in power. So what impact might this opportunity to choose an MP, and indirectly a government, have had upon people's sense of external political efficacy? When respondents were asked 'How much do you think the British government listens to majority opinion?', and were given an 11-point scale from 0 ('not at all') to 10 ('a great deal'), we see in Table 1 that the mean score rose significantly from 4.25 to 4.79.

A general election is likely to be the single most important domestic event in providing the average person with an incentive to think about and discuss politics. Did our respondents find politics more interesting, and did they

FIGURE 1
SATISFACTION WITH DEMOCRACY

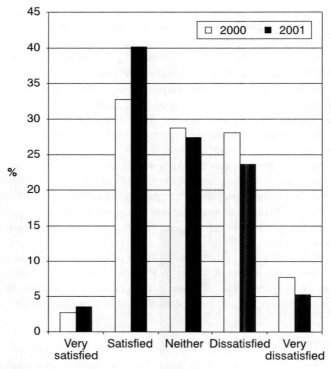

'Thinking about Britain, how satisfied are you with the way democracy works?'

become more involved in political discussions? Or was Labour's constant lead
in public opinion polls during the campaign enough to depress political interest and political discussion? We find that interest in all forms of politics –
local, regional, national, European and international – rose. The percentages
of those 'very interested' in international and national politics rose by eight

TABLE 1
POLITICAL EFFICACY

Year	Mean	Standard deviation	t	p
2000	4.25	2.44	6.04	0.00
2001	4.79	2.24		

'How much do you think the British government listens to majority opinion?'

FIGURE 2
CHANGES IN LEVELS OF POLITICAL INTEREST

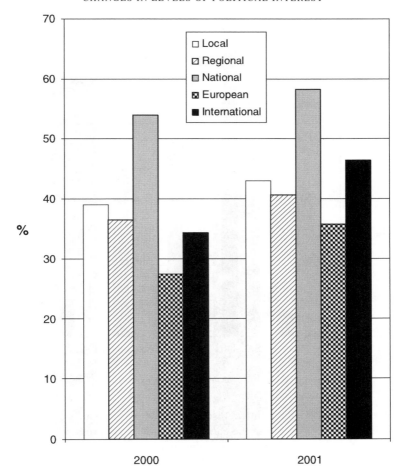

'How interested are you personally in each of the following levels: local politics; regional politics; national politics, European politics; international politics?'

per cent and four per cent respectively. In Figure 2 we have merged the 'very interested' and 'fairly interested' categories and we see that interest in international politics rose by 12 per cent and national politics by four per cent.

We have already noted that during the 4-week run-up to the 2001 general election television news was dominated by the campaign. Radio and newspapers similarly gave prominence to it. And, as we see in Figure 3, our respondents increased their consumption of political news. Over this 12-month period those

FIGURE 3
CHANGES IN THE USE OF THE MEDIA FOR POLITICAL NEWS

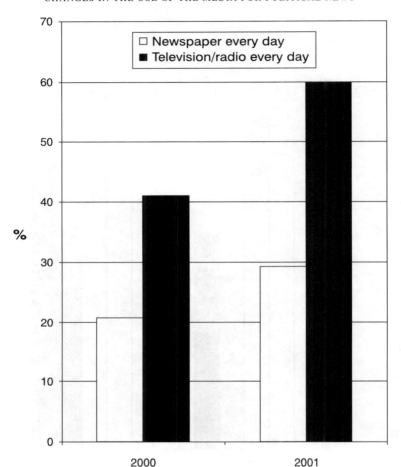

'In an average day, how often do you read a newspaper/listen to radio/watch television for political news?'

watching television or listening to the radio every day for political news rose by 19 per cent, and the numbers reading a newspaper every day for political news rose by eight per cent.

Did our respondents discuss politics more or less during this 12-month period? Very few talk politics with their neighbours: even with the heightened political interest generated by the general election few people were prompted to talk politics over the garden fence. However, as we see in Figure 4, the

FIGURE 4
CHANGES IN THE LEVEL OF POLITICAL DISCUSSIONS

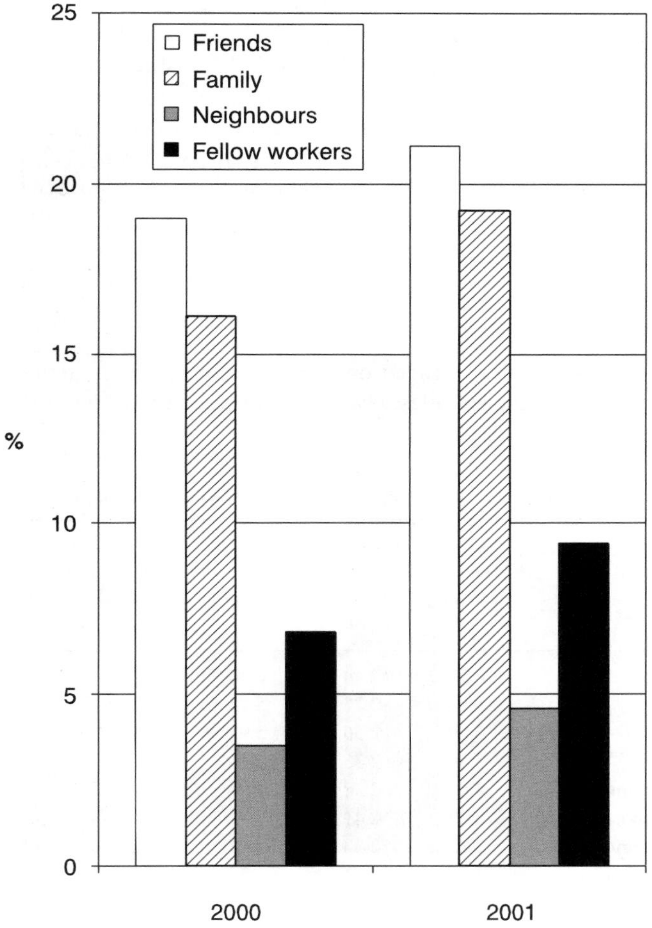

'How often would you say you discuss political matters when you get together with the following groups of peoples...' (Figures represent those responding 'often'.)

numbers 'often' discussing political matters with their family, friends, or fellow workers increased. Twelve months after our original survey, one in five talked politics with their family or friends, and one in ten with their fellow workers.

Discussing political trust elsewhere, we made the point that the public distrusted political institutions more than other public institutions in which politicians were absent (Pattie et al., forthcoming). However, we note in Table 2 that while these non-political institutions – the police, banks, courts and civil service – continue to be trusted by the public, only very slight (and generally insignificant) increases in trust occurred over 12 months. By contrast, the public's trust of political institutions, political parties and politicians rose. In the case of the new, devolved Scottish and Welsh institutions, trust rose very strikingly. For example, the mean score of the Scots' trust of their Parliament rose by 1.4 points and of the Scottish National Party by 0.7 points. Among the Welsh, their mean score of trust of their Assembly rose by 1.2. Among all respondents, trust of the government, the Labour Party, the House of Commons, and politicians rose substantially. Overall, people's trust in all of the 16 institutions listed rose.

The Dynamics of Citizen Behaviour

In 2000 our respondents engaged on average in 4.0 political actions, defined as attempting 'to influence rules, laws or policies', in the 12 months before the

TABLE 2
CHANGE IN LEVELS OF INSTITUTIONAL TRUST

| | 2000 | | 2001 | | | |
	Mean	Standard deviation	Mean	Standard deviation	t	p
Police	6.35	2.40	6.36	2.23	0.05	0.958
Courts	5.61	2.35	5.72	2.26	1.20	0.231
Banks	5.59	2.56	5.93	2.33	3.88	0.000
Civil service	5.56	2.35	5.75	2.11	2.19	0.029
Local government	4.66	2.38	4.91	2.15	3.02	0.003
Liberal Democrat Party	3.92	2.41	4.42	2.20	5.70	0.000
House of Commons	3.97	2.38	4.69	2.22	8.23	0.000
Scottish Parliament*	3.91	2.71	5.27	2.24	2.55	0.014
Government	3.84	2.56	4.67	2.32	9.35	0.000
Scottish National Party*	3.84	2.77	4.57	1.97	1.63	0.110
Labour Party	3.80	2.67	4.72	2.44	10.34	0.000
Conservative Party	3.35	2.62	3.72	2.27	4.14	0.000
Politicians	3.33	2.23	4.08	2.17	9.43	0.000
European Union	3.30	2.29	4.17	2.21	10.70	0.000
Welsh Assembly*	3.23	2.62	4.42	2.64	3.22	0.003
Plaid Cymru*	3.04	2.88	4.06	2.58	1.71	0.100

'And now your views on various institutions: Do you trust....' Respondents were given an 11-point scale ranging from 0 ('do not trust at all') to 10 ('trust completely').
*Asked of respondents residing in Scotland or Wales only.

TABLE 3
CHANGES IN THE LEVELS OF POLITICAL ACTIONS

	2000	2001
	%	%
Donated money to an organization	62.8	64.0
Voted in local government election	57.8	73.8
Signed a petition	47.2	47.3
Boycotted certain products	36.1	33.9
Bought products for ethical reasons	33.4	33.4
Raised funds for an organization	32.0	30.3
Contacted a public official	28.7	31.4
Worn or displayed a campaign badge	23.4	24.2
Contacted a solicitor	19.2	20.0
Contacted a politician	15.6	17.4
Contacted an organization	12.6	11.6
Contacted the media	10.6	9.6
Attended rally or political meeting	6.9	6.4
Taken part in public demonstration	4.7	3.6
Formed a group of like-minded people	4.7	5.1
Taken part in a strike	2.5	2.6
Participated in illegal protest	1.5	1.5

'During the last 12 months, have you done any of the following to influence rules, laws or policies?'

general election. However, when we asked them the similar question after the general election the average number of actions they had taken had risen to 4.1. We see in Table 3 that in nine of the 17 listed actions an increase in activity was recorded. Not surprisingly, the largest increase was recorded for those claiming to have voted in a local government election (a rise from 58 to 74 per cent).[2] People had also become significantly more active in contacting a public official.

Not only had our respondents become more politically active during these 12 months, but their potential for political action increased considerably. Asked whether they would take any of the 17 actions to influence political outcomes, in all but one of the potential actions the responses were higher than one year earlier.[3] The most notable growth was recorded in contacting the media and solicitors or judicial bodies (+9 per cent each); contacting public officials, and voting in a local government election (+8 per cent); and contacting politicians (+7 per cent). The mean number of potential actions rose from 8.4 to 9.1.

Just as potential political actions grew between the two time points, so also did potential participation in a wider range of citizen activities. People became more likely to participate in a neighbourhood watch scheme, or assist with meals on wheels or with a local amenity renovation project. The participation potential to become school governors or local councillors was low in 2000, which explains some of the difficulties today in attracting people to become directly involved in politics. The figures remain low 12 months later but again, as we see in Figure 5, the participation potential rose.

Finally, do we detect changes in people's associational engagement, whether by belonging to, participating in, volunteering for, or donating to organized groups, or participating in more informal friendship or support networks? As far as people's combined total of activities with organized groups are concerned, in other words, their membership, participation, volunteering and donating, in only four of the 26 types of organization that we listed was there an overall decline. The four types which experienced a decline in public involvement were peace, sports or outdoor activities, gymnasia and, finally, cultural organizations. In 2000, people on average belonged to 1.0 types of organizations and in 2001 on average they belonged to 1.7 types of organizations.

We see in Figure 6 that our respondents' informal networks increased during the 12 months. The percentage belonging to an informal friendship or acquaintance network, such as the pub quiz team, the reading group, or the child support group, rose from 23 to 25, and providing regular neighbourhood support, such as shopping for neighbours or visiting old people, rose from 17 to 18.

Finally, the total time people had spent on associational activities and networks, formal and informal, in the previous month before they were interviewed stayed fairly constant, as can be seen in Figure 7. There was a small rise in the percentage of people saying they had not spent any time during the last month associating with others (from 38 per cent to 39 percent), but the change was not significant.

As the above results show, therefore, civic attitudes and behaviours are far from static. Even over just one year, net levels of attitudes and activity changed substantially. But what underlies these changes? In other work, we examined some theories of civic activism from the perspective of a single point in time (Pattie et al., forthcoming). Here, we extend that investigation to examine change over time. We will focus mainly on change in two different areas: changes in people's perceptions of civic life (their trust in others, in state institutions, and so on); and changes in the actions they undertake. The aim is to explain who is likely to change their ideas or actions, and in which direction they are likely to move.

FIGURE 5
CHANGES IN POTENTIAL CITIZEN ACTIONS

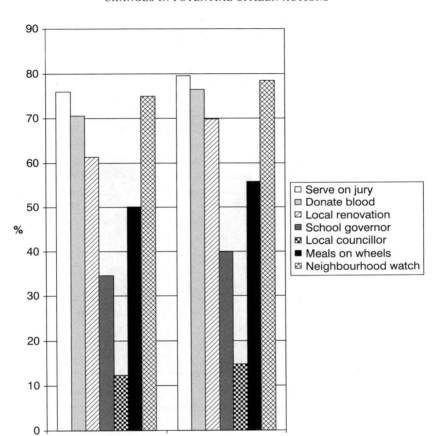

'Would you be willing: to serve on a jury; to donate blood; to help renovate a local park or amenity; to serve as a school governor; to stand as a local councillor; to assist a meals on wheels service; to participate in a neighbourhood watch scheme?'

Explaining the Changes in Civic Attitudes and Behaviour

We rely on regression models for much of our analysis here. However, since we are now interested in change over time, we take a particular approach to the modelling. The basic problem we face is that of causation: just because two factors are correlated, it does not mean that one causes the other. Nor

FIGURE 6
CHANGES IN INFORMAL, PERSONAL NETWORKS

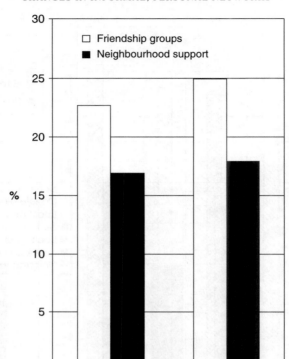

'... do you belong to an informal network of friends or acquaintances with whom you have contact on a regular basis?'; 'Do you actively provide any support beyond your immediate family for ill people, elderly neighbours, or acquaintances ...?'

does it mean that causation runs in a particular direction. So, for instance, does social capital 'cause' civic participation, or does civic participation 'cause' social capital? With cross-sectional data (gathered at one point in time), it is very hard indeed to disentangle such conundrums. However, time-series and panel data, by providing information for two or more time points, do allow us to begin to unpick cause from effect. The approach used to achieve this here draws on recent work in econometrics, stressing so-called Granger causality (Granger, 1988). The idea is simple, and rests on the analogy of time's arrow. Events in the past might cause events in the present, but events in the present are generally unlikely to cause events in

FIGURE 7
CHANGE IN TIME DEVOTED TO ASSOCIATIONAL ENGAGEMENT

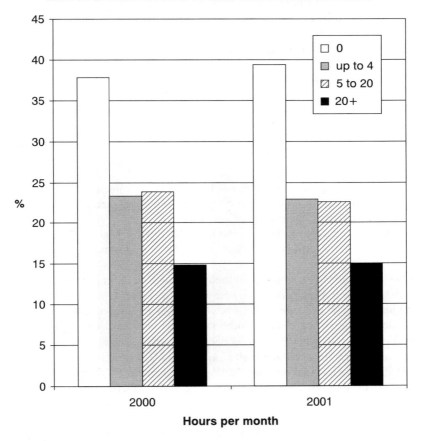

'During the last month, approximately how much time in total did you spend on activities in clubs, associations, groups, networks, or in supporting other people?'

the past. So current income levels might reflect (say) educational qualifications gained in the past. But current income cannot cause past education – it has already happened (though clearly there are exceptions, usually involving some form of anticipated actions: in a well-known example, the sales of Christmas cards rise as Christmas approaches – but selling Christmas cards does not cause Christmas!). More formally, 'x is a Granger cause of y, if present y can be predicted with better accuracy by using past values of x rather than by not doing so, other information being identical' (Charezma and Deadman, 1997: 165).

The analytical strategy adopted here, therefore, is to try to model variations in key variables measured at wave 2 of the panel in terms of explanatory variables measured at the earlier first wave of the survey. Included among the explanatory variables is the wave 1 version of the dependent variable. So, for instance, we can model civic activism at wave 2 by fitting the following model:

$$C_{i2} = a_{11} + b_{11}C_{i1} + b_{12}M_{i1} + b_{13}I_{i1} + b_{14}TV_{i1} + \ldots + u_{i1}$$

Where:

C_{i2} is the dependent variable, a measure of civic activism from wave two of the panel;

C_{i1} is the same measure of civic activism, at wave one of the panel;

M_{i1} is an index of interest in politics reporting in the media, at wave 1;

I_{i1} is an index of interest in politics at wave 1;

TV_{i1} is a measure of exposure to television at wave 1; and

U_{i1} us an error term in which $E(u_{i1})=0$ and σ_u^2 is constant.

Other independent variables, also measured at wave 1, can be added to the model. However, the key points to note are that we control for each individual's previous score on the dependent variable, and that all independent variables are measured using wave 1 data. Under these circumstances, the b_{1n} regression coefficients tell us whether each independent variable can effect change in the dependent variable, according to the principle of Granger causality.

In the following analyses, we employ wave 1 measures of the independent variables used in other work to evaluate the various theories of civic engagement (Pattie et al., forthcoming: details of the independent variables and models are given in Table 4).

However, before discussing the results, we need to look at our dependent variables in more detail. We will concentrate on change in two separate sets of factors. The first group comprises changes in individuals' attitudes and intentions concerning civic life. The second group concentrates on changes in their civic behaviour.

The 'attitudes and intentions' measures cover a range of different dimensions of civic life. The first three measures are related to different aspects of trust: trust in other citizens, trust in elected politicians, and trust in state institutions. The measures are built by summing respondents' answers to the relevant questions in the Audit. Although these measures are similar to measures used in other work (see Pattie et al., forthcoming), we employ slightly different methods of calculating the scales here to ensure complete comparability of scales between waves 1 and 2. The three trust measures are based on

TABLE 4
THE INDEPENDENT VARIABLES AND EXPLANATORY MODELS

ALL independent variables are measured using wave 1 data from 2000

Cognitive engagement

Age left education	Higher scores indicate longer period in education
Political knowledge	Higher scores indicate greater political knowledge
Media exposure	Higher scores indicate more attention paid to media coverage of politics
Interest in politics	Higher scores indicate greater interest in politics
Policy dissatisfaction	Higher scores indicate greater dissatisfaction with government policy management

General incentives

Collective benefits:

Satisfaction with democracy	Higher scores indicate greater dissatisfaction with democracy
Costs	Higher scores indicate greater perceptions of costs to actions

Selective benefits:

Process incentives	Higher scores indicate greater perceived personal benefits from political involvement (e.g. enjoyment from participation)
Outcome incentives	Higher scores indicate greater perceived privatized benefits from the act of participation (e.g. doing a good job as a councillor)
Group incentives	Higher scores indicate greater perceived benefits from participation for groups the respondent cares about
System (altruistic) benefits	Higher scores indicate a greater sense of participation as a public duty
Social norms	Higher scores indicate more perceived pressure to participate from peers
Expressive benefits	Higher scores indicate greater pride in being part of the civic community

Civic voluntarism

Political efficacy	Higher scores indicate a greater sense of political efficacy
Party identification	A series of dummy variables for identification with Conservative, Labour, Liberal Democrats and 'other parties' ('no party ID' is the comparison group)
Occupational status	Social class: higher scores indicate more middle class individuals
Free time	Higher scores indicate individuals with more free time
Mobilization	Higher scores indicate individuals who have been asked to participate

Equity-fairness

Outcomes and expectations	Higher scores indicate a greater gap between individual expectations of life, and perceived outcomes (with expectations falling well short of outcomes)

TABLE 4
CONTINUED

Economic deprivation	Higher scores indicate a greater perception that the economy is performing badly
Unemployed	Dummy variable: unemployed coded 1, else=0
Retired	Dummy variable: retired coded 1, else=0
Female	Dummy variable: women coded 1, else=0
Non-white	Dummy variable: non-white coded 1, else=0
Social capital	
Number groups joined	Number of types of organization of which respondent is a member
Trust others	Additive scale: higher scores indicate more trust
Trust elected politicians	Additive scale: higher scores indicate more trust
Trust state institutions	Additive scale: higher scores indicate more trust
Informal networks	Higher scores indicate more involvement in informal networks
TV watching	Higher scores indicate more time on average spent watching TV
Years in area	Higher scores indicate longer periods living in the same area
Family nearby	Higher scores indicate individuals with family living in the neighbourhood

Details of the scales can be obtained from the authors.

responses to a series of 11-point scales, all discussed earlier. The scales are coded so that the most 'trusting' reply possible is 10, and the least 'trusting' is scored 0. The 'trust in others' scale is produced by summing responses to three of these scales: whether the respondent thinks other people can be trusted, will be helpful, or will be fair. 'Trust in elected politicians' is also the sum of three scales: trust in the government; trust in the House of Commons, and trust in politicians. And 'trust in state institutions' is the sum of: trust in the courts, the civil service, the police, and local government. In all three cases, the higher an individual's score, the more trusting they are. In each case, Cronbach's alpha for the summary scales at both wave 1 and wave 2 confirms that the scales are robust (Table 5). Examining the averages for each of these scales at wave 1 and wave 2 confirms the patterns revealed earlier: on the whole, members of the Citizen Audit panel became more trusting of both elected and unelected political institutions between waves 1 and 2 of the survey. There was no significant change over time in the 'trust in others' scale, however.

The scale for political efficacy is based on the summed responses to four propositions: 'people like me have no say in what the government does'; 'people like me can have a real influence on politics if they are prepared to get

TABLE 5
CHANGE CITIZENSHIP SCALES

Wave	Mean				Cronbach's alpha	
	2000	2001	t	p	2000	2001
a) Attitudes and intentions						
Trust in others[1]	19.31	19.40	0.48	0.629	0.81	0.85
Trust in elected politicians[2]	10.85	13.43	11.31	0.000	0.87	0.90
Trust in state institutions[3]	21.53	22.73	4.71	0.000	0.82	0.84
Political efficacy[4]	11.75	12.04	2.95	0.003	0.46	0.49
Satisfaction with democracy[5]	3.05	2.87	4.79	0.000		
Interest in politics[6]	5.91	6.74	6.55	0.000	0.90	0.90
Exposure to politics on media[7]	3.66	4.88	11.60	0.000	0.72	0.63
Undertake private services[8]	3.32	3.60	5.50	0.000	0.63	0.69
Undertake public services[9]	0.47	0.55	2.99	0.003	0.45	0.50
b) Civic activities						
Political conversations[10]	8.16	8.42	2.49	0.013	0.77	0.76
Number of groups joined	1.03	1.71	11.48	0.000	0.60	0.60
Number of civic actions	3.97	4.14	1.65	0.099	0.76	0.74
Individualistic civic actions	2.93	3.07	1.97	0.049	0.70	0.68
Contacting civic actions	0.87	0.90	0.81	0.418	0.61	0.58
Collectivist civic actions	0.18	0.17	0.57	0.569	0.48	0.47
Time for associational engagement	2.97	2.89	0.97	0.333		

Notes:
1 sum q5a-q5c (wave 1): q2a-q2c (wave 2): high = high trust
2 sum q5d1, q5d2, q5d12 (wave 1): q2d1, q2d2, q2d12 (wave 2): high = high trust
3 sum q5d10 q5d11 q5d13 q5d14 (wave 1); q2d10 q2d11 q2d13 q2d14 (wave 2): high = high trust
4 sum q17a-q17d (wave 1)' q11a-q11d (wave 2): High = high efficacy
5 q8b (wave 1); q5b (wave 2): high = very dissatisfied.
6 sum q16a1 to q16a5 (wave1): q10a1 to q10a5: high = interested
7 sum q44c1, q44c3 (wave 1): q1c1 q1c3: high = high exposure
8 sum q32a q32b q32c q32g q32f (wave 1): q18a q18b q18c q18g q18f (wave 2): high = high willingness
9 sum q32e q32d (wave 1); q18d q18e (wave 2): high = high willingness
10 sum q61b1-q16b4 (wave 1): q10b1-q10b4 (wave 2): high = high conversation

involved'; 'sometimes politics and government seem so complicated that a person like me cannot really understand what is going on'; and 'it really matters which party is in power, because it will affect our lives'. Responses were on a five-point scale, from strongly agree to strongly disagree: they were coded so that 1 indicated low efficacy responses, and 5 high efficacy. So the higher an individual's score on the political efficacy scale, the greater their sense of political efficacy. Echoing Table 1, the results suggest a small but significant increase in individuals' sense of political efficacy between 2000 and 2001: people became more likely, on the whole, to feel their views mattered. A related issue, satisfaction with the way in which British democracy works, was measured using the five-point scale displayed in Figure 1 (with 5 indicating greatest dissatisfaction): as the figure implied, there was a small but significant drop in levels of dissatisfaction with democracy between 2000 and 2001.

As we saw earlier, interest in politics generally, and the extent to which people followed political news both increased between 2000 and 2001. We have created scales for each of these at each wave of the panel. The 'interest in politics' scale is the sum of scores on five questions asking how interested individuals were in local, regional, national, European and international politics. Responses to each were coded from 0 (no interest) to 3 (very interested), giving a scale that has a potential range running from 0 to 15: higher scores suggest greater interest in politics. The scale measuring exposure to political news in the media, meanwhile, was constructed by summing responses to two questions asking respondents how often, in an average week, they read political news in a paper, or used television or radio for political news. Responses to each were coded from 0 (never sought out political news) to 4 (sought out political news every day). The scale's theoretical range runs, therefore, from 0 to 8: the higher the score, the more frequent is the individual's exposure to political news. Both scales are robust in both waves of the panel (with good Cronbach's alphas), and they clearly demonstrate significant increases over time in interest in politics and in exposure to the media.

The last two measures of respondents' views examined here focus on the extent to which individuals claim they would be willing to undertake a series of 'civically-minded' activities: serving on a jury; donating blood; renovating a local amenity; serving as a school governor; serving as a local councillor; helping with meals on wheels; or participating in a Neighbourhood Watch scheme. What is clear is that people distinguish between these potential 'citizen acts'. Principal components analyses of answers to the relevant questions reveal similar structures of opinion in 2000 and in 2001 (Table 6). In both years, respondents distinguish between, on the one hand, citizen actions which involve mainly private effort (donating blood, serving on a jury, renovating a local park, helping with meals on wheels, joining Neighbourhood Watch) and those involving taking an active part in the operation of some more public body (being a school governor or a local councillor). We have therefore constructed two separate scales to summarize individuals' claimed willingness to undertake these citizen actions. The first is the number of 'private' citizen activities each individual claimed to be willing to undertake. The second is the number of 'public' citizen activities they are willing to perform. Looking at the averages for each scale in 2000 and in 2001, it is clear that, once

TABLE 6
WILLINGNESS TO UNDERTAKE POTENTIAL CITIZEN ACTIONS: PRINCIPAL
COMPONENTS ANALYSES

	Wave 1 2000		Wave 2 2001	
	Private service	*Public service*	*Private service*	*Public service*
Willing to donate blood	0.73		0.68	
Willing to serve on jury	0.67		0.60	
Willing to renovate local amenity	0.61		0.72	
Willing to join Neighbourhood Watch	0.51		0.62	
Willing to help meals on wheels	0.42	0.46	0.65	
Willing to stand as local councillor		0.80		0.87
Willing to serve as school governor		0.69		0.74
Eigenvalue	2.33	1.08	2.56	1.05
% variance accounted for	33.27	15.46	36.52	14.99

again, members of the panel became slightly – but significantly – more likely on average to say they were willing to undertake both kinds of activity over time (Table 5).

The other area we focus on here is change in actual civic behaviour over time. Three different areas are examined: conversations between citizens; membership of clubs, societies and voluntary organizations; and 'civic activism' – undertaking some act aimed at influencing laws, rules or policies.

Conversations about politics are an important channel through which individuals can express their opinions, and find out the views of others. It is also clear that, in electoral politics especially, political conversations between voters can mobilize support for particular parties and can also either encourage or discourage participation (depending on the composition of individuals' conversation networks: Huckfeldt and Sprague, 1995; Pattie and Johnston, 1999; Mutz, 2002). As demonstrated in Figure 4, political conversations were, on the whole, more common in 2001 than in 2000, not surprising in an election year. Our scale measures the frequency of political discussion with four groups of people: family members, friends, neighbours and workmates. Respondents were asked how often they spoke to people in each group: never (coded 1), rarely, sometimes, or often (coded 4). The political conversation scales were constructed by adding respondents' answers to all four questions: Cronbach's alphas are high suggesting the scale is reliable. The theoretical range of the scale runs from 4, for respondents who never talk politics to anyone in any of the groups, to 16, for respondents who often have political conversations with people in all of the groups. In both 2000 and 2001, the average respondent scored just over 8, suggesting some political conversation was taking place, with moderate frequency (though, as Figure 4 demonstrates, conversations were much more frequent with friends and family than with neighbours and co-workers: see also Pattie and Johnston, 1999). And there was a slight but significant increase in the political conversation scale between 2000 and 2001, consistent with a citizen body that was talking politics more often.

Associational engagement, as measured by the number of types of organizations joined in the previous year, also increased significantly between 2000 and 2001. The average panel respondent was a member of 1.0 types of organization in 2000, but of 1.71 (almost double) a year later (Table 5).

Clearly, we wish to know about changing levels of political action. We used four measures of political participation (based on the responses outlined in Table 3). The first counts the total number of activities undertaken by each panel respondent in both 2000 and 2001. Our remaining measures of civic activism differentiate between the various forms of participation identified in other work (Pattie et al., forthcoming). The second measure concentrates on what we have termed 'individualistic' political actions (petition signing, ethical consumption for example), and counts the number of such activities undertaken by each respondent. Third, we count the number of 'contact' actions undertaken (contacting politicians and officials). And the fourth measure concentrates on the number of 'collective' political actions (taking part in a demonstration, attending a meeting for example) undertaken. Intriguingly, there is little sign that most of these activities became more or less frequent between 2000 and 2001 (Table 5). Only 'individualistic' actions were significantly more frequent at the latter date than at the former.

Finally, what of the time given to associational life? In both 2000 and 2001, panel members were asked how much time they had spent in the previous month on activities that involved some sort of associational engagement with others – in clubs, associations, groups, networks, or in supporting others. Responses were coded on a six-point scale: those who spent no time on such activities were coded as 1, while those who spent 20 hours or more were coded 6. There was little change between 2000 and 2001 in the average amount of time spent in associational engagement (Table 5). In each year, the average panel respondent scored just below 3, equivalent to spending just under five hours a month on this form of associational life. There was no net change in the average time spent on such activities.

The Results

Our main interest is in accounting for change over time in civic attitudes and behaviour at the individual level. Even where there has been no net change on average, there may still have been considerable overall change. Some individuals may have become more active, or developed a more 'civic' outlook, while others may have become less active or civic in their views: but if movement in one direction is 'cancelled' by movement in the other, then the overall picture of volatility will not be well-captured by examining average levels of activity in 2000 and 2001. We need to go further, and model change at the level of the individual citizen. To do so, we estimate the panel data regression model outlined above.

In line with the logic of Granger causality discussed earlier, the dependent variables are individuals' scores on the measures just discussed at the time of the second interview in 2001. The independent, or explanatory, variables are taken from the same individuals' replies in the first interview, in 2000, and include their 2000 score on the dependent variable. Also included is a range of factors from leading theories of participation, and employed elsewhere to examine cross-sectional variations in civic activism in 2000 (Pattie et al, forthcoming). We concentrate here on a number of measures. From the cognitive engagement model (e.g. Dalton, 2002), we take age at which individuals left education, political knowledge scores, media exposure, interest in politics, and a measure of policy dissatisfaction. From the civic voluntarism model (Verba et al., 1995) come measures of political efficacy, mobilization, free time, occupational status and partisanship. The equity-fairness model (Runciman, 1966) contributes measures of perceived outcomes and expectations, economic deprivation, and variables assessing whether respondents are members of a deprived group. The social capital model (Putnam, 2000) contributes measures of interpersonal trust, trust in institutions, membership of associational groups and informal networks, exposure to TV, and ties to the local community. And from the general incentives model (e.g. Whiteley and Seyd, 2002), we examine the effects of perceived costs and benefits (both collective and selective) of action, as well as of social norms towards participation.

For the most part, the independent variables are defined in the same way as their cross-sectional equivalents in our other work (Pattie et al., forthcoming). There are two main sets of exceptions. One is party identification, which is defined here in terms of which party an individual identifies with, rather than by the strength of party identification. We make this change here to reflect the potentially important partisan impact of the 2001 election. The result of that contest was widely and correctly anticipated well in advance of the election itself: a second Labour landslide. If the election were to prove a factor in accounting for changes in civic activity over time, therefore, we might anticipate that supporters of different parties would be affected in different ways. Two different scenarios are possible. Conservative supporters, for instance, might have found the prospect of a second major defeat profoundly demotivating, while Labour supporters might have been more susceptible to mobilization. One could also anticipate the opposite reaction, with Conservatives keen to minimize the damage to their party, and hence becoming more active, while Labour supporters, assured of victory, might have become complacent and so less likely to become active.

The second group of explanatory variables to be calculated in a slightly different way here compared to our definitions in earlier work are the wave 1 measures of trust in others, in institutions and in politicians, political efficacy, and levels of individualistic contact, and collectivist civic action. As noted above, the versions adopted here are designed to allow strict comparability in these measures between waves 1 and 2 of the panel.

A general to specific modelling strategy is adopted here. Although all independent variables have the potential to be entered into the model, only those that prove significant are retained for the final model. As such, this provides relatively parsimonious models. There is, however, a risk that, by allowing variable selection to be driven by statistical rather than theoretical considerations, spurious results might result. We have, therefore, also conducted analyses that enter all possible independent variables simultaneously. The results of both exercises are very similar, reassuring us that we have neither missed something important nor misrepresented the results by adopting the general to specific procedure.

We start by examining change over time in perceptions and intentions concerning civic participation. The first set of models to be considered look at changing attitudes towards the political system. In particular, we are interested in changes in: interest in politics; exposure to political news on the media; levels of satisfaction with democracy (which is also our measure of collective benefits in the general incentives model); and political efficacy (Table 7).

Remember that the panel regression models all control for the dependent variable measured a year previously. As we would expect, in each case, this was the single most important variable accounting for 2001 scores on each issue. In all four equations, the respondent's score on the measure a year earlier is significantly and positively related to their score on the same measure in 2001 (the relevant coefficients are printed in bold in the table). In other words, people who were interested in politics in 2000 still tended to be interested in politics in 2001. Those who followed politics closely in the media in 2000 were on the whole still doing so in 2001. The more satisfied someone was with British democracy in 2000, the more likely they were still to be satisfied in 2001. And the greater a person's sense of political efficacy in 2000, the more likely it was that they would still feel efficacious in 2001.

This is exactly what we would expect from panel data (most people tend not to change their views radically over the course of a year). However, it is also worth noting that people's views in 2000 did not completely explain their

TABLE 7
THE DYNAMICS OF PARTICIPATION: CHANGING ATTITUDES TOWARDS POLITICS (REGRESSION)

	Perceptions and intentions scales 2001			
	Interest in politics	*Media exposure*	*Satisfaction with democracy*	*Political efficacy*
Independent variables (2000)				
Constant	1.88	3.86	1.86	8.89
Cognitive engagement				
Age left education				0.17**
Media exposure	0.12**	**0.31****		
Interest in politics	**0.40****	0.07**		0.10**
General incentives				
Collective benefits:				
Satisfaction with democracy			**0.35****	−0.17*
Selective benefits:				
Process incentives	0.21**			
Group incentives		−0.12*		
Civic voluntarism				
Political efficacy				**0.24****
Party ID (comparison = no party ID)				
Conservative ID			0.21**	
Labour ID				0.59**
Other ID			0.67**	
Occupational status	0.25**			
Equity-fairness				
Outcomes and expectations				−0.37**
Retired		0.51**		
Social capital				
Trust elected politicians	0.06**			
Trust state institutions			−0.12**	
Informal networks				0.56**
TV watching	−0.14*	−0.11**		−0.10*
Years in area		0.21*	0.07*	
R^2	0.38	0.21	0.20	0.30

Notes: *significant at $p = 0.05$; **significant at $p = 0.01$.

views in 2001. The R^2 values, while respectable for survey data, are not over-whelming, suggesting that much of the variation in each of our measures in 2001 remains to be accounted for. And, of more immediate interest to us, opinions in 2001 were related to a range of other factors from a year earlier, even when we control for people's views on the same measures in 2000. Because we have controlled for the 2000 score on the dependent variable, these other significant coefficients tell us about who was likely to change their views, and in what direction.

Looking first at interest in politics, those who followed political news closely in 2000 were more likely to become more interested in politics over the ensuing year than were those who did not make as much use of media politics reporting. The more middle-class the individual (as measured by occupational status), the more likely it was that their interest in politics would grow. And people who scored relatively high on the scale for trust in elected politicians in 2000 were also more likely to get more interested in politics than were those who did not trust politicians. From the general incentives model, process incentives (related mainly to how rewarding an activity people think politics is) were positively related to interest in politics: the more process incentives a person could identify in 2000, the greater the increase in their interest in politics over the following year. But not everything increased interest in politics. Frequent television viewers in 2000 became less interested in politics over time, compared to those who watched little television. This clearly pulls in the opposite direction to the effects of the 'exposure to politics on the media' variable, suggesting that Norris' (1996) critique of Putnam's (1995) indictment of television is correct. While over-exposure to television does seem demotivating, it depends what sort of media is being consumed. Those who use the media to follow politics can actually be mobilized by it. As we will see, this turns out to be a fairly persistent story.

The model for change in exposure to political reporting in the media looks relatively similar. The more interested a person was in politics in 2000, for instance, the more likely they were to pay increased attention to political news over the following year. TV watching was once again a disincentive, however. Frequent TV watchers in 2000 paid less attention to political news a year later than they had in 2000, while those who watched little TV at the first point in time paid an increasing amount of attention to it (remember that we have already controlled for exposure to politics in the media in 2000). Perceptions of group incentives are also related to changing media exposure to politics. Interestingly, the relationship was negative: the more likely people were in 2000 to feel that politics was a good way of obtaining benefits for groups they cared about, the greater the relative decline in the attention they paid to political news between 2000 and 2001. This is striking. It might be a consequence of disillusion, if, for instance, those who felt strong group incentives in 2000 felt let down by the results of the 2001 election. However, the correlation between perceptions of group incentives in 2000 and in 2001 is positive and significant: there is little sign of selective disillusion here.

Two other factors are associated with increasing exposure to political reporting in the media. First, those who were retired in 2000 were more likely to pay increased attention to political news than were those not retired (perhaps related to the greater time flexibility enjoyed by the retired, or perhaps to concerns over government pension plans which became an issue during the 1997–2001 Parliament.) And the longer people had lived in their neighbourhoods in 2000, the greater their increase in attention to television news.

Satisfaction with democracy, meanwhile, fell over time among those who in 2000 had identified with the Conservative Party or with some other party (compared, in both cases to those who identified with no party: the variable is coded so that high values reflect dissatisfaction). That supporters of the party which lost the 2001 election should become less satisfied with the workings of British democracy is hardly surprising. Conservative supporters were among the least satisfied with British democracy at that time (as they had been since 1997: Pattie and Johnston, 2001b). And the longer individuals had lived in their neighbourhood in 2000, the less their satisfaction with democracy increased. But the more people had trusted state institutions in 2000, the more their satisfaction with democracy improved over the subsequent year.

A sense of political efficacy, meanwhile, increased more among the relatively well-educated than among those who had left education early. It also grew faster among those who had been interested in politics a year before than among those who had not. And being a member of an informal network in 2000 contributed to an improved sense of political efficacy: feelings of political efficacy grew more among those who were members of such networks in 2000 than among those who were not. However, in keeping with Putnam's claims, television watching made people feel relatively powerless. The more frequently individuals watched television in 2000, the less their sense of political efficacy grew over the following year. And the more satisfied they had been with British democracy in 2000, the more their sense of political efficacy increased subsequently (remembering that the 'satisfaction with democracy' variable is coded so that high values indicate dissatisfaction). Finally, the higher scores on the 'outcomes and expectations' measure in 2000, the less their sense of political efficacy grew (and for some it fell) between 2000 and 2001. The outcomes and expectations measure, based on responses to questions such as 'politicians only look after themselves' and 'there is a big difference between what I expect from life and what I get', is coded so that high scores indicate a large disparity between expectations and results. In other words, those with high scores on the measure are the most disgruntled with their lot in life. It is hardly surprising, therefore, that they feel less politically effective as time goes on.

TABLE 8
THE DYNAMICS OF PARTICIPATION: CHANGING TRUST (REGRESSION)

	Perceptions and intentions scales 2001		
	Trust others	Trust elected politicians	Trust state institutions
Independent variables (2000)			
Constant	10.33	10.30	14.84
Cognitive engagement			
Age left education		−0.31*	
Political knowledge	0.20*		
General incentives			
Collective benefits:			
Satisfaction with democracy	−0.40*	−0.65**	−0.49*
Selective benefits:			
Process incentives	0.25*		
Outcome incentives	−0.28**		−0.30*
Civic voluntarism			
Party ID (comparison = no party ID)			
Labour ID		1.30**	
Occupational status	0.20*		
Equity-fairness			
Outcomes and expectations	−0.26	−0.80**	−0.85**
Retired	1.01**		
Social capital			
Trust others	**0.38****		0.13**
Trust elected politicians		**0.23****	
Trust state institutions		0.14**	**0.40****
TV watching	0.19*		
R^2	0.26	0.28	0.33

Notes: * significant at p = 0.05; ** significant at p = 0.01.

What of changes in levels of trust (Table 8)? Once again, not surprisingly, the more trusting people were in 2000 on each of our three trust scales, the more trusting they were a year later (all the relevant coefficients, picked out in bold, are positive and highly significant – indeed, they are the most significant variables in their respective equations). Two other factors stand out quite consistently in all three equations. First, the more dissatisfied with British democracy people were in 2000, the less likely they were to become more trusting of other people, of elected politicians or of state institutions over the subsequent year: dissatisfaction bred distrust. Second, the perceived greater

THE DYNAMICS OF CITIZENSHIP

the gap between outcomes and expectations in 2000, the less trusting did individuals become over time. On all three scales, trust fell most among those who in 2000 had felt they were receiving less than they expected: it increased most among those who had felt their expectations and outcomes were more in balance. Relative deprivation, therefore, was inimical to growing trust.

But these were not the only factors affecting change in the trust scales. Trust in other people grew most among those who scored well on the political knowledge scale in 2000, those who felt there were strong process incentives to action, the more middle class, the retired and (intriguingly) those who watched most television. It fell among those who had felt there were strong outcome incentives to action in 2000. Trust in elected politicians fell among the best educated, meanwhile, but (not surprisingly, given that their party had just won a second landslide victory), it grew among Labour partisans. It also grew more among those who had previously trusted other state institutions than among those who had not. And trust in state institutions also grew most among those individuals who trusted other citizens most. But it fell more among those with strong outcome incentives in 2000 than among those whose outcome incentives were weaker (presumably reflecting their general dissatisfaction with the state system – remember the outcome incentives scale is built from questions which tap into a sense that 'things would be better if I was involved in running them').

What of change in peoples' willingness to undertake different forms of civic activity? Our two scales cover willingness to undertake private services (such as blood donation), and public services (such as becoming a local councillor). As ever, the best predictor of an individual's views on these scales in 2001 is their score on the equivalent scale the previous year (Table 9: coefficients in bold). Education emerges as an important factor accounting for change: the longer people had spent in education the more their willingness to undertake both private and public responsibilities increased over the year. Outcome incentives were important – not surprisingly – in accounting for change in willingness to undertake public sector duties. Those who in 2000 had felt that people like themselves would do a good job as a councillor or an MP became more likely over time to claim a willingness to act in those capacities. But retired people's willingness to undertake private service activities declined over time relative to those who were not retired. This latter may reflect the relatively physical nature of several of the tasks in the scale: giving blood, renovating a park and helping with meals on wheels being cases in point.

The discussion so far has focused on changes in people's civic attitudes. What of their actions? Can we identify which factors mobilize people, and which demotivate them? We focus first on people's associational lives. What influenced changes in organizational membership, time given to associational

TABLE 9
THE DYNAMICS OF PARTICIPATION: CHANGES IN
WILLINGNESS TO ACT (REGRESSION)

	Perceptions and intentions scales 2001	
	Willing private service	Willing public service
Independent variables (2000)		
Constant	1.76	−0.12
Willing private service	**0.49****	
Willing public service		**0.34****
Cognitive engagement		
Age left education	0.06*	0.06**
Interest in politics	0.03**	0.02**
General incentives		
Selective benefits:		
Outcome incentives		0.04**
Civic voluntarism		
Equity-fairness		
Retired	−0.36**	
Social capital		
R^2	0.31	0.20

Notes: *significant at $p = 0.05$; **significant at $p = 0.01$.

activities, and frequency of political conversations (Table 10)? Once again, unsurprisingly, levels of activity in 2001 were best predicted by levels of the same activity in 2000 (coefficients in bold). The more types of organization people had joined in 2000, the more they joined a year later. The more time they spent associating in 2000, the more time they devoted to it in 2001. And those disposed to frequent political discussions in 2000 were also the most active political conversationalists in 2001. Education was positively associated with both group membership and with political conversation: the better educated an individual was in 2000, the bigger the increase in the number of types of organization they joined over the following year, and the more frequently they discussed politics. Occupational status, too, played a consistent role: more middle-class individuals became more active, spent more time associating, and became more frequent political discussants over time than did working-class individuals. And as we saw earlier, media effects were both

	Number of groups joined	Civic activities scales 2001 time associational engagement	Political conversations
Independent variables (2000)			
Constant	0.50	1.55	3.41
Time associational engagement		**0.24****	
Political conversations			**0.43****
Cognitive engagement			
Age left education	0.12**	0.14**	
Political knowledge	0.08*		
Media exposure	0.06**		0.14**
General incentives			
Selective benefits:			
Group incentives		0.08*	
Civic voluntarism			
Political efficacy			0.11**
Party ID (comparison = no party ID)			
Other ID		−0.94*	
Occupational status	0.12**	0.07*	0.11*
Free time		−0.05*	
Equity-fairness			
Retired		0.46**	−0.88**
Social capital			
Number groups joined	**0.45****		
Informal networks		0.42**	0.46*
TV watching	−0.10**	−0.08**	−0.10*
R^2	0.34	0.16	0.36

Notes: *significant at $p = 0.05$; **significant at $p = 0.01$.

evident and nuanced. In line with Norris's (1996) argument, how much attention people paid to political news had a motivating effect: the greater a person's exposure to politics in the media in 2000, the greater the increase in their associational membership and political conversation over time. But, as suggested by Putnam, television viewing in general was demotivating: the more TV a person watched in 2000, the less their associational activity increased over time, the less likely they were to spend more time on those activities, and the less likely they were to talk politics frequently (presumably because there was insufficient time to fit those activities and discussions around the demands of the TV schedules). Informal networking encouraged participation. Those in such a network in 2000 increased the time they spent associating, and the frequency of their political discussions more, on the whole, over the following year than those who did not belong to such a network. And the retired spent increasing amounts of time associating with others – but they became less frequent political discussants.

Those most politically knowledgeable in 2000 were more likely than the less-knowledgeable to increase their membership of different types of groups over the following year. And the more group incentives people saw in 2000, the greater was the increase in time they gave to associational activities between then and 2001. But people who identified with parties other than Labour, Conservative or Liberal Democrat, and people with most free time in 2000 were less likely than their counterparts to spend more time associating in 2001 than in 2000. And not surprisingly, perhaps, the greater the sense of political efficacy felt by individuals in 2000, the greater the increase in the frequency of their political conversations over the following year. People who felt that political activity mattered presumably saw political discussion as a key part of that activity, and, it is likely, responded to the 2001 election by talking more to their fellow citizens about politics.

Finally, what about changes in activities aimed at influencing rules, laws or policies? We examine not only change in the total number of activities undertaken, but also change in the number of individualistic, contacting and collective actions (Table 11). As before, levels of activity a year before were the best predictors: the more activities, both in total and of each kind, a person had undertaken in 2000, the more they undertook in 2001. Active people tended to stay active (coefficients in bold).

Education was associated with increasing levels of both total and of individualistic activism. The longer a person had spent in full time education, the more likely it was that they would undertake more activities in total, and more individualistic activities in particular, in 2001 than in 2000. And television watching discouraged both. The more TV people had watched in 2000, the less their total level of civic activity grew between 2000 and 2001, and the less their levels of individualistic activity increased. The more middle class someone's occupation, the greater the increase over time in total, contacting, and collective civic activities. Women were more likely than men to increase the level of their individualistic civic activities between 2000 and 2001. And (in line with Putnam's social capital argument), the more types of associational groups a person had joined in 2000, the greater the increase in their levels of individualistic civic action over the following year. Outcome incentives, meanwhile, were associated with change in levels of contacting: the more a person thought politics would benefit from the involvement of a person like

TABLE 11
THE DYNAMICS OF PARTICIPATION: CHANGING POLITICAL
ACTIVITIES (REGRESSION)

	Number of political activities scales 2001			
	Political activities	*Individualistic activities*	*Contacting activities*	*Collective activities*
Independent variables (2000)				
Constant	2.92	2.08	0.05	−0.14
N political activities	**0.42****			
N individual political actions		**0.34****		
N contacting political actions			**0.41****	
N collectivist political actions				**0.19****
Cognitive engagement				
Age left education	0.13*	0.13**		
General incentives				
Collective benefits:				
Satisfaction with democracy				0.04*
Costs				−0.02*
Selective benefits:				
Process incentives				0.03*
Outcome incentives			0.05*	
System (altruistic) benefits				0.02*
Civic voluntarism				
Party ID (comparison = no party ID)				
Conservative ID				−0.12**
Other ID				0.31**
Occupational status	0.10*		0.05**	0.02**
Equity-fairness				
Female		0.40**		
Social capital				
Number groups joined		0.10*		
Trust state institutions	−0.02*			
TV watching	−0.13**	−0.12**		
R^2	0.29	0.24	0.22	0.11

Notes: *significant at $p = 0.05$; **significant at $p = 0.01$.

themselves in 2000, the greater the increase over the next 12 months in their levels of contacting. People who thought they could make a difference tried to do so.

Finally, what of increases in levels of collective action? General incentives and rational choice factors played an important role here. Changes in levels of collective action were associated with dissatisfaction with democracy (our measure of collective benefits). Those who felt, in 2000, that British democracy was not working as well as they would like were more likely than those satisfied with it to take collective steps to remedy things. But (not surprisingly) those who perceived significant costs to involvement in 2000 were less likely to increase their collective activities than were those who saw few such costs. But the more process and altruistic benefits people could see in 2000, the more likely they were to become more collectively active in 2001. Partisanship mattered here too. Conservative identifiers became less collectively active over time, compared to those with no party identification, while those who identified with 'other' parties were more likely than non-identifiers to increase their collective activities.

Conclusion

The period between the 2000 and 2001 waves of our panel was a dramatic one. British political life was stirred up not only by a general election in June 2001, but also by the fuel protests of autumn 2000, by protests over a proposed ban on fox hunting, and by the political fall-out of the foot and mouth crisis of the first half of 2001. International tensions grew dramatically after the events of September 11, 2001. Although we cannot completely disentangle the effects of each of these events from the others, our panel evidence does suggest that an unusually 'political' year did have an effect on the civic attitudes and behaviour of the British public. In general, people became more concerned about politics, were more interested in it, paid greater attention to it, and did more about it. On a variety of measures, Britain was a more 'civic' society after the 2001 election than it had been before it.

Accounting for that change is more difficult, however. Here we have focussed on the attributes of individual members of the public. Who was likely to become more engaged with civic life, and who less? On the whole, the more interested people were in politics to start with, the more they felt they got out of their lives, the greater the resources they had to draw on, and the better integrated they were into informal networks of friends and acquaintances, the more active they became over time, and the more positive they felt in their civic attitudes. In other words, the 'civic culture' grew most among those who were already most likely to be civically minded. To them that have shall be given.

The villain of the piece however is, as Putnam (2000) suggested, television. In model after model, the more TV a respondent reported watching on average in 2000, the less likely they were to 'improve' their 'civicality'. Television is, of course, generally 'consumed' in the privacy of the home. Frequent TV watchers just did not get out and get involved to the same extent as those not glued to the screen. But – again a feature of many models – not all media exposure was bad. Those who paid close attention to political news in 2000 generally became more active, and thought better of civic life, over the following year. TV may be a 'villain', therefore, but it is not always so. As with so many things, it isn't what you do, it's the way that you do it.

ACKNOWLEDGEMENT

The Citizen Audit survey was funded by a grant from the Economic and Social Research Council (award no L215252025) of its Democracy and Participation programme. We are grateful to the ESRC for its support.

NOTES

1. For example, in the Citizen Audit we asked our respondents whether they were satisfied or dissatisfied with the delivery of a range of local authority services, including schools, care for the elderly, social services, road maintenance, and street cleaning, and on all these the percentages of dissatisfied had increased.
2. The local elections in 2001 were delayed as a result of the foot and mouth crisis, and therefore coincided with the general election, undoubtedly helping turnout (Butler and Kavanagh, 2001: 83).
3. The exception was forming a group of like-minded people.

REFERENCES

Almond, Gabriel A. and Sidney Verba (1963) *The Civic Culture: Political Attitudes and Democracy in Five Nations*. Princeton: Princeton University Press.
Banducci, Susan A. and Jeffrey A. Karp (2003) 'How Elections Change the Way Citizens View the Political System: Campaigns, Media Effects and Electoral Outcomes in Comparative Perspective', *British Journal of Political Science*, 33, 443–67.
Butler, David and Dennis Kavanagh (2001) *The British General Election of 2001*. Basingstoke: Palgrave.
Charezma, Wojciech and Derek F. Deadman (1992) *New Directions in Econometric Practice*. London: Edward Elgar.
Clarke, Harold D. and Allan Kornberg (1992) 'Do National Elections Affect Perceptions of MPs' Responsiveness? A Note on the Canadian Case', *Legislative Studies Quarterly*, 17, 183–204.
Dalton, Russell J. (1999) 'Political Support in Advanced Industrial Democracies', in Pippa Norris (ed.), *Critical Citizens: Global Support for Democratic Governance*. Oxford: Oxford University Press, pp. 57–77.
Dalton, Russell, J. (2002) *Citizen Politics*. New York: Seven Bridges Press.
Finkel, Steven E. (1985) 'Reciprocal Effects of Participation and Political Efficacy', *American Journal of Political Science*, 29, 891–913.
Granger, Clive J. (1988) 'Some Recent Developments in a Concept of Causality', *Journal of Econometrics*, 2, 111–20.
Huckfeldt, R. and John Sprague (1995) *Citizens, Politics and Social Communication: Information and Influence in an Election Campaign*. Cambridge: Cambridge University Press.

Inglehart, Ronald J. (1999) 'Postmodernization Erodes Respect for Authority, But Increases Support for Democracy', in Pippa Norris (ed.), *Critical Citizens: Global Support for Democratic Governance.* Oxford: Oxford University Press, pp. 236–56.

Jowell, Roger and Richard Topf (1988) 'Trust in the Establishment', in Roger Jowell, Sharon Witherspoon and Lindsay Brooks (eds.), *British Social Attitudes: The 5th Report.* Aldershot: Gower, pp. 109–26.

Kavanagh, Dennis (1980) 'Political Culture in Britain: the Decline of the Civic Culture', in Gabriel A. Almond and Sidney Verba (eds.), *The Civic Culture Revisited.* London: Sage, pp. 124–76.

Mortimore, Roger (1995) 'Politics and Public Perceptions', in F.F. Ridley and Alan Doig (eds.), *Sleaze: Politicians, Private Interests and Public Reaction.* Oxford: Oxford University Press, pp. 31–41.

Mutz, Diana (2002) 'The Consequences of Cross-Cutting Networks for Political Participation', *American Journal of Political Science,* 46, 838–55.

Norris, Pippa (1996) 'Does Television Erode Social Capital? A Reply to Putnam', *PS: Political Science and Politics,* 29, 474–80.

Norris, Pippa (ed.) (1999a) *Critical Citizens: Global Support for Democratic Governance.* Oxford: Oxford University Press.

Norris, Pippa (1999b) 'Introduction: the Growth of Critical Citizens?' in Pippa Norris (ed.), *Critical Citizens: Global Support for Democratic Governance.* Oxford: Oxford University Press.

Norris, Pippa (2002) *Democratic Phoenix: Reinventing Political Activism.* Cambridge: Cambridge University Press.

Norris, Pippa, John Curtice, David Sanders, Margaret Scammell and Holli A. Semetko (1999) *On Message.* London: Sage.

Pattie, Charles J. and Ronald J. Johnston (1999) 'Context, Conversation and Conviction: Social Networks and Voting at the 1992 British General Election', *Political Studies,* 47, 877–89.

Pattie, Charles J. and Ronald J. Johnston (2001a) 'A Low Turnout Landslide: Abstention in the British General Election of 1997', *Political Studies,* 49, 286–305.

Pattie, Charles J. and Ronald J. Johnston (2001b) 'Losing the Voters' Trust: Evaluations of the Political System and Voting at the 1997 British General Election', *British Journal of Politics and International Relations,* 3, 191–222.

Pattie, Charles J., Patrick Seyd and Paul Whiteley (2003) 'Citizenship and Civic Engagement: Attitudes and Behaviour in Britain', *Political Studies,* 51, 443–68.

Pattie, Charles J., Patrick Seyd and Paul Whiteley (forthcoming) *Citizenship in Britain: Values, Participation and Democracy.* Cambridge: Cambridge University Press.

Pharr, Susan J. and Robert D. Putnam (eds.) (2000) *Disaffected Democracies: What's Troubling the Trilateral Countries?* Princeton NJ: Princeton University Press.

Putnam, Robert D. (1995) 'Tuning in, Tuning Out: the Strange Disappearance of Social Capital in America', *PS: Political Science and Politics,* 28, 664–83.

Putnam, Robert D. (2000) *Bowling Alone.* New York: Simon & Schuster.

Rahn, Wendy, John Brehm and Neil Carlson (1999) 'National Elections as Institutions for Generating Social Capital', in Theda Skocpol and Morris P. Fiorina (eds.), *Civic Engagement in American Democracy.* Washington, DC: Brookings Institution, pp. 111–60.

Runciman, W.G. (1966) *Relative Deprivation and Social Justice.* London: Routledge, Kegan & Paul.

Seyd, Patrick and Paul F. Whiteley (2002a) *New Labour's Grassroots.* Basingstoke: Palgrave.

Seyd, Patrick and Paul F. Whiteley (2002b) 'Party Election Campaigning in Britain: The Labour Party'. Paper presented to the Annual Meeting of the Canadian Political Science Association, University of Toronto.

Verba, Sidney, Kay Lehman Schlozman and Henry E. Brady (1995) *Voice and Equality: Civic Voluntarism in American Politics.* Cambridge, Mass: Harvard University Press.

Whiteley, Paul F. and Patrick Seyd (2002) *High-Intensity Participation: The Dynamics of Party Activism in Britain.* Ann Arbor: University of Michigan Press.

Public Attitudes towards Political Protest in Britain, 2000–02

David Sanders, Harold Clarke, Marianne Stewart and Paul Whiteley

Since the beginning of the twenty-first century, there has been something of a revival of protest activity in Britain. The 'fuel protests' of September 2000 led to a brief crisis of public confidence over the government's ability to run the country effectively, and the sharp fall in Labour's opinion poll ratings provoked a serious review of the taxes levied on different categories of fuel. In 2002, a major demonstration by the Countryside Alliance, which was aimed at raising the political profile of 'rural issues', left support for the government largely unaffected. Nonetheless, the demonstration appeared to mobilize conservative parts of the body politic that earlier waves of protest had consistently failed to reach. Finally, the widespread protests against the war with Iraq, which took place in February and March 2003, produced the largest demonstrations that Britain had witnessed for over a generation. What is it that leads people to participate in protest activity? Are there any underlying factors that, regardless of the specific characteristics of a particular appeal, encourage people to join a protest or a demonstration? If so, is it possible to identify these factors and to assess their relative explanatory importance?

This article considers these questions using a new dataset – still under construction as we collect more data – which explores the changing propensities of the British public to engage in a variety of sorts of non-electoral political action. The data have been collected on a monthly basis, using representative sample surveys of the British electorate, since July 2000. We report here on the data collected up to and including December 2002. We will report on the impact of the Iraq War on public opinion – and, in particular, on 'protest potential' – in a later study. The first part of the article outlines six different, though in some respects complimentary, theoretical accounts of the sources of protest activity. The second part discusses how we attempt to specify the different models and describes our operational measures in a little more detail. It also provides an illustration of how key variables changed during the 2000–2002 period, focusing in particular on the roles played by the September 2000 fuel protests and by the June 2001

British Elections & Parties Review, Vol. 14, 2004, pp. 147–167
ISSN 1368-9886 print
DOI: 10.1080/1368988042000258817   © 2004 Taylor & Francis Ltd.

general election. Finally, the third part reports the results of formally testing the various models using individual-level data taken from the repeated monthly cross-section surveys between July 2000 and December 2002. The results show that none of the extant theoretical models provides an encompassing explanation of protest activity in Britain. People turn to protest for three main reasons: because they make rational calculations about its costs and benefits; because they believe that it can rectify the sense of dissatisfaction or deprivation that they feel; and because they are mobilized into action by personal social contacts. Successful protests by a minority also act as a spur for the majority to increase its 'protest potential'.

Models of Protest Activity

A considerable amount of research has been conducted into the sources of non-electoral forms of political participation. The types of behaviour analysed have ranged from signing petitions and boycotting goods through to full-scale rebellions and revolutions. We focus here on protests and demonstrations because, although they are outside the electoral arena, they represent a legitimate vehicle in democratic countries for people to make their voices heard. Previous research has sought to analyse the sources of non-electoral political activity under six main headings: Relative Deprivation, Cognitive Engagement, Civic Voluntarism, Social Capital, Rational Actor and General Incentives. In this section, we outline the core theoretical claims of each of these models in turn.

The Relative Deprivation Model. The Relative Deprivation account of political participation focuses on the role played by the sense of injustice that can impel people to act when they feel that current political or social arrangements are inequitable or unfair (Muller, 1979; Hochschild, 1981). In his classic study of the problem, Gurr (1970) argues that people feel a sense of relative deprivation when there is a gap between their 'value expectations' (what they think they ought to get out of life) and their 'perceived value capabilities' (what they think they will get). These feelings of deprivation in turn provide an emotional mobilizing spur to political participation. We operationalize the relative deprivation model here by differentiating among (1) feelings of inequity or unfairness, (2) feelings of economic deprivation, and (3) dissatisfaction with life in general. We hypothesize that heightened feelings of inequity, economic deprivation or life dissatisfaction are all assumed to invoke a greater chance that the individual will participate in protest activity.

The Cognitive Engagement Model. The Cognitive Engagement model stresses the importance of education and political knowledge as sources of political mobilization (Dalton, 1996; Nie, Junn and Stehlik-Barry, 1996). It argues that well-educated people are more aware of political events and public affairs. They are more capable of processing politically relevant information. They are also more inclined to make responsibility attributions to governmental institutions and political actors for policy outcomes. And they are in turn potentially more dissatisfied with government performance in key policy areas. All of these characteristics mean that the cognitively engaged are more likely to participate in all forms of political activity, including protest, in order to effect meaningful change in the political system and in the wider social order.

The Civic Voluntarism Model. The Civic Voluntarism model argues that churches, voluntary associations and workplaces are important social settings that encourage their members to acquire the information, resources and civic skills that are necessary for effective political participation. This participation can involve 'conventional' activities like voting and involvement in local party organizations, as well as communal and protest politics like demonstrations and marches (Verba, Schlozman and Brady, 1995; Huckfeldt and Sprague, 1995; Mutz, 1998). The Civic Voluntarism model suggests that participation in protest politics is driven by three key sets of variables. First, participation is more likely if the individual is psychologically engaged with the political system. Such engagement is variously manifested through people's sense of political efficacy (the feeling that politicians respond to the citizens' concerns), interest in politics, and the extent to which they identify with established political parties. An efficacious, interested partisan, it is claimed, will be much more psychologically engaged than an inefficacious, uninterested non-identifier. Second, individuals who possess politically relevant resources (such as education, income and the access to more free time that is typically associated with a higher social class) are more likely to participate than individuals who lack resources. Third, participation is more likely among people who are in a position to be mobilized into activity by the persuasive efforts other people. To put it simply, some people do things because they are asked. Others are more available to participate in new forms of political activity because, as a result of having volunteered to participate in the past, they have more social contacts that are conducive to future participation. Reflecting these various explanatory factors, the Civic Voluntarism model suggests that Psychological Engagement, Resources and Mobilization are all conducive to protest activity.

The Social Capital Model. Social Capital consists in the existence of informal social networks that link people in a community, and in the presence of relatively high levels of social trust between the members of that community.

Like physical capital, social capital is alleged to have important productive consequences. First, network activities and trust together facilitate reciprocity in social relations and reduce the transactions costs of monitoring compliance with public goods provision (Becker, 1976; Coleman, 1988; Jackman and Miller, 1998; Putnam, 1993, 2000). Second, high levels of social capital are conducive to citizens' active engagement with the political system. Although social capital theorists typically associate this engagement with relatively high levels of voting, the idea that social engagement lends itself to political involvement can be extended to other forms of political activity. Indeed, the social capital model implies that people who are relatively involved in their local communities will be more likely than those who are uninvolved to engage in protest activity. By the same token, those who exhibit higher levels of social trust should be more inclined to embrace the sort of collective action that is engendered by protest activity.

The 'Core' or 'Minimal' Rational Actor Model. The Rational Actor model has been deployed in a variety of political and economic contexts. However, its potential value in explaining political participation is readily apparent. Individuals undertake actions only if the benefits accruing from them outweigh the costs (Downs, 1957; Olson, 1965). The core version of the model, introduced by Riker and Ordeshook (1968), can be expressed as

$$U_i = pB - C$$

That is, the utility of a given action (U_i) is a function of the perceived benefits of the action *discounted by probability of receiving those benefits* (hence the multiplicative pB term) minus the perceived costs of participation in the action itself. It follows that the probability that an individual will take part in protest action can be expressed as

Probability of Protest = f (Efficacy*Benefits – Costs)

where Efficacy measures the individual's perception of the extent to which the government is responsive to their concerns; Benefits measures the individual's perceptions of the benefits 'for people like me' that are derived from participation; and Costs measures the individual's perception of the costs of participation. Protest is predicted to be more likely when efficacy*benefits is relatively high and when costs are relatively low.

The General Incentives or Modified Rational Actor Model. The Core Rational Actor model embraces a very narrow definition of rationality. The General Incentives model seeks to extend the boundaries of rationality so that the calculus of action is not based exclusively on personal costs and benefits (Whiteley and Seyd, 1994). This formulation was anticipated in Riker and Ordeshook's addition of a 'civic duty' term to their $U_i = pB - C$ equation for electoral participation, thereby converting it into $U_i = pB - C + D$. A variety of possible terms could be added to the core formulation in a model of protest. Given that the notion of civic duty has little relevance to participation in protest activity, three further terms stand out as being of obvious importance. The first refers to the possibility that people may participate in protests not to obtain benefits for people like themselves but for other groups that they care about. In order to take account of this possibility we add a term for Group Benefits to the 'core' Rational Actor equation. Our second additional term concerns people's Risk Orientations. There is always a possibility that any given protest might transmute into an activity that many of the original participants did not intend. Accordingly, we hypothesize that individuals who are generally highly acceptant of risks will be more likely to join protests and demonstrations than those who are generally risk averse. Finally, we add a term for Expressive Benefits. We associate these benefits with the expression of the individual's *dissatisfaction* with the operation of the democratic process and with life in general. We hypothesize that the more intense these dissatisfactions are, the more they will act as a stimulus for the individual to express them in the form of protest activity.

Data and Model Specifications

In this section we describe the specific measures that we employ to test each of the theoretical models outlined above. In outlining these measures, we also provide an illustration of how key variables in the models changed, on a monthly basis, during the July 2000–December 2002 period. Figure 1 outlines the distribution of our dependent variable – the propensity to engage in protest activity – averaged across the 30-month period analysed. Respondents were asked to indicate, on a 0–10 scale, how likely it was that they would participate in a protest or demonstration over the next few years.[1] We use this measure of *protest potential* rather than respondents' recall of their actual protest activity because the percentage of people who have recently protested is so small that it produces a highly skewed distribution (Marsh, 1977; Barnes and Kaase, 1979). Measures of actual protest behaviour also fail to distinguish between people who are very likely to participate in protest – but who, for whatever reason, do not – and those for whom protesting is only the remotest possibility. The distribution of 'protest potential' responses shown in Figure 1 is similar to that reported in Marsh (1977) and Moyser, Parry and Day (1984). A large plurality of respondents (38 per cent) indicates that there is no chance of their protesting; a large majority (68 per cent) respond with a

FIGURE 1
PROBABILITY OF PARTICIPATING IN A PROTEST

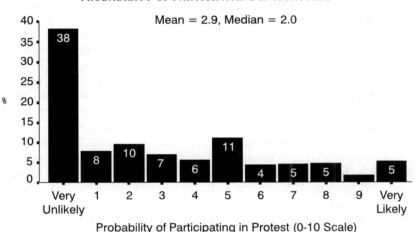

Probability of Participating in Protest (0-10 Scale)

probability under 0.5; and only 20 per cent indicate that there is a greater than 0.5 chance.

Figure 2 indicates how the *average* propensity to engage in protest activity *varied* between July 2000 and December 2002. The trend line shown is fitted using a Loess regression model. This model understates the extent to which the September 2000 fuel protests affected the behavioural dispositions of the British electorate. The average probability of protesting, as measured on the 0–10 scale, increased from 2.8 in August to 3.3 in September, and then declined progressively until the period just after the general election in June 2001. The figure rose gradually after the election period, averaging 3.1 in the last quarter of 2002. These broad trends suggest two important conclusions. First, waves of protest like the fuel protests may themselves lead people to adjust their perceptions of their own likely behaviour. In September 2000, the fuel protesters appear to have provided a sort of role model that other members of the public felt they might reasonably imitate. Although this 'contagion' effect appeared to decay fairly rapidly, the very occurrence of well-publicized protests by a relatively small minority of citizens appeared to render the majority of the public more prepared to engage in such activity. Second, the period around the general election itself is associated with relatively low levels of protest potential. This implies that one consequence of general elections might be to lower the level of protest potential, as more citizens focus their attention on the electoral process. In any event, the apparent effects of the fuel protests and of the general election shown in Figure 2

FIGURE 2
TREND IN LIKELIHOOD OF PARTICIPATING IN A PROTEST, JULY 2000 –
DECEMBER 2002

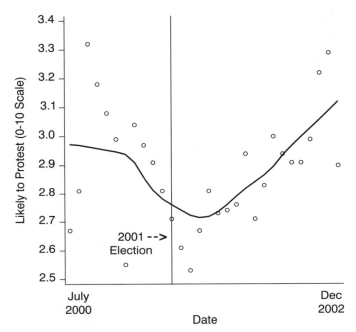

suggest that appropriate controls need to be incorporated into the relevant models that we estimate below.

We have analysed the aggregate-level dynamics of public attitudes towards protest in a separate article, where we show that protest potential tends to fall in economic good times and to rise when economic conditions are less favourable (Sanders et al., 2003). In this article we use individual-level data to test each of the six theoretical models outlined above.

Table A1 (see Appendix) summarizes the individual-level indicators that we employ to test the Relative Deprivation model outlined above. We measure the individual's Sense of Inequity by two indicators. The first is the extent to which people consider there is a gap between what they deserve to get out of life and what they actually get. The second is the extent to which they believe that the government treats people like them unfairly. We measure Economic Deprivation in terms of people's evaluations of their retrospective and prospective personal economic circumstances and in terms of their emotional reactions to those circumstances (Conover and Feldman, 1986; Frank, 1988). We assume that both negative evaluations and negative emotional reactions connote higher levels of economic deprivation.[2] Finally, we measure (dis)satisfaction with life in general by the individual's response to a general question about how satisfied they are with their 'life as a whole'. The responses yield a 4-point scale where 4 connotes a high level of satisfaction and 1 a high level of dissatisfaction. Our formal specification for the Relative Deprivation model is:

$$\begin{aligned} \text{Probability of Protest} = \beta_0 &+ \beta_1 \text{ Expectations / Outcome Gap} \\ &+ \beta_2 \text{ Government Unfair} + \beta_3 \text{ Economic Evaluations} \\ &+ \beta_4 \text{Economic Emotions} + \beta_5 \text{ Life (Dis)satisfaction} \quad (1) \\ &+ \beta_6 \text{ Age} + \beta_7 \text{ September 2000} \\ &+ \beta_8 \text{ October 2000} + \varepsilon_i \end{aligned}$$

where β_1 and β_2 measure Inequity effects; β_3 and β_4 measure Economic Deprivation effects; β_5 measures the effects of Life (Dis)satisfaction; age is the respondent's age, included in all our models for control purposes; β_7 and β_8 measure the effects of the autumn 2000 fuel crisis, again included all of our models for control purposes;[3] and ε_i is a random error term.

Table A2 (see Appendix) outlines our operational measures of the Cognitive Engagement model. We measure Interest in Politics in terms of an 11-point 'attention to politics' scale; Education as a 6-point scale which reflects the age at which the respondent completed full-time education; and Evaluation of Government Record in terms of the respondent's assessment of whether or not the government is doing a good job managing the economy. Our formal specification of the Cognitive Engagement model is

$$\begin{aligned} \text{Probability of Protest} = \beta_0 &+ \beta_1 \text{ Attention to Politics} + \beta_2 \text{ Level of Education} \\ &+ \beta_3 \text{ Evaluation of Government's Economic Record} \\ &+ \beta_4 \text{ Age} + \beta_5 \text{ September 2000} \quad (2) \\ &+ \beta_6 \text{ October 2000} + \varepsilon_i \end{aligned}$$

where β_4, β_5, β_6 and ε_i are defined as in (1).

Table A3 (see Appendix) lists the measures we employ to operationalize the Civic Voluntarism model. We use three indicators of Psychological Engagement: personal political efficacy, attention to politics (as in the Cognitive Engagement model), and strength of partisanship. Resources are operationalized in terms of education, income band and social class. Mobilization is measured in two ways: by whether or not the respondent has recently been asked to participate in politics and community affairs; and by whether or not they have volunteered to participate in such activity. We accordingly specify our individual-level model of protest potential as:

$$
\begin{aligned}
\text{Probability of Protest} = {} & \beta_0 + \beta_1 \text{ Political Efficacy} + \beta_2 \text{ Attention to Politics} \\
& + \beta_3 \text{ Strength of Partisanship} + \beta_4 \text{ Education} + \beta_5 \text{ Income Band} \\
& + \beta_6 \text{ Social Class} + \beta_7 \text{ Asked to Participate} \\
& + \beta_8 \text{ Volunteered to Participate} + \beta_9 \text{ Age} + \beta_{10} \text{ September 2000} \\
& + \beta_{11} \text{ October 2000} + \varepsilon_i
\end{aligned}
\tag{3}
$$

where β_1, β_2 and β_3 measure Engagement effects; β_4, β_5 and β_6 measure Resource effects; β_7 and β_8 measure Mobilization effects; and other terms are as defined in (1).

Our operational measures of Social Capital are shown in Table A4 (see Appendix). Note that the two 'mobilization' indicators employed in the Civic Voluntarism (being asked to participate and volunteering) are also used in the Social Capital model. In the latter context, however, 'being asked' and 'volunteering' are interpreted as representing the extent of the individual's involvement in local political and social networks. The second aspect of Social Capital is measured by the extent to which the individual believes people can generally be trusted. All three of these measures are expected to exert positive effects on people's chances of engaging in protest. Our formal Social Capital model specification is:

$$
\begin{aligned}
\text{Probability of Protest} = {} & \beta_0 + \beta_1 \text{ Asked to Participate} + \beta_2 \text{ Volunteered} \\
& + \beta_3 \text{ Social Trust} \\
& + \beta_4 \text{ Age} + \beta_5 \text{ September 2000} \\
& + \beta_6 \text{ October 2000} + \varepsilon_i
\end{aligned}
\tag{4}
$$

where β_1 and β_2 measure Social Network effects; β_3 measures the effect of trust; and other terms are defined as in (1).

Table A5 (see Appendix) summarizes the indicators that we use in the 'core' Rational Actor model and in the more extended Rational Actor or General Incentives model. Our specification of the core model views the probability of an individual engaging in protest as:

$$
\begin{aligned}
\text{Probability of Protest} = {} & \beta_0 + \beta_1 \text{ pB} - \beta_2 \text{ Costs} \\
& + \beta_3 \text{ Age} + \beta_4 \text{ September 2000} \\
& + \beta_5 \text{ October 2000} + \varepsilon_i
\end{aligned}
\tag{5}
$$

where 'pB' represents the Personal Benefits accruing from participation discounted by the individual's sense of Political Efficacy; Costs measures the time and effort involved in participating; and other terms are as defined in (1). The General Incentives model adds further terms to (5) for Group Benefits, Risk Orientations and Expressive Benefits as follows:

$$\text{Probability of Protest} = \beta_0 + \beta_1 \, pB - \beta_2 \, \text{Costs}$$
$$+ \beta_3 \, \text{Group Benefits} + \beta_4 \, \text{Risk Orientations}$$
$$+ \beta_5 \, \text{Democracy Dissatisfaction} + \beta_6 \, \text{Life Dissatisfaction (6)}$$
$$+ \beta_7 \, \text{Age} + \beta_8 \, \text{September 2000}$$
$$+ \beta_9 \, \text{October 2000} + \varepsilon_i$$

where β_3 and β_4 are self-explanatory; β_5 and β_6 denote the effects of Expressive Benefits; and other terms are defined as in (5).

Empirical Results

In this section, we report the results of estimating equations (1)–(6) using individual-level pooled cross-section for the period, July 2000–December 2002.[4] Table 1, Column 1 reports the results of estimating (1), our equation for the Relative Deprivation (RD) model. The results of this model are mixed. On the positive side, in line with theoretical expectations, both negative economic emotions and the perception that the government treats 'people like me' unfairly exert positive and significant effects on the probability of protesting. Similarly, Life Satisfaction has a significant negative effect. The control variables – age and the dummy variable terms for September and October 2000 – are all significant and 'correctly' signed. Older people were less likely to protest; and the probability of protesting across all respondents was disproportionately high in September and October 2000, at the time of the successful fuel protests. However, the R^2 value for the model is weak (.02) and two of the terms – the Expectations/Outcome Gap and Personal Economic Evaluations – are both non-significant. Overall, although the Relative Deprivation model produces some significant effects, it clearly fails to offer a convincing explanation of protest potential in contemporary Britain.

Table 1, Column 2 examines the extent of the empirical support for the Cognitive Engagement model. The results are an improvement on the RD model. All the coefficients are significant and correctly signed (Interest and Education both increase the chances of protest; approval of the government's record reduces it) and the R^2 (.09) is noticeably higher than in Column 1. The pattern of coefficients on the control variables reproduces

TABLE 1
ESTIMATED RELATIVE DEPRIVATION, COGNITIVE ENGAGEMENT AND CIVIC
VOLUNTARISM MODELS OF PROTEST, 2000–02

	Column 1 Relative Deprivation Model	Column 2 Cognitive Engagement Model	Column 3 Civic Voluntarism Model
Expectations/Outcome gap	−.05 (.05)		
Government is unfair	.15* (.05)		
Personal economic evaluations	.02 (.02)		
Negative economic emotions	.32** (.06)		
Life satisfaction	−.15** (.03)		
Government record		−.30** (.04)	
Attention to politics		.32** (.05)	.22** (.01)
Personal efficacy			.17** (.01)
Partisanship strength			.08** (.02)
Asked to participate			.73** (.07)
Volunteered to participate			1.14**(.07)
Level of education		.09** (.02)	.09** (.02)
Income level			−.12** (.02)
Social class			−.14** (.02)
Age	−.02** (.00)	−.03** (.00)	−.03** (.02)
September 2000	.39** (.10)	.38** (.10)	.32** (.10)
October 2000	.32** (.10)	.33** (.10)	.28* (.10)
Constant	4.08** (.18)	2.31** (.07)	2.66**(.16)
Corrected R^2	.02	.09	.15
N	16686	16248	16367

Notes: OLS estimates, standard errors in parenthesis; *significant at .01; **significant at .001.
Dependent variable is Probability of Participating in a Protest.
Source: Democracy and Participation Project monthly surveys, July 2000 – December 2002.

that observed in Column 1 (as indeed it does in all of our estimated models in Tables 1 to 3), reinforcing our confidence in the importance of including these controls.

The Civic Voluntarism model is tested in Column 3. The evidence is again broadly supportive. Most of the coefficients are all significant and correctly signed. All three measures of Psychological Engagement (Efficacy, Interest and Strength of Partisanship) exert positive effects on protest, as do the two Mobilization measures (Asked and Volunteered to Participate). The Resource measures, however, produce rather more ambiguous results. As predicted,

TABLE 2
ESTIMATED SOCIAL TRUST, CORE RATIONAL ACTOR AND GENERAL INCENTIVES
MODELS OF PROTEST, 2000–02

	Column 1 Social Trust Model	Column 2 Core Rational Actor Model	Column 3 General Incentive Model
Asked to participate	.95** (.06)		
Volunteered to participate	1.44** (.07)		
Social trust	.00 (.01)		
Efficacy* Individual benefits		.26** (.01)	.25** (.01)
Costs		−.83** (.05)	−.75** (.05)
Group benefits			.56** (.06)
Positive risk orientation			.50** (.03)
Democracy satisfaction			−.41** (.03)
Life satisfaction			−.16** (.03)
Age	−.02** (.00)	−.02** (.00)	−.02** (.02)
September 2000	.42** (.10)	.38** (.10)	.34** (.10)
October 2000	.30** (.10)	.29** (.10)	.27* (.10)
Constant	3.38** (.09)	4.08** (.07)	3.63**(.16)
Corrected R2	.09	.07	.10
N	17892	18056	16905

Notes: OLS estimates, standard errors in parenthesis; *significant at .01; **significant at .001.
Dependent variable is Probability of Participating in a Protest.
Source: Democracy and Participation Project monthly surveys, July 2000–December 2002.

Education exerts a positive effect, but both income and class – contrary to the
Civic Voluntarism model's claims – have negative effects. In the British
context, it appears that income and class position are not necessarily the sort
of 'resource' for non-electoral participation that they are in the United States.
Rather, richer and more middle-class people seem to prefer to leave the
protesting – if they wish to do it at all – to others. In the Civic Voluntarism
model's favour is its relatively high R^2 in comparison with Columns 1 and 2.
However, even this figure (R^2=.15) indicates that a large proportion of the
variance in protest potential remains unexplained.

Table 2 Column 1 reports the results of testing the Social Capital Model. In
line with the findings about 'mobilization' in Table 1, the two terms for Social
Networks (being asked or volunteering to participate) are significant and
correctly signed. However, the term for Social Trust is clearly non-significant,
suggesting that this dimension of social capital is not important in explaining
the British public's propensity to protest.

Columns 2 and 3 of Table 2 respectively report the 'core' Rational Actor and the more extended General Incentives models. As predicted, in both tables the pB (Efficacy*Personal Benefits) term is positive and significant, while the Costs term is significant and negative. These results suggest that there is an important element of individual rational calculation in people's dispositions to engage in protest. The other results in Column 3 of Table 2, however, show that this 'core' rationality is supplemented by other, soft-rational incentives. Again as predicted, both the belief that political action can benefit groups the respondent cares about and a broad willingness to take risks makes people more likely to engage in protest. Similarly, satisfaction with democracy and with life in general both exert a reductive effect on the propensity to protest. The R^2 value in the General Incentives model (.10) is higher than in the Cognitive Engagement equation, but not as high as in the Civic Voluntarism model.

How can we make sense of these various findings? Each model appears to derive some support from the data, but some yield incorrectly signed coefficients, some produce non-significant coefficients, and none has a particularly impressive R^2 value.[5] Although we do not report the results here, we conducted a series of 'encompassing tests' to determine whether or not any one of the six models was encompassed any of the others (see Charemza and Deadman, 1997: 250). Two results of the exercise are worth reporting. First – and unsurprisingly – the Civic Voluntarism model encompasses the Social Capital model. This is unsurprising because two of the variables in the Civic Voluntarism (the indicators of Mobilization) also appear as indicators of Social Networks in the Social Capital model – whilst the only remaining variable in the Social Capital model (Trust) is non-significant. This suggests to us that 'being asked to participate' and 'volunteering' are probably best regarded as measures of 'mobilization' rather than as measures of 'social networks'. It is likely that our operationalization of Social Capital was probably inadequate in the first place, and that alternative indicators need to be found if the model is to be properly tested in the future.

The second result of our encompassing tests is more important. With the exception of the Social Capital model being encompassed by Civic Voluntarism, none of the remaining models was encompassed by any of the others. The simple implication is that, Social Capital apart, each model has a distinctive role to play in explaining protest in Britain. Although each model makes a distinct set of theoretical claims, they are not intrinsically inconsistent with one another. For example, merely because there is a rational actor component to the calculus of protest participation, it does not follow that there cannot also be a component that reflects either cognitive engagement or relative deprivation. People are complicated and the calculus that underpins their actions is a complex mix of rationality, emotion and circumstance. The quintessentially hybrid Civic Voluntarism model already recognizes this, in combining considerations of Engagement, Mobilization and Resources.

In our final model, therefore, we combine the different components of all six of our models in order to construct a 'best' model. This model was initially specified to include the independent variables from equations (1)–(6). Following the principles of Hendry's (1995) general-to-specific econometric methodology, we then re-estimated the model including only those variables that achieved statistical significance at the first stage. The results are reported in Table 3. The pattern of coefficient signs and significance levels is identical to that reported in the earlier 'distinct' models reported in Tables 1 and 2. The table suggests three broad conclusions. First, protest potential in Britain is affected by a wide range of independent factors. These include relative

TABLE 3
ESTIMATED COMPOSITE 'BEST' MODEL OF PROTEST, 2000–02

Government is unfair	.18** (.06)
Negative econ emotions	.25** (.06)
Life satisfaction	−.12** (.04)
Government record	−.12** (.06)
Personal efficacy	.13** (.01)
Attention to politics	.19** (.01)
Partisanship strength	.11** (.03)
Asked to participate	.67** (.07)
Volunteered	.99** (.07)
Level of education	.09** (.02)
Efficacy*Indiv benefits	.09** (.02)
Costs	−.35** (.05)
Group benefits	.38** (.07)
Positive risk orientation	.37** (.03)
Democracy satisfaction	−.35** (.04)
Age	−.02** (.00)
Income level	−.09** (.02)
Social class	−.13** (.03)
September 2000	.25** (.10)
October 2000	.24** (.10)
Constant	2.61** (.22)
Corrected R^2	.19
N	13123

Notes: OLS estimates, standard errors in parenthesis; *significant at .01; **significant at .001. Dependent variable is Probability of Participating in a Protest.

Source: Democracy and Participation Project monthly surveys, July 2000– December 2002.

deprivation (government is unfair, negative economic emotions and dissatisfaction with life in general); psychological engagement (efficacy, interest and
partisanship); mobilization (being asked and volunteering); resources (education); narrow rational cost-benefit calculation (pB – Costs); soft-rational
calculation (perceptions of group benefits, risk orientations and dissatisfaction
with democracy); demographic position (age, income, class); and 'events' (the
autumn 2000 fuel crisis). Second, the importance of most of these various
factors has been acknowledged in previous research – which is why they were
included in the various models that we tested in the first place. Two important
and novel features of our best model, however, merit emphasis. The model
shows, for the first time in the UK context, that people's risk-orientations
represent one of the most powerful influences on their propensities to protest.
It also shows that events – especially successful events like the September
2000 fuel protests – can stimulate others, albeit temporarily, seriously to
consider to participating in protest. Finally, the R^2 value reported in the table
indicates that just under 20 per cent of the variance in protest potential can be
explained by the independent variables in the model. Although this figure is
not high in absolute terms, it represents an improvement on all of our original
models.

Our final set of findings is reported in Table 4. The table does not report the
full results of the estimated models. Rather, it shows what happens if we add a
series of further 'timing' variables to our Table 3 'best' model. Consider, first,
the 'Extend fuel crisis' column of Table 4. This shows that if we add dummy
variable terms for November and December 2000 to the best model, the
results are non-significant – which supports the notion that the effects of the
September fuel crisis had dissipated almost entirely by November. Our second
timing experiment concerns the possible impact of the June 2001 general election. It will be recalled from our discussion of Figure 2 that the average level
of protest potential fell before the election and rose thereafter. We explore the
possible implications of this potential 'election effect' in two ways. First, we
create a dummy variable ('Post-Election Period') that takes the value 0 if a
respondent was interviewed before the election and the value 1 thereafter.
Second, we create a further dummy ('February–October 2001') that represents the period of the run-up to and the immediate aftermath of the 2001 election. If the anticipation and/or occurrence of the election were exerting some
sort of independent effect on protest potential, then we would expect that
either or both of these terms would yield significant coefficients when they are
added to the Table 3 model. However, as the two right-hand columns of Table
4 indicate, this is clearly not the case: both variables are clearly non-significant. It is, of course, possible that the election played a role in determining the
values of some of the independent variables in our 'best' model – though this
is not an issue that we are able to explore here. Nonetheless, the results of

TABLE 4
CONSEQUENCE OF ADDING ADDITIONAL 'TIME' CONTROLS TO THE BEST
MODEL

	Best model	Extend fuel crisis	Add post election	Add before/ after election
September 2000	.25** (.02)	.23* (.10)	.21* (.11)	.22* (.11)
October 2000	.24* (.02)	.23* (.11)	.23* (.11)	.24* (.11)
November 2000		.23 (.15)		
December 2000		.00 (.16)		
Post-election period			−.00 (.05)	
Feb–Oct 2002				−.00 (.06)
Corrected R^2	.19	.19	.19	.19
N	13132	12590	12590	12590

Notes: OLS estimates, standard errors in parenthesis; *significant at .01; **significant at .001.
Dependent variable is Probability of Participating in a Protest.
Source: Democracy and Participation Project monthly surveys, July 2000–December 2002.

Table 4 show that the election itself did not exert an independent effect, over and above those specified in our best model, on the preparedness of the British public to engage in protest activity.

Summary and Conclusions

Relatively few people actually engage in protest during any given time period. But lots of people seriously consider doing it. The core of our research design here has involved using representative sample survey data to measure people's own estimates of the chances that they will protest. In this context, we have made two important sets of empirical observations. First, the propensities of British citizens to engage in protest vary quite considerably over time. It is also possible that they vary *systematically* over time – though this is a matter for our subsequent research. Second, we have shown that people's preparedness to participate in protest is not the result of random circumstance. Our models show that we can understand many of the factors that lead some people to protest while others do not. To be sure, no single theoretical perspective can provide a complete, or perhaps even a satisfactory explanation of protest potential. Even in combination, the various models struggle to explain 20 per cent of the variance in protest activity. This said, our results suggest that three 'old' factors, and two 'new' ones, exert consistent and powerful influences on people's preparedness to protest. The 'old' – the frequently researched – factors are rational calculation, relative deprivation and mobilization. These factors have featured in many previous analyses, though not always in the complimentary, non-encompassing, fashion that we have shown here. The 'new' factors are people's 'risk orientations' and the timing effects of 'events'. The pronounced timing effect that we observed – the imitative, 'contagion' effect on popular protest-intentions of the 2001 fuel protests – decayed quite rapidly. Nonetheless, it is clear that such effects do exist. If a series of relatively 'successful' protests were – for whatever reason – to occur, the cumulative effects on popular consciousness could be quite considerable. In this sense, the potential for greater protest activity in Britain in the future is non-trivial.

APPENDIX

TABLE A1
INDICATORS OF RELATIVE DEPRIVATION

(a) *Sense of Inequity/unfairness*
1. Agreement with: 'There is often a big gap between what people like me expect out of life and what we actually get' (dummy).
2. Agreement with: 'The Government generally treats people like me fairly' (dummy).

(b) *Sense of Economic Deprivation*
1. Score on 1-5 scale: How does the financial situation of your household now compare with what it was 12 months ago? (lot better = 5; little better = 4; no change = 3; little worse = 2; lot worse = 1)
2. Score on 1-5 scale: How do you think the financial situation of your household will change over the next 12 months? (lot better = 5; little better = 4; no change = 3; little worse = 2; lot worse = 1)
3. Number (0–4) of negative responses ('angry', 'disgusted', 'uneasy' or 'afraid') when asked to describe her/his 'feelings about the financial position of [her/his] household'.

(c) *Dissatisfaction with life in general*
Score on 1-4 scale: 'Thinking about your life as a whole, are you…very satisfied (4), fairly satisfied (3), fairly dissatisfied (2), or very dissatisfied (1)?'

TABLE A2
INDICATORS OF COGNITIVE ENGAGEMENT

(a) *Interest in Politics*
    Score on 0-10 Attention to Politics scale: 'On a scale from 0 to 10… how much attention do you pay to politics and public affairs?'

(b) *Level of Education*
    Score on 1-6 scale: 'At what age did you complete your fulltime education?' (14 or under = low, 15, 16, 18, 19 or 20, 21 or over = high).

(c) *Evaluation of Government Record*
    Agrees that 'The government is doing a good job managing the economy' (dummy).

TABLE A3
INDICATORS OF CIVIC VOLUNTARISM

(a) *Psychological Engagement with the political system*
1. Personal Political Efficacy: Score on 0-10 Personal Influence scale – 'On a scale from 0 to 10... how much influence do you have on politics and public affairs?'
2. Interest in Politics: Score on 0-10 Attention to Politics scale – 'On a scale from 0 to 10... how much attention do you pay to politics and public affairs?'
3. Strength of partisanship: Score on 4-point scale (none=1, not very strong=2, fairly strong=3, very strong=4); partisanship assessed using traditional BES battery.

(b) *Mobilization*
1. Asked to participate: Over the past few years, has anyone asked you to get involved in politics or community affairs? (Yes=1; No=0)
2. Volunteered to participate: Over the past few years, have you volunteered to get involved in politics or community affairs? (Yes=1; No=0)

(c) *Resources*
1. Level of Education (as in Cognitive Engagement model)
2. Income band: 7-point scale (Under £5k=1; £5-10k; 10-15k; £15-25k; £25-35k; £35-50k; Over £50k = 7).
3. Class: 4-point scale (DE=1, C2=2, C1=3, AB=4).

TABLE A4
INDICATORS OF SOCIAL CAPITAL

(a) *Extent of the individual's involvement in informal social (and political) networks*
1. Asked to participate: Over the past few years, has anyone asked you to get involved in politics or community affairs? (Yes=1; No=0)
2. Volunteered to participate: Over the past few years, have you volunteered to get involved in politics or community affairs? (Yes=1; No=0)

(b) *Level of Social Trust*
Generally speaking would you say that most people can be trusted, or that you can't be too careful dealing with people? Please use the 0 – 10 scale to indicate your view, where 0 means can't be too careful and 10 means most people can be trusted.

TABLE A5
INDICATORS OF THE RATIONAL ACTOR AND GENERAL INCENTIVES MODELS

(a) *Core Rational Actor model, pB - C*
1. Personal Political Efficacy (0-10 scale as in Civic Voluntarism model) multiplied by
    Personal Benefits (1-3 scale where 1 denotes disagreement with 'Being active in politics is a
    good way to get benefits for me and my family'; 2 denotes neither agree nor disagree; 3
    denotes agreement).
2. Costs: Score on 1-3 scale where 1 denotes disagreement with 'It takes too much time and
    effort to be active in politics and public affairs'; 2 denotes neither agree nor disagree; 3
    denotes agreement.

(b) *Group Benefits*
    Score on 1-3 scale where 1 denotes disagreement with 'Being active in politics is a good way
    to get benefits for groups that people care about like pensioners or the disabled'; 2 denotes
    neither agree nor disagree; 3 denotes agreement.

(c) *Risk Orientation*
    Score on 1-4 scale: Generally speaking, how willing are you to take risks? (1 denotes very
    unwilling; 2 somewhat unwilling; 3 somewhat willing; 4 very willing).

(d) *Expressive Benefits*
1. Dissatisfaction with Democracy. Score on 1-4 scale: 'On the whole, are you very satisfied
    (=4), fairly satisfied (=3), fairly dissatisfied (=2), or very dissatisfied (=1)?'
2. Dissatisfaction with Life in general. Score on 1-4 scale: 'Thinking about your life as a whole,
    are you...very satisfied (=4), fairly satisfied (=3), fairly dissatisfied (=2), or very dissatisfied
    (=1)?'

ACKNOWLEDGEMENTS

This article is based on a paper presented at the Political Studies Association Annual Conference,
University of Leicester, 15–17 April 2003. The authors are grateful to the editors for their helpful
comments on the earlier draft. The research was supported by a grant from ESRC's Democracy
and Participation Programme.

NOTES

1. 'Thinking about the next few years, on scale from 0 to 10, how likely is it that you
    will...participate in a protest, like a rally or a demonstration, to show your concern about a
    public issue or problem?'
2. To simplify the presentation, we combine our measures of retrospective and prospective
    personal assessments into a single index of 'Economic Evaluations'. When we estimate indi-
    vidual-level Economic Evaluations effects in Part 3, we combine two 5-point scales (one
    retrospective, one prospective) where a high score denotes things have got/will get a lot better
    and a low score denotes things have got/will get a lot worse. With regard to Emotional Reac-
    tions to the economy, in presenting the aggregate data, we follow an analogous practice to
    that employed with Economic Evaluations and report the average monthly balance of Posi-
    tive minus Negative Emotional Reactions. When we estimate the individual-level effects, we
    simply count the number of Negative Emotional Reaction words that the individual cites as
    describing the condition of their household's financial position, yielding a 0–4 scale.

3. We include terms only for September and October because preliminary analysis – as well as
    the graphical results presented in Figure 2 – indicated that the fuel crisis effect on protest
    potential had disappeared by November 2000. Including terms for months after October 2000
    yield non-significant effects in all of the models specified here.
4. There were some months (for example, in June 2001) when our RDD survey was not
    conducted. In the later months of the project (after February 2002) financial constraints
    obliged us to reduce the monthly sample size from 1000 to 500. Nonetheless, the dataset is a
    large one, containing over 20,000 cases over a 30-month period.
5. The relatively modest R^2 scores reported in all of our models should not be interpreted as
    indicating that those models are without value. The fact that the models provide statistically
    significant and robust parameter estimates is far more important than the overall level of
    'variance explained'. The low R^2 values simply reflect the fact that it is extraordinarily diffi-
    cult to predict the protest potential of an individual voter. The magnitudes of the significant
    coefficients, however, indicate the extent to which the protest potential of the average voter
    changes in response to changes in the independent variables in the model.

REFERENCES

Barnes, Samuel and Max Kaase (1979) *Political Action: Mass Participation in Five Western
    Democracies.* Beverly Hills: Sage.
Becker, G.S. (1975) *Human Capital: A Theoretical and Empirical Analysis.* New York: National
    Bureau of Economic Research.
Charemza, Wojciech W. and Derek F. Deadman (1997). *New Directions in Econometric
    Practice,* 2nd Edn. Aldershot: Edward Elgar.
Coleman, J.S. (1988) 'Social Capital in the Creation of Human Capital', *American Journal of
    Sociology* 94: 95–120.
Conover, P.J. and S. Feldman (1986) 'Emotional Reactions to the Economy: I'm Mad as Hell and
    I'm Not Going to Take It Anymore.' *American Journal of Political Science.* 30: 50–78.
Dalton, R. J. (1996) *Citizen Politics in Western Democracies,* 2nd Edn. Chatham: Chatham
    House.
Downs, A. (1957) *An Economic Theory of Democracy.* New York: Harper & Row.
Frank, R.H. (1988) *Passion within Reason: The Strategic Role of the Emotions.* New York: W.W.
    Norton.
Gurr, T.R. (1970) *Why Men Rebel.* Princeton: Princeton University Press.
Hendry, David F. (1995) *Dynamic Econometrics.* Oxford: Oxford University Press.
Hochschild. J.L. (1981) *What's Fair? American Beliefs about Distributive Justice.* Cambridge:
    Harvard University Press.
Huckfeldt, R. and J. Sprague (1995) *Citizens, Politics and Social Communication.* Cambridge:
    Cambridge University Press.
Jackman, R.W. and R.A. Miller (1998) 'Social Capital and Politics', in N.W. Polsby (ed.),
    American Review of Political Science, vol. 1. Palo Alto: Annual Reviews.
Marsh, A. (1977) *Protest and Political Consciousness.* London: Sage.
Muller, E.N. (1979) *Aggressive Political Participation.* Princeton: Princeton University Press.
Mutz, D.C. (1998) *Impersonal Influence: How Perceptions of Mass Collectives Affect Political
    Attitudes.* New York: Cambridge University Press.
Nie, N.H., J. Junn and K. Stehlik-Barry (1996) *Education and Democratic Citizenship in
    America.* Chicago: University of Chicago Press.
Olson, M. (1965) *The Logic of Collective Action.* New York: Schocken Books.
Parry, Geraint, George Moyser and Neil Day (1992) *Political Participation and Democracy in
    Britain.* Cambridge: Cambridge University Press.
Putnam, Robert D. (1993) *Making Democracy Work: Civic Traditions in Modern Italy.* Princeton:
    Princeton University Press.
Putnam, Robert D. (2000) *Bowling Alone: The Collapse and Revival of American Community.*
    New York: Simon & Schuster.

Sanders, D. (1991) 'Government Popularity and the Next General Election', *Political Quarterly* 62: 235–61.

Sanders, D. (1996) 'Economic Performance, Management Competence and the Outcome of the Next General Election', *Political Studies,* 44: 203–31.

Sanders, D. (1999) 'Conservative Incompetence, Labour Responsibility and the Feel Good Factor: Why The Economy Failed to Save the Conservatives in 1997', *Electoral Studies* 18: 251–70.

Sanders, D., H. Clarke, M. Stewart and P. Whiteley (2003) 'The Dynamics of Protest in Britain, 2000–2002'. *Parliamentary Affairs,* 56: 687–99.

Verba, S., K.L. Schlozman and H.E. Brady (1995) *Voice and Equality: Civic Voluntarism in American Politics.* Cambridge: Harvard University Press.

Whiteley, P.F. et al. (1994) 'Explaining Party Activism: The Case of the British Conservative Party', *British Journal of Political Science* 24: 79–94.

DEVOLUTION

Opinion Polling in Scotland: An Analysis of the 2003 Scottish Parliament Election

Nicola McEwen

Opinion polls measure the attitudes, beliefs and preferences of a given population. In the context of an election, snapshots of the voting intentions of relatively small samples of the population are taken, within accepted margins of error, as reliable representations of the likely voting behaviour of the electorate as a whole.

There is some evidence to suggest that, in addition to representing voting preferences, the results of published opinion polls may also shape these preferences. It is notoriously difficult, however, to isolate the impact of opinion polls from other factors influencing the vote, and the available evidence is conflicting. Some studies point to a 'bandwagon effect' in which voters drift towards the party leading in the polls to conform to the majority view, while others suggest an 'underdog effect' where the losing party or parties gain voters' sympathy (Marsh, 1984; Whiteley, 1986; McAllister and Studlar, 1991).

Although the direct effect of polls on voting behaviour is inconclusive, there may be less doubt about the polls' influence on the behaviour of political elites and parties. In British general elections, prime ministers are said to pay close heed to the polls in determining when to call an election (Hodder-Williams, 1970: 83–4; Butler and Kavanagh, 1992: 135) – an option not open to Scotland's First Minister, who must operate within the constraints of a fixed four-year term. Opinion polls can also enthuse or demoralize party activists, and inform the development of the strategies of parties contesting the election (Denver, 2003a: 147–8). For example, in the 1999 Scottish Parliament election, when a mid-campaign poll suggested the Scottish National Party was trailing Labour by some 19 per cent in the constituency vote and 13 per cent in the regional list vote, the Scottish Nationalist Party (SNP) all but abandoned its election strategy, cancelled its daily press conferences and launched its own daily 'newspaper' in a bid to bypass negative press coverage (Jones, 1999: 6; McCrone, 1999: 32).

The potential influence of opinion polls on the conduct, reporting and possibly the outcome of election campaigns underlines the need for polls to be of the highest standard, and to be an accurate representation of public opinion

British Elections & Parties Review, Vol. 14, 2004, pp. 171–190
ISSN 1368-9886 print
DOI: 10.1080/1368988042000258826   © 2004 Taylor & Francis Ltd.

as it stands when the poll snapshot is taken. Strictly speaking, opinion polls are not intended to predict election outcomes. They can only ever identify opinion on the day or days on which the poll is conducted (Broughton, 1995: 85–9). However, the degree to which the final polls accurately foretell the election result can provide insight into the extent to which they offer a true representation of the population's political preferences. Such assessments of polling accuracy thus inform perceptions of the credibility of the individual polls, of polling in general, and of the wider market research industry. Indeed, assessing the credibility of the polls in this way is often encouraged by the reactions of polling companies and their clients who seek to take credit when they 'get it right'.

While the long record of British electoral polls is generally positive, it has been marred by two significant failures. The first was in the 1970 general election, when four of the five organizations conducting campaign polls wrongly predicted a Labour victory. Only Opinion Research Centre (ORC) correctly forecast a Conservative victory, adjusting its final poll to take into account a late swing towards the Conservatives and an increased likelihood of Conservative voters to turn out on election day (Hodder-Williams, 1970: ix–xx; Teer and Spence, 1973: 182–98). The second, more notorious, occasion was the 1992 general election. The four final polls suggested Labour and the Conservatives were level in terms of their percentage share of the vote, generating predictions that the election would result in a hung parliament and a likely coalition government. In the event, the Conservatives won comfortably with a 7.6 per cent lead over Labour. According to one observer, it was the 'worst disaster' in the 50-year history of the polling industry (Crewe, 1997: 61).

Following the failures in 1970 and, especially, in 1992, opinion polls in British elections have been subject to intense scrutiny within and outwith the industry (Market Research Society, 1994; Jowell et al., 1993; Broughton, 1995: 85–99; Moon, 1999: 106–33). In response, polling companies have sought to refine sampling and weighting techniques, in particular, to address the apparent unwillingness of Conservative voters to participate in opinion polls or to disclose their voting intentions. The 1997 and 2001 general elections avoided repeating the debacle of 1992, but the verdict on their success was mixed (Curtice, 1997; Curtice and Sparrow, 1997; Crewe, 1997, 2001; Travis, 2001).

Opinion polls in Scotland have never been subject to the same degree of scrutiny. Surveys of Scottish party and constitutional preferences have been periodically conducted since the Second World War, and separate Scotland-wide opinion polls have featured in every general election since February 1974. System Three's monthly series of voting preferences has been running since April 1974 (Miller, 1974: 134; Macartney, 1979). Although the outcome of British general elections is rarely determined by the voting preferences of Scots, Scotland's distinctive party system and political arena have sustained interest in the Scottish result, while its extensive media network has ensured a client-base for polling firms. Trends in Scottish opinion polls have been monitored since the mid-1970s, most notably in the *Scottish Government Yearbook* and its successor, *Scottish Affairs*. However, the results presented by the polls have seldom been examined and the sampling and reporting techniques rarely questioned.

The lack of scrutiny of Scottish opinion polls may be a reflection of the aforementioned tendency to judge the success or failure of opinion polls on whether or not they correctly predict the winner. In British general elections, it is the winner of the British election that matters most. Perhaps as a result, Scotland-wide polls were largely ignored in the post-mortem that followed the 1992 election. The establishment of the Scottish Parliament, however, heightens the potential impact of opinion polls on the development and outcome of Scottish elections, strengthening the case for a greater degree of scrutiny of opinion polls in Scotland.

This article aims to take a step towards filling the 'scrutiny gap'. Its principal concern is with published polls conducted in the run-up to the Scottish Parliament election of 1 May 2003. Neither the honesty nor the objectivity of companies conducting pre-election polling is placed in question. Rather, the article is focused upon assessing the accuracy of the pre-election polls, and examining the effect of the sampling techniques employed in conducting them.

Did the Polls Get it Right in 2003?

Eleven polls of voting intentions were published in the month preceding the 2003 Scottish Parliament election. Notably, most were commissioned from companies other than the five members of the Association of Professional Opinion Polling Organisations (APOPO) that have dominated UK election polling.[1] Five companies conducted opinion polls in the 2003 Scottish election: NFO System Three for the *Herald*; Scottish Opinion for the *Daily Record/Sunday Mail*; Populus for the *Times*; YouGov for the *Mail on Sunday* and *Daily Telegraph*; and Mori for the *Daily Mail* (see Table 1). With the exception of Scottish Opinion and NFO System Three, who conducted weekly and fortnightly polls respectively, the polls were fairly sporadic.

The Scotsman, Scotland's second national broadsheet, abandoned polling the electorate, relying upon secondary reporting of other polls. Its online edition, *scotsman.com*, conducted surveys of its registered readers and these were only occasionally reported in the *Scotsman* and *Scotland on Sunday*. A *scotsman.com* internal review included among its objectives that the panel

TABLE 1
OPINION POLLS IN THE 2003 SCOTTISH PARLIAMENT ELECTION

Polling company	Newspaper	Publication date	Sample
NFO System Three	The Herald	5 April	969
Scottish Opinion	Sunday Mail	6 April	362
Populus	The Times	15 April	500
Scottish Opinion	Daily Record	16 April	1005
NFO System Three	Herald	17 April	2122
YouGov	Mail on Sunday	20 April	952
Scottish Opinion	Daily Record	23 April	1000
YouGov	Daily Telegraph	28 April	1081
Mori	Scottish Daily Mail	29 April	1017
NFO System Three	Herald	29 April	875
Scottish Opinion	Daily Record	30 April	1000

would give 'an unprecedented insight into the thoughts of the Scottish people on key issues and voting intentions' (*scotsman.com*, 2003). Such an insight is not possible with such an unrepresentative sample that, at best, could only provide insight into the opinions and voting intentions of online readers of the *Scotsman/Scotland on Sunday*. Indeed, the published data had no pretences of being anything other than a readers' survey. Consequently, the *scotsman.com* surveys are excluded from this analysis.

The published polls in 2003 were fewer in number than in the 1999 Scottish Parliament election. Greater media attention was perhaps inevitable on such an historic occasion, when voters elected the first Scottish Parliament for almost 300 years. Interest in monitoring voting intentions may also have been heightened by the monthly series of System Three polls, which pointed to a closely fought contest between Labour and the SNP (McCrone, 1999: 34).[2] In the 1999 campaign, five companies, including ICM, NOP and Mori, collectively produced 15 polls commissioned by seven different newspapers (BBC, 1999).

The paucity of polls in 2003, and particularly the absence of most of the big polling firms, may be attributed to the fact that it seemed a foregone conclusion that Labour would emerge as the largest party and form a coalition with the Liberal Democrats. Even when an NFO System Three poll in early April suggested that Labour and the SNP were on level-pegging on the constituency vote, and put the SNP ahead on the list vote, a Labour–Liberal Democrat coalition seemed assured. Labour continues to benefit from a favourable geographic distribution of its vote in the first-past-the-post constituency election, and was expected to emerge with the largest number of seats. In addition, the Liberal Democrats had all but ruled out forming a coalition with the SNP. In the context of a predictable election, expensive opinion polls may have seemed a luxury for some media outlets. Moreover, the news media was dominated by coverage of the war in Iraq, making it difficult for any election issue to capture the headlines. This was exacerbated by a dull campaign that was most notable for its lack of policy or ideological debate (McEwen, 2003).

How, then, did the opinion polls fare? Opinion can change over the course of a campaign; thus, in assessing the accuracy of the polls in 'predicting' the final result, we can only fairly consider those polls conducted in the final days of the campaign. The results from the four final polls are set out in Table 2.

If the criterion for judging the success of opinion polls is that they predict the winner (Moon, 1999: 12–13), then the opinion polls in the 2003 Scottish election were successful. All of the polls predicted that Labour would emerge as the largest party, comfortably ahead of their SNP rivals, but short of an overall majority. This would be a rather crude measure of success, however. According to Crewe (1997: 72), the true test of a poll's accuracy is measured by the mean difference between each party's percentage share of the vote, and the poll's forecast of that share. As Table 2 indicates, the mean error on the parties' share of the constituency vote ranged from 1.6 to 3.3, producing an average error across the polls of 2.7. In the list vote, the range in mean scores was 2.6 to 4.5, an overall average error of 3.5. In both the constituency and list vote, the YouGov internet poll was closest to the actual election result, while the worst performers were Mori and Scottish Opinion.

Table 3 conducts a similar exercise to assess the accuracy of the final three polls of the 1999 Scottish Parliament election campaign,[3] and finds similar degrees of error. Again, polls accurately foresaw that Labour would emerge as the largest party short of an overall majority, but Table 3 also reveals substantial inaccuracies in their forecasts of vote share. The mean error on the parties' share of the constituency vote in 1999 ranged from 1.8 to 3.9, with an error range of 2.8 to 5.6 in the regional list vote. This produced an average error across the polls of 3.0 and 4.1 for the constituency and regional list votes respectively.

The polls may have predicted the winner in 1999 and 2003, but their performance was hardly a roaring success. To put these errors in perspective, Table 4 presents details of the accuracy of forecast polls in general elections since 1945. Measured against previous performance at general elections, the errors produced by polling firms aiming to forecast the Scottish Parliament elections have been historically rather high. Indeed, the average error across the final four polls in 1992 – the election referred to by Crewe as the worst disaster in the history of the polling industry – was 3.0. This is matched by the error in the constituency forecast of the final three polls in 1999, and the error

TABLE 2
FINAL POLLS, SCOTTISH ELECTION 2003

Polling Company	NFO System Three	Mori	Scottish Opinion	YouGov	
Client	The Herald	Scottish Daily Mail	Daily Record	Telegraph	
Fieldwork	23–27 April	25–27 April	23–25 April	1 May	
Sample size	875	1,017	1,000	1,081	Election Result
Constituency Voting Intentions					
Labour	38	43	40	36	34.6
SNP	28	26	27	24	23.8
Cons	10	12	11	16	16.6
Lib Dem	14	9	14	19	15.3
SSP	6	6	5	5	6.2
Greens	3	1	–	–	0 (uncontested)
Others	2	3	3	1*	3.4
Labour Lead	10	17	13	10	10.8
Error on lead	−0.8	+6.2	+2.2	−0.8	
Average error on share (±)	2.9	3.3	2.9	1.6	
Regional List Voting Intentions					
Labour	28	35	26	26	29.3
SNP	28	26	25	23	20.9
Cons	9	10	9	16	15.5
Lib Dem	13	11	19	14	11.8
SSP	10	9	9	10	6.9
Greens	7	6	–	–	6.7
Others	5	3	12	11*	8.9
Labour Lead	0	9	1	3	8.4
Error on lead	−8.4	+0.4	−7.4	−5.4	
Average error on share (±)	3.3	3.7	4.5	2.6	

Note: *In YouGov polls on first and second vote, the category 'others' include the Scottish Green Party.

in the constituency voting intentions in the final polls of the 2003 election was not far behind. In the regional list vote, the error in 1999 and 2003 was considerably higher than that recorded in the 1992 general election. This highlights the comparatively poor record of the pollsters in Scotland. Moreover, the greater inaccuracies in forecasting regional list vote share suggest added

TABLE 3
FINAL POLLS, SCOTTISH ELECTION 1999

Polling Company	NOP	ICM	Scottish Opinion	
Client	Scottish Daily Express	Scotsman	Daily Record	
Fieldwork	30 April-2 May	2–3 May	1–4 May	Election result
Sample size	750	1,005	1,108	6 May 1999
Constituency Voting Intentions				
Labour	46	42	46.8	38.8
SNP	31	30	28.3	28.7
Cons	12	14	12.4	15.6
Lib Dem	8	12	12.5	14.2
Others	3	2	–	2.7
Labour Lead	15	12	18.5	10.1
Error on lead	+4.9	+1.9	+8.4	
Average Error on share (±)	3.9	1.8	3.2	
Regional List Voting intentions				
Labour	36	41	42.2	33.6
SNP	32	30	30.0	27.3
Cons	14	14	12.7	15.4
Lib Dem	10	10	15.1	12.4
Others	8	5	–	11.3
Labour Lead	4	11	12.2	6.3
Error on lead	−2.3	+4.7	+5.9	
Average Error on share (±)	2.8	4.0	5.6	

Note: Scottish Opinion did not measure support for smaller parties or independent candidates in its 1999 pre-election poll.

difficulties for pollsters in achieving true representations of voting preferences in an election conducted under the additional member electoral system.

All polls include a degree of sampling error. A random probability sample of 1,000 respondents assumes a standard error of up to ± 3 per cent.[4] Several of the polls produced in advance of the 2003 election drew upon quota samples. Generating a sampling error for quota polls is more difficult. Although similar ranges of sampling error are usually assumed, quota samples are thought to produce greater errors than those calculated under the assumptions of random probability sampling, especially where respondents are

TABLE 4
AVERAGE ERRORS IN PRE-ELECTION POLLS IN UK GENERAL ELECTIONS AND
SCOTTISH PARLIAMENT ELECTIONS

Year	No. of forecast polls	Mean error per party
UK General Elections		
1945	1	1.5
1950	2	1.3
1951	3	2.3
1955	2	1.0
1959	3	0.3
1964	4	1.0
1966	3	1.3
1970	5	2.0
Feb. 1974	6	1.0
Oct. 1974	5	1.5
1979	5	0.3
1983	7	1.5
1987	7	1.3
1992	4	3.0
1997	6	2.0
2001	3	1.8
Scottish Parliament Elections		
1999 – constituency	3	3.0
1999 – list	3	4.1
2003 – constituency	4	2.7
2003 – list	4	3.5

Source: British results extracted from Crewe (2001: 97) with Scottish results added.

clustered in concentrated geographical areas as in the face-to-face interviews conducted by NFO System Three (Moon, 1999: 39–40). As Table 2 illustrates, in many cases, the errors on estimates of each party's vote share in the 2003 election often went beyond the sampling error of ±3 per cent. Moreover, the errors were often in a similar direction. To varying degrees, Mori, Scottish Opinion and NFO System Three over-estimated support for Labour and the SNP (although NFO System Three had broadly accurate predictions of Labour's share of the regional list vote, and Scottish Opinion under-estimated Labour's list vote). At the same time, all three polling companies under-estimated support for the Conservative Party. Similar tendencies were evident in the polls conducted on the eve of the 1999 Scottish Parliament election, most notably in their over-estimation of the Labour vote.

There are several possible explanations for these polling discrepancies. First, we cannot fully discount the possibility of a late swing. As noted above, late swing was considered the primary cause of polling discrepancies in the 1970 general election. On that occasion, polling had stopped a few days before the election and, as a result, most polls apparently failed to identify a shift in support towards the Conservative Party. Nowadays, the final polls in UK general elections are usually published on election day, to help ensure they detect any evidence of a late swing towards one or other party, or any change in the estimated percentage of electors who will vote at all. In the 2003 Scottish election, however, the final polls were conducted between 23 and 27 April, and published on 28, 29 and 30 April, before the election on 1 May. Theoretically, then, the difference between the polls and the election results may have been a result of last-minute changes of heart on the part of the elec- torate. This is impossible to test given the absence of exit polls or efforts to re- interview respondents immediately prior to the election, but there is little evidence from the campaign of any events that may have provoked such late swings.

A second possible explanation may be the result of differential turnout between different groups in society. Turnout in the 2003 Scottish Parliament election fell to 49.4 per cent, down from 58.8 per cent in 1999. Trends in Scot- land and elsewhere suggest that voter abstention is concentrated among the urban working class and the young (Denver, 2003b; Electoral Commission, 2003: 17–27). If opinion polls do not adequately take account of differential participation rates, we may expect that the vote share attributed to the parties with greatest appeal to the young and the working class – in the Scottish case, Labour, the SNP and the Scottish Socialist Party – would then be exaggerated in the polls. Indeed, this seems to have been the case in the pre-election polls in 2003, and was given by one company as the main reason for polling discrepancies (Enyon and Martin, 2003). In an effort to counteract the effect of differential turnout, British pollsters often ask respondents to indicate their likelihood to vote. This is encouraged within the ESOMAR/WAPOR guide- lines (ESOMAR, 1998: para. 6.2.7) The common practice in British election polling is to publish the voting intentions of only those respondents who say they are 'certain to vote'. In the Scottish election, only Mori followed this practice. Even then, 59 per cent of its sample said they were 'absolutely certain to vote', a considerably higher figure than the actual turnout. In its mid-campaign telephone poll and its final poll, NFO System Three gathered data on likelihood to vote, but it was the overall figures that were published in the *Herald*.[5]

The biggest surprise of the 2003 election result was the success of the small parties and independents. Some of the polls under-estimated this support, perhaps in part because of the options offered in the voting intention question.

Based on available published survey results, Mori asked respondents to choose one of the six main parties or 'some other party', thus excluding independent candidates. YouGov and Scottish Opinion appeared to merge the Scottish Green Party with the category 'others'. This may help to explain why this category produced YouGov's biggest error. It is important to acknowledge that polling for an election conducted under the additional member electoral system (AMS) presents a challenge for the pollsters. Samples of 1,000 or less may be less likely to identify support for smaller parties, such as the Senior Citizens Unity Party which won a seat in Central region, and local independent candidates, three of whom found success in the constituency and list ballots. As Hodder-Williams noted, opinion polls are more effective when opinions can be slotted into broad categories, as this heightens the probability of catching the 'right' number of respondents in each category. The more parties and candidates on offer to the electorate, the narrower the categories, and the narrower the chances of opinion polls reflecting accurate representations of voting intentions (Hodder-Williams, 1970: 16). It remains to be seen whether the success of the small parties and independents was a peculiar feature of the 2003 election, or an enduring feature of Scottish parliamentary AMS elections to which polling companies may need to adapt.

The Scottish polls also highlighted some problems generic to opinion polling across Britain, which have been evident to varying degrees since the 1992 general election. With the exception of YouGov, the polls under-estimated support for the Conservatives. This has less serious ramifications in Scottish elections because the Conservatives are not in a position to pose a serious challenge for government, and there is little or no prospect in the foreseeable future of the Conservatives being entertained as potential coalition partners for either Labour or the SNP. Nevertheless, an under-estimation of the Conservative vote is a persistent problem in polling, evident to varying degrees in every Scottish and British election since 1992.

One explanation for the under-representation of Conservative voters in opinion polls emerges from Noelle-Neumann's 'spiral of silence' theory (Noelle-Neumann, 1977). Instead of adopting the conventional understanding of public opinion as a reflection of the attitudes and judgements of rational individuals, Noelle-Neumann returned to Rousseau's conceptualization of public opinion as the pressure to conform. She suggested that individuals who believe that they hold minority views will be less likely to voice them, while those believing that their views conform to the majority will be more self-confident in expressing them. These acts of expression and reticence, in turn, influence the 'climate of opinion' encouraging those who believe themselves to hold unpopular views to keep them to themselves (Noelle-Neumann, 143-5). Such a 'spiral of silence' may explain why the analyses which followed the opinion polling failures of 1992 found that those who refused to declare a voting intention, or said they were undecided, disproportionately identified with the Conservative Party. This may be partly a result of a perceived selfishness or embarrassment in favouring a traditionally tax-cutting party, or a result of a perceived hostility towards the Conservatives in the wider society. Inasmuch as this affects those who refuse to declare an intention to vote, it may also imply that Conservative voters are disproportionately among those who refuse to take part at all (Broughton, 1995: 89–99; Crewe, 1997: 62–3). We must take care not to assume causality here. Evidence also suggests that those refusing to take part in poll interviews are disproportionately female and elderly, two social groups that are disproportionately Conservative for reasons beyond shame or fear of isolation (Broughton, 1995: 91). Nevertheless, the idea of a 'spiral of silence' among Conservative voters may be plausible in Scotland. Antipathy towards the Conservative Party ran deep in Scotland throughout the 1980s and 1990s, and represented an important dimension explaining support for Scottish home rule. In the 1997 devolution referendum, one analysis found that 'not identifying with the Conservative Party' was by far the most significant characteristic of YES YES voters (Denver et al., 2000: 166–8). Under David McLetchie's leadership, the Scottish Conservatives may have regained some respect, if not much support, but a 'shy Tory' factor may remain a problem for pollsters.

An associated problem in British election polling has been a tendency to over-estimate Labour's share of the vote. This was evident in some of the Scottish polls, often alongside an over-estimation of support for the SNP. In part, this may be reflective of the same problem. In Scotland, Labour is not the only party to appeal disproportionately to young, working-class and male voters. The SNP, and increasingly the Scottish Socialist Party (SSP), also fairs well among this group (Bennie et al., 1997: 97–107). Furthermore, an over-estimation of support for Labour and the SNP is associated with an under-estimation of support for the smaller parties and independents, whose success in 2003 was at Labour's and especially the SNP's expense (Denver, 2003b).

The size of the errors in the 2003 Scottish polls, and the consistency in the direction of error, suggests that we are not just dealing with the effects of sampling error alone. A degree of sampling bias is also at work. Furthermore, even allowing for the effect of late swings and differential turnout, Table 2 illustrates that there were considerable variations between polls conducted over the same time period. Thus, even if we accept that one can never assess the accuracy of pre-election opinion polls in light of the election result, when simultaneous polls tell a different story, they cannot all be right. Inaccuracies in polling forecasts, as well as the differences between simultaneous polls, suggest that the manner in which polls are conducted may influence the results they generate.

Polling Techniques

Do the methods involved in conducting opinion polls influence the picture of the electorate they portray? To address this question, consideration will be given to three distinctive dimensions of polling technique: the size of the sample; the form of sampling; and the weighting procedures used to rectify the under-representation and over-representation of particular groups.

Sample Size

The size of a sample is not, in itself, a measure of its representativeness or reliability, but smaller sample sizes increase the range of sampling error. Consequently, the reported findings of an opinion poll based on very small samples have less chance of being accurate. Given the sensitive and potentially influential nature of pre-election polls, the ESOMAR/WAPOR guidelines recommend that samples of less than 1,000 respondents should be avoided (ESOMAR, 1998: para. 6.2.3). As Table 1 indicates, some of the polls published in the Scottish election campaign had sample sizes that were considerably smaller than 1,000. The Scottish Opinion poll for the *Sunday Mail* (6 April 2003) had a sample size of just 362. The Populus poll for the *Times* had a sample of 500. The final poll for NFO System Three was 875, though its previous omnibus poll in early April was a little bigger, with 969 respondents, and its telephone poll considerably larger, with over 2,122 respondents (*The Herald*, 5 April 2003; 17 April 2003).

Forms of Sampling and Interviewing

Consideration of sampling technique falls into two broad categories: the form of sampling and the mode of interviewing. As Table 5 reveals, opinion polls conducted on the eve of the 2003 Scottish election involved considerable variation in both sampling form and interview mode.

There are two main forms of sampling: random probability sampling and quota sampling. Random probability sampling is the purest and most reliable form of sampling from a statistical point of view, but it has been historically problematic in opinion polling. Until recently, surveys had to be conducted in face-to-face interviews and the time and cost constraints involved in reliably surveying the population by means of face-to-face, random probability sampling proved prohibitively high. Among other things, it made it difficult to identify late swings from one party to another, as was evident in the 1970 general election. By contrast, face-to-face quota sampling can be more efficient with respect to time and cost (Broughton, 1995: 53–7). Indeed, between the 1974 and 1992 general elections, face-to-face quota sampling was the most common method of conducting opinion polls. Increasing household access to the telephone opens up new opportunities, however. It is estimated

TABLE 5
SAMPLING AND WEIGHTING TECHNIQUES

Pollster	NFO/System Three	Mori	Scottish Opinion	YouGov
Sample type	Clustered Quota, Omnibus	Households selected randomly Respondents by Quota	Random, Omnibus	Internet panel
Interview method	Face-to face	Telephone	Telephone	Online self-completion questionnaire
Scope	51 constituencies	All 73 constituencies	All 73 constituencies	Internet panel of approx. 3000 Scottish electors
Quota controls	Gender interlocked with working-status with age interlocked socio-economic group	Gender interlocked with working-status; age interlocked with housing tenure	Range of socio-demographic and political quota	Rim weighting, controls inc. past voting and newspaper readership
Weighting	Demographic	Demographic	n.a.	Demographic, social, political

Source: Information gathered from company websites and in interviews with companies involved. Scottish Opinion refrained from responding to repeated requests for information regarding the technical details of their surveys.

that over 94 per cent of the population now live in households with a telephone (Curtice, 1997: 456), making the telephone a more reliable means of conducting surveys than has been possible hitherto. Telephone polling is commonly combined with quota sampling, but polling by telephone also makes random probability sampling more feasible. Consequently, some polling firms, notably Gallup and ICM, have switched to random or semi-random forms of sampling (Curtice, 1997: 456).

Among the four companies producing polls in the run-up to the Scottish election, Mori and System Three relied upon a form of quota sampling. In Mori's case, as in the System Three mid-campaign telephone poll, households are selected randomly using random digit dialling, with quotas used thereafter to identify individuals to be interviewed. YouGov's polls also use quotas, but draw their sample from a registered panel rather than from the electorate as a whole. The only company conducting random probability sampling was Scottish Opinion. Its election polls formed part of a weekly telephone omnibus survey, with random samples drawn from the electoral register. The website boasts of 'the huge financial investment' it made by purchasing 'the entire electoral roll'.[6] Using the electoral register as a sampling frame is problematic, however. Not only does it exclude that proportion of the population who are not registered to vote, but it also becomes dated rather quickly. Writing in the early 1970s, Teer and Spence estimated that around 1 per cent of the electorate dies or moves house each month, 4 per cent of names listed on returns in October are ineffective when the register comes into force in February, and at the end of its 12-month lifespan, around 16 per cent of those listed on the register will have died or moved house (Teer and Spence, 1973: 31).

A broad range of interview methods was also evident in pre-election polling in 2003. Both Mori and Scottish Opinion conducted interviews by telephone. Although System Three conducted a mid-campaign telephone poll of 2122 voters across all 73 constituencies, its monthly omnibus polls (including the final poll) are conducted using face-to-face interviews in clustered units across approximately 50 constituencies. In YouGov's case, samples are drawn from its registered panel. Potential respondents are contacted by email and invited to participate in an online questionnaire (www.yougov.com).

Few British polling firms still rely on the face-to-face method of interviewing which System Three continues to practice. Face-to-face interviews tend to be more expensive, associated with low (and often unrecorded) response rates, and susceptible to the influence of individual interviewers (Broughton, 1995: 60–72). Curtice and Sparrow suggested that there is strong evidence of a pro-Labour bias in British face-to-face quota samples, and offer a number of explanations as to why (Curtice and Sparrow, 1997). First, since interviewers are given a degree of freedom about where and whom to interview, concerns over timing, efficiency, access and safety may increase the likelihood that they choose mixed council/private areas, excluding wealthier and more deprived estates. In general, this risks encountering neighbourhood effects, which lead to an over-estimation of the Labour vote, as well as risking an over-estimation of the proportion of those voting at all. Furthermore, face-to-face quota polls provide interviewers with little incentive to minimize the number of people refusing to participate. Faced with a refusal from a would-be respondent, the interviewer need merely find someone else who fits the quota. As Curtice and Sparrow surmise, inasmuch as those less inclined to declare a voting intention are disproportionately Conservative voters, then those less inclined to participate in surveys at all may also be disproportionately Conservative (Curtice and Sparrow, 1997: 442–3).

As noted above, widespread telephone use now makes telephone polling much more feasible. Access to the internet, however, is still much more restricted and is heavily biased towards the young and the middle class. This makes internet polling of the sort conducted by YouGov somewhat controversial.

There are a number of advantages to internet polls. Relative to telephone or face-to-face polls, they are cheap, efficient and convenient, permitting respondents to complete questionnaires in their own time, within a set period (usually around a week). However, there are a number of serious drawbacks. The main problem is one of coverage error. Internet polls are restricted to that section of the population that have internet access. Moreover, they are reliant on those willing to join an on-line internet panel (Best and Krueger, 2002: 74–5). As a result, internet polling can never be representative. Since representativeness is an essential criterion of opinion polls, strictly speaking, internet polls are not opinion polls, a point underlined in the ESOMAR/WAPOR guidelines (ESOMAR, 1998, s.3).

In a trial commissioned by ICM and the *Guardian*, Baker et al. conducted a study of a random telephone sample of 4,104 adults across the country, to contrast the characteristics and attitudes of internet users with those of non-users (Baker et al., 2003). Within their sample, 52 per cent had internet access at home or elsewhere (excluding those who only had access at work), while only 16 per cent indicated a willingness to join an internet panel. Compared to the sample as a whole, would-be internet panellists were more likely to be younger, wealthier, owner-occupiers. Advocates of internet polls would argue that the under-representation of certain socio-demographic groups within internet panels can be corrected by weighting to conform to the profile of the target population. However, as Best and Krueger point out, this assumes that accessible email users, inaccessible email users and those without access to the internet or email all form their opinions in the same way. Yet, Best and Krueger argue that internet users obtain information from different sources, participate in different social activities and socialize in different ways from non-users and, consequently, their decision-making and opinion-formation processes are likely to be different (Best and Krueger, 2002: 76–8). Indeed, in the ICM trial, even after weighting for demographic characteristics and past voting, would-be internet panellists were more likely to be more politically aware and politically engaged, more socially liberal, more left-wing and more likely to say they would vote Labour or Liberal Democrat than in the larger telephone sample.

Nevertheless, YouGov has a strong track record. As well as coming closer than any other polling organization in forecasting the 2003 Scottish election result, they previously found success in predicting the outcome of the 2001 general election, the Australian election, and the Conservative leadership contest in 2001. Internet polls, in themselves, cannot be representative of the population, although in the context of differential turnout in a low-turnout election, where the voting population is more middle class and politically engaged, at least some of the differences between the profile of internet panellists and the voters may be diminished. With respect to the election polls, however, YouGov's success in the 2003 election is unlikely to be any more a vindication of internet polling than Mori and Scottish Opinion's lack of success is a condemnation of telephone polling. Rather, YouGov's track record in accurately forecasting election results may be a vindication of its quota-setting and weighting techniques.

Quota-setting, Weighting and Adjustment

In quota sampling, individuals are selected by interviewers according to pre-determined quotas. Traditionally, quota controls are set using standard demo-graphic controls, including gender, age, working status and social class. The latter is the most difficult for interviewers to identify and apply. Some polling companies use housing tenure as a substitute for class. As outlined in Table 5, NFO System Three and Mori used interlocking quotas along these lines. Once the data is collected, it is standard practice in opinion polling to weight the raw data according to these socio-demographic quota controls, to adjust for any residual unrepresentativeness (Crewe, 1997: 63).

Inappropriate quota-setting and weighting has long been recognized as a flaw in standard opinion polling, and was identified in the aftermath of the 1992 general election as one of the factors contributing to polling inaccura-cies. It was suggested that the social benchmarks used to set quotas failed to fully reflect changes in society, such as a growing elderly population, a declin-ing proportion of council tenants, and an expanding middle class. As a result, the quotas were biased towards Labour (Butler and Kavanagh, 1992: 141; Crewe, 1997: 61–2; Curtice and Sparrow, 1997: 443). Moreover, sampling and weighting according to socio-demographic quota settings will only be reliable if quotas correlate strongly with the dependent variable, in this case, voting intention. Age, gender and working status are only weakly correlated with voting preferences (Curtice and Sparrow: 1997: 443). Relying on stan-dard demographic quota controls may therefore be inadequate. In the 2003 Scottish election, YouGov was alone among the polling companies in using politically-sensitive controls in addition to social and demographic character-istics, drawn from the information gathered in detailed questionnaires during the process of registering for the YouGov panel. Such controls include weighting by past voting and newspaper readership. YouGov's success can only reinforce demands for more widespread use of politically-sensitive quota controls. However, it should not be assumed that those quotas which correlate well with voting preferences in England will also correlate well with voting preferences in Scotland. Class identity is usually more strongly associated with Scottish voting behaviour than is any objective categorization of class group. Other variables such as national identity and constitutional preference may also be more effective means of political weighting (Bennie et al., 1997: 97–107).

Historically, it has been standard practice in opinion polling to ignore those who refuse to respond to the voting intention question, or who remain undecided. This practice was based on the assumption that those who did not declare support for a party were similar with respect to their distribution of political preferences to those who did declare. However, analyses conducted in the wake of the 1992 election revealed this assumption to be false (Moon, 1999: 122–7). Whether based upon a 'spiral of silence' or some other factors, those who did not declare a preference were found to disproportionately favour the Conservatives. Since 1992, several of the APOPO polling firms have engaged in efforts to resolve this problem by seeking to identify party preferences by other indirect means, and reallocating the non-disclosers accordingly. For example, in 1997, Gallup reallocated its non-disclosers on the basis of their preferences among the party leaders and on the party that respondents considered most competent at handling the economy. Similarly, NOP reallocated on the basis of party identification and perception of economic competence. ICM used past voting and evidence from the British Election Study to estimate the voting preferences of its non-disclosers (Crewe, 1997; Moon, 1999: 189–92). These adjustments have been successful in generating more accurate representations of the Conservative vote, although as Crewe noted in his assessment of polling in the 1997 and 2001 general elections, polls are continuing to exaggerate the Labour vote (Crewe, 2001: 86–100).

Poll projections in the 1999 and 2003 Scottish Parliament elections suggest that polling in Scotland suffers from the same tendencies to under-estimate the Conservative vote and over-estimate the Labour (and sometimes SNP) votes. Yet, none of the companies conducting polls in 2003 made any adjustments to address the problem of bias in non-disclosure. Instead, non-disclosers were eliminated from the published results. Mori – the only APOPO member conducting polls in the 2003 election – has been the least inclined to adopt adjustment strategies developed by its competitors. For those outside the APOPO network, it would seem that there is a lack of engagement with such issues and perhaps a lack of acceptance that the problems exist. If this is a reflection of complacency, it is surely a consequence of the lack of scrutiny of opinion polling in Scotland.

Conclusion

This article has advocated the need for greater scrutiny of opinion polling in Scotland. As a contribution to this end, it has examined the extent to which the final polls in elections to the Scottish Parliament have differed from the election results, revealing substantial inaccuracies that are surely a cause for concern. Set within a comparison of polling in post-war British general elections, the average errors in the Scottish polls are considerable. This is subject to the qualification that interviews in the final polls in Scottish elections have tended to stop earlier than has been the case in recent British elections, though there is little evidence to suggest that the inaccuracies are the result of late swings in public opinion. Historically, errors in estimates of the constituency vote share in the Scottish Parliament polls approach the levels of the 1992 general election polling debacle; and there is clearly an even greater problem in accurately representing voting intentions on the regional list. This is in part a consequence of the electoral system, and a reflection of the support for a range of smaller parties and independents whose support is difficult to identify in samples of c.1,000.

Scottish polls also appear to suffer from difficulties common to British pollsters, most notably the tendency to over-estimate support for the Labour Party and to under-estimate support for the Conservatives. However, there is little evidence of similar efforts being made in Scotland to address these problems through appropriate compensatory adjustments to raw data, beyond simple demographic weighting. In the last Scottish Parliament election, YouGov was alone among the pollsters in employing politically-meaningful quota-setting and weighting techniques, and their polls proved to be the best performer in 2003. One of the worst performers, Scottish Opinion, was reluctant to disclose its sampling and weighting techniques (see note 6). This lack of transparency reinforces the need for greater scrutiny.

It is not the intention of this article to under-estimate the challenge of achieving accurate representations of voting preferences within the time and cost constraints of election polling. Nor is it the intention to question the integrity of the polling companies engaged in this process in Scotland. However, this overview of polling in elections to the Scottish Parliament suggests there is room for improvement. The influence that opinion polls can have over the nature of election campaigns, and the strategies and behaviour of those contesting them, suggests that polls may at least have an indirect effect on election outcomes. This imposes an obligation on those engaged in the conduct, reporting and analysis of poll results to ensure that the results obtained are as accurate as possible. Greater scrutiny of opinion polls ought to play a part in informing that process. Pollsters in Scotland can learn from the efforts of other pollsters to address some generic problems; but there may also be a need to find Scottish solutions to Scottish polling problems. Such solutions ought to take into account Scotland's distinctive six-party system, as well as the challenges of polling in an additional member electoral system. To this end, there may be scope for looking beyond British shores to learn from polling practices in other multi-party, proportional systems.

ACKNOWLEDGEMENTS

This research was conducted with the aid of an ESRC postdoctoral fellowship (Award Ref No TO26271402). I am grateful to all those who provided assistance and technical information, in particular, Chris Enyon at NFO System Three, Peter Kellner at YouGov, Mark Diffley at Mori Scotland, and Dianne Newman at the Scotsman. Thanks also to Ailsa Henderson, David Denver, John Curtice and the editors, all of whom offered very useful advice which informed the development of the article.

NOTES

1. These are Gallup, ICM, NOP, Harris and Mori. Mori were commissioned to conduct one opinion poll in the final week of the campaign. The dominant polling company in Scotland, NFO System Three, is an associate member of APOPO.
2. ICM also conducted regular polls for the Scotsman and its sister paper, Scotland on Sunday, in the year preceding the 1999 election. In contrast to the System Three polls for the Herald, most of ICM's polls placed Labour comfortably ahead of the SNP in constituency voting intentions and, to a lesser extent, in voting intentions for the regional lists.
3. These three final polls were conducted between 30 April and 4 May, and published 4–5 May. The election took place on 6 May. Three polls were published on Sunday 2 May – by NOP, Mori and ICM – but since they were conducted 27–29 April, they cannot be considered final polls. System Three's last poll was published seven days before the election.
4. Calculations of sampling error are derived from number theory, and a standard error of ±3 per cent is based upon an observed value of 50 per cent. Most observations of a party's share of voting intentions are less than 50 per cent, some substantially so. The smaller the party's share, the smaller will be the range of error around this value (see Moon, 1999: 27–33 for an excellent explanation of sampling error).
5. In the NFO System Three 'eve of election' poll, 52 per cent of the sample indicated they were 'certain to vote', close to the actual turnout of 49 per cent. Had these estimates been published by the *Herald*, there would still have been an over-estimate of support for the SNP and (on the constituency vote) Labour, and an under-estimate of the Conservative vote, but the degree of discrepancy is reduced (see Enyon and Martin, 2003).
6. Information on Scottish Opinion's polling techniques has been derived from the company's website (www.scottishopinion.com), and considerable questions remain unanswered. Repeated requests for information on technical details, submitted in numerous email and telephone messages, failed to elicit any satisfactory response.

REFERENCES

Baker, Ken, John Curtice and Nick Sparrow (2003) *Internet Poll Trial,* Research Report prepared for ICM/the *Guardian*, January.

BBC (1999), online at *http://news.bbc.co.uk/1/hi/events/scotland_99/opinion_polls/309944.stm.*

Bennie, Lynn, Jack Brand and James Mitchell (1997) *How Scotland Votes.* Manchester: Manchester University Press.

Best, Samuel J. and Brian Krueger (2002), 'New Approaches to Assessing Opinion: The Prospects for Electronic Mail Surveys', *International Journal of Public Opinion Research,* 14.1: 73–92.

Broughton, David (1995) *Political Opinion Polling and Politics in Britain.* Hemel Hempstead: Harvester Wheatsheaf.

Butler, David and Dennis Kavanagh (1992) *The British General Election of 1992.* Houndmills: Macmillan.

Crewe, Ivor (1997) 'The Opinion Polls: Confidence restoreR?', in Pippa Norris and Neil T Gavin
    (eds), *Britain Votes, 1997*. Oxford: Oxford University Press, pp. 61–77.
Crewe, Ivor (2001) 'The Opinion Polls: Still Biased to Labour', in Pippa Norris (ed), *Britain
    Votes 2001*. Oxford: Oxford University Press, 86–101.
Curtice, John (1997) 'So how well did they do? The Polls in the 1997 Election', *Journal of the
    Market Research Society*, 39.3: 449–61.
Curtice, John and Nick Sparrow (1997) 'How accurate are traditional quota opinion polls?
    Journal of the Market Research Society, 39.3: 433–48.
Denver, David (2003a) *Elections and Voters in Britain*. Houndmills: Palgrave Macmillan.
Denver, David (2003b) 'A "wake up!" call to the parties? The Results of the Scottish Parliament
    Elections 2003', *Scottish Affairs*, 44: 31–53.
Denver, David, James Mitchell, Charles Pattie and Hugh Bochel (2000), *Scotland Decides: The
    Devolution Issue and the Scottish Referendum*. London: Frank Cass.
Electoral Commission (2003) *Scottish Elections 2003: The official report on the Scottish Parlia-
    ment and local government elections, 1 May 2003*, November.
Enyon Chris and Chris Martin (2003) 'What the opinion polls tell us about voting behaviour', in
    Ross Burnside, Stephen Herbert and Stephen Curtis (eds), *Election 2003*, Scottish Parlia-
    ment Information Centre Research Report. Edinburgh: The Scottish Parliament), pp. 21–3.
ESOMAR (1998) *ESOMAR/WAPOR Guide to Opinion Polls including the ESOMAR
    International Code of Practice for the Publication of Public Opinion Results*, accessed on
    http://www.esomar.org.
Hodder-Williams, Richard (1970) *Public Opinion Polls and British Politics*. London: Routledge
    & Kegan Paul.
Jones, Peter (1999) 'The Scottish Parliament Elections: From Anti-Tory to Anti-Nationalist
    Politics', *Scottish Affairs*, 28: 1–9.
Jowell, Roger, Barry Hedges, Peter Lynn and Graham Farrant and Anthony Heath (1993) 'The
    British General Election: The Failure of the Polls', *Public Opinion Quarterly*, 57.2: 238–63.
Macartney, W.J. Allan (1979) 'Summary of Scottish opinion polls relating to voting intentions
    and constitutional change', in Henry M. Drucker and Nancy L. Drucker (eds), *Scottish
    Government Yearbook 1979*. Edinburgh: Paul Harris Publishing.
McAllister, Ian and Donley T. Studlar (1991) 'Bandwagon, Underdog or Projection? Opinion
    Polls and Electoral Choice in Britain, 1979–1987'. *Journal of Politics*, 53.3: 720–41.
McCrone, David (1999) 'Opinion Polls in Scotland, July 1998–June 1999', *Scottish Affairs*, 28:
    32–43.
McEwen, Nicola (2003) 'Is Devolution at Risk? Examining Attitudes towards the Scottish Parlia-
    ment in Light of the 2003 Election', *Scottish Affairs*, 44: 54–73.
Market Research Society, (1994) *The Opinion Polls and the 1992 General Election*. The Market
    Research Society.
Marsh, Catherine (1984) 'Back on the Bandwagon: The Effect of Opinion Polls on Public
    Opinion', *British Journal of Political Science*, 15.1: 51–74.
Millar, William L. (1981), *The End of British Politics?: Scots and English Political Behaviour in
    the Seventies*. Oxford: Clarendon Press.
Moon, Nick (1999) *Opinion Polls: History, Theory and Practice*. Manchester: Manchester
    University Press.
Noelle-Neumann, Elisabeth (1977) 'Turbulences in the Climate of Opinion: Methodological
    Applications of the Spiral of Silence Theory', *Public Opinion Quarterly*, 41, 143–58.
Scotsman (2003) *2003 Panel: Project Evaluation*, internal document.
Scottish Opinion, online at scottishopinion.com.
Teer, Frank and James D. Spence (1973) *Political Opinion Polls*. London: Hutchinson University
    Library.
Travis, Alan (2001) 'Poll scars', *The Guardian*, 13 June.
Whiteley, Paul (1986) 'The Accuracy and Influence of the Polls in the 1983 General Election', in
    Ivor Crewe and Martin Harrop (eds), *Political Communications: The British General
    Election Campaign of 1983*. Cambridge: Cambridge University Press, pp. 312–24.

Minor Tremor but Several Casualties: The 2003 Welsh Election

Richard Wyn Jones and Roger Scully

In May 1999, the inaugural election to the devolved National Assembly for Wales (NAW) produced a sensation. The election result, which saw the Labour Party's hegemony in Wales disturbed and an unprecedented advance by Plaid Cymru, has been widely described as a 'quiet earthquake' in Welsh politics (Trystan et al., 2003). The result did much to shape the first four years of devolution in Wales. Four years on, the second NAW election produced a substantially lower turnout,[1] and a rather less surprising result – if one that is still important for Welsh politics. In this article, after discussing the background to the election and presenting an overview of the result, we explore why the 2003 election produced the outcome that it did, and consider its implications for the future of Welsh politics.

Four Years On

The road to devolution in Wales was rocky and somewhat tortuous.[2] In sharp contrast to the 1997 referendum in Scotland, which demonstrated that devolution was indeed the 'settled will' of the Scottish electorate, the referendum one week later in Wales served only to confirm the deep ambivalence of the Welsh electorate to the Labour government's plans for a National Assembly for Wales. The very narrow victory for the pro-devolution camp – in a low turnout poll – was, however, enough to facilitate the establishment of the devolved chamber. This institution, its proponents argued, would underpin a new style of politics in Wales – a politics that was more effective, more accountable and, above all, more 'inclusive'.[3]

As a means of revitalizing the political process in Wales, devolution failed its first test. Electoral turnout for the first NAW election was a mere 46 per cent. Those who did vote, however, produced a sensational result. Few expected the Labour Party, long hegemonic in Welsh politics, to have much trouble securing a majority in the 60-seat Assembly under the semi-proportional voting system being used. However, the months preceding the election saw severe internal Labour difficulties – notably the embarrassing resignation of Welsh Secretary Ron Davies in autumn 1998, followed by a bitter and

British Elections & Parties Review, Vol. 14, 2004, pp. 191–207
ISSN 1368-9886 print
DOI: 10.1080/1368988042000258835

protracted leadership battle between Alun Michael and Rhodri Morgan. And election day witnessed a surge in support for the Welsh Nationalist party, Plaid Cymru. Labour gained only 28 Assembly seats, while Plaid exceeded all expectations to become Labour's major opposition with 17. Among Labour casualties were totemic 'heartland' seats in Islwyn, Rhondda and Llanelli.

The aftershocks of this result continued for some time and, eventually, fatally undermined Alun Michael's position as Assembly First Secretary. Having chosen to form a minority administration, Michael's autocratic style of government alienated not only other parties, but also many in Labour's ranks (Rawlings, 2003). After six months, Michael was deposed and replaced by Rhodri Morgan – the very man that Tony Blair and other senior Labour figures had striven to keep from leading the party in Wales. Morgan undertook the re-launching of his party as 'Welsh Labour' under the slogan 'the true party of Wales';[4] in the autumn of 2000 he also signed a 'partnership' agreement with the Liberal Democrats that put in place a coalition government until May 2003.

The extent to which the 1999 result had transformed the Welsh electoral landscape was illustrated a week before the 2003 poll. Prime Minister Blair made a high-profile campaign visit to what news media termed 'the key marginal of The Rhondda' – a description no-one could have used prior to 1999. The Labour campaign aimed explicitly at winning an Assembly majority, with party resources heavily targeted towards winning back the constituencies lost to Plaid four years previously. The 2001 UK election result – which had seen Labour in Wales regaining most of the ground lost two years previously – encouraged many in the party to see 1999 as essentially an aberration, and hope that 2003 would see 'business as usual' being resumed. Plaid Cymru had, since 1999, lost their erstwhile and popular party leader, Dafydd Wigley, and there was a general expectation that they would struggle to hold the gains made in 1999. For the Conservatives and Liberal Democrats, the battle in Wales in 2003 was essentially to avoid coming fourth; while, unlike in Scotland, no significant advances seemed likely by other parties beyond the 'big four'.

Survey evidence has suggested that while support for the principle of devolution has grown substantially since the referendum, there has also been considerable public disappointment with the lack of identifiable benefits attributable to devolution (Wyn Jones and Scully, 2003). The election campaign did little to change matters or raise public awareness of the achievements of the NAW, being a lacklustre affair that generated little informed debate in Welsh news media. However, to be fair, politicians and journalists alike could do little about the domination of the news agenda by Iraq in the months and weeks preceding the election. As election day approached, pollsters and pundits almost uniformly predicted turnout to fall below that in

1999. The fate of the parties was less clear; the final campaign poll (conducted by NOP for HTV-Wales) indicated that things were very much in the balance. Labour were well in the lead, at 39 per cent for the constituency vote, and 35 per cent for the second (regional list) vote. However, Plaid retained a clear second place with 26 per cent and 23 per cent respectively, with the Tories on 16 per cent and 17 per cent, the Liberal Democrats on 13 per cent and 11 per cent. Assuming a uniform swing across Wales from the 1999 results, this poll predicted a final result of 30 seats for Labour, 15 for Plaid, 9 for the Conservatives and 5 for the Liberal Democrats.[5]

The Election Outcome

The aggregate results of the election are presented in Table 1. Although increasing its vote share only modestly over a 1999 performance then seen as disastrous, Labour captured sufficient seats to have effective control over the Assembly.[6] Despite losing the Wrexham constituency seat to erstwhile colleague John Marek, and their Mid and West Wales list seat to the Conservatives, Labour decisively defeated Plaid Cymru in the Rhondda and Iswlyn, and also (though far more narrowly) won back the Conwy and Llanelli constituencies; at the same time, Labour held off strong challenges from the Conservatives in Clwyd West and from Plaid Cymru in Carmarthen West. By contrast, Plaid Cymru saw a substantial decline from its 1999 performance – particularly on the second vote, where they lost more than a third of their vote share – and they paid the inevitable price in terms of representation, losing a list seat (in South Wales East) and four constituency seats to Labour. The Liberal Democrats comfortably held the three constituencies they had won four years previously, and also retained their three list seats. The biggest surprise, perhaps, was the relatively strong Conservative showing. Increasing their share on both votes, the Tories comfortably held the Monmouth constituency seat (a constituency won by Labour in the previous two Westminster

TABLE 1
VOTE SHARES AND SEATS (CHANGE FROM 1999), 2003 NATIONAL ASSEMBLY FOR WALES ELECTION

	First vote (% share)	Second vote (% share)	Seats
Labour	40.0 (+2.4)	36.6 (+1.1)	30 (+2)
Plaid Cymru	21.2 (−7.2)	19.7 (−10.8)	12 (−5)
Conservatives	19.9 (+4.0)	19.2 (+3.2)	11 (+2)
Liberal Democrats	14.1 (+0.6)	12.7 (+0.1)	6 (−)
Others	4.8 (+0.1)	11.8 (+6.9)	1 (+1)

Turnout = 38.2% (−7.7%)

elections) and garnered two additional list seats (in Mid and West Wales, and in South Wales East).

The Labour victory was a personal triumph for Rhodri Morgan, around whom the Labour campaign had been heavily based. Amidst a chorus of claims that Wales had 'Come Home to Labour', Morgan chose to ditch his erstwhile coalition partners: the post-election Cabinet was drawn entirely from Labour AMs. Labour's position was strengthened further by the shambolic state into which Plaid Cymru quickly lapsed. The disappointment of defeat provoked an immediate and public round of nationalist blood-letting. In the face of widespread criticism, and despite initially indicating that he would carry on, Ieuan Wyn Jones resigned as Plaid leader one week after the election. But he left no obvious successor; he also left a party that, for many, required not merely a new leader, but a new direction.[7] Accompanied by surprisingly strong showings from the party in the Scottish Parliament and English local government elections, the Tory recovery in Wales was hoped by some Conservatives to indicate a wider revival. For the Liberal Democrats, however, modest gains in vote share from 1999 were scant compensation for the loss of ministerial office and a return to the status of the third party of opposition.

Analysing the Election

The remainder of this article will begin to explore why the 2003 Welsh election produced the result it did. Our empirical analysis will draw heavily on the 2003 Wales Life and Times Survey.[8] While this survey lacks the panel component that would make understanding changes in voting behaviour from 1999 much easier, it nonetheless provides substantial information on public attitudes and voting behaviour. Our analysis proceeds in two stages. First, we identify a number of potential influences on the outcome of the election, and present some initial tabular data pertaining to these factors. Second, we construct a multivariate analysis of voting behaviour.

For the initial stage in our analysis, we examine three things: first, the immediate inferences we can draw from voting patterns themselves; second, changes in longer-term influences on voting (specifically, public attitudes towards the various parties); and third, the possible impact of some more immediate factors surrounding the May 1st election.

'Differential Voting'?

The 1999 NAW election result was shocking primarily because it contrasted so sharply with previous general election results in Wales. Labour's victory in 2003, and Plaid's slump in support, would appear to suggest that 1999 was aberrant and that Welsh politics has now returned to 'business as usual'. But a closer look at the results suggests otherwise. Labour's 2003 success occurred despite their attaining a vote share nearly 10 per cent below that garnered in the 2001 UK general election (which was itself down 6 per cent on that of 1997); Plaid Cymru's 2003 vote share was one of their best ever across Wales.[9] As we have observed in other work, election results and survey evidence indicate Welsh voting preferences differ systematically between the National Assembly and Westminster contexts (Trystan et al., 2003; Scully, 2003). In both good years and bad, Labour and the Conservatives do systematically better in Westminster elections than in National Assembly ones; for Plaid Cymru, the opposite is true. These patterns appear to reflect voter perceptions of the core concerns of the respective parties, and their relevance to particular electoral environments. Despite the efforts of Labour and the Conservatives to project a more Welsh identity in recent times, both parties fell *below* their 2001 general election vote share in 2003; Plaid did substantially *better* than two years previously. Moreover, as shown in Table 2, if we compare reported behaviour in the 2003 NAW election with how our survey respondents claim they would have voted in a Westminster poll, we find continued disparities in party preferences, and in the expected direction. Labour and the Tories continue to do worse in NAW elections than in those for the UK Parliament. Meanwhile, Plaid Cymru's main problem in 2003 was simply a general decline in support in elections at all levels.[10] Plaid continue to do better in NAW elections than in Westminster ones in both good and bad years; but 2003 was definitely a bad year.

Attitudes Towards the Parties

If 2003 was a bad year for Plaid Cymru, the question remains why that was so. An obvious place to begin exploring this is with fundamental public attitudes towards Plaid and the other political parties. Our data from 1999 and 2003

TABLE 2
VOTE SHARE (IN % TERMS), ACTUAL NAW AND HYPOTHETICAL
WESTMINSTER ELECTION, 2003

	NAW vote (first vote)	Hypothetical Westminster vote
Labour	42.7	50.0
Plaid Cymru	23.8	10.1
Conservative	17.4	23.0
Liberal Democrats	12.1	14.8
Others	4.0	2.2
Weighted N	466	754

Source: 2003 Wales Life and Times Survey.

TABLE 3
PARTY IDENTIFICATION (IN PERCENTAGE TERMS) IN THE WELSH
ELECTORATE, 1999 AND 2003

	1999	2003
Labour	46.2	44.3
Plaid Cymru	15.9	10.3
Conservatives	16.4	17.9
Liberal Democrats	8.3	9.0
Other/None	13.2	18.5
Weighted N	1256	988

Note: Figures reported are for respondents claiming any degree of party identification or to feel
          'closer' to one party.
Sources: 1999 Welsh Assembly Election Study, 2003 Wales Life and Times Survey

contain evidence both on the traditional measure of party identification, and also on voter attitudes to all the parties.

Table 3 reports party identification figures for each of the major parties in both 1999 and 2003. As can be seen, the pattern is generally one of continuity except for the fairly substantial decline in identification with Plaid Cymru. Whatever position is taken on wider questions concerning the appropriate measurement of the concept or its place in models of voting behaviour (e.g., Bartle, 2003), Plaid by 2003 attracted fewer identifiers than in 1999.

Another measure, used in both our election surveys, gauged respondents' summary evaluative feelings about each major party. As seen in Table 4, on this measure three of the four parties became less popular between 1999 and 2003, and none attracted particularly high levels of public affection. The one party whose rating improved was the Conservatives; although they remained the least-liked party, the scars of 18 years of Conservative government had begun to heal. But perhaps the most important finding is that the party experiencing the greatest decline in public esteem was Plaid Cymru.

Quite why Plaid declined so much in popularity requires investigation beyond the scope of this article. In part it may reflect the loss of the popular leadership of Dafydd Wigley and the ineffectiveness of his successor, Ieuan Wyn Jones (see below). But it may also indicate the effectiveness of the sustained campaigns against Plaid by Labour and its tabloid ally, the Welsh Mirror. The paper's political stance was characterized by repeated virulent attacks on Plaid Cymru and causes closely associated with the party, most notably the Welsh language,[11] aimed at labelling the party as 'extreme', while even those sections of the Labour Party regarded as

TABLE 4
FEELINGS ABOUT THE PARTIES (2003 PERCENTAGE AND 1999/2003
MEAN SCORES)

Response	Labour	Plaid	Tories	Liberal Democrats
Strongly in favour	12.4	5.0	4.3	3.7
In favour	35.3	25.3	16.2	20.3
Neither	28.9	42.7	40.7	56.8
Against	15.0	19.1	23.0	15.4
Strongly against	8.4	7.9	15.8	3.7
Mean (out of 5)*	**3.28**	**3.01**	**2.70**	**3.02**
1999 Mean	**3.39**	**3.30**	**2.52**	**3.17**
Weighted N	979	949	978	966

Note: *Where 'Strongly in favour' = 5, down to 'Strongly against' = 1.
Source: 2003 Wales Life and Times Survey.

insufficiently hostile to nationalism felt the wrath of Wales' biggest-selling newspaper. Plaid Cymru was singularly unsuccessful at combating these accusations.

The Iraq War

By dominating much news attention during March and April 2003, the Iraq war overshadowed the campaigns for the devolved and local elections across the UK on May 1. Nonetheless, given considerable disquiet within the Labour Party about the war, and the substantial public protests prior to military action commencing, 'pro-war' parties might have been expected to suffer in the elections, and more clearly 'anti-war' parties benefit. However, public opinion in the UK swung strongly behind the government with the start of war, and the fall of Baghdad occurred some three weeks prior to the polls. Thus it becomes less surprising that the most clearly pro-war party, the Conservatives, did unexpectedly well across the UK, while Labour largely held its ground in Scotland and made gains in Wales. Although doing quite well in the English local elections, the Liberal Democrats, who had voiced some criticisms of war, under-performed against expectations in both Scotland and Wales; the clearly anti-war nationalist parties in both Scotland and Wales lost votes and seats. As we can see from Table 5, with military action an established fact – and, indeed, apparently successful – by the time of the election, most Welsh voters were unwilling to criticize the government's policy. There was thus little chance of a large anti-war vote occurring, and even some scope for a 'Baghdad bounce'.

TABLE 5
'BRITAIN WRONG TO SUPPORT IRAQ WAR'

Response	%
Agree strongly	15.2
Agree	23.7
Neither agree nor disagree	12.9
Disagree	37.5
Disagree strongly	10.6
Weighted N	*985*

Source: 2003 Wales Life and Times Survey.

The Iraq war might have been expected to have another important impact, raising the salience of 'British' considerations, and making 2003 a less 'Welsh' election than it might otherwise have been. However, the findings reported in Table 6 suggest otherwise. At least for those engaging in the minority sport of voting in NAW polls, Welsh matters seem to have had a somewhat greater import in 2003.[12]

The Party Leaders

Table 7 presents data concerning respondents' feelings about the main UK and Welsh party leaders. While none of the leaders are much loved, Rhodri Morgan towers over the other Welsh party leaders in terms of popularity. Both Nick Bourne, the Conservative leader, and Mike German for the Liberal Democrats, fare poorly. It thus seems safe to assume that Nick Bourne was not a major factor in the Conservatives' relative success in 2003. And despite having had three years as Opposition Leader in the NAW in which to develop a profile, Ieuan Wyn Jones possessed precious little public appeal. That his

TABLE 6
SALIENCE OF WELSH AND BRITISH MATTERS TO VOTING DECISION
(IN PERCENTAGE TERMS), 1999 AND 2003

	1999	*2003*
Welsh Matters	42.2	50.1
British Matters	32.5	32.1
Both Equally	20.2	11.5
Other	5.1	6.4
Weighted N	*683*	*485*

Sources: 1999 Welsh Assembly Election Study, 2003 Wales Life and Times Survey.

TABLE 7
FEELINGS ABOUT PARTY LEADERS

Leader	Mean score (out of 10)	Don't knows (%)
Blair	5.81	0.9
IDS	4.35	13.6
Kennedy	4.74	21.0
Morgan	5.46	17.3
Wyn Jones	4.32	39.1
Bourne	3.63	62.1
German	3.50	51.2

Source: 2003 Wales Life and Times Survey.

rating was lower than that of Iain Duncan Smith tells us most of what we need to know about Wyn Jones' stature as an electoral asset for his party. Morgan also enjoyed a far higher profile than the other party leaders in Wales – one that bore comparison with the opposition leaders at Westminster, and is again in stark contrast with the other Welsh party leaders. While the impact of leaders on election outcomes in parliamentary elections remains a matter of considerable dispute,[13] and their impact upon sub-state elections remains largely unexplored, it is surely reasonable to assume that the popularity of a party's leadership has *some* impact upon their fortunes.

A Multivariate Analysis of Voting Behaviour

While the discussion above is interesting and suggestive, probing further into the 2003 Welsh election requires a more sophisticated multivariate analysis. In the absence of panel data, and with vote recall over the 1999–2003 period subject to substantial error and bias,[14] our analysis is inevitably somewhat restricted: we cannot reliably point to those who switched their electoral support between the first and second NAW elections and then analyse what factors might lie behind such changes. Instead, we develop our analysis in two stages. First, we run identical multivariate models on both our 1999 and 2003 survey data, comparing the manner in which a number of potential explanatory variables help to predict voting for each of the four major parties. Second, we develop a more detailed model to apply to our 2003 data.

For the first stage of our analysis, we replicate – with some minor differences in coding of variables – a model used in previous analysis of the 1999 election (Trystan et al., 2003), and apply it to our 2003 survey data. The independent variables include standard socio-demographic controls (age, sex and social class),[15] as well as several other variables found to be of importance in explaining the result of the first NAW election. These are: whether the respondent was born in Wales (a dummy variable coded '1' for yes, '0' otherwise); whether they were a Welsh speaker (two dummy variables entered for fluent and non-fluent speakers, with non-speakers as the comparison); a set of dummy variables measuring voters' constitutional preferences; a further set of dummy variables based around the 'Moreno' national identity scale; a measure of attitudes to the Westminster government;[16] and dummy variables (coded '1' if yes, '0' otherwise) if the respondent reported according priority to 'Welsh' or 'British' considerations in deciding how to vote. This model was developed largely to test whether the 1999 result could be adequately explained via a 'second order election' understanding, but can also be used as a useful means of comparing 1999 with 2003.

Table 8 reports estimates from a series of logistic regressions run on both the 1999 and 2003 data. The dependent variable in each column is whether the respondent reported casting their first (constituency) vote for that party or not, with non-voters excluded from the analysis. For each party, the model is run in an identical specification on both the 1999 and 2003 data. The results show a reasonable model fit, and some interesting contrasts between 1999 and 2003.

- One important finding that does not substantially differ is the extent to which the Welsh language has been and remains a central feature of the political landscape in Wales. Even when allowance is made for factors like national identity and place of birth, the language has a role in defining partisan preferences in Wales that is quite unthinkable east of Offa's Dyke.
- Labour's performance in 2003 was most impressive in many of its heartland seats, but we see its appeal improving across the social class profile. Furthermore, Labour in 2003 was much less dependent for support on those thinking about the vote primarily in UK terms; politically, Welsh Labour was more able to stand on its own feet and was less dependent on the popularity of Tony Blair's government.
- National identity became more important for defining Conservative support in 2003. The rise in Conservative support appears to have involved them drawing disproportionately from the more 'British' sections of the Welsh population. Given that these sectors are generally declining in number, this is not necessarily encouraging for the future of the Welsh Tories. Somewhat relatedly, while Conservative support has become less defined by anti-devolution attitudes, there is still a strong link between Conservative support and opposition to the further extension of Welsh self-government.
- The Liberal Democrat vote in 2003 remains the hardest to predict statistically. One very interesting finding, however, is the sharp change in the relationship between Liberal Democrat support and the Welsh language, which

between 1999 and 2003 has gone from a strong negative relationship to a modest (if non-significant) positive one. This may reflect in part the declining appeal of Plaid Cymru even among many Welsh speakers; but it may also be associated with the record of the Liberal Democrats in government from 2000 to 2003, and particularly the role played by Jenny Randerson as Culture Minister in developing policies supportive of the Welsh language.

- Plaid Cymru support is most readily predicted by our model for both elections. In 2003, competence in the Welsh language remained central to Plaid support, but the nationalists slipped badly among non-fluent speakers, their votes becoming more concentrated among fluent Welsh speakers, as well as amongst exclusively Welsh identifiers. Once language and identity are accounted for, Plaid did much less well in 2003 among those born in Wales, and across the main social classes, and its support was more concentrated among those concerned mainly with Welsh matters in making their vote choice.

For the second stage of our analysis, we specified a more developed model to apply to the 2003 survey data. This model incorporated variables plausibly related to voting patterns in 2003, but not available in the 1999 data. Specifically, we include: evaluations of the four Welsh party leaders on the 0–10 scale reported in Table 7 (with non-responses coded at the mean value for each leader to avoid losing excessive numbers of cases); responses to the question on the Iraq war reported in Table 6 (entered as a quasi-interval scale variable, with strong opposition to the war coded as '1', through to strong support coded as '5'); and a variable measuring the extent of negative evaluations of the policy performance of the Welsh Assembly government.[17] Logit estimates for the four parties are reported in Table 9. These results are broadly consistent with those of our earlier model, suggesting that the findings are robust and not an artefact of model specification peculiarities. The inclusion of the additional variables does, however, produce significantly enhanced model 'fit' for all four parties, indicating the relevance of the additional variables.

Among the new variables specified, attitudes to performance of the Assembly Government do not attain a significant relationship with vote choice; nor do attitudes to the Iraq war. However, attitudes to Welsh political leaders are important in shaping voting behaviour. The signs for the individual coefficients are strikingly unsurprising: all party supporters see good in their leader and little positive in the other leaders. If we assume that the statistical relationship to at least some degree involved leader evaluations generating voting support (i.e., that a voter favouring Morgan or Wyn Jones would be more likely to support their respective parties) then the fact that Morgan had both a higher profile and substantially more positive evaluations than the

TABLE 8A
LOGIT ESTIMATES (STANDARD ERRORS) FOR MODELS OF NAW
ELECTION VOTING, 1999

Variable	Labour	Conservative	Liberal Democrat	Plaid Cymru
Age	−.01 (01)	.01 (.01)	.00 (.01)	.00 (.01)
Female	.12 (.19)	.19 (.27)	−.16 (.27)	.01 (.23)
Social Class:				
Salariat	−.51 (.30)*	.57 (.45)	.32 (.43)	−.14 (.37)
Routine Non-man.	−.45 (.32)	.10 (.49)	.27 (.46)	.17 (.39)
Petty bourg.	−.72 (.39)*	.48 (.54)	−.25 (.57)	.43 (.47)
Skilled man.	−.25 (.40)	.56 (.58)	−.39 (.62)	.25 (.50)
Work. class	.17 (.31)	−.02 (.50)	−.41 (.49)	.09 (.38)
Born in Wales	.53 (.25)**	−.38 (.33)	−.60 (.32)*	−.12 (.30)
Welsh Speaking:				
Fluent	−1.09(.29)***	−1.43 (.57)**	−1.60 (.62)**	2.32 (.30)***
Non-fluent	−.13 (.22)	−.62 (.35)*	−.32 (.32)	1.05 (.26)***
National Identity:				
More British	.23 (.38)	.04 (.49)	.54 (44)	−.36 (.55)
Equal Welsh/Brit.	.01 (.30)	.31 (.38)	.04 (.38)	.35 (.39)
More Welsh	−.12 (.34)	−.29 (.50)	−.16 (.50)	.94 (.41)**
Welsh, not Brit.	−.30 (.36)	−.50 (.56)	.17 (.50)	.77 (.43)*
Constitutional Preference:				
Assembly	.57 (.23)**	−.77 (.29)***	.04 (.30)	.06 (.30)
Parliament	.42 (.24)	−1.23 (.36)***	−.02 (.34)	.66 (.30)**
Independence	−.40 (.39)	−.93 (.60)	−2.54(1.33)*	1.88 (.41)***
Level of Vote Decision:				
Mainly Wales	−.12 (.22)	−.61 (.34)*	−.22 (.31)	.72 (.25)***
Mainly UK	.49 (.23)**	.33 (.29)	−.26 (.31)	−1.03 (.32)***
'Anti-Government' Views	−.37(.10)***	.32 (.10)***	−.05 (.12)	.15 (.09)*
Constant	−.35 (.48)	−1.88 (.67)	−1.28 (.67)	−2.67 (.63)
Log Likelihood	804.57	453.33	463.46	587.94
Model Improvement	92.63	96.35	45.82	248.10
Nagelkerke Pseudo R^2	.17	.24	.12	.43
Weighted N	679	679	679	679

Note: *p<.10, **p<.05, ***p<.01.

TABLE 8B
LOGIT ESTIMATES (STANDARD ERRORS) FOR MODELS OF NAW ELECTION
VOTING, 2003

Variable	Labour	Conservative	Liberal Democrat	Plaid Cymru
Age	.01 (01)	.00 (.01)	−.02 (.01)	−.01 (.01)
Female	.17 (.23)	−.20 (.30)	.15 (.34)	.10 (.29)
Social class:				
Salariat	−.28 (.33)	.30 (.41)	.75 (.43)*	−.32 (.39)
Routine non-man.	.59 (.31)*	.60 (.39)	−.29 (.52)	−.78 (.42)*
Petty bourg.	.30 (.44)	.42 (.50)	.88 (.57)	−1.72 (.61)***
Skilled man.	.99 (.40)**	−2.26 (1.02)**	−6.74 (14.87)	.42 (.48)
Work. class	.83 (.31)***	−.62 (.46)	.12 (.50)	−.36 (.41)
Born in Wales	1.06 (.30)***	−.13 (.37)	−.43 (.46)	−1.10 (.39)***
Welsh Speaking:				
Fluent	−1.51 (.34)***	−1.49 (.69)**	.60 (.48)	2.23 (.36)***
Non-fluent	−.48 (.28)*	−.51 (.39)	.46 (.40)	.36 (.35)
National Identity:				
More British	.03 (.47)	.33 (.46)	.24 (.63)	−.75 (.68)
Equal Welsh/Brit	.05 (.39)	−.26 (.44)	.60 (.60)	−.10 (.53)
More Welsh	.74 (.41)*	−.87 (.51)*	−.18 (.64)	.56 (.52)
Welsh, not Brit.	−.07 (.45)	−1.59 (.69)**	−.11 (.72)	1.22 (.56)**
Constitutional Preference:				
Assembly	.47 (.29)	−.44 (.34)	.66 (.46)	.07 (.44)
Parliament	.49 (.29)*	−1.17 (.37)***	.36 (.46)	.57 (.40)
Independence	.60 (.40)	−.95 (.63)	−.79 (.83)	.90 (.48)*
Level of Vote Decision:				
Mainly Wales	−.03 (.28)	−.13 (.41)	−.23 (.43)	1.02 (.38)***
Mainly UK	.39 (.30)	.62 (.40)	−.31 (.47)	−.25 (.45)
'Anti-Government' Views	−.34 (.10)***	−.08 (.14)	.23 (.14)*	.15 (.12)
Constant	−2.18 (.61)	−.47 (.75)	−1.44 (.91)	−1.80 (.82)
Log Likelihood	570.01	349.74	290.41	382.52
Model Improvement	90.78	92.40	37.47	142.72
Nagelkerke Pseudo R^2	.23	.29	.15	.39
Weighted N	488	488	488	488

Note: *p<.10, **p<.05, ***p<.01

other leaders must have been of importance to Labour. Such a 'leadership effect' must be tested more thoroughly; but our results do suggest that the narrow Labour victory may have owed even more to Rhodri Morgan than was generally realized at the time.

TABLE 9
LOGIT ESTIMATES (STANDARD ERRORS) FOR EXTENDED MODEL OF NAW
ELECTION VOTING, 2003

Variable	Labour	Conservative	Liberal Democrat	Plaid Cymru
Age	.01 (01)	−.01 (.01)	−.03 (.01)**	−.01 (.01)
Female	.24 (.25)	.09 (.32)	.02 (.36)	.10 (.31)
Social Class:				
Salariat	−.04 (.35)	.11 (.44)	.95 (.47)**	−.33 (.42)
Routine non-man.	.54 (.34)	.65 (.42)	−.32 (.55)	−.58 (.44)
Petty bourg.	.38 (.49)	.71 (.56)	.81 (.60)	−1.78 (.64)***
Skilled man.	1.11 (.43)**	−2.07(1.03)**	−6.74 (14.30)	.53 (.49)
Work. class	1.02 (.33)***	−.40 (.49)	−.07 (.53)	−.57 (.44)
Born in Wales	1.01 (.33)***	−.12 (.40)	−.42 (.50)	−1.19 (.43)***
Welsh Speaking:				
Fluent	−1.36 (.37)***	−1.58 (.72)**	.72 (.52)	2.17 (.39)***
Non-fluent	−.30 (.31)	−.76 (.43)*	.71 (.42)*	.25 (.38)
National Identity:				
More British	−.14 (.49)	.69 (.51)	.21 (.68)	−.53 (.71)
Equal Welsh/Brit	−.03 (.43)	−.21 (.49)	.83 (.66)	−.15 (.57)
More Welsh	.72 (.45)	−.67 (.56)	−.01 (.68)	.75 (.57)
Welsh, not Brit.	−.18 (.49)	−1.42 (.73)*	.05 (.76)	1.32 (.61)**
Constitutional Preference:				
Assembly	.20 (.33)	−.15 (.37)	.94 (.51)*	.16 (.48)
Parliament	.34 (.32)	−.86 (.40)**	.48 (.51)	.61 (.44)
Independence	.65 (.45)	−1.04 (.69)	−.20 (.89)	.67 (.55)
Level of Vote Decision:				
Mainly Wales	.08 (.28)	−.23 (.44)	−.17 (.47)	.93 (.40)**
Mainly UK	.48 (.33)	.60 (.44)	−.20 (.50)	−.21 (.47)
Leadership Evaluations:				
Morgan	.34 (.07)***	−.14 (.08)*	−.16 (.09)*	−.12 (.08)*
Wyn Jones	−.24 (.08)***	−.03 (.10)	−.25 (.10)**	.42 (.09)***
Bourne	−.32 (.10)***	.49(.12)***	−.31 (.13)**	−.09 (.11)
German	.09 (.08)	−.26 (.11)**	.57 (.13)***	−.32 (.10)***
'Anti-Government' Views	−.31 (.11)***	−.09 (.15)	.19 (.14)	.13 (.13)
'Anti-WAG' Views	−.11 (.19)	.21 (.20)	−.02 (.24)	−.29 (.24)
Iraq War Right	.09 (.09)	.09 (.12)	−.25 (.14)*	−.04 (.11)
Constant	−2.43 (.80)	−.80 (1.01)	−.12 (1.11)	−1.80 (.82)
Log Likelihood	505.26	312.88	261.34	348.03
Model Improvement	149.07	127.83	65.68	173.87
Nagelkerke Pseudo R^2	.36	.39	.26	.46
Weighted N	484	484	484	484

Notes: *p<.10, **p<.05, ***p<.01.

Conclusion

The first election to the National Assembly for Wales in 1999 saw a substantial, if quiet, earthquake in Welsh electoral politics. Four years on, the second election witnessed a more minor tremor, but with some significant casualties. The result has had, and will have, important implications for Welsh politics and the future of devolution. The return to one-party government has already seen changes to the day-to-day functioning of the Assembly, and the rejection of proposals for proportional representation to be introduced for Welsh local government elections. The election result will also surely influence the ultimate impact of the Richard Commission, whose report on the powers and electoral arrangements of the NAW is due in 2004. And election defeat has prompted an implosion of the main opposition party, Plaid Cymru, which may take some years to arrest. Not all elections produce major earthquakes. But even apparently dull elections can matter.

NOTES

1. For more discussion of turnout in the 1999 election and its implications, see Scully et al. (forthcoming).
2. For a thumbnail sketch of the history of Welsh devolution as well as an extensive bibliography, see Wyn Jones and Scully (2003).
3. For an excellent discussion of the 'cult of inclusivity', see Chaney and Fevre (2001).
4. Labour's 're-branding' exercise was a direct response to Plaid Cymru's adoption of the bilingual 'Plaid Cymru – The Party of Wales' as its official title in 1998. For further discussion, see Wyn Jones (2001).
5. The final seat was expected to go to the Independent candidate John Marek. Marek had been Labour AM for Wrexham in the 1999–2003 Assembly, and was standing as an independent after being de-selected by his constituency Labour party. Marek was expected to win after an HTV/NOP constituency poll conducted during the campaign had shown him comfortably ahead.
6. Labour was given an effective majority in the Assembly by the decision of Plaid Cymru's Dafydd Elis Thomas to stand again for the position of Presiding Officer, a position that Thomas had held during the Assembly's first term.
7. See, for example, Hywel Williams, 'Now What's the Point of Plaid?' The Guardian May 14th 2003, p.24. Both candidates to succeed Ieuan Wyn Jones as Plaid President – Cynog Dafis and the eventual victor, Dafydd Iwan – acknowledged that Plaid's recent direction had been mistaken. Both argued that the party should have made more of its ultimate constitutional aim, and that that should be stated to be 'Independence' rather than the cumbersome formula of 'full national status within the EU' that had prevailed previously. There was also widespread acceptance in the party during the leadership election that it became too closely associated with the National Assembly (and therefore, associated with its failings) in the minds of many voters.
8. The 2003 Wales Life and Times Survey was funded by the ESRC Devolution and Constitutional Change programme (grant L219252042) and co-directed by Anthony Heath and Richard Wyn Jones. Fieldwork was conducted by the National Centre for Social Research.
9. Outside European Parliament elections, the 2003 NAW poll was Plaid's second best election performance ever in an all-Wales election.

10. As further evidence for the thesis of a general decline in Plaid support, note that the 2001 survey reported Westminster support for Plaid at slightly above 14 per cent, and support for Plaid on the first vote in a hypothetical NAW poll at above 26 per cent. (For further details, see Scully (2003).)

11. The Welsh Mirror's stance on the Welsh language has been subjected to searching critical examination by Patrick McGuiness. See Patrick McGuiness, 'Reflections in the "Welsh" Mirror,' Planet: The Welsh Internationalist, No. 153 (June/July 2002), pp. 6-12; and Patrick McGuiness, '"Racism" in Welsh Politics,' Planet: The Welsh Internationalist, No. 159 (October/November 2003), pp. 1-12.

12. Of further interest, the Iraq war or any other foreign affairs matters were nominated as the issue that 'mattered most to you' in deciding how to vote by only 1.4 per cent of the 2003 survey respondents who answered this question (ie, 7 actual respondents!).

13. For a useful summary, and important contribution to the debate, see Andersen and Evans (2003)

14. Our 2003 survey included vote recall questions for both the 1999 National Assembly election and the 1997 devolution referendum. According to respondents, the distribution of their first (constituency) votes in 1999 among those who voted was: 57.6 per cent Labour, 17.7 per cent Plaid Cymru, 14.8 per cent Conservative and 9.1 per cent for the Liberal Democrats. Even making every allowance for sampling error and the changes in the electorate over the four year period, this is patently ridiculous.

15. Age is coded in years; sex is a dummy variable coded '1' for female, '0' for male; social class is coded as a series of dummy variables for each class categorization, with those not classified used as the comparator category.

16. This variable was originally developed in Trystan et al. (2003) to gauge anti-government attitudes as a possible stimulus for 'protest' voting. The scale was created from responses to questions on changes in the health service, the general standard of living, and the education system. For each issue area a respondent scored one point if they felt that the situation had worsened a little since the last election and believed that this was mainly as a result of government policies, and two points if they felt that the situation had worsened a lot since the election and was a result of government policies. Thus a respondent blaming the government for substantial declines in all three areas would score 6, while a respondent not blaming the government for any worsening would score 0. For the 1999 survey, the comparison against which voters are assessing government performance is 1997; for 2003, voters were asked how things have changed in Wales since 1999.

17. The variable measuring the perceived performance of the Assembly Government is identical to that specified in note 16 for the Westminster government, except that here respondents scored points if they attributed blame for perceived decline to the Assembly Government.

REFERENCES

Andersen, Robert and Geoffrey Evans (2003) 'Who Blairs Wins? Leadership and Voting in the 2001 Election', in C. Rallings, J. Fisher, J. Tonge and P. Webb (eds.) British Elections & Parties Review, Vol. 13. London: Frank Cass.

Bartle, John (2003) 'Measuring Party Identification: An Exploratory Study with Focus Groups', Electoral Studies 22: 217–37.

Chaney, Paul and Ralph Fevre (2001) 'Ron Davies and the Cult of 'Inclusiveness': Devolution and Participation in Wales', Contemporary Wales 14: 21–49.

Rawlings, Richard (2003) Delineating Wales. Cardiff: University of Wales Press.

Scully, Roger (2003) 'Comparing Westminster and National Assembly Elections in Wales', Contemporary Wales, 16: 75–82.

Scully, Roger, Richard Wyn Jones and Dafydd Trystan (forthcoming) 'Turnout, Participation and Legitimacy in Post-Devolution Wales', British Journal of Political Science.

Trystan, Dafydd, Roger Scully and Richard Wyn Jones (2003) 'Explaining the Quiet Earthquake: Voting Behaviour in the First Election to the National Assembly for Wales', *Electoral Studies* 22: 635–50.

Wyn Jones, Richard (2001) 'On Process, Events and Unintended Consequences: National identity and the Politics of Welsh Devolution,' *Scottish Affairs,* 37: 34–57.

Wyn Jones, Richard and Roger Scully (2003) 'A Settling Will? Wales and Devolution, Five Years On', in C. Rallings, J. Fisher, J. Tonge and P. Webb (eds.) *British Elections & Parties Review,* Vol. 13. London: Frank Cass.

PARTIES AND POLITICAL ELITES

When Sheep Bark: The Parliamentary Labour Party since 2001

Philip Cowley and Mark Stuart

Throughout the 1997 parliament the Parliamentary Labour Party (PLP) was routinely discussed in terms that would have been unrecognizable to MacDonald, Attlee, Wilson or Callaghan. Backbench MPs were said to be trooping loyally (most said far *too* loyally) through the division lobbies. If the complaint used to be that Labour leaders were not in control of their party, after 1997 it soon became that they were too much in control. Labour MPs were routinely described as timid, gutless, sycophantic and cowardly. They acquired a reputation for excessive cohesion, excessive loyalty and an overall lack of backbone. They were variously described as sheep, poodles, clones, robots or – most bizarrely of all – daleks (Cowley, 2002: 37, 41, 96).

These phrases now seem distinctly old hat. Since the 2001 election the focus has instead been on how rebellious the PLP has become. At a remarkably hostile Prime Minister's Questions on 4 July 2001, Labour MPs began the parliament making clear their opposition to reforms to incapacity benefit – an encounter described as 'Day One of the Intifada' (White, 2001; also see Sylvester, 2001). Several private meetings of the PLP were similarly rumbustious.[1] More than 100 Labour MPs then voted against frontbench advice (albeit on a free vote) over the membership of departmental select committees (Cowley, 2001b). In May 2002 the government was forced to back down over its plans for Lords reform in the face of backbench pressure (Cowley and Stuart, 2003a: esp. 192–3). February and March of 2003 saw two enormous backbench revolts over Iraq, followed by a series of rebellions over Foundation Hospitals, one of which reduced the government's majority to just 17, the lowest on a whipped vote since 1997. And the issue of university top-up fees saw the government forced into a series of retreats and concessions in a desperate bid to stave off their first Commons defeat.

How did it come to this? This article examines the voting behaviour of Labour MPs from the 2001 election to the end of the second session of the parliament. It has four substantive sections. First, it details the rebellions that have taken place so far, placing them in their historical context. Second, it identifies the most rebellious backbenchers, and discusses the changing behaviour of some MPs. Third, it examines the behaviour of the 2001 intake

British Elections & Parties Review, Vol. 14, 2004, pp. 211–229
ISSN 1368-9886 print
DOI: 10.1080/1368988042000258844   © 2004 Taylor & Francis Ltd.

in some detail, to study the effect of changes in Labour's selection procedures. Fourth, it examines the factional nature of the voting behaviour. We begin, however, with a short methodological note, explaining the nature of the data employed in the article.

Methodology

MPs are not of equal importance. In an important article on legislative studies in 1976, Anthony King noted that although commentators often talked about 'parliamentary control' as if Parliament was one entity, there were in fact three groups within Parliament who wanted to 'control' the executive – the Opposition frontbench, the Opposition backbench, and the government's own backbenchers. Of these, it was the relationship between the government's own backbenchers and the executive – what he termed the 'intra-party' relationship – that was crucial. 'As far as the Government is concerned, government back-benchers are the most important Members of the House' (King, 1976: 16).[2]

Although the voting procedures in the House of Commons score highly in terms of transparency (Rekosh, 1995: 229–39, 294–5) – electors can see how their elected representatives have voted – one drawback of divisions in the Commons is that, unlike in some legislative chambers, abstentions cannot be formally recorded. The whips may formally sanction an absence from a vote, it may be accidental, or it may be deliberate. There is no information on the record that allows us to establish, at least not systematically, the cause of absences. We cannot therefore necessarily read anything into non-voting. For the purpose of systematic analysis over time, therefore, we have to rely on the votes cast.

The focus here therefore is on dissenting votes cast by government back-bench MPs; that is, those occasions when one or more Labour Members vote against their own party whip or the apparently clear wishes (sometimes implicit) of their own frontbench. This is the definition employed in earlier research (see for example, Norton, 1980: x). This article examines the votes cast by Labour MPs from the start of the parliament in June 2001 to the end of the second session in November 2003. As in previous research, excluded from the analysis are mistaken or mis-recorded votes and votes on matters of private legislation, private members' bills, matters internal to the House of Commons and other free votes.[3]

The Rebellions

There were 141 separate backbench rebellions by Labour MPs in the first two sessions of the 2001 parliament: 76 in the first session (from June 2001 to November 2002), with 65 in the second session (from November 2002 to

November 2003). These rebellions have ranged across the whole gamut of government policy, but 11 issues (broadly defined) saw rebellions in which at least 15 Labour MPs cross-voted:

1. In July 2001 40 Labour MPs voted against the timetabling motion for a debate on the membership of select committees.
2. Throughout November and December 2001 there were 22 separate back-bench revolts during the passage of the Anti-Terrorism, Crime and Security Bill. The largest saw 32 Labour MPs support an amendment to allow judicial review of the Home Secretary's decisions to detain terrorist suspects without trial.
3. In January 2002 26 Labour MPs backed a backbench amendment to the NHS Reform and Health Care Professions Bill, opposing the abolition of Community Health Councils (CHCs).
4. There were three rebellions during the passage of the Education Bill, including one in February 2002 in which 46 Labour backbenchers supported an amendment moved by the former Health Secretary, Frank Dobson, on faith schools.
5. Throughout June and November 2002 there were 17 separate rebellions during the passage of the Nationality, Immigration and Asylum Bill. The largest, insisting on the education of asylum seeker children in mainstream education, saw 43 Labour MPs vote against their whips.
6. In June and October 2002 the Enterprise Bill saw two rebellions, the largest of which saw 24 Labour MPs support an attempt to compel the Office of Fair Trading to take into account damage to the public interest and employment levels when determining competition policy on mergers and acquisitions.
7. The biggest rebellions of all came over the possibility of military action in Iraq, the largest of which saw 139 Labour MPs vote for an amendment that 'the case for war against Iraq had not yet been established, especially given the absence of specific United Nations authorisation'.
8. The subject of firefighters' pay and conditions saw rebellions during both the Local Government Bill and the Fire Services Bill; the largest saw 41 Labour MPs vote against their whips.
9. There were 20 rebellions throughout April, May and November against aspects of the Criminal Justice Bill. The two largest saw 33 Labour backbenchers vote against the abandonment of trial by jury in complicated serious fraud cases, or where there was thought to be a danger of a jury being interfered with.
10. There were nine rebellions during the passage of the Health and Social Care (Community Health and Standards) Bill that sought to establish Foundation Hospital Trusts. May saw the largest rebellion, when 65

Labour MPs defied their whips to back a Reasoned Amendment to Second Reading, and a subsequent revolt in November saw the government's majority cut to 17, the lowest since Labour entered government in 1997.

11. In July 2003 15 Eurosceptic Labour MPs opposed a government motion welcoming the draft Constitutional Treaty produced by the Convention on the Future of Europe.

These 11 issues between them accounted for 90 of the 141 rebellions. There were also an additional 51 smaller revolts covering a wide range of issues, including opposition to the war in Afghanistan, Sinn Fein's access to facilities in the House of Commons, commonhold and leasehold reform, student finance, community care, licensing laws, social security, the suspension of elections and justice issues in Northern Ireland, reproductive cloning, Post Office closures, pensions, ministerial conduct, regional assemblies, the European Communities (Amendment) Bill and other European issues.

A total of 141 rebellions meant that there were rebellions by Labour MPs in 18.8 per cent of divisions. In *absolute* terms, this is clearly not a high level of dissent: it means that around one out of every five divisions saw a rebellion – no matter how small – by a Labour MP. The others see complete cohesion. But, given that party cohesion has been a marked feature of British parliamentary life since the end of the nineteenth century (see, for example, Lowell, 1926), this should not be surprising. Of more interest, therefore, is to view the rebellions in *relative* terms. How does this behaviour compare to the behaviour of government MPs in previous parliaments?

Table 1 shows the number of backbench rebellions in the first session of every parliament in which Labour has been in government, going back to MacDonald in 1924. You do not need to be a statistical whiz to spot the key finding: there were more backbench revolts in the first session of 2001 parliament (which is marked in bold in the table) than in the first session of *any* parliament when Labour has been in power. The comparison with the first session of the 1997 parliament is especially sharp: there were almost five times as many revolts in the first session of the 2001 parliament than there were in the first session of the last. But there were also more rebellions in the first session of the 2001 parliament than there were in the first session of the parliament elected in October 1974, the parliament in which backbench dissent was to reach its post-war height (Norton, 1980: 427–46).

Table 2 extends the analysis, including the first two sessions of every post-war parliament, covering periods of both Labour and Conservative government. (We lack systematic data on periods when the Conservatives were in government before 1945 to enable us to extend the analysis back further).

TABLE 1
BACKBENCH REBELLIONS IN THE FIRST SESSION OF EVERY LABOUR
GOVERNMENT, IN RANK ORDER

Parliament	N
2001	**76**
1974O	54
1924	52
1929	33
1997	16
1945	10
1966	9
1974F	8
1950	1
1964	0

Again, the finding is fairly clear. A total of 141 revolts in two sessions is more than in the first two sessions of every post-war parliament.[4] As the table shows, this remains true when the 141 revolts are expressed as a percentage of the number of divisions taking place. The rate of rebellion faced by the whips'

TABLE 2
BACKBENCH REBELLIONS IN THE TWO SESSIONS OF ALL POST-WAR
GOVERNMENTS, IN RANK ORDER

Parliament	N	Rebellions as % of divisions
2001	**141**	**18.8**
1983	137	17.4
1970	135	16.2
1992	119	16.1
1974O	115	13.7
1987	111	12.3
1959	52	12.2
1979	64	7.8
1974F	8	7.3
1945	38	5.6
1997	35	5.0
1966	31	3.8
1950	5	2.1
1955	7	1.5
1951	2	0.4
1964	1	0.3

office in the 2001 parliament is higher than that faced by government whips in any other post-war parliament.

Yet here – as so often in life – size does matter. If each of these revolts consisted of a single MP, then the Labour whips could sleep soundly in their beds. Unfortunately for the whips, this is clearly not the case. The two largest Iraq rebellions were the biggest revolt against the whip since the mid-19th century, easily breaking all the modern records: the 110 Labour MPs who rebelled over agricultural rent reform in 1975 (Norton, 1980: 179–80), or the 95 Conservatives who voted against the post-Dunblane firearms legislation (Cowley and Norton, 1999: 93). To find a bigger revolt, you have to go back to the Corn Laws (see, for example, McLean, 1998). The rebellion in favour of a reasoned amendment to the Second Reading of the Health and Social Care (Community Health and Standards) Bill – which saw 65 Labour MPs cross-vote – was the largest against the Second Reading of a Government Bill by its own backbenchers since the Shops Bill in 1986 (Bown, 1990; Regan, 1990). And as the list above showed, there were also large revolts over faith schools, anti-terrorism legislation, immigration and asylum, community health councils and the fire service. Indeed, such was the frequency with which Labour MPs were rebelling that even some large revolts began to go unreported. A rebellion in mid-November 2003 saw 41 Labour MPs vote against their whip, but the revolt went almost entirely unreported in the media, as did a series of large revolts over the Criminal Justice Bill later in the month.

That said, as Table 3 makes clear, the majority of the rebellions since 2001 were considerably smaller than this. Over half consisted of fewer than ten backbenchers; just 21 (15 per cent) saw 30 or more Labour MPs break ranks. Whilst the government may suffer a rebellion every five votes, it only suffered a large rebellion – of 30 or more backbenchers – roughly every 35 votes.

The mean size of the rebellions since 2001 is 14. In absolute terms, this is greater than the average size of backbench rebellions in every Conservative period of government from 1945 to 1997, although this figure is partly

TABLE 3
SIZE OF BACKBENCH REBELLIONS, 2001–03

Number of MPs voting against the whip	N	As % of revolts
1–9	82	58
10–29	38	27
30–50	13	9
50+	8	6
Total	141	100

distorted by two variables. The first is the overall size of the parliamentary party, which varies as a result of the electoral success of the party in government. Fairly obviously, governments that win landslides have more MPs than those that scrape in. The second variable is the size of the 'payroll vote', those MPs who are part of the government (broadly defined) and who are bound to support it in the division lobbies. This latter group has increased over time, with the result that similar sized parliamentary parties from the 1950s and 1990s would have very different numbers of backbenchers. As a result, the number of backbenchers during the post-war period has ranged from under 200 (in 1964, and the two parliaments of 1974) to over 300 (in 1945).

The parliament of 2001 saw an average revolt of around 5 per cent of the backbench party, which (as Table 4) shows is the seventh largest in the post-war period. The contrast between the parliaments of the 1960s and 1970s and today is particularly strong.[5] The parliament of 1966 saw rebellions that were – in relative terms – almost twice as large as those of 2001. The parliament of February 1974 saw rebellions that were almost four times as large. Labour MPs may therefore be rebelling more often than they did in the 1960s and 1970s, but they are not (yet) rebelling in anywhere near the same quantity.

TABLE 4
AVERAGE SIZE OF BACKBENCH REBELLIONS IN THE TWO SESSIONS OF ALL
POST-WAR GOVERNMENTS, IN RANK ORDER

Parliament	Mean size of rebellion	Mean rebellion as % of backbench party
1974F	35	19.0
1974O	23	11.7
1966	22	9.1
1997	21	7.4
1992	12	5.9
1950	13	5.8
2001	**14**	**5.2**
1951	12	5.1
1945	14	4.6
1970	8	3.5
1983	8	2.9
1987	7	2.9
1979	6	2.8
1959	5	1.9
1955	4	1.6
1964	1	0.5

Who are the Rebels?

From the 2001 election to the end of the second session, a total of 197 Labour MPs voted against their whip.[6] This is more than did so in the whole of the preceding (1997) parliament. It is also more than the number of Conservative MPs who did so in the whole of the 1992 parliament under John Major (Cowley, 1999: 21). As a proportion of those MPs on the backbenches, 197 rebels means that almost two-thirds (65 per cent) of those who have been on the backbenches at some point during the parliament rebelled. Of those who have been on the backbenches solidly since 2001, just over three-quarters (77 per cent) rebelled. Yet if we take a longer perspective, this is not an especially high figure. The 1987 parliament saw 213 government MPs defy their whips in total, 165 of whom had done so by the end of the second session, and the parliament of 1983 saw some 226 MPs defy their whips by the end of the second session, 13 more than the current parliament – and from a smaller parliamentary party as well (also see Norton 1978: 214; 1980: 435).

Most of the 197 did not rebel often: almost three-quarters (140) rebelled on fewer than ten occasions; just 25 voted against their party whip 20 or more times. The identity of the 25 most rebellious MPs (listed in Table 5) is unlikely to be a huge surprise to anyone with a passing knowledge of Westminster or the politics of the PLP. Jeremy Corbyn heads the list (with 87 votes against the party whip), closely followed by John McDonnell (79). There is then a sharp drop, down to three MPs with over 50 dissenting votes each (Jones, Sedgemore and Marshall-Andrews), closely followed by another six with 40 or more dissenting votes.

It is worth stressing that this means that even the most rebellious Labour MP only votes against the party once every eight votes. And – as the table shows – Corbyn and McDonnell are exceptional in their behaviour, even when compared to some of the other more rebellious Labour MPs. Even Lynne Jones, the third most rebellious Labour MP (and the most rebellious woman), has voted against the party line 57 times, just once in every 13 votes. Even the rebels, therefore, are overwhelmingly 'loyal' in the division lobbies.[7]

The turnover caused by the 2001 election was the lowest at the end of any full-length parliament since 1945 (Cowley, 2001a: 258). Just 38 Labour MPs (discussed in more detail below) were new to the Commons.[8] This small influx of new MPs means that the changes in the PLP's behaviour cannot have been caused by changes in its membership. For the most part, the PLP consisted of the same people as it did four years before – but behaving very differently. It is, however, possible to identify three explanations for the difference in behaviour.

First, there are all the ex-members of the government sitting on the backbenches. After the reshuffle in 2003, this group totalled over 90.[9] It is not

TABLE 5
MOST REBELLIOUS LABOUR MPS SINCE 2001

Name	Number of votes cast against the whip since 2001
Jeremy Corbyn	87
John McDonnell	79
Lynne Jones	57
Brian Sedgemore	53
Robert Marshall-Andrews	51
Alan Simpson	48
Harry Barnes	47
Kelvin Hopkins	47
Robert Wareing	47
Dennis Skinner	43
Neil Gerrard	40
Denzil Davies	38
Andrew Bennett	37
Alice Mahon	37
Diane Abbott	36
Jim Marshall	32
Mark Fisher	31
Llew Smith	29
Kevin McNamara	28
George Galloway*	27
Mike Wood	25
Kate Hoey	24
Glenda Jackson	24
Terry Lewis	24
Tam Dalyell	22

Note: *includes only votes cast whilst in receipt of the party whip. Galloway only cast one vote – with or against the government – from his suspension from the PLP on 6 May 2003 (and subsequent expulsion on 23 October) until the end of the second session, and that was to participate in the anti-Foundation Hospitals vote on 19 November.

necessarily that ex-ministers have begun to vote against the government out of bitterness at leaving government (although some may be doing so), but that believing that their ministerial career is over gives them a freedom to act which is denied to others. Over half of this group (49) had voted against the government by the end of the second session, although this leaves almost half who had not done so, and even many of the rebels are less rebellious than they sometimes seem. Many of the better-known ex-ministers have in fact been fairly selective in their rebellions (the most rebellious ex-Cabinet Minister,

Frank Dobson, only voted against the whip nine times between 2001 and November 2003). If they have inflicted damage to the government, then it has usually been by voice as much as by vote.

Second, there is a large group of MPs who know that they are unlikely ever to get onto even the first rung of the ministerial ladder (at least under the present leadership). Of the huge 1997 intake, there were 75 who have not received even the lowest of government positions after six years in Parliament. Of these, all but 11 (85 per cent) rebelled between 2001 and 2003. Of course, some – John McDonnell or Bob Marshall-Andrews, for example – were never likely candidates for ministerial office. But there were 27 MPs from the 1997 intake who were on the backbenches for all of the last parliament without rebelling once, but who have begun to do so since 2001. They include the much-maligned Helen Clark, who (as Helen Brinton) became synonymous with excessive loyalty, but who voted against the party line five times between 2001 and 2003.

Third, partly as a result of the two factors listed above (what one senior whip described as 'the dismissed and the disappointed'), and partly simply because of the passage of time, the overall number of MPs to have defied the whip climbs ever-upwards. The number of MPs to have rebelled against the government at least once rose steadily from 77 at the end of the 1997 session to 133 by the end of the last parliament. Just over 20 rebels then left at the 2001 election, lowering the total temporarily, but it had reached 122 by the end of the first session of the 2001 parliament and had risen to 197 by the summer recess in 2003. Once an MP has rebelled once, they are much more likely to rebel for a second time (and then a third, and a fourth, and a fifth, and so on). And so with each new rebellion, the number of likely rebels for any subsequent rebellion increases.

Largely unnoticed, the government attempted in the much-maligned reshuffle of 2003 to ameliorate all three of these problems. Back into government came some ex-ministers – such as Chris Mullin or Bridget Prentice – thus sending out the message that resurrection is possible. Into government also came a group of 1997 loyalists – such as Nick Palmer or David Stewart – who might otherwise have come to the conclusion that they had no chance of ever making it even slightly up the greasy pole. And third, into government came a handful of MPs who had rebelled very occasionally – such as Jackie Lawrence or David Borrow – in order to show that sporadic rebellion does not of itself result in an eternity in darkness. The much-publicized cock-up in the changes at the top of government therefore distracted attention from the (much better thought through) changes at the lower levels.

But there is a limit to the extent to which problems can be ameliorated in this way. Promoting rebellious MPs can create resentment from overlooked loyalists. Promoting one MP into government almost always means sacking another. There is therefore an obvious limit to the number of ex- or would-be-ministers who can be brought into government, without simply creating more disgruntled ex-ministers in the process. The only way round this is to try to create more governmental posts. Although the government has been criticized for doing exactly this – by increasing the number of PPSs (see for example *The Guardian*, 5 August 2003) – the recent increases were in fact minute when viewed in long-term perspective (cf Alderman and Cross, 1966) and the tactic can anyway only bring in a very small extra number of MPs. For the most part, therefore, these problems will just continue to get worse the longer the government is in office.

The 2001 Intake

Complaints about the behaviour of MPs have been fuelled in recent years by the changes to the procedures used by Labour to select its parliamentary candidates (Shaw, 2001). For example, the pamphlet *Parliament's Last Chance*, from a group of senior parliamentarians called Parliament First, complained of the increasing centralization of political parties, and the resulting decline of the independent-minded parliamentarian (2003: 6, 26). The accusation is a simple one: Labour's ruthless Head Office weeds out dissenting voices. All those who might think for themselves and cause the whips sleepless nights are blocked, with the result that only Blairite clones make it to the Commons.

It was difficult to test this argument in 1997, because the scale of Labour's victory meant that it won many constituencies that were widely assumed to be safe Conservative seats, with the result that the very large 1997 intake included MPs who had not been properly vetted by the party's HQ (Cowley, 2002: 11). The 2001 intake, however, constitute a good test case for the effects of Labour's selection procedures, because in 2001 there was very little change in the number of seats held by each party, and so nearly every new Labour MP inherited their seat from a retiring Labour incumbent. As a result, they had all been vetted properly; and the party hierarchy had plenty of warning about its new MPs.

The 40 new Labour MPs (including the two by-election entrants) are listed in Table 6. Of the 40, 23 had voted against their whip by the end of the second session in November 2003. This constitutes 58 per cent of the 2001 intake. (By the end of the second session of the last parliament, by contrast, just 19 per cent of the 1997 intake had rebelled).

Notwithstanding the difficulties with abstentions (noted above), because of the extremely high profile of the issue we also looked at those who were absent from one or more of the Iraq votes, where there would have to be an extremely good reason for an absence. In fact, this makes relatively little

TABLE 6
THE BEHAVIOUR OF THE 2001 INTAKE

Name	Cast rebellious votes	Absent over Iraq	Backed 100% appointed Lords	Backed Cook on select committee reform
Vera Baird	•	•	•	•
Ian Lucas	•	•	•	
Dai Havard	•	•	•	
Khalid Mahmood	•	•	•	
Kevin Brennan	•	•		•
Colin Challen	•	•		•
Parmjit Dhanda	•	•		•
Paul Farrelly	•	•		•
Hywel Francis	•	•		•
Mark Lazarowicz	•	•		•
Rob Marris	•	•		•
Ann McKechin	•	•		•
Albert Owen	•	•		•
David Heyes	•	•		
David Wright	•	•		
Anne Picking	•		•	•
Kevan Jones	•		•	
Iain Luke	•		•	
John MacDougall	•		•	
James Sheridan	•		•	•
David Hamilton	•			•
John Lyons	•			•
Chris Mole	•			•
Mark Tami	(•)	•	•	
Paul Daisley*		•		
Tom Harris			•	•
David Cairns			•	
Tony Cunningham			•	
James Purnell		(•)	•	
Sion Simon			•	
Tom Watson			•	
Chris Bryant				•
Andrew Burnham				•
David Miliband				•
Meg Munn				•
Jon Cruddas				
Wayne David				
Huw Irranca-Davies				•
Jim Knight				
John Mann				

Note:　*died on 19 June 2003.

difference to the figures, since most of those who were absent have also cast dissenting votes at one point or other. Just three of the 2001 intake who have yet to cast a dissenting vote were absent from one or more of the main Iraq votes. James Purnell was absent from the votes on 26 February for personal reasons; Paul Daisley was opposed to the government's position but was terminally ill and unable to vote and Mark Tami abstained once on 18 March.[10]

On whipped votes therefore, including abstentions on Iraq, 24 of these 40 MPs have defied the whips to date.[11] In itself, this is a fairly remarkable figure: just two years after their election, almost 60 per cent of the 2001 intake had already defied their whips.

We then took a wider view, and included two key free votes. First, the votes on reform of the House of Lords. The vote may well have been free, but the Prime Minister's preference for a 100 per cent appointed chamber was well known (see for example, McLean et al., 2003). Of the 40 members of the 2001 intake, just 16 backed the PM's preferred position. Second, we examined a key vote on the nomination of select committees held at the beginning of the parliament (Cowley, 2001b), which again was free but where the known preference of many within the whips' office was to reject Robin Cook's reforms (Kelso, 2003). Of the 40, just over half backed the proposals.

Table 6 shows the behaviour of the 2001 intake across these various votes. There are just five MPs from the 2001 intake who (a) have not yet defied the whips on a whipped vote; (b) backed the PM's position on the Lords; and (c) rejected Cook's proposals on select committee reform.[12] These are marked in bold in the table: David Cairns, Tony Cunningham, James Purnell (notwithstanding his absence from one of the Iraq votes), Sion Simon, and Tom Watson.

If the aim of Labour's selection process was to ensure that only Blairite clones made it to the Commons, then it failed dismally. Over half defied the whips before the second anniversary of their election, making them roughly three times more rebellious than the 1997 intake had been. (It also makes them more rebellious in percentage terms than the group of ex-ministers discussed above). On 'free' votes they show no inclination to do as either the PM or the whips' office would like. The majority did not back the PM's position on Lords reform; the majority defied the known preferences of the whips over select committee reform. Just five – a mere 13 per cent – have not yet rebelled or defied either their whips or their Prime Minister.

It is, however, worth noting that this behaviour has its costs. Ten of the 2001 intake were promoted to government in the first two years of the parliament – nine as Parliamentary Private Secretaries (PPSs) and one, David Miliband, as a Minister of State. Of these ten, none voted against the party line. By contrast, of the 23 who voted against the party whip none has made it into

government, even at the lowest level. Of the five most 'super loyal' MPs identified above, four – Cairns, Cunningham, Purnell, and Watson – entered
government as a result of the reshuffle of 2003. The promotion rates are therefore: of the 23 who rebelled, none are now in government; of the 11 who did
not rebel but who did not necessarily do the whips' or the PM's bidding on
free votes, just over 50 per cent are now in government; of the five who did
not rebel and who did both the whips' and the PM's bidding on free votes, 80
per cent are in government.[13] This is unlikely to be coincidental.

Rebels with Causes

Richard Rose famously identified a classic distinction between factions and
tendencies in political parties. The Conservatives were a party of tendencies –
in which *ad hoc* groups of MPs (or others) joined together in temporary coali-
tions over specific individual issues. Labour, by contrast, was a party of
factions, in which groups of MPs (or others) campaigned together over a
range of issues (Rose, 1964). The Conservatives' classification as a party of
tendencies is now disputed (see, for example, Heppell, 2002; Cowley and
Norton, 2002). But what about Labour? To what extent are the rebels on each
issue the same people?

    To examine this, we first grouped the 121 individual rebellions into the 11
broad issue categories listed above, excluding the smaller, more idiosyncratic,
rebellions. We then looked at the number of issues over which MPs rebelled
(see Table 7). One of the phrases often used to describe MPs participating in a

TABLE 7
NUMBER OF ISSUES OVER WHICH LABOUR REBELS DISSENTED, 2001–03

Number of issues	Number of rebels	% of rebels
1	69	36
2	36	19
3	26	14
4	11	6
5	18	9
6	6	3
7	4	2
8	5	4
9	7	4
10	5	3
11	3	2
Total	190	102

rebellion is 'the usual suspects'. It is a phrase that many of the rebels dislike, believing that it is used to make light of their actions. To imply that those who oppose the government are just the 'usual suspects' is to imply that their opposition is predictable, only to be expected, and should not therefore be taken seriously. It is a (doubtless deliberately) vague phrase, but if by it we mean rebelling over, say, three-quarters of the issues to see backbench dissent, then (as Table 7 shows) the 'usual suspects' comprise just 15 MPs. If we widen the definition as far as it can possibly go, to include those MPs who rebelled on over 50 per cent of the issues that triggered backbench dissent (by its very nature, 'usual' cannot surely mean less than 50 per cent), then we are still talking about just 30 MPs. These 30 are listed in Table 8. To avoid offending anyone, we shall avoid describing them as the usual suspects – but when there is a rebellion you can suspect they will usually be involved.

There is therefore a hard core of rebels in the PLP, who participate in most serious rebellions, but this group numbers no more than 30. Around them, there is a much larger group of MPs who are willing to rebel but who do so less frequently, and less predictably. This latter group includes many who might be casually dismissed as 'the usual suspects', but whose voting is more discerning than this label implies – including Peter Kilfoyle (who rebelled over five issues out of the 11), Ann Cryer (five), Austin Mitchell (five), Gwyneth Dunwoody (four), Tam Dalyell (three) and Graham Allen (three).

Conclusion

The 2001 election did not mark the point at which the PLP changed from being sheep to rottweillers – both because Labour MPs were not sheep before, and because they have not become rottweillers since.

The supposed spinelessness of the 1997 parliament was always a myth. Although there were relatively infrequent rebellions in the last parliament, there were still 96 separate backbench revolts, and (as Table 4 indicates) those that did take place were sizeable. For poodles, Labour MPs could bark loudly when provoked (see, for example, Cowley and Stuart, 2003b). Moreover, the growing restlessness of the PLP had begun *before* the 2001 election. The number of rebellions grew throughout the last parliament, session-on-session (at least until the stunted, pre-election session of 2000–2001).

Rebellion therefore was on the increase before the 2001 election, and it has continued to increase since. The 2001 parliament has seen the largest revolt since the middle of the 19th century and has seen more revolts than any comparable period of post-war government. The widespread impression that Labour MPs are causing trouble for their leadership is far from erroneous.

But it is wise not to exaggerate the changes that have occurred. There has been no collapse in party discipline. Cohesion remains the norm, dissent the

TABLE 8

LABOUR MPS WHO REBELLED ON MORE THAN HALF OF MAIN ISSUES, 2001–03

Number of issues rebelled on (out of 11)

6	7	8	9	10	11
Harold Best	Ronnie Campbell	Dr Ian Gibson	Neil Gerrard	Harry Barnes	Kelvin Hopkins
Bill Etherington	Michael Clapham	Kate Hoey	Alice Mahon	Jeremy Corbyn	John McDonnell
David Taylor	Harry Cohen	Diane Abbott	Bob Marshall-Andrews	Dr Lynne Jones	Dennis Skinner
Mike Wood	John Cryer	Andrew Bennett	Alan Simpson	Brian Sedgemore	
Michael Connarty		Llew Smith	John Austin	Robert Wareing	
Gordon Prentice			Terry Lewis		
			Jim Marshall		

exception. Most votes still see complete cohesion. Even when Labour MPs do break ranks, they do not usually do so in huge numbers. Things may be bad, but they are not as bad as they were in the 1960s or (especially) the 1970s. There may be lots of would-be rebels, but they have yet to form into any organized resistance against the government. The good news for the government therefore is that although there are lots of MPs who are willing to rebel against it, it does not yet face any large-scale factional opposition on the backbenches of the PLP. The flip side of this, however, is that when it gets into trouble with its backbenchers, it cannot simply dismiss its problems as the result of the behaviour of the usual suspects – because there are not enough of them to cause it trouble.

ACKNOWLEDGEMENTS

This article draws on research funded by the University of Nottingham's Research Strategy Fund and the ESRC (RES-000-23-0028). We are grateful to all those MPs who have helped with the research, in whatever capacity.

NOTES

1. The very first PLP meeting after the election, for example, saw criticism from several normally loyal MPs, such as Peter Pike (who spoke about conditions on council estates in his constituency) and Debra Shipley (who spoke passionately about the state of her local hospitals).
2. He continued: 'One discounts the disapproval of the other party; the disapproval of one's own is harder to bear' (King, 1976: 16). See also Hurd (1997: esp. 3).
3. For example, excluded are the apparent (but incorrect) dissenting votes cast by George Howarth (Division 133, 15 Jan. 2002), Paul Goggins (Division 170, 14 April 2003), and John MacDougall (Division 200, 15 May 2003).
4. For the record, it also exceeds the figure for the government of May 1929–Aug. 1931, which saw 95 separate rebellions.
5. Indeed, when viewed as a percentage of the parliamentary party even the size of the Iraq rebellion becomes (just very slightly) less impressive. The largest Iraq revolt saw 34 per cent of the PLP vote against their whip. But in 1924, 73 Labour MPs – constituting 40 per cent of the PLP – voted against the MacDonald government over the right of strikers to claim unemployment benefit. As a proportion of the parliamentary party, this still remains the largest revolt by members of the PLP.
6. Of these, one (Ray Powell) has since died, one (Paul Marsden) defected to the Liberal Democrats, and one (George Galloway) has had the whip removed. By the end of the second session, this left 194 MPs sitting on the government benches, and in receipt of the whip, who had rebelled.
7. Moreover, because some of the more rebellious MPs are often refused leave of absence from the Commons as a punishment for their actions, some of them argue that they in fact cast more 'loyal' votes in favour of the government than do some of the less rebellious MPs.
8. This figure excludes Shaun Woodward, elected for the first time as a Labour MP in 2001 but first elected to the Commons in 1997 as a Conservative. In addition, Huw Irranca-Davies and Chris Mole both came in at by-elections since 2001.
9. This figure includes those who were in the government (broadly defined) as PPSs.

10. Tami had also once been in a dissenting lobby, albeit by mistake. On 26 November 2001, he was one of the first Labour MPs to arrive at the lobby to vote on introducing a new offence of religious hatred to the Committee stage of the Anti-Terrorism, Crime and Security Bill. One of the whips indicated that the Labour line was to vote against the clause, when in fact they were supposed to vote aye. Tami (along with Martyn Jones, who did the same) then had to cancel out their first vote by entering the aye lobby.
11. Or 25, if one includes Paul Daisley, who would have rebelled had he been well enough.
12. Extending the analysis to include other unwhipped votes – such as those over whether Gwyneth Dunwoody and Donald Anderson were to remain on select committees – makes no difference to the analysis. All five of the MPs identified here had voted to support the whips' original nominations.
13. The late Paul Daisley has been excluded from these calculations.

REFERENCES

Alderman, R.K. and J.A. Cross (1966) 'The Parliamentary Private Secretary – A Danger to the Free Functioning of Parliament', *Political Studies* 14: 199–208.
Bown, Francis A.C.S. (1990) 'The Defeat of the Shops Bill', in Michael Rush (ed.) *Parliament and Pressure Politics.* Oxford: Clarendon Press, pp. 213–33.
Cowley, Philip (1999) 'Chaos or Cohesion? Major and the Conservative Parliamentary Party', in Peter Dorey (ed.) *The Major Premiership.* London: Macmillan, pp. 1–25.
Cowley, Philip (2001a) 'The Commons: Mr Blair's Lapdog?', in Pippa Norris (ed), *Britain Votes 2001.* Oxford: Oxford University Press, pp. 251–64.
Cowley, Philip (2001b) 'Don't Panic! Putting those select committee votes into perspective', *Renewal* 9: 102–5.
Cowley, Philip (2002) *Revolts and Rebellions: Parliamentary Voting Under Blair.* London: Politico's.
Cowley, Philip, and Philip Norton (1999) 'Rebels and Rebellions: Conservative MPs in the 1992 Parliament', *British Journal of Politics and International Relations* 1: 84–105.
Cowley, Philip, and Philip Norton (2002) 'What a ridiculous thing to say! (which is why we didn't say it): A response to Timothy Heppell', *British Journal of Politics and International Relations* 4: 325–9.
Cowley, Philip, and Mark Stuart (2003a) 'Parliament: More Revolts, More Reform', *Parliamentary Affairs* 56: 188–204.
Cowley Philip and Mark Stuart (2003b) 'In Place of Strife? The PLP in Government, 1997–2001', *Political Studies* 51: 315–31.
Heppell, Timothy (2002) 'The Ideological Composition of the Parliamentary Conservative Party, 1992–97', *British Journal of Politics and International Relations* 4: 299–324.
Hurd, Douglas (1997) 'The Present Usefulness of the House of Commons', *Journal of Legislative Studies* 3: 1–9.
Kelso, Alexandra (2003) 'Where were the massed ranks of parliamentary reformers? 'Attitudinal' and 'Contextual' Approaches to Parliamentary Reform', *The Journal of Legislative Studies* 9: 57–76.
King, Anthony (1976) 'Modes of Executive-Legislative Relations', *Legislative Studies Quarterly* 1: 11–34.
Lowell, A.L. (1926) *The Government of England*, vol. 2. London: Macmillan.
Mclean, Iain (1998) 'Irish Potatoes, Indian Corn, and British Politics: Interests, Ideology, Heresthetics, and the Repeal of the Corn Laws', in A. Dobson and J. Stanyer (eds) *Contemporary Political Studies 1998.* Nottingham: Political Studies Association, pp. 114–21.
Mclean, Iain, Arthur Spirling and Meg Russell (2003) 'None of the Above: The UK House of Commons Votes on Reforming the House of Lords, February 2003', *Political Quarterly* 74: 298–310.
Norton, Philip (1978) *Conservative Dissidents.* London: Temple Smith.

Norton, Philip (1980) *Dissension in the House of Commons, 1974–1979*. Oxford: Clarendon Press.

Parliament First (2003), *Parliament's Last Chance*. London.

Regan, Paul (1990) 'The 1986 Shops Bill', *Parliamentary Affairs* 41: 218–35.

Rekosh, E. (ed.) (1995), *In the Public Eye: Parliamentary Transparency in Europe and North America*. Washington DC: International Human Rights Law Group.

Rose, Richard (1964) 'Parties, Factions and Tendencies in Britain', *Political Studies* 12: 33–46.

Shaw, Eric (2001) 'New Labour: New Pathways to Parliament', *Parliamentary Affairs* 54: 35–53.

Sylvester, Rachel (2001) 'Labour grumbles are emblems of a deeper unease', *Daily Telegraph,* 5 July.

White, Michael (2001) 'Why Labour MPs are the new opposition', *The Guardian,* 7 July.

The Irish Labour Party Leadership Election, 2002: A Survey of Party Members

Peter Fitzgerald, Fiachra Kennedy and Pat Lyons

The election of party leaders is often based on the votes of a small number of electors, normally a party's elected representatives in parliament. Internal party elections are of enormous importance to students of democratic theory and practice because such 'organizational' elections determine the choices offered to the electorate in general elections. Those who lead political parties into government generally find themselves, if not leading the government, then playing very important roles in government (Marsh, 1993a, 1993b; Müller, 2000).

The election of Iain Duncan Smith as leader of the British Conservative Party in 2001 is a salient example of the issues which may arise for a party that embarks upon leadership elections based on a one-member, one-vote (OMOV) ballot of all members.[1] Although Duncan Smith had the legitimacy of being elected by party members, this did not make him an effective or respected leader among his parliamentary colleagues, nor did it make the Conservatives a more potent opposition party. In view of this, it would be fascinating to understand the factors that motivated Conservative Party members to support Duncan Smith in 2001. Unfortunately, no detailed academic survey of party members' preferences was undertaken (although ICM ran a short survey commissioned by *The Daily Telegraph* in August 2001).[2] Instead, we are forced to rely mainly on official electoral and anecdotal evidence.

In the past, explanations of party leadership contests have often been based on the views of expert commentators or the published views of participants. In essence, such explanations are based on opinion. However, where parties have adopted inclusive methods of election, new opportunities arise to study in greater detail the operation and nature of representation in parties (LeDuc, 1999). The study of internal party leadership elections opens up new opportunities to examine voter choice in an environment where the franchise is restricted to party members whose general profile is quite often different to that of the general electorate.[3]

There have been leadership elections in Australia, Britain, Belgium, Canada, Denmark, Finland, Germany, Israel and the United States where

British Elections & Parties Review, Vol. 14, 2004, pp. 230–244
ISSN 1368-9886 print
DOI: 10.1080/1368988042000258853

party members have decided who will lead the party (Davis, 1998; Carty and Blake, 1999). However, to our knowledge there has not previously been a post-election survey of voters in such elections. Our survey of the Irish Labour Party leadership election is the first conducted in a national party selecting a new leader by balloting members. For this reason, we believe our survey is of interest not only to students of electoral behaviour but also to those interested in political representation more generally. Our aim here is simply to describe this unique election and illustrate briefly the utility of undertaking leadership surveys.

Candidates

The leadership election in the Irish Labour Party came about when Ruairí Quinn resigned as party leader on August 27, 2002. Nominations for the contest to replace him were opened on September 4 and remained open until September 18. This gave potential candidates an opportunity to take soundings in the party as to their likely level of support. In the end, four candidates came forward to contest the leadership election: Brendan Howlin announced his candidacy on September 10, Róisín Shortall and Pat Rabbitte entered the race on September 12 and Eamon Gilmore entered on September 15.[4] The immediate favourite was the outgoing deputy-leader, Brendan Howlin, a TD from the rural constituency of Wexford.[5] Howlin, whom Quinn had defeated for the party leadership in 1997, was seen as the candidate representing continuity. He was also the party's spokesperson on Finance and was the most experienced of the candidates in that he had held the portfolios of Health (1993–94) and the Environment (1994–97).

The main challenge to Howlin was seen as coming from Pat Rabbitte, a TD for Dublin South-West and party spokesperson on Justice. There was a view within the party that Rabbitte's background as a Democratic Left TD, who had only recently joined the party, might lessen his appeal among longstanding Labour Party members (there were approximately 250 former Democratic Left members in an electorate of about 3,900). However, his declaration prior to the general election that he would not serve as a Labour minister in a government involving Fianna Fáil gave him the status of challenger of the *status quo* within the party and the candidate for change. He was also perceived as the most media-friendly candidate, given his penchant for sharp sound bites and regular appearances in the media. In terms of government experience he had been a Minister of State in the Department of Enterprise and Employment (1994–97) with the (unusual) right of attendance at cabinet meetings.

A problem for Rabbitte's challenge was the entry into the race of Eamon Gilmore, another Dublin based, former member of Democratic Left.

Gilmore's policy output and work rate as the Labour Party's Environment spokesperson had impressed, and he had previously been a Minister of State in the Department of the Marine (1994–97).

The fourth and final candidate, Róisín Shortall, had no previous ministerial experience. She opposed both the merger with Democratic Left in 1998 and the coalition with Fianna Fáil in 1992, and was also regarded as suspicious of the so-called 'liberal agenda'. Moreover, she was critical of Quinn's leadership and had refused a position on the party front bench after the 2002 general election.

Campaign

The election campaign ran from the close of nominations on September 18 and lasted just over five weeks.[6] During the initial phase of the campaign there was little to distinguish the candidates. For the most part they focused on claims that they would lead a vigorous and critical opposition to the Fianna Fáil – Progressive Democrat government.[7] The main division that emerged at this early stage related to the issue of how the candidates would deal with the new intake of 'leftish' TDs.[8] While Howlin talked of 'forging new alliances on the broad left',[9] Rabbitte saw 'formal alliances on the left' as 'problematic' and not a priority.[10]

The election campaign was focussed around a series of 14 debates that were organized by the party's Head Office and constituency organizations. The frequency of the debates (12 of the 14 meetings were held in the first two weeks of October) and time involved travelling to and from them, was an important feature of the election, as it restricted candidates' ability to undertake other kinds of campaign activity. Nonetheless, each candidate was issued with the contact details of all party members entitled to vote.[11] All of the candidates sent out election leaflets and some contacted members through emails and text messages. Another common strategy involved campaign teams telephoning party members on behalf of the candidates, with the candidates themselves calling key members or 'opinion leaders' in the party who were regarded as likely to influence fellow voters.

Each of the candidates sought the endorsement of prominent members of the party, with particular attention being paid to the constituencies with large numbers of voters. Rabbitte was perhaps the most successful at this as he garnered the support of seven TDs (as well as 17 councillors and six trade union leaders); these supporters were from different parts of Ireland (which was important given that three of the four candidates were based in Dublin) and were willing to support him in public. Two senior party officers issued letters of support for Howlin, whereas the 'youth wing' of the Labour Party came out in support of Gilmore. While Gilmore and Shorthall were believed to have the support of a number of prominent trade unionists and some Dublin TDs, none issued public statements of support.

As the election campaign progressed it became obvious from published opinion polls and contacts with party members that Rabbitte had emerged as the frontrunner, despite the fact that Howlin had originally been tipped as the leading candidate. Consequently, the only strategy open to the less popular candidates was to embark on a vote-management strategy, whereby they instructed their supporters how to rank their preferences on the ballot paper – a common strategy in many constituencies during general election campaigns (Kennedy, 2002). There were a number of attempts to form electoral alliances among the less popular candidates, though in the end these came to nothing.[12] In any case, the proportion of first preference votes that Rabbitte won meant that even the most disciplined of vote transferring between the remaining candidates was very unlikely to cost him the election. There was, however, media speculation of a cross-ballot alliance between Rabbitte and Willie Penrose (who was contesting the deputy leadership election).[13] The attraction of such an alliance for Rabbitte was that it might deliver a large number of votes (Penrose's constituency had the largest number of voters, 275) and also enhance his credibility amongst rural voters and long-term members of Labour.[14] Significantly, when Penrose originally announced his candidacy for the deputy leadership, he denied that he would be running on a 'joint ticket'.[15]

There were few policy differences among the candidates. Indeed, an examination of the literature produced by the four candidates reveals very little policy content at all, even though Labour Party members often debated issues such as the Nice Treaty, Northern Ireland and the economy. That said, questions raised at the public meetings did elicit some differences. For example, a question on the issue of abortion at the 'Labour Women' hustings brought differing responses from the candidates.[16] Gilmore was the only candidate to state unambiguously that he was in favour of 'a woman's right to choose'. While Shortall was opposed to this view, Howlin explained that he disagreed with the liberal pro-choice position but was in favour of expanding the current circumstances under which abortion would be allowed. Rabbitte avoided the issue by deferring comment until an internal party committee on the issue had reported. Despite significant differences in the candidates' positions on the issue, and some media coverage of their responses, the abortion issue played no major part in the rest of the campaign.

In terms of involvement in the campaign by the media, there were a number of debates, discussions and interviews with the candidates on radio, television and in the print media. It should be remembered that this election campaign took place in the midst of the government's campaign to pass the Nice Treaty at the second attempt. Where the media may have had an impact was with the publication of two opinion polls by *The Irish Times*. The results of the first

TABLE 1
IRISH TIMES/MRBI POLL RESULTS SHOWING PUBLIC SUPPORT FOR LABOUR
LEADERSHIP CANDIDATES, SEPTEMBER–OCTOBER 2002 (%)

	Amongst the general public	Amongst Labour supporters	Amongst the general public	Amongst Labour supporters
Survey date	September 30	September 30	October 18	October 18
Rabbitte	30	42	35	40
Howlin	21	31	20	25
Shortall	10	11	10	10
Gilmore	8	13	8	16
No Opinion	31	3	27	4
N	1,000	95	1,001	96

Notes: 'As you are probably aware, nominations have closed for the election of a new leader of the Labour Party. Which one of the following candidates would you personally like to see as the new leader of the Labour Party?' SHOW CARD. (1) Eamon Gilmore; (2) Brendan Howlin; (3) Pat Rabbitte; (4) Róisín Shortall; (5) No opinion. Irish Times/MRBI/6218/02, 23–24 September 2002, question 8, and 14–15 October 2002, question 8.

poll were published on September 30, though the main focus of this, and the later poll, was the Nice Treaty Referendum.

From Table 1 it can be seen that Rabbitte established a clear lead among both the general public and Labour Party supporters, and that the race was clearly between him and Howlin. While those polled did not constitute the electorate (i.e., eligible Labour Party members), it did have an effect in shifting the status of media pundits' 'favourite' from Howlin to Rabbitte.[17] While this no doubt provided a boost to the Rabbitte campaign, more importantly it presented him as the most popular candidate with the general electorate and therefore the leadership candidate most likely to improve the party's standing at the next election. Near the end of the campaign (18 October), *The Irish Times* published the results of a second poll. The results showed that support for Rabbitte had increased amongst both the public and Labour Party supporters.[18]

Election Result

The electoral system used for this contest is the same as those used in Irish general elections, the Single Transferable Vote (STV). However, as with Irish presidential and by-elections, the electoral rules are more appropriately considered an Alternative Vote (AV) system because there is only one winner (Sinnott, 1995: 16). Initially most commentators saw the leadership election as a contest between Rabbitte and Howlin. When the first opinion poll was

TABLE 2
THE RESULT OF THE LABOUR PARTY'S LEADERSHIP ELECTION
(25 OCTOBER 2002)

Leadership candidates	First count	Second count	Total
Pat Rabbitte	1,587	541	2,128
Brendan Howlin	1,005	306	1,311
Eamon Gilmore	598	Eliminated	
Róisín Shortall	282	Eliminated	
Spoiled or non-transferable	2	33	
Total	3,474		

Source: Labour Party Report, 2001–03.

published it became clear that Rabbitte had a substantial lead over the other three candidates among the general public as well as among Labour Party members. The result of the election confirmed Rabbitte's popularity among the latter group (see Table 2). Winning 46 per cent of first preferences put Rabbitte within touching distance of the party leadership. After the first count Howlin was in second place with 29 per cent of the vote while the other two candidates together had 25 per cent of the vote.

Rabbitte's dominance of the first preference votes meant that if Howlin was to have any hope of winning he would have had to pick up almost all of the transferred votes of the two eliminated candidates. Both Shorthall and Gilmore were eliminated after the first count, because even if Gilmore had received all of Shorthall's second preferences, he would not have had enough votes to put him ahead of Howlin. As it was, Rabbitte picked up almost two-thirds of the transferable votes in the second count and was duly elected leader.

Data

Before using our survey to examine the election result in more detail, a brief overview of the data is necessary. A random sample was selected drawing on 50 per cent of the membership database of those eligible to vote in the leadership election. This resulted in a sample of 1,791 questionnaires being posted to members on 5 February 2003 – a little more than three months after the leadership election.[19] Attempts to get the survey in the field at an earlier date were constrained by the practical consideration of a potentially low response rate for a questionnaire sent during the Christmas period. In any event, 548 surveys were returned, yielding a response rate of 31 per cent, which is reasonable for a postal survey. Furthermore, 70 per cent of the completed surveys were returned within two weeks. As the survey slightly overestimates support for Rabbitte and Gilmore, and underestimates support for Howlin and Shorthall, we have weighted the data so that it reflects the result of the support for each candidate in the election itself. Given the post-election nature of the survey, there is always a danger that members of a party will row in behind the leader of the election contest. However, Rabbitte's support among respondents to our survey was just over 50 per cent, so almost half of our respondents were willing to say they opted for a candidate other than the party leader. This is very close to the actual result and supports the reliability of our data.

Candidates' Campaign Activities

Our survey of party members entitled to vote in the leadership election facilitates examination of the factors influencing their choices. In line with election studies based on the Michigan voter model, the emphasis here is primarily on the voters (Curtice, 2002: 161). The results shown in Figure 1 offer an indication of the most salient campaign channels perceived by party members in this

FIGURE 1
WAYS IN WHICH THE LEADERSHIP CAMPAIGN CAME TO PARTY MEMBERS

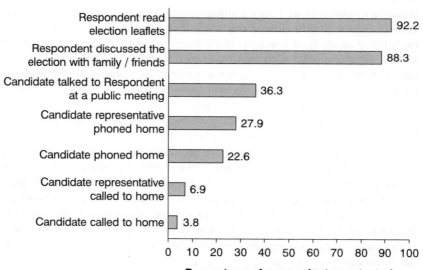

Source: Labour Leadership Election Survey, 2003.

election. Almost all (92 per cent) respondents learned about the campaign through leaflets sent to them. Almost as important was the impact of discussing the election with family or friends (88 per cent).

If we take a closer look at what the candidates did during the five-week campaign, we can see the importance of the party debates, at which 36 per cent of the respondents met at least one of the candidates. Telephone canvassing was also a significant feature of the campaign with candidates or their representatives phoning the homes of over a third of all respondents. Only a small number of respondents were canvassed personally by a candidate who called to their house in a manner typical of general election campaigns. These results indicate two important features of internal party elections. First, the style of campaigning is different to that in general elections, in the sense that voters went to meet the candidates rather than vice versa. Second, while voters may have gone to meet candidates this did not diminish the importance of personal contact with (potential) leaders, a prominent feature of many types of election campaign.

In Table 3 we measure the level of support for each candidate by the respondent's experience of the election campaign. We then compare the support for each candidate within each of these categories with the overall level of first preferences they achieved in the actual election. For example, of those respondents who were contacted by phone by Rabbitte, 69 per cent gave him their first preference. This percentage is significantly greater than the 46 per cent of first preferences that he received from Labour Party members in the actual result overall. Howlin and Shorthall also won larger shares of the vote from those whom they personally phoned than they did from party members overall. With regard to Howlin, his share of the vote among those voters who were contacted by Rabbitte and Shorthall is significantly less than the share of the vote he won in the election. This suggests that candidates personally contacting party members by phone significantly boosted their own support and undermined that of other candidates.

A similar pattern is evident when we consider whether or not the respondent met each of the candidates at a public meeting. As noted earlier, public meetings organized by the party offered members the best chance of meeting the candidates. The evidence in Table 3 suggests that meeting voters significantly boosted a candidate's support. In the 'meet candidate at public meeting' section of the table, all of the percentages along the principal diagonal are significantly different, and greater, than the vote share won in the election. Interestingly, Rabbitte's share of the vote amongst those who met Howlin at one of these meetings is significantly less than the share of the vote he won in the election.

One campaign factor not shown in Table 3 is candidates calling on respondents' homes. The problem with this item is selection bias, in that candidates

TABLE 3
CANDIDATE CAMPAIGN ACTIVITIES BY FIRST PREFERENCE VOTE CHOICE IN
THE LEADERSHIP ELECTION (%)

	Rabbitte	Howlin	Gilmore	Shorthall	Total
Vote share	45.7	28.9	17.2	8.1	536
Candidate phoned the respondent					
Rabbitte	**69.0**	**11.9**	14.3	4.8	42
Howlin	42.9	**42.9**	14.3		56
Gilmore	41.2	31.4	25.5	2.0	51
Shorthall	57.6	**15.2**	**6.1**	**21.2**	33
Representative of candidate phoned					
Rabbitte	**59.0**	24.6	9.8	6.6	61
Howlin	50.0	27.3	13.6	9.1	44
Gilmore	39.1	34.8	23.9	2.2	46
Shorthall	41.9	32.3	16.1	9.7	62
Met candidate at public meeting					
Rabbitte	**53.9**	23.0	15.8	7.2	152
Howlin	**37.1**	**40.5**	15.5	6.9	116
Gilmore	41.9	23.9	**27.4**	6.8	117
Shorthall	37.7	24.7	23.4	**14.3**	77
Read election leaflets	47.6	27.9	17.2	7.3	494
Discussed election with family/ friends	46.8	28.0	17.6	7.6	472

Note: Data weighted to reflect result of election. Figures in bold indicate that the proportion is
significantly different from overall share of the vote at the 5 per cent level of significance
(one-tailed test).
Source: Labour Leadership Election Survey, 2003.

generally used this tactic to make 'courtesy calls' to known supporters in the
hope that these 'opinion leaders' would attract support from other party
members. More importantly, the number of respondents influenced in this
manner was very small (less than 5 per cent of the total electorate).

Analysis of the Election Result

Was Rabbitte generally popular across the Labour Party membership or did he
appeal only to particular sections? Did Howlin and the others lose out because
they failed to win over particular groups? It is clear from Table 4 that in all but
one case, the support Rabbitte won in each social and political group within

TABLE 4
SOCIAL PROFILE OF SUPPORT FOR EACH OF THE LEADERSHIP CANDIDATES (%)

	Rabbitte	Howlin	Gilmore	Shorthall	Total
Vote share	45.7	28.9	17.2	8.1	536
Female	44.7	32.1	16.4	6.9	159
Male	45.8	27.4	18.2	8.7	358
25 or younger	40.0	0.0	**46.7**	13.3	15
26–35 years	35.3	37.3	19.6	7.8	51
36–45 years	51.8	23.5	15.3	9.4	85
46–55 years	46.6	28.6	14.3	10.6	161
56–65 years	46.6	29.8	18.3	5.3	131
66 or older	45.1	34.1	15.4	5.5	91
Degree	40.3	**22.4**	**24.9**	**12.4**	201
Not	49.1	33.1	**12.5**	5.3	320
Trade Union Member	45.9	27.2	17.9	9.0	368
Not	47.9	30.3	16.2	5.6	142
Dublin	40.9	**18.2**	**27.3**	**13.6**	198
Rest of Country	49.1	**35.3**	**10.7**	**4.9**	326
Former DL Member	**60.5**	0.0	**34.9**	4.7	43
Not	44.8	31.4	15.4	8.3	493
Before Campaign	48.9	28.9	15.4	6.8	226
During Campaign	43.4	28.7	18.9	9.1	265
No Degree-Dublin	51.2	**15.0**	22.5	10.0	80
No Degree-Rest of Country	48.1	**39.1**	**8.9**	**4.2**	235
Degree-Dublin	**33.0**	**20.0**	**30.0**	**16.5**	115
Degree-Rest of Country	51.2	24.4	15.8	7.3	82

Note: Data weighted to reflect result of election. Figures in bold indicate that the proportion is
significantly different from overall share of the vote at the 5 percent level of significance
(one-tailed test.

Source: Labour Leadership Election Survey, 2003.

the party was not significantly different from his overall level of support. In essence, Rabbitte was popular right across the party. However, he did receive especially high support among those who were also former members of Democratic Left, though this can have done little to influence the overall outcome of the election since it accounted for a small proportion of party members.

With regard to the other three candidates, it would seem that they appealed to particular groups of voters. Moreover, the evidence suggests that Howlin's attempts to win this election were severely undermined by his failure to win sufficient support from two large groups of party members. First, Howlin trailed Gilmore by almost ten percentage points among party members who lived in Dublin. Second, support for Howlin was also less than that for Gilmore among those members with a university degree. In contrast to Howlin, Gilmore appealed more to those who had higher levels of education, who were former members of Democratic Left and who lived in Dublin. Unfortunately for him, Gilmore's popularity amongst the youngest age group was of little use to him since they constituted such a small proportion of the sample. Finally, Shorthall, who won only a very small percentage of the vote, was more popular among those with higher levels of education and those who lived in Dublin.

Since some of these social and political groups contain very few cases, it is especially important to focus on the relative support achieved by the candidates amongst the largest groups showing different patterns of preference. From this it is evident that support for Rabbitte was weakest among those who lived in Dublin and who had a university degree. One of the problems for Howlin was that he was not able to benefit from this weakness. Instead of supporting the candidate who was in second place in the opinion polls, this group of voters opted for the two candidates that trailed from the outset, Gilmore and Shorthall. The interesting implication here is that such potentially 'sophisticated' voters decided to vote sincerely rather than strategically, which is a little surprising given their likely extensive experience of a variety of electoral contests.

While Rabbitte might have been relatively unpopular amongst this group of Dublin party members, he captured 50 per cent of those Dublin voters who did not have a degree. Howlin, on the other hand, suffered from his unpopularity among Dublin voters, again finishing in third place, behind Gilmore. The largest group of party members consisted of those not resident in Dublin and lacking higher educational experience. Howlin actually did quite well amongst this group, but his success was at the expense of Gilmore and Shorthall. Rabbitte was as popular among this group of voters as he was across the party as a whole. In summary, the evidence suggests that while Rabbitte was popular among all groups of Labour Party members, Howlin's failure to appeal to those who lived in Dublin and who had higher levels of education undermined his ability to pose a threat to Rabbitte.

Conclusion

Using a post-election survey we have examined one of the most important examples of intra-party democracy in action – the selection of a new party leader. The election of party leaders by members is a relatively new phenomenon and thus far there have only been a few examples of leadership election surveys of provincial parties in Canada. We believe that the survey reported in this article represents the first such survey of a national party's leadership electorate. Endeavouring to undertake surveys of these new and emerging forms of elections would seem to help provide answers to some key questions.

First, what criteria do party members use in deciding who would make the best choice for party leader? Second, do voting preferences in leadership elections have a similar basis to preferences made in other types of elections where the general electorate participate? Third, do party members vote strategically in supporting candidates that are not necessarily their first choices – on the basis of policy proximity for example – but whom they regard as likely to have the most positive impact on the general electorate in future elections? Fourth, are internal party election campaigns very different in style and content to general elections and, if so, why? Is it, for instance, a consequence of the party organization not wishing to undermine its own cohesion? Fifth, given the considerations that parties must make of the costs and benefits of internal party democracy, how are the election rules and campaign management engineered to ensure maximum benefits for the party? Finally, it should be noted that leadership election surveys may give extra leverage in studying important questions raised in previous research such as Mair's (1997) 'paradox'. They have an advantage over traditional membership surveys in that there is something very tangible at stake in leadership elections and therefore surveys based on such elections can examine more critically how party members decide on concrete and important issues.

In our survey, we have begun the task of trying to answer some of these important questions. One significant finding from our research is that for almost a third of the party the election campaign had no effect, since such members had already acquired sufficient information to make a firm choice for leader before the election campaign commenced. This indicates that success in a leadership election is in part determined by how a parliamentarian performs during their career within the party, parliament, government, general elections, and in representing the party in the media. In short, a potential leader's reputation is of crucial importance.

The Labour leadership election also indicated an important campaign strategy that party organizations may use to 'manage' their elections. One important feature of the Labour Party's leadership campaign was that it lasted about the same length as a typical general election campaign. The danger with relatively long leadership campaigns is that they are costly to the party and have the potential to be divisive. Leadership candidates often only need plurality support to be successful and they do not need either majority or plurality support among parliamentary members in membership ballots. This implies that successful leadership contests may prove to be Pyrrhic victories for leaders who find they face an apathetic or even hostile parliamentary party. The demise of Iain Duncan Smith in November 2003 tends to demonstrate as much.

The danger for any party that embarks on democratization is that greater inclusiveness may result in a decline in subsequent electoral effectiveness, as the general electorate ignore a party that is perceived to lack effective unity and leadership. The Irish Labour Party sought to reduce these potential costs by constraining candidates to campaign largely within the rules of a series of time-consuming internal party debates. However, such successful management of leadership campaigns, while minimizing costs and adverse publicity, has the potential disadvantage of throwing away the benefits of increased public legitimacy – a key motivation that often lies behind the introduction of such elections in the first place.

More generally, future research can address the question of whether leadership elections within parties can be understood using the voting models employed in national election studies. But it should be noted that leadership elections have a number of unique features. By definition, party attachment is not a factor, and neither is voting on the basis of the economic assessments (egocentric or sociotropic) likely to be directly applicable. On the other hand, other policy or ideological effects may well be important, and there are likely to be strong 'candidate effects'. Furthermore, voter assessments in leadership elections will probably be uniquely influenced by the expectations of how the wider public will react to a new leader at future national elections.

It is our hope that some of the issues raised in this article will encourage greater interest in pursuing post-leadership election surveys of party members. There are, of course, important methodological and ethical issues to be considered, but post-election surveys promise to neutralize at least one such potential problem – the well-known 'Hawthorne effect', whereby researchers risk influencing the outcome they are supposed to be studying. More generally, the changing nature of political parties has opened up new opportunities to study not only how they operate internally, but also how they are changing and what implications this may have for popular conceptions of political participation, representation and legitimacy. It would be a pity to miss this opportunity in an era of declining voter turnout, party attachment and party membership.

ACKNOWLEDGEMENTS

The authors are grateful for the financial support provide by the Public Opinion and Political Behaviour Research Programme of the Institute for the Study of Social Change (ISSC), University College Dublin. The authors also wish to thank Ronan Murphy, Prof. David Farrell (University of Manchester), Prof. Michael Marsh (Trinity College, Dublin), Bill Cross (Mount Allison University, Canada) and Lisa Young (University of Calgary, Canada) for helpful comments.

NOTES

1. Alderman and Carter (2002: 583) note that this 'contest revealed numerous weaknesses in the leadership election procedures … such as the failure to anticipate a tie in the first ballot and the inadequacy of the national membership lists. More serious is the provision for only two candidates to go forward to the final membership ballot … the elimination of Portillo by only one vote in a parliamentary party that was split almost equally between three candidates prompted vigorous protests. The point was underlined by the fact that tactical voting might have resulted in any two of the three candidates entering the run-off. The procedures may well have played a part in shaping the outcome in Portillo's case.'
2. See http://www.icmresearch.co.uk/reviews/2001/telegraph-tory-members-aug-2001.htm. MORI also conducted a survey of local Conservative Constituency Association Chairs in July 2001. See www.mori.com/polls/2001/MS010721.shtml.
3. The undertaking of specialized studies in fields such as leadership election surveys fits in with the research agenda proposed by Franklin and Wlezien (2002) for 'reinventing election studies'.
4. An interesting feature of the election was that two possible leadership candidates – Joan Burton and Willie Penrose – opted instead to contest the deputy leadership. Joe Costello and Liz McManus also sought the deputy leadership.
5. *The Irish Times*, 28 August 2002.
6. The ballots were posted out to voters on October 4 and were to be returned no later than noon on October 25.
7. Howlin set himself the objective of 'getting rid of this awful government' and talked of 'change in the way we organise ourselves' (Press Release, 10 Sept.). Rabbitte talked of rebuilding the party and returning to 'full-blooded opposition' (Press Release, 12 Sept.). Similarly, Gilmore talked of 'vigorously opposing' the government and 'building the Labour Party' (Press Release, 15 Sept.).
8. In the 2002 election the Green Party and Sinn Fein both increased their representation in the Dáil by four seats, while four non-party candidates who campaigned on the 'health issue' were also elected.
9. Press Release, 10 Sept. 2002.
10. Press Release, 12 Sept. 2002.
11. Initially, there was some confusion over who was entitled to vote, but when a member of the party was successful in being added to the list of electors the party headquarters was prompt in providing their contact details to the various candidates.
12. Interview with a member of Gilmore campaign.
13. *The Irish Times*, 13 Sept. 2002.
14. Membership figures from Labour Head Office.
15. *The Irish Times*, 16 Sept. 2002.
16. *The Irish Times*, 30 Sept. 2002.
17. There was criticism of these polls within the party. While the polls were a representative sample of the general electorate with 1000 respondents, the number of Labour Party identifiers was less than 100, with Labour Party members constituting a smaller portion and those eligible to vote constituting an even smaller number. For this reason Eamon Gilmore complained that 'asking two or three Labour members their opinion and publishing a result as if it were a valid poll of the leadership electorate is a disservice to the newspaper readership'. MRBI responded to such comments by arguing that it was valid to ask the public who they would like to see as party leader. See Brennock (2002).
18. With a sub-sample size of about 95 respondents the sampling error is about +/– 10 per cent, indicating that the changes noted in the MRBI polls could be attributed to sampling error. It could be argued that the changes in the larger national sample also did not change in a significant manner except in the case of Rabbitte.
19. This database, held in the Labour Party headquarters, contained 3,472 names and addresses, which is somewhat less than the total official electorate. This unfortunate situation seems to have arisen because the database was not updated quickly enough after appeals. More information about the survey is available upon request from the authors.

244 BRITISH ELECTIONS & PARTIES REVIEW

REFERENCES

Alderman K. and N. Carter (2002) 'The Conservative Party Leadership Election of 2001', *Parliamentary Affairs*, 55: 569–85.

Brennock, M. (2002) 'Gilmore criticises newspaper poll on Labour Party leadership', *The Irish Times*, 19 October.

Carty, R.K. and D.E. Blake (1999) 'The Adoption of Membership Votes for Choosing Party Leaders: The Experience of Canadian Parties', *Party Politics*, 5: 211–24.

Curtice, J. (2002) 'The State of Election Studies: Mid-life Crisis or New Youth?' *Electoral Studies*, 21: 161–8.

Davis, J.W. (1998) *Leadership Selection in Six Western Democracies*. Westport, CT.: Greenwood Press.

Franklin, M.N. and C. Wlezien (2001) 'Reinventing Election Studies', *Electoral Studies*, 21: 331–8.

Kennedy, F. (2002) 'Elite Level Co-ordination of Party Supporters: An Analysis of Irish Aggregate Data', *Representation*, 38: 284–93.

LeDuc, L. (2001) 'Democratizing Party Leadership Selection.' *Party Politics*, 7: 323–41.

Mair, P. (1997) *Party System Change: Approaches and Interpretations*. Oxford: Oxford University Press.

Marsh, M. (1993a) 'Introduction: Selecting the Party Leader', *European Journal of Political Research*, 24: 229–31.

Marsh, M. (1993b) 'Selecting Party Leaders in the Republic of Ireland', *European Journal of Political Research*, 24: 295–316.

Müller, W. (2000) 'Political Parties in Parliamentary Democracies: Making Delegation and Accountability Work', *European Journal of Political Research*, 37: 309–33.

Sinnott, R. (1995) *Irish Voters Decide: Voting Behaviour in Elections and Referendums since 1918*. Manchester: Manchester University Press.

The Labour Party (1991) *Constitution of the Labour Party*. Dublin: Labour Party.

The Labour Party (2003) *Report To National Conference 2001–2003*. Dublin: Labour Party.

None of that Post-modern Stuff around Here: Grassroots Campaigning in the 2002 Irish General Election

Michael Marsh

Election campaigns in Ireland provide some exceptions to the general trends in campaigning identified by prominent observers in recent years. Changes in the role of experts in marketing and PR, in the degree of central control and national focus, and the downgrading of labour intensive activities have given rise to an era of campaigning in liberal democracies variously, and somewhat fancifully, described as 'post-modern' (Norris, 2002), and even, ironically, as 'post-Fordist' (Denver and Hands, 2002). In particular there has been an increase in the central control of campaigning, making full use of the latest media and professional assistance and decreasing use – often through necessity – of local party workers. Campaigns are now seen as sophisticated PR operations, in which great effort is made to get professionally constructed messages straight to the voter with minimal opportunities for distortion by untrustworthy intermediaries such as journalists and party workers. This is not to say that everything takes place in the political capital. In fact, great attention is given to constructing a local element – not least through leaders' appearances at carefully chosen sites – but this is centrally directed and centrally controlled. The campaign itself is not decentralized.

Irish election campaigns have changed in ways that illustrate the general truth of some elements of this framework. As late as 1970, Chubb observed that the 'small and comparatively underdeveloped' resources of central offices left candidates dependent on their own efforts (Chubb, 1970). Generous funding from the public purse, which some parties have been able to supplement with considerable private donations, has provided central organizations with far more resources. Campaigns have become much more professional, making widespread use of marketing and PR skills and information. Fianna Fail's (FF) campaign in 2002 was a fine illustration of early planning using focus groups, as well as local and national polls, to develop an effective set of campaign themes and a well-staffed publicity operation to ensure that the media itself stayed 'on message' during the campaign. Fine Gael's (FG) was not like this, and a late change of leadership contributed to a badly planned

British Elections & Parties Review, Vol. 14, 2004, pp. 245–267
ISSN 1368-9886 print
DOI: 10.1080/1368988042000258862   © 2004 Taylor & Francis Ltd.

and focussed effort that certainly did not help the party maximize its opportunities (see Collins, 2003). Yet the local element remains a significant part – many would say a critical part – of the operation. Parties may put much effort into deciding who should run in each constituency but they do so within severe constraints. Selection remains a local operation and central controls are largely indirect (Galligan, 1999, 2003). The candidates themselves still fund their own campaigns for the most part, and they decide how far they will run with the party, how far they will run without it and, in some cases, how far they will run despite it. And these local campaigns generally take the very old-fashioned form of the door-to-door canvass, supplemented by a presence at schools, supermarkets, train stations and shopping centres. Candidates also put up many posters and seek publicity in the local press and, increasingly as the broadcast media market becomes decentralized, on local radio.

Where more than one candidate is fielded in a constituency, the national party must manage the inevitable competition between those candidates so that each works to the advantage, and not to the disadvantage, of the party. This is typically done first by 'bailiwicking': i.e., dividing the constituency into territories and getting the candidates to make agreements about who campaigns in each area. There are some areas exclusive to each candidate – usually their 'home' areas – and others where there is a free for all. Second, there is some attempt at vote management, whereby party supporters in an area are asked to vote for one particular candidate so as to obtain a reasonably even distribution of the vote across the candidate slate. This maximizes the chances of winning seats (see e.g. Gallagher, 2003 for a full explanation). This occurs with different degrees of success. Every election gives rise to a few stories of fights between the workers for rival candidates from the *same* party, and many stories of complaints to party HQ about canvassing agreements being broken; and every set of results throws up illustrations of instances where seats were lost that would have been secured by more effective vote management.

There are thus at least two campaigns in Ireland, the national and the local, and at every election the comment is made that in reality there are many more – one for each constituency – as well as an interrelationship between the local and the national. As elsewhere, parties in Ireland produce manifestos, promote their leaders and, with varying degrees of success, seek to influence, if not control, the election agenda in the mass media (see Collins, 2003; Brandenburg and Hayden, 2003). The national campaign also impinges significantly on the local one, not least in the selection and promotion of candidates (Galligan, 2003). To date, most academic coverage has focussed on these aspects of campaigning. The focus here is on the local, and in particular on the old-style door-to-door style of constituency campaigning, which seems redundant in most other countries.

What We Know

In contrast to the literature stressing the nationalization of campaigning, there has been a significant revival of academic interest in local campaigning and in particular in the importance of personal contact with voters. Experimental evidence has long suggested a role for personal appeals in boosting the vote (Bochel and Denver, 1971) and some recent US studies have served to underline the importance of this aspect of campaigning for turnout in what are usually seen as television dominated elections (Gerber and Green, 2000; Green et al., 2003; Gerber et al., 2003). In the UK, a succession of studies has demonstrated the importance of the local campaign for party vote shares. These have relied on a variety of methods. Surveys of party agents or candidates in constituencies provide measures of general campaign activity (e.g. Denver and Hands, 1997; Denver et al., 2002; Denver et al., forthcoming). Surveys of party members have provided measures of the incidence of grass roots contact (e.g. Whiteley and Seyd, 2003). Campaigning has also been measured more indirectly by the use of local campaign expenditure (e.g. Pattie et al., 1995). Finally, there has been a limited degree of individual-level analysis using election study data to explore the link between contact and voting (Butler and Stokes, 1970; Whiteley and Seyd, 2003; Johnston and Pattie, 2003; Pattie and Johnston, 2003). Denver et al. (forthcoming) report strong correlations between these several measures. In general, these analyses have reinforced the argument that local campaigns matter in terms of vote share, with the individual level analyses giving added weight to the aggregate data analyses by showing that local campaigning works by mobilizing or reinforcing the predispositions of those contacted directly.

There is also US evidence on the impact of personal contact on the vote choice (Kramer, 1970; Huckfeldt and Sprague, 1992; Weilhouwer and Lockerbie, 1994; Krassa, 1988; Wielhouwer, 1999; Beck et al., 2002; Wielhouwer, 2003). These studies largely reject the argument that local campaigning is irrelevant but do not all agree on how much and in what ways campaigns matter.

The Irish evidence is much less extensive. Gallagher and Marsh (2002) examined the impact of FG member activity on the FG vote, and Benoit and Marsh (2003a, b, c) have assessed the impact of campaign expenditure in Ireland. However, there has been little work on the importance of individual contacts for the vote and no work on its importance for the party share of the vote. Using evidence from the 2002 Irish election study a start will be made here to redress that situation. Ireland is somewhere that we would expect to see local campaigning effects if we were going to find them anywhere. The institutional setting encourages candidate-centred voting (Swindle, 2002; Carey and Shugart, 1994; although see also Bowler et al., 1996), and hence, perhaps, local considerations, and this is reinforced by the small size of constituencies, the nature of the party system and the political culture. Personal appeals provide a means of getting through the perceptual screen that many voters might put up to avoid political information from the media. Moreover, candidates themselves can make the most personal of appeals, asking not for a vote for their party but for a vote for them as an individual, an individual the voter will probably have met on other occasions prior to the campaign.

In what follows, we will first look at the extent of local campaigning and then examine the association between contact and voting preference. Then we will develop a multivariate model in order to provide a stronger test of the argument that 'contact matters'. It will be seen that it does; contact between a voter and a party apparently makes support for that party by the voter more likely. Finally – and this is important where parties run more than one candidate – we will provide some preliminary evidence that the candidate who contacts is also likely to be the candidate who wins the vote.

Local Campaigning in 2002

The experiences of the candidates have been well documented in the now well-established series of *How Ireland Voted* books dating back to 1987, each of which contains a number of accounts by candidates themselves of their experiences. In all cases they emphasize the importance of the canvass. Taking comments from the 2002 study we note that one candidate sees it as 'by far the best method of making direct contact with the individual voters'; another explains that 'every single house in the constituency had to be canvassed by a member of my campaign team, or myself' (Fleming et al., 2003). Even so, 'some [canvassers] found that, as has been the case in other recent elections, more often than not people were not at home, so a second canvass was required midway through the election campaign'. Another candidate, recognizing the problems of the door-to-door campaign when a higher proportion of voters are now in the labour force, explained the need for 'a very early morning start at commuter railway stations, bus queues, traffic congestion points, school drop off points and early morning shopping or breakfast stop cafes'. She still found voters who complained that 'they saw few candidates actually coming door to door looking for votes'. Not surprisingly, candidates realize they must make rational use of their scarce resources. A candidate from the Greens expressed regret that 'as a small party, a full door to door canvass in a three-week election campaign period was not going to be possible' and so his team 'canvassed more intensively areas where we already polled well'. This sort of targeting must be expected, even in relatively small constituencies.

As part of their canvass, candidates will typically distribute leaflets extolling their achievements and, where it seems helpful, the achievements of their party; they ensure that their names are displayed prominently through the extensive use of posters hung on lampposts and telegraph poles. One independent candidate (Liam Twomey, Waterford) explained how his team postered the road that would be used by a television team coming to make an election programme on his constituency, in order to build the impression of himself as a 'credible candidate'. There will be party posters, some bearing the names of the local candidates, but these are usually supplemented by personal candidate posters, which may or may not carry the party name conspicuously, and may or may not mention any running mates. Advertisements in local papers were less widespread in the 2002 election as candidates had to confine their spending within legal limits. Most of the reported expenditure went on posters and leaflets.

The Attentiveness of the Voters

Before we look at the effect the campaign may have had on the vote we must ask how much it was noticed by the voters: were they in fact contacted by a candidate or those working on behalf of a candidate, and did they see posters or read leaflets? Respondents were asked whether or not a candidate or party worker had called to their home during the campaign.[1] Table 1 shows that over half of the electorate who voted reported that a candidate did call to the house, and over half also reported being contacted by a party worker. This is a much higher figure than we find elsewhere. In Britain less than a quarter reported such contact in 2002 (Pattie and Johnston, 2003), and in the US it is also no more than about 25 per cent nationwide (Huckfeldt and Sprague,

TABLE 1
THE EXTENT OF THE LOCAL CAMPAIGN – HOUSEHOLD CONTACT

Number of candidates/ parties who called	By candidates		Party wkrs phoned		Any
	Candidates	Parties	Parties	Parties	Parties
0	45	46	46	95	23
1	26	28	21	5	24
2	15	17	15	*	26
3	8	7	9	*	15
4 or more	4	2	9	0	11

Note: Self-reported voters only. Independents treated as a single group here.

1992). In Scandinavia, less than 5 per cent of voters report a personal contact (Esaiasson, 1992), while in Japan such campaigning is prohibited by law. A comparative study of general elections in eight countries emphasizes how untypical is the Irish case: 23 per cent reported contact in New Zealand, 18 per cent in Portugal, 13 per cent in Germany and less than 10 per cent in Bulgaria, France, Hungary, and Poland.[2] Karp et al. (2003: Figure 1) show that the Irish experience was at least equally remarkable in the context of a European Parliament election campaign.

The personal contact is face-to-face. Very few voters were telephoned. This medium seems to be used much more extensively in Britain and the US, particularly to identify party supporters: so-called 'voter identification' (e.g. Denver and Hands, 2002). Its lack of use in Ireland may indicate that parties already have this information, but it may also underline the importance placed, by parties and by voters, on face-to-face contact. A few voters were visited by several candidates, but contact by one candidate is the norm. The figures for each particular type of contact are individually quite high, but even more striking is the total proportion of people who are contacted (or rather whose home is contacted) in at least one of these several ways: by the candidates or party workers in person or by phone. This formulation increases the extent of contact to almost 80 per cent with the typical household contacted in one way or another by at least two separate parties. When the fact that not all respondents would have necessarily known of the contact made (or would have recalled correctly) is taken into account, the real level of contact may well be even higher (see Bochel and Denver, 1971).

Which parties were most active? As we might expect, Table 2 shows that the larger parties were able to make a more extensive effort. Of course they fielded more candidates, although with 138 nominees independents were the largest group. Candidates are supported by people from their party as well as by personal supporters (Gallagher and Marsh, 2002). FF's potential advantage in terms of members (it claims around 40,000 members to 20,000 in FG, 4,000 in Labour and less than 1,000 in the smaller parties) did not translate into the same sort of dominance in terms of door-to-door coverage that we might have expected. Its activity was not much greater than that on behalf of FG. The smaller parties did not run candidates everywhere, so the extent to which they cover their potential electorate is greater than these figures suggest. If we limit analysis to the voters from the target constituencies of the smaller parties, we might expect their activity to come quite close to that of the larger parties. Sinn Féin (SF) ran candidates in almost three quarters of all constituencies but activity would have been low in most of them. In the ten or so where it had a serious chance, it reached the homes of 35 per cent of voters. In contrast, using the same criterion, the Greens and the Progressive Democrats (PDs) only reached 18 per cent – a confirmation of the relative scale of SF's machine.[3]

TABLE 2
THE EXTENT OF THE LOCAL CAMPAIGN – HOUSEHOLD CONTACT BY PARTIES

	Share of candidates	Visit by candidates	Visit by party workers	Visit or phone by workers or candidates
Contacting Party				
FF	23	33	35	55
FG	18	24	28	43
Greens	4	2	5	5
Labour	10	12	15	24
PD	7	4	5	7
SF	8	6	12	16
Ind	30	10	13	19
Total	100	91	113	169
N	463			

Notes: Self-reported voters only. Totals in columns 2, 3 and 4 do not sum to 100 because not all respondents were contacted but some of those contacted were contacted by several parties.

A majority of voters were contacted by several parties. Table 3 shows, for each group of voters (by first preference), the extent of contact from each of the seven parties (treating independents/others as a single group). Each party's efforts were far from being concentrated merely on its own voters. In fact, FF and FG voters were contacted by 2.6 and 2.8 candidates (on average) respectively and other voters by more than 3. This makes good sense from the perspective of the parties because of the operation of the single

TABLE 3
CONTACT WITH EACH PARTY'S VOTERS

Vote	Percentage of each party's voters with a contact from						
	FF	FG	Green	Lab	PD	SF	Ind/other
FF	65	42	4	24	6	15	19
FG	52	63	4	18	7	11	17
Green	39	32	29	12	6	9	22
Lab	42	30	5	51	7	12	17
PD	47	36	11	16	35	4	7
SF	39	34	5	21	4	57	20
Ind	53	37	4	20	6	19	50

Notes: Self-reported voters only. Multiple contacts mean that rows do not sum to 100.

transferable vote. A lower preference can make the difference between success and failure. Certainly candidates who won no second or third preferences would find it hard to get elected as few make the quota on the first count. All parties contacted more than 50 per cent of their eventual voters with the exception of Greens and PDs who each fall well short of that figure.

In addition to considerations of political strategy we might expect overall levels of canvassing to vary locally with resources. The two largest parties report relatively low levels of membership in Dublin so activity should be lower there. However, we might also expect levels to vary with the costs of such canvassing, and these are higher where housing density is lower. In fact, over the country as a whole there is relatively little variation, but the proportion of voters in Dublin City and County reporting contact (68 and 71 per cent respectively) is about 10 percentage points lower than elsewhere, despite the fact that there are generally more parties running in Dublin.

Voters were also asked what sort of attention they paid to the campaign: what sorts of communication they noticed. What is clear is that, in addition to the direct contacts already mentioned, voters read leaflets, noticed posters and saw election advertisements in the press, but very few of them attended meetings or used the Internet (Table 4).[4] The number seeing press advertisements may be lower than it might have been in previous elections since there were fewer such advertisements this time, but posters are clearly visible to almost all voters, and leaflets also seem to be looked at by most people.

Effects of the Campaign

Campaigns can have three main objectives. First, campaigners may set out to firm up their potential support, to try to ensure that they will realize all of that potential on election day. Second, campaigners may seek to convert those leaning towards another party. Finally, they will seek to mobilize all supporters to

TABLE 4
VOTERS' ATTENTIVENESS TO THE CAMPAIGN

	%
Looked at candidate's campaign posters	83
Read election leaflets put in letter box, given in street etc.	68
Looked at advertisements for parties and candidates in the newspapers	52
Saw information about parties and candidates on the Internet	5
Attended public meetings related to the election	4

Note: Self-reported voters only.

ensure that they actually vote on election day. The last of these may be very significant but we will not examine such effects here, as the validated voting records of respondents are not yet available. This leaves confirmation and conversion. This is perhaps a continuum rather than a dichotomy: all voters have some likelihood of voting for a party and, particularly in the STV system, campaigners will seek to increase that likelihood. Even if they cannot secure a first preference they will ask for a vote of some kind. Hence, in examining the apparent effects of campaigning we should consider effects on both first preferences and on lower preferences.

At the aggregate level, there is little sign that the campaign changed many minds when it came to party choice. If we simply look at the change between the first and last poll carried out by each of the main organizations, the picture is one of considerable stability. In the MRBI polls, FG dropped 2 per cent and Independents rose by a similar margin; IMS polls showed rising FF and SF support, with FG falling to a similar degree. However, FF support was overestimated and FG underestimated in these polls by a rather larger margin (McElroy and Marsh, 2003). Even so the average change over the couple of weeks between first and last polls was less than two percentage points, and required that no more than 3 per cent (MRBI) and 5 per cent (IMS) of voters actually changed their minds. This should not be surprising. The election came at the end of a five-year term of office and was flagged well in advance, so we would not have expected to see a lot of movement. MRBI's adjusted poll figures, taking into account the error between poll findings and likely outcomes, had FF on 42 per cent well before the campaign started and this was the eventual result. This, it is worth emphasizing, does not mean the campaign did not matter. It may well have mattered a great deal at the level of the individual making up their mind, and it may have mattered a lot for particular candidates, but there is no evidence that the campaign had a big impact on the party share of seats. Party efforts either cancelled out one another, or served only to cement the loyalties of those already leaning in their direction.

It could well be that many made their final decision during the campaign, but that these final decisions did not alter the result signalled in earlier opinion polls. The Election Study survey indicates that 70 per cent of those who voted made up their mind before the campaign, with only 30 per cent reporting that they made their decision after that point. This is a slightly smaller number than is typical in Britain, but more than do so in Australia and the US (where of course the campaign is much longer) (McAllister, 2002: 28). We may be sceptical about whether people really know when they decided but this at least suggests that there is nothing odd about Ireland in this respect.[5]

The ideal tool for exploring the impact of campaigning on individuals is information on each respondent's voting intention before and after contact was made. In the absence of this, as here, we cannot provide any definitive evidence on the impact of the canvass on the vote. We can measure the association between local contact and vote, but if we find a link this will not tell us whether contact actually persuades voters to support a particular party, or whether parties are simply being efficient at keeping in touch with their most likely supporters. In other words, is a correlation between contact and vote evidence that a party is good at convincing voters, or simply evidence that it has been efficient in concentrating its resources on those most likely to support it anyway?

We will turn to the latter consideration shortly. To begin with we will look at the association between contact and vote from the viewpoint that the contact makes a difference. To assess how much difference we will compare the voting behaviour of those contacted by a party with the behaviour of those not contacted. It should be remembered that several parties might have called. Hence we will distinguish those who were contacted by one particular party from those who were not, and those contacted by another party from those who were not. This gives us a fourfold distinction for each party-voter association. If we take FF as illustrative, there are (1) voters not contacted by FF who were contacted by another party, (2) voters not contacted by any party, (3) voters contacted by FF and at least one other, and finally (4) voters contacted only by FF. When we are considering the effectiveness of campaigning in convincing voters we need to compare the proportions within each of these four groups of voters who voted FF. Table 5 does this using, first, contact with a candidate from the party and second, contact with party workers. It should be recalled that the unit for calling is in every case the house, not the individual. This can be expected to weaken any relationship we might find.

There are several important features of this table. We may take 'no contact' as the benchmark and indeed the distribution of party support in that column comes very close to the distribution in our sample.[6] First, we can see that contact is associated with higher levels of voting for the contacting party; and contact only with some other party is associated with lower levels of support. Moreover, monopoly contact is particularly effective. For FF, contact increases support by 8 per cent when it is competitive and 23 per cent when it has sole contact; when it is only some other party who contacts a voter, support is depressed by 15 percentage points. A second point is that while this pattern appears to hold for all parties it would seem to have a stronger 'impact' in the case of the smaller ones. Contact increases SF support by a factor of four, and a monopoly of contact by a factor of 11. A third point is that in almost all cases the 'impact' of *workers* calling is less than that of a *candidate*, either negatively or positively. We can surely conclude that contact is quite strongly associated with vote, that a monopoly of contact is associated

TABLE 5
ASSOCIATION BETWEEN TYPE OF CONTACT AND FIRST PREFERENCE VOTE

		Contact only by a party other than the row party	No contact at all	Contact by row party and at least one other	Contact only by row party
FF	cand	28	45	53	67
	wkrs	37	46	48	59
FG	cand	9	21	29	43
	wkrs	12	21	24	33
Green	cand	3	5	29	+
	wkrs	2	4	19	+
Labour	cand	5	10	26	47
	wkrs	7	12	14	20
PD	cand	2	3	19	+
	wkrs	2	3	11	+
SF	cand	2	5	25	66
	wkrs	4	5	11	29
Ind/O/	cand	5	11	23	50
	wkrs	8	8	26	21

Notes: Self-reported voters only. Cell entries show % of each cell voting for row party. Smallest
cell n is 26. + cells have too few cases for sensible analysis.

even more strongly, and that a visit by candidates of a party is associated more strongly with a vote for that party than a visit by party workers.

Before exploring further the meaning of this association in terms of the likely impact of the canvass on the vote, we should also look at the picture with respect to lower preferences. By using a simulated ballot we were able to measure second and lower preference votes, and so we can see whether contact is associated with getting not simply first preference votes but second and third ones too. Of course some preferences may not indicate support. Being ranked 10/10 is hardly an endorsement. However, very few voters express such a complete preference order. Most indicate no more than a few preference votes. Table 6 replicates Table 5 but defines support not as a first preference vote but as a lower preference for a party, other than that of the first preference candidate. In effect it is a second *party* preference. The sample for each row of Table 6 thus excludes those who have already cast a first preference for that party. We have shown the analysis in this way to emphasize the association of contact with lower preferences.

The main result here is the existence of clear differences between the second and third columns. These are much smaller than in Table 5, but for

TABLE 6
ASSOCIATION BETWEEN TYPE OF CONTACT AND SECOND PARTY VOTED FOR

		Contact only by a party other than the row party	No contact at all	Contact by row party and at least one other	Contact only by row party
FF	cand	19	31	46	36
	wkrs	26	30	36	26
FG	cand	15	21	31	41
	wkrs	19	19	27	42
Green	cand	6	8	11	+
	wkrs	6	8	13	+
Labour	cand	14	17	37	58
	wkrs	16	17	27	16
PD	cand	13	14	39	+
	wkrs	11	17	26	+
SF	cand	6	7	26	66
	wkrs	4	8	17	20
Ind/O/	cand	14	16	38	29
	wkrs	15	19	27	44

Notes: Self-reported voters only. Cell entries in each row show % of each group voting for row party as second or third choice party. Smallest cell n is 18. + cells have too few cases for sensible analysis. In each row, those who gave a first preference to a candidate from that party are excluded.

most parties there is a stronger association with support when contact is made, whether it is contact by candidates or by party workers. The low numbers in column 4 are surprising at first glance but what these indicate is probably a ceiling effect. For instance, 67 per cent of those who are contacted only by FF give that party a first preference. If only 36 per cent of those who do not give FF their first preference make the party their second choice, this is still a relatively high figure. Those in this contact group who intend to support FF clearly tend to do so with a first preference. The greater 'impact' of contact with party workers may be due in part to the fact that first preferences were lower within this group, so there is less of a ceiling effect. We can conclude that contacts by either workers or candidates are both linked to support, but that candidate contact is associated with higher preferences than contact by party workers.

It would be unwise to infer from this that all candidates and parties need to do is contact more voters directly in order to be guaranteed a seat in the Dáil. As we have pointed out, the data may say simply that parties are quite efficient at targeting likely supporters, something parties may not do so well elsewhere (Kramer, 1970; Huckfeldt and Sprague, 1992). And of course to the extent that they are efficient, it may *appear* that contact has an effect which in fact quite misleading. Some targeting certainly goes on, as the quotation from a Green party candidate above demonstrates. We might be somewhat sceptical about the precision of such activity. The nature of personal campaigning on the streets, as opposed to by phone, is that it lends itself easily to canvassing by areas but not to targeting individuals. Candidates also know the areas in which they should do well even if they are not so sure about the individuals who support them. They can work on unofficial ballot box tallies at local elections and previous general elections as well as information from previous door-to-door canvassing. Ballot boxes will contain at most only a few hundred votes, in many cases fewer than that. This tells parties where they are strong and where they are weak, and so they are in a position to place particular emphasis where they feel it is most required. They also know what sorts of people support them, at least in the smaller, more socially homogenous parties. All this information suggests that parties who have limited resources should target areas, not that they should target individual voters for an initial contact. Hence there is a chance that parties are more likely to contact supporters than not, particularly if they are less well-resourced parties that have to limit their canvass to the areas most likely to reward them. For the smaller parties, activity is much greater in constituencies where they have a chance to win a seat and this will also tend to strengthen the link between contact and support without necessarily implying that contacts bring additional votes.[7]

We need to make some allowance for this if we are to estimate more precisely the true impact of contact. Essentially, it may be that rather than contact determining the likelihood of support, it is the likelihood of support that determines contact. Contact is possibly endogenous, not exogenous, to the relationship between contact and vote. Furthermore, it might also be possible that there is some memory bias, with respondents tending to remember contact with parties to which they feel favourable and forget the rest. The conventional solution to this problem is to use a separate set of variables to predict contact, and then to use predicted contact as the independent variable in the relationship. This has not proved to be possible in as much as we have not been able to predict contact with any reasonable degree of accuracy.[8] In such a situation the cure can be worse than the disease (Bartels, 1991). Instead, we have simply chosen to include in a multivariate analysis those variables that can be expected to be associated with contact and with vote. This is similar to a recent study by Pattie and Johnston (2003). We then assess the degree of relationship between contact and vote that remains after these other factors have been controlled. There are several controls:

- attachment to the party in contact (1, 0);
- voting for that party in the previous general election (1, 0);
- thermometer rating of party leader (0–100);
- thermometer ratings of FF and FG party leaders [as main prime ministerial alternatives] (0–100);
- euro spent by the party in the campaign, divided by constituency size;
- euro spent by all parties together, divided by constituency size;
- evaluation of last government (1–5).

This is a fairly standard set of variables for a party choice model, with the addition of the spending variables. We have included these to control for the indirect effects of the local campaign as opposed to those related to personal contact (see Pattie and Johnston, 2003).

We then estimated a number of logit models for candidate and for worker contact, taking each of the parties in turn. Dependent variables were first preference and then second party preference as in Tables 5 and 6. These 28 sets of estimates are not displayed in full because most of the coefficients are not of primary interest here. We display only the coefficients for the contact variables and their significance, as well as summary statistics for each of the models. This is done in Table 7. In most instances links between contact and support remains significant even with the several controls. This is particularly so for candidate contact and for first preference vote, but contact is also highly significant as a predictor of a lower preference vote for most parties, at least when contact is by a candidate. Contact by the party is generally significant; contact by another is less often so. In all, 20/28 coefficients for contact by the row party are statistically significant at the .05 level and only 9/28 coefficients indicating contact by another party are significant. For candidate contacts, 19/28 coefficients are significant; for contacts by party workers the figure is only 10/28.

These controls obviously leave an association in many instances, but is this association attenuated? Does it appear to be the case that those contacted are people who might in any case be expected to vote for the party which contacts them? We can see this best by reproducing Tables 5 and 6 (as Tables 8 and 9) using the predicted probabilities of party support based on the multivariate models. In each case we have set all other independent variables to their mean values.[9]

Taking Table 8 first, we can see that the differences between the columns are smaller than in Table 5. Uncontrolled, candidate contact appeared to be worth 8 per cent of the vote to FF and monopoly contact worth 22 per cent. In Table 8 the figures are 1 per cent and 13 per cent. For FG, differences also of 8 per cent and 22 per cent have dropped to 4 per cent and 17 per cent. The attenuation of the effects is more marked for SF. Differences of 20 and 61 per

TABLE 7
LOGIT ESTIMATES OF VOTE

	Contact by row party		Contact by another party		Pseudo R^2	N
	Coef	P≤	Coef	P≤		
First preference: Contact by candidate						
FF	.53	.001	−.47	.003	.36	1775
FG	1.01	.000	−.73	.000	.41	1775
Greens	1.89	.007	.20	.589	.41	1300
Labour	2.03	.000	−.71	.009	.41	1605
PD	1.41	.001	−.41	.232	.28	843
SF	1.62	.001	−1.20	.005	.58	1412
Ind/othr	1.96	.000	−1.10	.000	.18	1485
First preference: Contact by party workers						
FF	.36	.048	−.56	.001	.36	1775
FG	.33	.161	−.60	.005	.40	1775
Greens	1.62	.007	.01	.978	.41	1300
Labour	.54	.140	−.28	.339	.35	1605
PD	.62	.284	−.41	.233	.26	843
SF	.42	.471	−.41	.373	.55	1412
Ind/othr	1.29	.000	−.06	.796	.13	1485
Second party pref: Contact by candidate						
FF	.76	.000	−.22	.234	.16	983
FG	.86	.000	−.46	.005	.09	1398
Greens	.02	.981	−.16	.580	.19	1238
Labour	1.31	.000	−.17	.392	.11	1465
PD	1.16	.003	.23	.391	.13	779
SF	.98	.037	−.06	.858	.29	1340
Ind/othr	1.08	.000	−.32	.073	.07	1346
Second party pref: Contact by party workers						
FF	.18	.384	−.10	.606	.14	983
FG	.41	.030	−.16	.369	.07	1398
Greens	.82	.087	−.01	.963	.19	1238
Labour	.49	.028	.29	.150	.09	1465
PD	.43	.283	−.61	.015	.12	779
SF	.98	.004	−.32	.270	.29	1340
Ind/othr	.71	.002	−.19	.299	.06	1346

Notes: Self-reported voters only. Models also contain row party attachment, past vote, thermometer ratings of row and major party leaders, euros spent by row party, euros spent by all parties and evaluations of the last government.

TABLE 8
ASSOCIATION BETWEEN TYPE OF CONTACT AND FIRST PREFERENCE PARTY:
PREDICTED PERCENTAGES FROM MODELS IN TABLE 7

		Contact only by a party other than the row party	No contact at all	Contact by row party and at least one other	Contact only by row party
FF	cand	31	43	44	56
	wkrs	32	46	41	55
FG	cand	7	15	19	32
	wkrs	10	17	13	22
Green	cand	1	0	6	5
	wkrs	1	1	4	4
Labour	cand	1	3	11	20
	wkrs	*	*	*	*
PD	cand	2	4	9	14
	wkrs	*	*	*	*
SF	cand	0	1	2	6
	wkts	*	*	*	*
Ind/Other	cand	3	9	19	41
	wkrs	6	6	18	19

Notes: Self-reported voters only. Cell entries show % of each cell voting for row party. * neither
coefficient significant.

cent fall to 1 per cent and 5 per cent. What this suggests is that the people who got such a visit were very likely to vote for SF anyway, not because of contact but because of a combination of other factors. The impact of party worker contact is also attenuated, and that was weaker to begin with. Even so it is evident that support amongst those contacted is generally higher than amongst those not contacted.

Turning to the importance of contact for lower preferences, illustrated in Table 9, the effects of contact are generally weaker but it still appears that contact matters. The entries in the cells in columns 3 and 4 are in almost all cases higher than those in columns 1 and 2. In FF, FG and Labour in particular, as well as amongst Independents, those contacted are generally more likely to vote for the party making contact than those who are not contacted. Again, this is less pronounced when contact is by party workers than when it is by candidates.

Overall then, even with controls there remains a clear association between contact and vote. This is still not conclusive evidence of causation, but the inference that there is a causal link is much more plausible when these

TABLE 9
ASSOCIATION BETWEEN TYPE OF CONTACT AND SECOND PARTY VOTED FOR:
PREDICTED PERCENTAGES FROM MODELS IN TABLE 7

		Contact only by a party other than the row party	No contact at all	Contact by row party and at least one other	Contact only by row party
FF	cand	20	24	35	40
	wkrs	24	26	27	29
FG	cand	14	21	28	39
	wkrs	18	20	24	27
Green	cand	*	*	*	*
	wkrs	*	*	*	*
Labour	cand	11	12	32	35
	wkrs	14	11	22	17
PD	cand	10	9	28	24
	wkrs	7	14	12	20
SF	cand	2	3	6	6
	wkrs	2	3	5	7
Ind/Other	cand	12	16	29	36
	wkrs	13	15	23	27

Notes: Self-reported voters only. Cell entries show % of each cell voting for row party.
            * neither coefficient significant.

controls are in place. The degree of attenuation we see in the relationships suggests that there is some targeting, that all parties, even the largest ones, do tend to contact their potential supporters more than they do other voters. The attenuations are most marked in the case of the smaller parties who have more incentive to target, having fewer campaigners and more socially homogenous support bases. It is also worth underlining the fact that candidate contact seems to matter more than general party worker contact, and that this holds for both first and lower references. Visits by candidates asking for a second, third or even fourth preferences appear to pay dividends.

Local Campaigns and Candidate Choice

Most voters make decisions about candidates as well as parties, either because they are voting for a candidate rather than a party, or because they have chosen a party that runs more than one candidate. Campaigns are focussed on candidates as well as parties. We have seen that there is a strong link between party contact and party support. What is the situation as regards candidates?

Of respondents who voted, 64 per cent said they had decided on their first preference candidate in advance of the start of the official campaign as opposed to70 per cent who had decided their party. Perhaps there is just a little more uncertainty about candidate than there is about party. However, the distinction between picking a party and picking a candidate may be problematic for some respondents. Given that the smaller parties did not run two candidates in many instances, and the questions followed one on another very closely, someone who decided on party before the campaign must logically have decided on candidate (and vice-versa) but this is not the case; early deciders for SF, Greens and PDs had also decided on which candidate they would vote for in only 87, 77 and 85 per cent of cases respectively,[10] very similar proportions to those found in the larger parties where about 90 per cent of those who have decided party have also decided on candidate. However, the total number of cases this involves is very small and it is possible that respondents simply meant they did not know who the candidates were.

What is the connection between candidate contact and votes for those particular candidates? We confine ourselves here to those who were contacted by a candidate in situations where a party ran more than one candidate. In such cases over 80 per cent of those contacted and who voted for a party contacting them, voted for a candidate who contacted them: 81 per cent in the case of Labour and 86 per cent in the cases of FF and FG. In other words, only 14 per cent of the FF voters who were contacted by a FF candidate gave their first preference to a FF candidate who did not contact them ahead of one who did. The same is true for FG. Much of this might be attributed to a combination of bailiwicking and vote management, as contact will be made typically by only one FF candidate who would also be the most local one.[11]

Discussion

This article has examined the campaign in the 2002 Irish general election, paying particular attention to the extent and pattern of personal campaign links. While Irish campaigns do show many signs that parties have observed and learned from the style and tactics of parties elsewhere in the world, Irish elections are certainly not prime examples of the post-modern, post-fordist era of campaigning which some have claimed to see elsewhere. Personal contact is felt to matter by politicians, and all parties make considerable efforts to knock on as many doors as possible during the weeks of the official campaign. Despite the glossy posters of party leaders, the extensive use of opinion poll and focus group research, central management, and sometimes extensive teams of media watchers and controllers all seeking to shape the agenda, the essential style of campaigns remains personal, with individual candidates seeking to make an impact and doing so for the most part by the traditional method of meeting the folks. Almost 80 per cent of voters report that a party worker or candidate called to their home.

The big parties, with more candidates and more party workers – members and personal candidate supporters – naturally achieve a wider coverage. Given its much larger organization it might be expected that FF would do even better than it does, but in fact FG runs it quite close. There is a strong connection between these direct contacts (at least to the home) and the vote, whether we are looking at parties or at individual candidates. What is less clear is the process by which this correlation is achieved: is it that contact produces electoral support, or is it that (likely) electoral support attracts contact. Are parties 'chasing' new voters or 'mobilizing' existing ones? (Rorschneider, 2002). Our evidence addressing this question is necessarily indirect, as the Irish election study lacks a campaign panel element. The fact that so many contactees report making up their mind *before* the contact was made also suggests mobilization, or reinforcement, may be dominant. FF and FG, and to a lesser extent Labour, do make contact with a much higher proportion of voters who do not support them and so, at least in theory, may be seen to spend more resources chasing new voters. This difference could stem simply from differences in size but it could also reflect the fact that SF, the PDs and the Greens do have a more focussed appeal. They are 'niche' parties, who will have a much clearer ideological message and a more homogenous pattern of social support. Arguably it is this fact, as well as differences in resources, that explains the different pattern of contacts.

The analysis here has tried to describe the extent of grassroots campaigning and explore its possible impact on each party's share of the vote. It is very clear that there is extensive grassroots campaigning, by candidates and by party workers. Most voters are contacted, and a majority of voters are contacted by more than one party. Elections take place on the airwaves, but they also take place on the doorsteps. We did not see much aggregate change in the 2002 campaign, but many voters say they decided late and it seems possible that the doorstep campaign was a factor for some of those voters. It is very clear that contact is strongly associated with vote: those contacted by FF or by SF, for example, are more likely to vote for those parties than are those not contacted. This association could be an artefact of the strategy all parties use of concentrating resources in areas where they are more popular. When we controlled the relationship, using a number of possible predictors of contact (following this logic) and of vote the relationships are weaker. However, they remain very apparent, and are generally substantively and statistically significant. It could be argued that more controls are possible. We have controlled for party related factors, but candidates too have their natural supporters, typically drawn from their own hinterland. That too could be controlled. If the relationship between contact and vote then disappeared would that mean the association between contact and support was spurious? That conclusion would be unwarranted, and a dangerous one for any would-be politician to draw. Contact could be the mechanism that transforms potential support into votes. That contact may not simply be at election time. Candidates will typically be known around their districts and maintain an active presence there, although they will seek to make that final visit in the last few weeks before an election.

The links between support and contact are most pronounced when it comes to candidates. Arguably, individual candidates are more careful of their own resources and so give their personal time where it will be of most use, but it may also be that such personal contacts are especially effective, and effective at winning a vote if not a first preference vote (No. 1). Even if this is not the case, the conviction amongst politicians that the personal door-to-door style is necessary ensures it will be some time yet before the only link between the campaign and the voter's home is merely an electronic one.

ACKNOWLEDGEMENTS

This article uses data from the 2002 Irish Election Study, directed by Michael Marsh (Trinity College Dublin) and Richard Sinnott (University College Dublin), as principle investigators, together with John Garry (The Queen's University, Belfast) and Fiachra Kennedy (University College Dublin). The election study was funded under the National Development Plan: Programme for Research in Third-Level Institutions. I am grateful to Chris Wlezien and Justin Fisher for comments on an earlier draft.

NOTES

1. 'Called to' means personally, not by phone. This was the topic of a separate question: see below.
2. Author's analysis of CSES Wave 2, Summer 2003 release: www.umich.edu/cses.
3. 'Serious' is defined here as where it won at least 10 per cent of the vote.
4. Of course this last channel may come to be more important in future years. Many candidates did put up attractive websites. The parties have made some efforts to develop their own websites and party TDs all have standard ones but many challenging candidates also conveyed useful election information in this way.
5. Data from an IMS pre-/post-election panel survey also indicates that the question does provide a guide to the stability of vote intention. Of those who had 'definitely' decided how to vote the week before the election (and who did vote), 14 per cent did not follow their pre-election party choice, while of those who were not certain, 33 per cent apparently changed their mind. These late changes had a negligible impact on the result (McElroy and Marsh, 2003).
6. These are as follows: FF 46%, FG 20%, Greens 4%, Labour 10%, PDs 3%, SF 6% and independents and others 11%. While the sample is weighted to make it match the electorate in demographic terms we have not weighted it to correspond to the election outcomes. Consequently, there is a small overrepresentation of FF voters at the expense of FG in particular.

7. We also looked to see whether or not those who decided before the campaign were more or less likely to receive callers, and more or less likely to vote for a party which called. We find only a very small link between the time when respondents made their decision and whether contact has been made. Those contacted are marginally more likely to have decided prior to the campaign. Those giving their first preference to a calling party are also slightly more likely to be voters who decided prior to the campaign, not those who decided late.
8. It is possible that each voter's geographical proximity to a candidate might predict contact quite well and be exogenous but data on this is not available at present.
9. This means predicted probabilities for smaller parties, but not independents, are relatively low as, by definition, their supporters are not typical.
10. Moreover, none of these cases are in constituencies where SF and PDs ran multiple candidates.
11. In all only 4 per cent of candidates who call are covering territory already covered by a running mate.

REFERENCES

Bartels, L.M. (1991) 'Instrumental and "Quasi-instrumental" Variables', *American Journal of Political Science,* 35: 777–800.

Beck P.A., R.J. Dalton, S. Greene and R. Huckfeldt (2002). 'The Social Calculus of Voting: Interpersonal, Media, and Organizational Influences on Presidential Choices', *American Political Science Review* 96: 57–73.

Benoit, K. and M. Marsh (2003a) 'For a Few Euros More: Campaign Spending Effects in the Irish Local Elections of 1999', *Party Politics,* 9: 561–82.

Benoit, K. and M. Marsh (2003b) 'A fistful of euros: campaign spending effects under the single-transferable vote electoral system', presented to the annual conference of the Political Studies Association of Ireland, Portmarnock, Co Dublin, 12–14 October.

Benoit, K. and M. Marsh (2003c) 'Campaign Spending in the Irish Local Government Elections of 1999', *Irish Political Studies* 18 (2): 1–22

Bochel J. and D. Denver (1971) 'Canvassing, Turnout and Party Support: An Experiment', *British Journal of Political Science* 1: 257–69.

Bowler, S., D.M. Farrell and I. McAllister (1996). 'Constituency Campaigning in Parliamentary Systems with Preferential Voting: Is There a Paradox?' *Electoral Studies* 15: 461–7.

Brandenburg, H. and J. Hayden (2003) 'The Media and the Campaign', in M. Gallagher, M. Marsh and P. Mitchell (eds) *How Ireland Voted 2002.* London: Palgrave, pp. 177–96.

Carey, J. and M.S. Shugart (1994) 'Incentives to Cultivate a Personal Vote: A Rank Ordering of Electoral Formulas', *Electoral Studies* 14: 417–39.

Carty, R.K. and M. Eagles (1999) 'Do Local Campaigns Matter? Campaign Spending, the Local Canvass and Party Support in Canada', *Electoral Studies* 18: 69–87.

Chubb, Basil. (1970) *Government and Politics of Ireland.* Oxford: Oxford University Press.

Collins, S. (2003) 'Campaign Strategies', in M. Gallagher, M. Marsh and P. Mitchell (eds) *How Ireland Voted 2002.* London: Palgrave, pp. 21–36.

Denver, D., G. Hands, J. Fisher and I. MacAllister (2002) 'The Impact of Constituency Campaigning in the 2001 General Election', *British Elections and Parties Review* 12: 80–94.

Denver, D., G. Hands and I. MacAllister (forthcoming) 'The Electoral Impact of Constituency Campaigning in Britain 1992–2001' *Political Studies.*

Denver, D. and G. Hands (2002) 'Post-Fordism in the Constituencies? The Continuing Development of Constituency Campaigning in Britain', in D. Farrell and R. Schmitt-Beck (eds) *Do Political Campaigns Matter?* London: Routledge, pp. 108–26.

Denver, D. and G. Hands (1997) *Modern Constituency Electioneering: The Case of Britain.* London: Frank Cass.

Esaiasson, P. (1992) 'Sweden', in D. Butler and A. Ranney, *Electioneering.* Oxford: Clarendon Press.

Fleming, S., P. Bradford, J. Burton, F. O'Malley, D. Boyle, A. Ó Snodaigh and L. Twomey (2003) 'The Candidates' Perspective' in M. Gallagher, M. Marsh and P. Mitchell (eds) *How Ireland Voted 2002*. London: Palgrave, pp. 57–87.

Gallagher, M. (2003) 'Stability and Turmoil: Analysis of the Results', in M. Gallagher, M. Marsh and P. Mitchell (eds) *How Ireland Voted 2002*. London: Palgrave, pp. 88–118.

Gallagher, M. and M. Marsh (2002) *Days of Blue Loyalty: The Politics of Membership of the Fine Gael Party*. Dublin: PSAI Press.

Galligan, Y. (1999) 'Candidate Selection', in M. Marsh and P. Mitchell (eds) *How Ireland Voted 1997*. Boulder CO: Westview, pp. 57–81.

Galligan, Y. (2003) 'Candidate Selection: More Democratic or More Centrally Controlled', in M. Gallagher, M. Marsh and P. Mitchell (eds) *How Ireland Voted 2002,* London: Palgrave, pp. 37–56.

Gerber, A.S. and D.P. Green (2000) 'The Effects of Canvassing, Telephone Calls, and Direct Mail on Voter Turnout: A Field Experiment', *American Political Science Review* 94: 653–63.

Gerber A.S., D.P. Green and R. Shachar (2003) 'Voting May Be Habit-forming: Evidence from a Randomized Field Experiment', *American Journal of Political Science,* 47: 540–50.

Green D.P., A.S. Gerber and D.W. Nickelson (2003) 'Getting Out the Vote in Local Elections: Results from Six Door-to-door Canvassing Experiments', *Journal of Politics* 65: 1083–96.

Huckfeld, R. and J. Sprague (1992) Political Parties and Electoral Mobilization: Political Structure, Social Structure and the Canvass', *American Political Science Review* 86: 70–86.

Huckfeldt, R. and J. Sprague (1995) *Citizens, Politics and Social Communications*. Cambridge: Cambridge University Press.

Johnston, R. and C. Pattie (2003) 'Do Canvassing and Campaigning Work? Evidence from the 2001 General Election in England', in C. Rallings, R. Scully, J. Tonge and P. Webb, *British Elections & Parties Review,* Vol. 13: 210–28.

Karp, J., S. Bowler and S. Banducci (2003) 'Electoral Systems, Party Mobilization and Turnout: Evidence from the European Parliamentary Elections 1999', in C. Rallings, R. Scully, J. Tonge and P. Webb, *British Elections & Parties Review,* Vol. 13: 210–28.

Kramer, G.H. (1970) The Effects of Precinct Level Canvassing on Voter Behaviour', *Public Opinion Quarterly* 34: 560–72.

Krassa, M.A. (1988) Context and the Canvass: The Mechanisms of Interaction', *Political Behavior* 10: 233–46.

McAllister, I. (2002.) 'Calculating or Capricious? The New Politics of Late Deciding Voters', in D. Farrell and R. Schmitt-Beck (eds) *Do Political Campaigns Matter?* London: Routledge, pp. 22–40.

McElroy, G. and M. Marsh (2003) 'Why the Opinion Polls Got It Wrong in 2002' in M. Gallagher, M. Marsh and P. Mitchell (eds) *How Ireland Voted 2002*. London: Palgrave, pp. 159–76.

Norris, P. (2002) 'Campaign Communications', in L. Le Duc, R. Niemi and P. Norris (eds) *Comparing Democracies 2*. London: Sage, pp. 127–47.

Pattie, C. and R. Johnston (2003) 'Hanging on to the telephone? Doorstep and Telephone Canvassing at the British General Election of 1997', *British Journal of Political Science* 33: 303–22.

Pattie, C., R. Johnston and E. Fieldhouse (1995) 'Winning the Local Vote', *American Political Science Review* 89: 969–83.

Rorschneider, R. (2002) 'Mobilizing Voters verses Chasing Voters', *Electoral Studies* 21: 367–82.

Ruostetsaari, I. and M. Mattila (2002) 'Candidate-centred Campaigns and Their Effects in an Open List System: The Case of Finland', in D. Farrell and R. Schmitt-Beck (eds) *Do Political Campaigns Matter?* London: Routledge, pp. 92–107.

Schmitt-Beck, R. and D. Farrell (2002) 'Do Political Campaigns Matters? Yes, But It Depends', in D. Farrell and R. Schmitt-Beck (eds) *Do Political Campaigns Matter?* London: Routledge, pp. 183–93.

Swindle, S.M. (2002) 'The Supply and Demand of the Personal Vote', *Party Politics* 8: 279–300.

Whiteley, P. and P. Seyd (2003) 'How to Win a Landslide by Really Trying: The Effects of Local Campaigning on Voting in the 1997 British General Election', *Electoral Studies* 22: 301–24.
Wielhouwer, P.W. (1999) 'The Mobilization of Campaign Activists by the Party Canvass', *American Politics Quarterly* 27: 177–200.
Wielhouwer, P.W. and B. Lockerbie (1994) 'Party Contacting and Political-Participation, 1952–90', *American Journal of Political Science* 38: 211–29.

Reference Section

The reference section in this year's *Review* follows the same pattern as last year. It contains a chronology of major events in 2003, details of parliamentary by-elections during the current parliament, a comprehensive record of published public opinion polls in 2003, and the summary results of the 2003 devolution and local elections.

It has been compiled by members of the LGC Elections Centre at the University of Plymouth. Paul Lambe was responsible for the chronology, Dawn Cole gathered the opinion poll data, and Colin Rallings, Michael Thrasher and Lawrence Ware maintained the files from which the local election results were drawn.

British Elections & Parties Review, Vol. 14, 2004, pp. 268–313
ISSN 1368-9886 print
DOI: 10.1080/1368988042000258871   © 2004 Taylor & Francis Ltd.

Chronology of Major Political Events 2003

1. The Prime Minister Tony Blair in a sombre New Year message said that he could not 'recall a time when Britain was confronted, simultaneously, by such a range of difficult, and in some cases dangerous problems.'

    Iain Duncan Smith, the leader of the opposition, in an optimistic New Year message said that the Conservative Party 'over the past year ... had taken the first steps on the long road back to electoral victory' and flagged the forthcoming May local government elections as a test of his leadership.

    Greece's six months presidency of the EU began.

2. David Trimble, the Ulster Unionist leader, made the official disbanding of the IRA a prerequisite for resumption of the power-sharing Northern Ireland Assembly, suspended in October 2002.

3. The Pentagon ordered the despatch of thousands of marines to the Persian Gulf.

    President Bush, in an address to soldiers at Fort Hood, the biggest US military base, dismissed Iraq's claims that it was cooperating with UN weapons inspectors, denounced Saddam Hussein for showing contempt for the United Nations and said that if force became necessary they would not be conquering the Iraqi people but liberating them.

4. The Prime Minister and his family returned from a winter holiday to Egypt which Mr Blair had interrupted to meet with the Egyptian President, Hosni Mubarak, and King Abdullah of Jordan to discuss the continued Israeli-Palestinian crisis.

6. Lord Jenkins of Hillhead, politician and writer, died aged 82. Roy Jenkins twice Home Secretary (1965–67, 1974–76) and Chancellor of

the Exchequer (1967–70) retired from the Commons in 1976 and became the first British president of the European Commission (1977–81). Co-founder of the SDP, he returned to the Commons in March 1982 as the MP for Glasgow Hillhead and masterminded the electoral pact between the SDP and the Liberals under David Steel at the 1983 and 1987 general elections. Jenkins, who lost his seat at the 1987 election, was elevated to the Lords and elected Chancellor of the University of Oxford. In 1998 he headed the Independent Committee on Voting Systems and found in favour of proportional representation.

The FTSE 100 index closed at 3,603.7, its lowest level since December 1995.

7.   Israeli Prime Minister Ariel Sharon banned Palestinians from attending a planned peace summit called by Tony Blair to discuss reform of the Palestinian authority.

Both houses returned from the Christmas recess. Late night sittings became a thing of the past when the Commons sat from 11.30am to 7pm as the reforms of the all-party modernization committee came into effect. The Commons, henceforth, will sit early, at 11.30 am rather than 2.30pm and rise at 10.30pm on Mondays, 7.30pm on Tuesdays and Wednesdays, 6.30pm on Thursdays, with fewer Friday sittings and the PM at the dispatch box at midday Wednesdays to face PMQs.

At PMQs Charles Kennedy the Liberal Democrat leader asked Tony Blair 'if the UN inspectors find nothing and the US attacks anyway, will Britain be involved?'

In a statement to Parliament the Defence Secretary Geoff Hoon announced that thousands of reservists had been called up by the government in preparation for possible military action against Iraq and that the threat of force 'must remain and it must be real'.

8.   The Government's majority fell to 132 when 45 backbenchers defied ministers to vote against the motion welcoming the principle of NHS foundation trusts.

10.   North Korea withdrew from the global treaty limiting nuclear weapons.

12.   Leopoldo Galtieri, the former Argentine dictator who led his country into war with Britain over the Falkland Islands, died aged 76.

14.   Sir Edward Heath gave evidence at the judicial inquiry into 'Bloody Sunday' and said that it was 'absurd to suggest that Her Majesty's government intended or was prepared to risk the events that occurred'.

Rebekah Wade, former editor of the *News of the World*, became the first female editor of the *Sun* when she replaced David Yelland.

16.   Official figures from the federal statistics office revealed that the German economy grew by just 0.2% in 2002 and that the budget deficit had grown to 3.7% of gross domestic product and thereby had breached the EU's deficit limit of 3%.

22.   Charles Clarke, Secretary of State for Education and Skills, in a statement to the House on the future of higher education reaffirmed the government's commitment to a 50 per cent participation rate by the end of the decade and said that the 'social gap among those entering higher education is a national disgrace'. Damian Green, the then Conservative shadow education secretary, reminded Mr Clarke that 135 Labour members had signed an early day motion opposing the top-up fees proposed in his White Paper.

The Christian Democrats (CDA) with 44 seats narrowly won the Dutch general elections. A revival by the Labour Party (PvdA) saw it increase its number of seats from 23 to 42. The Pim Fortuyn List (LPF) saw its representation fall from 26 to 8 seats in the 150-seat assembly.

24.   President Bush's cabinet increased to 15 members with the appointment of Tom Ridge as the country's first secretary of homeland security.

27.   In his report to the Security Council Hans Blix, the UN's chief weapons inspector, concluded that Iraq had yet to accept the need for genuine disarmament.

28.   Ariel Sharon's Likud Party returned 37 MPs at the Israeli general election to give Sharon's right-wing bloc a majority with 67 seats in the 120-seat Knesset.

30.   Richard Reid, the so-called 'shoe bomber' who attempted to blow up a trans-Atlantic jet, was sentenced to life imprisonment by a US court.

An eight-nation EU statement initiated by the Spanish Prime Minister Jose Maria Aznar, signed by Britain, Denmark, Italy, Portugal and EU applicants Hungary, Poland and the Czech Republic, called for Europe to stand united behind the US. The initiative, taken without consultation with France or Germany, came only days after EU foreign ministers had agreed upon a policy of peaceful diplomacy.

31.   The Prime Minister Tony Blair urged President Bush to work with the United Nations to disarm Saddam Hussein and to avoid solitary US military action.

FEBRUARY

1.   Chancellor Gerhard Schroder's position was seriously weakened when his Social Democratic party was defeated in his home state of Lower-Saxony.

2.   Thirteen years after the 'velvet revolution' that brought him to power the president of Czechoslovakia and then of the Czech Republic, the erstwhile playwright Vaclav Havel, stepped down as head of state.

3.   All seven astronauts on board the space shuttle Columbia lost their lives when the craft disintegrated as it re-entered the earth's atmosphere.

        In a statement to the House on his talks with President Bush the Prime Minister Tony Blair said that if Saddam 'rejects the peaceful route ... he must be disarmed by force'. Iain Duncan Smith, the Conservative Party leader, expressed his party's support for the PM; however, the Liberal Democrat leader Charles Kennedy said the ' government still had to make a case'. Gordon Prentice, Labour backbench MP for Pendle, said 'he and many other people believed we were being led by the nose into war.'

4.   For the first time since becoming Prime Minister Tony Blair was on the losing side when his preferred option of a wholly appointed second chamber was defeated in a Commons vote. The Commons were unable to agree to any of the options put forward by the Joint Select Committee on Lords reform.

6.   Geoff Hoon, Secretary of State for Defence, told the House that the government had deployed one third of the RAF's aircraft to the Persian Gulf in preparation for war.

North Korea threatened an attack on South Korea in the event of a US strike against North Korean nuclear facilities.

10.   The Father of the House, Tam Dalyell, Labour MP for Linlithgow, was asked to withdraw following a confrontation with the Speaker of the House Michael Martin. Dalyell had failed to win an emergency debate from the Speaker, on what Dalyell termed 'the misleading of Parliament and the people' by the inclusion of a plagiarized PhD thesis in the recently released so-called 'dodgy dossier' on Iraq.

14.   Hans Blix updated the UN Security Council on the hunt for weapons of mass destruction in Iraq. Blix concluded in his report that 'many proscribed weapons and items are not accounted for' and that 'three months after the adoption of resolution 1441 the period of disarmament through inspection could still be short if immediate, active and unconditional cooperation were forthcoming'. France, Germany and Russia urged that the weapons inspectors be given more time. Britain and the US asserted the case for war.

15.   In what commentators have called the biggest peace rally in British history hundreds of thousands of anti-war protestors marched through London.

16.   NATO members agreed to make preparations for the defence of Turkey in the event of war with Iraq. The decision followed a bitter diplomatic row and a rift in the alliance when France, Germany and Belgium vetoed a request by the US a week earlier.

17.   A congestion charge of £5 was introduced for motorists in central London.

19.   President Robert Mugabe of Zimbabwe arrived in Paris, by invitation of the French government, to attend a two-day Franco-African summit albeit in violation of a travel ban imposed by the EU to punish his regime for its human rights record.

20.   In a joint statement the Archbishop of Canterbury and the Archbishop of Westminster outlined their doubts about the 'moral legitimacy' of a conflict with Iraq.

24.   North Korea test-fired a missile into the Sea of Japan.

25.   In a statement to the House Tony Blair revealed that a new resolution
       was to be tabled at the UN that Iraq was in material breach of UN reso-
       lution 1441 but voting would be delayed 'to give Saddam one further
       chance to disarm voluntarily'.

26.   In a debate in the Commons calling for support of the government's
       stance on Iraq, Labour backbencher and former cabinet minister Chris
       Smith moved an amendment saying that the case for military action
       was yet unproven. The amendment was lost by 199 votes to 393 when
       121 Labour backbenchers defied a three-line whip, and with 13
       Conservative, all 52 Liberal Democrats and 13 from other parties
       voted in favour of the amendment. The government motion was
       however approved by 434 votes to 124.

       Iain Duncan Smith apologized to the backbench 1922 committee for
       having sacked a number of officials from Conservative Central Office.
       The sacking of Mark MacGregor the party's chief executive, Rick Nye
       the director of research, and Stephen Gilbert the director of campaigns
       had precipitated a bitter feud between party 'modernizers' and 'tradi-
       tionalists' and threatened IDS's already tenuous grip on the leadership.
       Former Conservative shadow chancellor Francis Maude suggested that
       'the Conservative Party needs to lie down in a darkened room for a
       period and gather itself'.

27.   Rachel Lomax became the first female deputy governor of the Bank of
       England.

28.   Vaclav Klaus was elected president of the Czech Republic.

MARCH

1.   Khalid Sheikh Mohammed, suspected as having planned the al Qa'eda
       attacks in the US on 11 September, was arrested in Pakistan.

9.   Clare Short, International Development Secretary and Labour MP for
       Birmingham Ladywood, said that she would resign from the govern-
       ment if it sanctioned military action against Iraq without a second UN
       resolution.

       The Maltese voted in a referendum to join the EU.

10.   Yasser Arafat, the Palestinian president, nominated his deputy Mahmoud Abbas as prime minister.

11.   The world's first permanent international criminal court opened in The Hague.

        The FTSE index fell to an eight-year low.

12.   Charles Kennedy asked the Prime Minister Tony Blair if the Attorney General had advised that 'war on Iraq in the absence of a second UN resolution authorising force would be legal'. Mr Blair replied, 'we would not do anything as a country that did not have a proper legal basis'.

        The Serbian Prime Minister, Zoran Djindjic, was shot dead in Belgrade.

        Home Secretary David Blunkett published a White Paper, 'Respect and Responsibility – Taking a Stand Against Anti-Social Behaviour'. Following a statement by Mr Blunkett in the Commons, Oliver Letwin, then shadow Home Secretary, replied that the opposition 'did not disagree on diagnosis but on cure, with legislation seeping out of every pore of the Home Office'.

17.   The Attorney General, Lord Goldsmith, advised the government that the use of armed force against Iraq was legal.

        Britain and the US abandoned efforts to obtain UN authority for military action in Iraq.

        Robin Cook, Leader of the House resigned from the government. In a personal statement to the House Mr Cook explained that he had resigned because Britain was 'embarking on a war without agreement in any of the international bodies of which we are a leading partner'. Cook's statement was greeted by a standing ovation in the House.

        China announced the election of Wen Jiabao as prime minister.

        European Union commissioner Chris Patten was elected Chancellor of Oxford University. Mr Patten, who received 4,203 votes, surpassed the required 50 per cent of the vote after only one transfer under the single transferable voting system employed. Despite the convenience of holding the election on a weekend, agreeable weather, and the franchise being extended to include all who had taken a degree at Oxford – some 100,000 alumni – turnout was just over 8 per cent.

18.   In an historic nine and a half hour Commons debate 57 MPs spoke on a government motion that expressed support for the decision to use 'all means necessary to ensure the disarmament of Iraq's weapons of mass destruction'. Ian Duncan Smith gave his party's support to the government. Charles Kennedy for the Liberal Democrats spoke in favour of an amendment moved by Peter Kilfoyle, former Labour Defence Minister, that the 'case for war against Iraq has not yet been established, especially given the absence of specific UN authorisation'. The amendment was defeated by 396 votes to 217, with 139 Labour, 16 Conservative and all 53 Liberal Democrat MPs voting against the government. However, at the end of the debate the main motion was carried by 412 votes to 149.

20.   The invasion of Iraq began.

       The Northern Ireland Assembly Elections Act attained Royal Assent. The act provided for postponement of elections to the assembly in order to attempt to resolve the deadlock in the peace process.

24.   It was announced that the body of the ITV journalist Terry Lloyd, missing whilst covering the war in Iraq, had been found in a hospital in Basra.

25.   President Bush asked Congress for $75 billion additional funding for the war in Iraq.

26.   The Scottish People's Alliance became the UK's newest political party.

27.   The Clerk of Parliament announced that in the first hereditary peers by-election Viscount Ullswater had been the victor.

       Albeit with a swing of 12.6 per cent to the Liberal Democrats and on a 13.6 per cent turnout, the Labour Party's candidate held on to the Hayes division of Staffordshire County Council by just 66 votes at the first council by-election to be held since the start of the Iraq war.

APRIL

8.   US President George Bush and Prime Minister Tony Blair announced, at a war summit held at Hillsborough castle, that the UN would play a 'vital role' in post-war Iraq. Bush, on his first visit to Northern Ireland, endorsed a joint statement by Blair and the Irish premier, Bertie Ahern, which called for a 'complete and irrevocable' end to paramilitary activity in the province. The US President urged all parties to accept the British and Irish blueprint for restoration of the devolved power-sharing Stormont government.

9.   Gordon Brown, the Labour Party's longest serving Chancellor of the Exchequer, presented his budget and told the Commons, 'Britain, even in difficult world conditions, is able to meet our military and security costs abroad and at home and the costs of building peace, while maintaining in full our record investment in schools, hospitals, transport and policing. The Chancellor announced the abolition of hospital charges for all pensioners and an additional £100 winter fuel payment for every household with a pensioner over the age of 80. The leader of the opposition, Iain Duncan Smith, said that Brown had 'imposed 53 tax rises since 1997'.

Approval was given by the European Parliament to the accession treaties of ten candidate countries to join the EU.

The Norwegian parliament voted to introduce a ban on smoking in bars, restaurants, cafés and nightclubs.

Jubilant Iraqis toppled a bronze statue of Saddam Hussein in the centre of Baghdad.

10.   Abul Majid al-Khoei, a prominent Shia Muslim cleric, was assassinated. The American- and British-supported peace broker had only recently returned to Iraq after an exile in London since the failed 1991 Shia uprising.

The Prime Minister Tony Blair and Taoiseach Bertie Ahern cancelled a meeting at Hillsborough castle planned as the occasion for the release of their blueprint to revive the Northern Ireland peace process and reinstate the devolved assembly at Stormont. According to Mr Blair's official spokesman 'sufficient progress' had not yet been made in talks with the pro-agreement parties. Ahern said he and Blair were 'not blaming anybody'; however, the failure to reach an agreement with republicans about an overt act of disarmament by the IRA was widely regarded as the stumbling block.

Clare Short, Secretary of State for International Affairs, said in the Commons that as the military phase of the crisis comes to an end, the priority will be to 'provide order and humanitarian relief and to establish an Iraqi interim authority so that the long-term reconstruction can begin'.

14.   In a House of Commons speech the Prime Minister Tony Blair declared victory in the war with Iraq.

17.   Sergei Yushenkov, a prominent opposition politician, was assassinated in Moscow.

        American-born billionaire philanthropist Sir John Paul Getty died aged 70.

19.   Following landslide victories in parliamentary and gubernatorial elections the leader of the People's Democratic Party, Olusegun Obasanjo, won a second term as Nigerian president. It was the first time in the country's 43 years of independence that an elected civilian government had successfully conducted an election.

23.   Greek and Turkish Cypriots were able for the first time since 1976 to cross the UN 'green line' that has divided the island's ethnic communities.

28.   Foreign Secretary Jack Straw told the House that Iraq was 'now under coalition control' and gave the government's support for the US 'road map' for peace in the Middle East.

30.   Two suicide bombers in Israel were found to have held British passports.

MAY

1.   India restored diplomatic and air links with Pakistan in a bid to reduce tension between the two states.

        Crispin Blunt, MP for Reigate and a shadow trade minister, resigned from the Tory front bench and called for a leadership election.

Mr Blunt commented that the party carries 'the handicap of a leader whom Conservatives in parliament and outside feel unable to present to the electorate as a credible alternative prime minister'. Tim Yeo, MP for South Suffolk declared that the party needed a leadership contest 'like a hole in the head'.

Hours after Blunt's action the Conservatives made net gains of some 660 seats at the local elections. Labour lost 880 seats and control of 36 English councils, including the country's largest council Birmingham. In both the Scottish Parliament and Welsh Assembly elections no party emerged with a clear overall majority (see Tables 4.1–4.4).

Paul Murphy, the Northern Ireland Secretary, announced that the Assembly elections scheduled for May 29 would be postponed after the IRA had failed to declare an unequivocal end to paramilitary activities.

6.   George Galloway was suspended from the Labour Party after complaints that his opposition to the war in Iraq had brought the party into disrepute. The party investigation came as a preliminary inquiry by the Parliamentary Commissioner for Standards was launched into allegations that Mr Galloway had received money from the former Iraqi government and had not declared this in the Register of Members' Interests.

7.   The Health and Social Care (Community Health and Standards) Bill was introduced in the Commons. David Hinchliffe, the Labour chairman of the Health select committee, moved a reasoned amendment declining to give the bill a second reading. The amendment was defeated by 297 votes to 117; however 65 Labour rebels voted against the government. The second reading of the bill was passed by 304 votes to 230 and the government's majority reduced to 64 when 31 Labour rebels voted with the Opposition parties against the government motion.

8.   The Regional Assemblies (Preparations) Act received the royal assent. The act provides for the holding of referendums on the establishment of elected assemblies for the regions of England (excluding London).

At business questions in the House the Shadow Leader of the Commons Eric Forth, MP for Bromley and Chislehurst, said that 'postal ballots in local elections were a threat to democracy as the secrecy of the ballot was effectively disappearing before our eyes'.

At prime minister's question time the leader of the Opposition, Ian Duncan Smith, urged Tony Blair to consent to a referendum on the new European constitution.

The European Parliament (Representation) Act gained the royal assent and thereby Gibraltar became part of a UK region for elections to the European Parliament.

11.   Lithuanians voted in favour of joining the European Community in a referendum.

Carlos Menem the former president of Argentina pulled out of the presidential election and Nestor Kirchener won by default to become the country's sixth president in 18 months.

12.   Clare Short, the International Development Secretary, resigned from the Cabinet and Baroness Amos was appointed in her stead.

15.   Tessa Jowell, the Secretary of State for Culture Media and Sport, announced that the government would back a bid by London to host the 2012 Olympic Games with a public funding package of £2.4 billion.

16.   John Prescott the Deputy Prime Minister announced plans to hold referendums on regional assemblies in the North East, the North West, and Yorkshire and the Humber in the autumn of 2004.

18.   Prime Minister Guy Verhofstadt's centre-left coalition was returned to power in the Belgium general election.

21.   In a House of Lords debate on the relationship between the judiciary, the legislature and the executive introduced by Lord Rogers of Quarry Bank, Lord Smith of Clifton said that 'unbridled presidentialism is now the operational basis of British government'.

22.   In a vote at the UN, which also ended 13 years of sanctions against Iraq and allowed for the use of oil revenues to fund reconstruction, the United States and Britain gained international legal backing for their occupation of the country.

28.   The Prime Minister Tony Blair flew to Iraq to visit British troops.

       The US Defence Secretary Donald Rumsfeld admitted that there was
       an element of doubt as to whether weapons of mass destruction would
       be found in Iraq.

29.   Andrew Gilligan accused the government of having exaggerated the
       threat posed by Iraq in order to strengthen its case for war and sparked
       a ferocious political debate between the government and the BBC.
       Speaking on Radio 4's Today programme, he claimed that the govern-
       ment had dishonestly included in an intelligence dossier the claim that
       'Saddam's military planning allows for some WMDs to be ready
       within 45 minutes of an order to deploy them'. Gilligan said that a
       British official who had been involved in the preparation of the dossier
       had told him that in the week before its publication in September 2002
       the dossier had been transformed at the 'behest of Downing Street ...to
       make it sexier'.

JUNE

1.   In his weekly column for a Sunday tabloid newspaper Andrew Gilli-
       gan alleged that Alastair Campbell had intervened in the preparation of
       the September intelligence dossier on Iraq.

2.   Queen Elizabeth II celebrated the 50th anniversary of her coronation.

       Vladimir Putin the Russian president and US President George Bush
       finalized the treaty of Moscow, a strategic arms reduction agreement
       set to reduce nuclear arms by two-thirds by 2012. The summit
       preceded a G8 meeting in St Petersburg at which world leaders prom-
       ised billions of dollars to fight AIDS and hunger.

3.   Among the recommended reforms published in the electoral commis-
       sion's policy reports was the proposal to abolish the £500 deposit
       required by candidates to stand in a general election. Lord Janner
       urged the government to reject the proposal, which he called 'a charter
       for the lunatic fringe'.

4.   At PMQs Sir Peter Tapsell, Conservative MP for Louth and Horncas-
       tle asked if the Prime Minister had deliberately sought to mislead the

House over Iraq's weapons of mass destruction or was his 'blunder based on unsound intelligence reaching him?' Menzies Campbell, Liberal Democrat MP for Fife North East, initiated a debate with a motion that called for an independent inquiry into information on weapons of mass destruction. The Foreign Secretary Jack Straw introduced an amendment that argued that an inquiry by Parliament's Intelligence and Security Committee would be appropriate. Mr Campbell's motion was defeated by 203 votes to 301.

9.   In a long-awaited statement the Chancellor of the Exchequer Gordon Brown announced that the 'five tests' for UK membership of the euro had not yet been passed. Michael Howard the Shadow Chancellor responded for the Opposition by saying of the Prime Minister and the Chancellor that they were 'united in rivalry, each determined to frustrate the other'.

12.   The Lord Chancellor, Lord Irvine of Lairg QC resigned. The resignation of the Secretary for Health Alan Milburn for personal and family reasons precipitated an earlier than planned Cabinet reshuffle. Dr. John Reid was appointed Secretary of State for Health and Peter Hain, who retained his post as Secretary of State for Wales, succeeded Reid as the Leader of the House of Commons. Alastair Darling who retained the post of Transport Secretary, replaced Helen Liddell as Secretary of State for Scotland. In a major constitutional change the Lord Chancellor's Department was abolished and, with Lord Falconer as its first Secretary of State, a new Department of Constitutional Affairs created. The change ended the political and legal anomaly of the post of Lord Chancellor as a compound of legislator, executive and judiciary, in the combined positions of Speaker of the House of Lords, cabinet minister and head of the judiciary.

14.   Lord Falconer unveiled three consultation papers as part of a range of constitutional reforms to separate the judiciary and politicians. The proposals included an independent judicial appointments commission for England and Wales comprised of five judges, five lawyers and five laymen, a range of options on their powers to select, appoint and promote judges and a new supreme court separate from Parliament to replace the House of Lords as the highest court of appeal in the UK.

13.   David Beckham was awarded the OBE in the Queen's Birthday Honours.

A further shuffle saw Estelle Morris, former Secretary of State for Education and Skills who resigned her post in October 2002, returned to government as Minister for the Arts in the Department for Culture, Media and Sports.

17. David Trimble the Ulster Unionist leader won marginal support from his party to endorse the proposals set out by the London and Dublin governments to break the impasse over the Good Friday Agreement. Ulster Unionist MPs Jeffery Donaldson, Revd. Martin Smyth and David Burnside resigned their party whip in protest at the party's decision.

Sir Stanley Kalms, multi-millionaire treasurer of the Conservative Party, stood down after a series of rows with the party leader Ian Duncan Smith over staff changes at Tory central office.

18. Iain Duncan Smith in reference to the Prime Minister's recent changes to government departments described them as the 'most botched, bungled and damaged reshuffle of modern times' and accused Mr Blair of having 'ripped up the constitution ... as though our constitution were the Prime Minister's personal plaything'.

19. Appearing before the Foreign Affairs select committee on the presentation of the government's case for war with Iraq, Andrew Gilligan described the source of his allegations as 'closely connected with the question of Iraq's weapons of mass destruction, easily sufficiently senior and credible to be worth reporting'.

23. Alan Johnson, Higher Education Minister, Labour MP for Kingston upon Hull West and Hessle, and former leader of the postman's union claimed that he would not be advocating the introduction of top-up fees for students of up to £3,000 a year if he thought it would jeopardize the chances of 'working class kids' going to university. In the Commons debate on proposals outlined in the government's White Paper on higher education George Mudie, Labour MP for Leeds East and former lifelong learning minister, enquired if Mr Johnson really believed 'the nonsense' he was reading.

25. Alastair Campbell the government's director of communications gave evidence to the Foreign Affairs select committee inquiry. Campbell said that 'the allegation ... that the prime minister put to the country and to parliament a false basis for putting at risk the lives of British servicemen' was a lie and demanded an apology from the BBC.

26.   Under what he described as an 'unprecedented level of pressure from Downing Street' the BBC news director Richard Sambrook announced that 'we stand by our entire story'.

27.   Strom Thurmond, Republican senator for South Carolina, the longest serving and oldest person ever to have served in the US Congress who retired in January 2002, died aged 100 years.

        In a joint press conference with Tony Blair on the last day of his state visit to Britain the Russian president Vladimir Putin said, 'Russia also thought that Iraq might possess weapons of mass destruction'. The leaders announced that the two countries had agreed to cooperate in the building of a sub-Baltic pipeline for Britain to import Russian natural gas.

30.   The Hunting Bill reappeared on the Common's agenda and in a free vote on the total ban clause the motion was carried by 362 votes to 154.

        The White Paper, 'Our Fire and Rescue Service', was published by the Deputy Prime Minister John Prescott.

        Mervyn King was appointed Governor of the Bank of England on the retirement of Sir Edward George.

JULY

3.   The US offered a $25 million reward for information on the where-abouts of Saddam Hussein.

6.   In a devolution referendum, with turnout higher than that for the recent French general and presidential elections, the electorate of Corsica rejected a central government plan to give the island more autonomy in the form of a single local assembly elected by proportional representation.

8.   The 'West Lothian' question of Scottish MPs voting through policy in England was raised when Conservatives claimed that 40 Labour MPs representing Scottish constituencies had been decisive in the narrow defeat of an amendment by 286 votes to 251 to block the government's plans to set up foundation hospitals.

9.   In the Commons the Hunting Bill was passed at its third reading by 317 votes to 145.

        Charles Clarke published a White Paper on the government's skills strategy intended to address the 'skills weaknesses that have dogged us for so long'.

10.   Dr David Kelly was named in leading newspapers as the source of Andrew Gilligan's allegations.

        The Licensing Bill received royal assent.

        The Bank of England cut interest rates to 3.5 per cent.

        Only hours before Iain Duncan Smith delivered a speech in Prague in which he challenged EU leaders to reject the single currency, former Chancellor of the Exchequer Kenneth Clarke condemned the Conservative Party leader for making the party unelectable by attempting to force Britain out of the EU.

15.   The House of Lords voted down by 210 votes to 136 the Home Secretary David Blunkett's proposals to restrict jury trials in cases of complex fraud or where there was a likelihood of jury intimidation.

        Dr David Kelly gave evidence to the Foreign Affairs select committee inquiry, which decided he was most unlikely to be the source of Gilligan's allegations.

17.   Tony Blair joined a select band of British prime ministers to become only the fourth to have addressed both houses of the US Congress (Winston Churchill in 1941, 1943 and 1952, Clement Attlee in 1945 and Margaret Thatcher in 1985).

        The bitter row over the government's presentation of the case for war with Iraq continued as the House of Commons broke for the summer recess.

18.   Dr David Kelly was found dead.

20.   Statements were issued by the BBC that, Andrew Gilligan 'did not misquote or misrepresent Dr David Kelly' and that the corporation believed it was 'right to place Dr Kelly's views in the public domain'.

21.   Lord Hutton was appointed head of an independent inquiry into the events surrounding Dr Kelly's death.

23.   Tony Blair returned from a week-long round the world diplomatic trip during which he had received 17 standing ovations in his speech to the joint houses of the US Congress and was asked by reporters in Japan if he felt he had blood on his hands.

       Guardian/ICM polls revealed the nation as polarized by the argument over whether the war against Iraq was justified, that Labour's lead over the Conservative Party was down to two points from 12 points in May, and that Mr Blair's personal rating was –17 points with 54 per cent unhappy and only 37 per cent happy with his performance as prime minister.

28.   The former international development secretary Clare Short accused the prime minister of being implicated in the death of the government scientist Dr David Kelly. The MP for Ladywood Birmingham said that the 'truth needs to be found and those responsible held to account. Alastair Campbell and Tony Blair work very, very closely together. They are all implicated, it seems to me'.

30.   At his monthly press conference the prime minister referred all questions on Dr Kelly's death to the judicial inquiry led by Lord Hutton and when pressed as to whether he would resign if no weapons of mass destruction were found in Iraq insisted that he remained confident that the intelligence the government had received was correct.

AUGUST

1.   The Hutton inquiry began.

       The US and North Korea ended months of tense diplomatic deadlock when agreement to hold talks was reached. The confrontation had begun in October 2002 over the US claim that North Korea was engaged in a secret uranium enrichment programme. In response North Korea had expelled international nuclear inspectors, abandoned the Nuclear Non-Proliferation Treaty and restarted a mothballed nuclear reactor. The crisis had deepened when earlier this year the North Koreans had admitted to possession of nuclear warheads and to having started to reprocess spent plutonium.

2. Tony Blair became the Labour Party's longest continuously serving prime minister overtaking the record set by Clement Attlee.

4. Diplomatic despatches released under the US Freedom of Information Act revealed that Ronald Reagan had prepared secret plans to counter the prospect of the anti-nuclear Labour leader Neil Kinnock winning power at the 1987 British general election. Publicly the Americans claimed to be neutral on the election, however the dispatches revealed how privately US diplomats warned that 'if the Labour party gains power, significant difficulties in the relationship can be expected'. In a prophetic warning, Charles Price the then US ambassador in London, told Washington that 'if Labour ever hopes to regain power, it will almost certainly have to confront the need to rethink its commitment to unilateral nuclear disarmament'.

5. Ken Macdonald QC, a founding member of Cherie Blair's Matrix chambers, was appointed Director of Public Prosecutions.

6. The former Pakistani Prime Minister Benazir Bhutto who lives in exile in London and her husband, who lives in a jail in Pakistan, were found guilty by a Swiss court of money-laundering and ordered to pay almost £7 million in reparations to the Pakistani state.

7. Conservative Party internal feuding was revived when Tim Yeo, in a thinly veiled attack on the party chairwoman Theresa May, said that Iain Duncan Smith's attempts to modernize the Conservatives were being blocked by elements in the party.

George Soros donated $10 million to America Coming Together, a group of political activists made up of liberals, environmentalists and unions whose aim is to assist the Democrat candidate at the 2004 US election. Mr Soros said, 'the fate of the world depends on the United States and President Bush is leading us in the wrong direction'.

11. Charles Taylor the warlord-turned-president of Liberia handed power to his vice-president Moses Zeh Blah and went into exile in Nigeria. In 1997, after eight years of bloody civil war Mr Taylor took 75 per cent of the vote at the presidential elections and had employed the campaign slogan, 'He killed my Ma, he killed my Pa, but I will vote for him'.

NATO began its first peacekeeping operation outside European borders when it took control of the International Security Assistance Force in Kabul.

12.   Lady Diana Mosley, widow of the late Sir Oswald Mosley, died in
        Paris aged 93 years. The couple had married in 1936 at Joseph
        Goebbels' Berlin home with Adolf Hitler in attendance.

13.   US troops were deployed in Liberia to support the peacekeeping
        operations of West African countries.

14.   Large areas of the US northeast, including New York, and two
        Canadian cities were plunged into darkness by a massive power cut.

15.   In a letter to the UN Security Council Libya admitted responsibility for
        the Lockerbie bombing in 1988.

19.   Sergio Vieira de Mello, a UN special representative, was killed in a
        suicide bomb attack on the UN headquarters in Baghdad.

        The three-year bloody war in Liberia ended when rebel groups signed
        a peace deal.

20.   Pauline Hanson and David Etteridge, the co-founders of Australia's
        far-right One Nation Party, were found guilty of electoral fraud by a
        Brisbane court and jailed for three years.

25.   In Rwanda's first official presidential election since the 1994 genocide
        took place, Paul Kagame, the incumbent president, gained more than
        95 per cent of the vote.

27.   Pierre Poujade died aged 82 years. The French shopkeeper rose to
        fame as a national demagogue in defence of the small trader against
        big business, state bureaucracy and high taxation. At the 1956 election
        his UDCA party won 52 seats in the French Assembly, including one
        by a young Jean-Marie Le Pen.

        Geoff Hoon, the Defence Secretary gave evidence to the Hutton
        inquiry.

28.   The Prime Minister Tony Blair told the Hutton inquiry that the 'respon-
        sibility is mine' for the decisions that led to the naming of Dr Kelly.

29.   Downing Street's director of communications Alastair Campbell
        resigned and David Hill, a former Labour Party press chief, was
        appointed as head of a reconstructed press operation.

SEPTEMBER

2.   As Charles Clarke told the Association of Commonwealth Universities conference in Belfast that 'there was no alternative to increasing student fees to pay for higher education', George Mudie, Labour's former education minister told the BBC that the prime minister faced his most serious domestic test yet over the issue. Martin Salter, Labour MP for Reading West and deputy convenor of the party's electoral campaign added, 'my job is to help the Labour Party win the next general election. This policy won't'.

4.   The British National Party won its eighteenth UK council seat when it took the Grays Riverside ward in Thurrock, Essex.

6.   Mahmoud Abbas the Palestinian prime minister resigned. According to aides Mr Abbas's position had been seriously undermined in a constant power struggle with Yasser Arafat.

11.   The Swedish foreign minister Anna Lindh died in hospital from stab wounds.

14.   The Swedish electorate rejected membership of the European monetary union in a referendum.

15.   World Trade Organization talks in Cancun, Mexico, collapsed after a walkout by African countries protesting at the west's failure to open its markets to third world nations.

        Four months after resigning the presidency of Plaid Cymru in the wake of the party's poor performance at the Welsh Assembly elections, Ieuan Wyn Jones was elected to lead the nationalist party in the assembly. Mr Jones had permanently relinquished the presidency, but a decision to separate the office of party leader from that of president cleared the way for his remarkable political recovery.

17.   Andrew Gilligan admitted his accusation that No. 10 inserted the 45-minute claim knowing it to be wrong was a 'slip of the tongue' and that the error he made was 'in expressing the understanding I had that the views had been conveyed to the government as something Dr Kelly had told me.'

18.   Defence Secretary Geoff Hoon denied that there was any conspiracy to reveal Dr Kelly's name.

The Labour Party lost its first parliamentary seat in a by-election since 1988 when Sarah Teather, the Liberal Democrat candidate, took the Brent East seat with 39.1 per cent of the vote. Support for the Labour Party collapsed in a swing of 29 per cent that left its candidate Robert Evans in second place. The by-election followed the death of the Labour MP Paul Daisley who was elected at the 2001 general election with 63 per cent of the vote and a 13,047 majority.

Plans unveiled in a government white paper by the constitutional secretary Lord Falconer included legislation to exclude the remaining 92 hereditary peers, a statutory commission to oversee and select appointments to the Lords and legislation to enable the expulsion of convicted peers, such as Lord Archer, retrospectively.

20.   Lord Williams of Mostyn, leader of the House of Lords died aged 62 years.

21.   In violation of the country's constitution that forbids the president to promote political parties or individual candidates, Vladimir Putin appeared alongside the Kremlin's approved candidate on television and on electoral posters at the St Petersburg gubernatorial elections. Turnout plummeted, with 70 per cent of voters remaining in their dachas and one in ten ballot papers of those who did bother to vote spoilt. City council chairman, Vadim Tyulpanov, said 'residents felt there was no point ... because everything was decided'.

22.   Chancellor Gerhard Schroder's Social Democrat Party suffered a crushing electoral defeat when Bavarian Premier Edmund Stoiber's Christian Social Union party won an historic two-thirds majority in the Bavarian state parliament.

24.   A Guardian/ICM poll put the Labour Party on 35, the Conservatives on 30 and the Liberal Democrats on a 28 per cent share of the vote at a general election.

26.   Iain Duncan Smith, the Conservative Party leader, already reeling from the party's poor performance at the Brent-East by-election, received another body-blow when the former Tory party deputy prime minister, Lord Heseltine told Radio 4 listeners that the Conservative Party could not win the next general election.

Charles Kennedy on the last day of his party's Brighton conference told Liberal Democrat delegates to 'be in no doubt: we are overtaking the Conservatives. Be in no doubt: we are the only credible challenge to the government.'

30.   In language redolent of former prime minister Margaret Thatcher, Tony Blair underscored his refusal to back down over NHS reform or student top-up fees and his decision to go to war with Iraq in his speech at the Labour Party conference in Bournemouth by saying of his vision of leadership, 'I can only go one way, I've not got a reverse gear'. Pre-conference predictions of a rank and file revolt against the prime minister by his party did not materialize.

OCTOBER

6.   The pro-Moscow candidate Akhmad Kadyrov, was elected president of Chechnya with over 80 per cent of the popular vote and on a turnout of 86 per cent after many of his challengers withdrew or were removed from the election and 10,000 local police backed by 3,500 Russian troops provided 'security' for voters.

7.   Arnold Schwarzenegger was elected as governor of California the world's fifth largest economy. Over 150 candidates stood at the election in what was the state's first ever attempt to sack a governor mid-term. Gray Davis, a Democrat, had been recalled just eight months into his second term. The only other governor to be recalled in US history was Lynn Frazier, in North Dakota who was voted out in 1921.

9.   At the Conservative Party conference in Blackpool, overshadowed by talk of plots against his leadership and improper payments to his wife, Iain Duncan Smith advised his critics to 'Get on board...or get out of the way'.

13.   Sir Kevin Tebbit, a top civil servant at the Ministry of Defence, told the Hutton inquiry that key policy decisions that led to the public naming of Dr Kelly had been taken at a Downing Street meeting chaired by the Prime Minister Tony Blair.

14.   The parliamentary standards commissioner Sir Philip Mawer announced the start of an investigation into the probity of the secretarial salary paid to Betsy Duncan Smith by her husband the Conservative Party leader.

15.   The Labour controlled 60-member Welsh Assembly approved an early
       retirement scheme for Welsh councillors by a majority of two votes.
       The scheme, aimed at encouraging a greater diversity in age, gender
       and race among candidates for council office, offered £1,000 for every
       year served up to a maximum of £20,000.

16.   BNP candidates were convincingly defeated by Liberal Democrats at
       council by-elections in the Lanehead ward of Burnley and the
       Mixenden ward in Calderdale. The Burnley council by-election had
       been triggered by the resignation of the BNP's Luke Smith, 21, after
       he was involved in a brawl at the BNP's annual summer bash. He had
       won the seat just five months before at the May council elections.

19.   The Prime Minister Tony Blair spent five hours in London's Hammer-
       smith hospital receiving treatment after complaining of chest pains.
       After a cardioversion, a procedure to regulate the heartbeat, he was
       declared fit and well and discharged.

       Switzerland's far-right People's party, the SVP, took 27.7 per cent of
       the vote in the country's general election to become the biggest party
       in Switzerland's new lower-house with 56 of the 200 seats.

22.   Stuart Wheeler, who donated £5 million to the Conservative Party
       under William Hague, called for the overthrow of Iain Duncan Smith
       as party leader.

23.   Madame Chiang Kai-shek died in New York aged 105.The widow of
       China's Nationalist leader whose forces lost the civil war to Mao
       Zedong's Communists in 1949, left Taiwan after her husband's death
       in 1975 and lived in relative seclusion in the US.

       George Galloway, MP for Glasgow Kelvin, was expelled from the
       Labour Party after being found guilty of bringing the party into disre-
       pute.

24.   Four members of the Welsh Assembly were alleged to have failed to
       declare employing their spouses in the member's register of interest.
       Although a criminal offence in Wales and Scotland, those at Westmin-
       ster who break such rules face only parliamentary censure.

28.   An official inquiry began into the escalating costs of the Scottish
       Parliament building. Initially projected to cost between £10m and

£40m the inquiry was told that current projections estimate the cost at over £400m.

29.   Twenty-five months after taking office the self-proclaimed 'Quiet Man' of British politics went quietly. Iain Duncan Smith lost a confidence vote on his leadership, 75 votes for and 90 against. In a short statement he said that the 'parliamentary party has spoken and I will stand down as leader when a successor has been chosen'. His departure thrust the Conservative Party into its fourth leadership election in eight years.

NOVEMBER

3.   The government launched its 'Your Say' campaign to encourage northern voters to consider the issues of devolution. In an all-postal ballot of 11 million voters, the North-West, North-East and Yorkshire and The Humber regions will be the first three of eight English regions to hold a referendum in the autumn of 2004. The Deputy Prime Minister, John Prescott and the local and regional government minister, Nick Raynsford , addressed meetings across the north of the country at the start of an awareness campaign aimed, according to Mr Prescott, at empowering voters to make an informed choice.

The Prime Minister, much to the chagrin of his chancellor Gordon Brown, appointed two junior ministers, Hazel Blears and Douglas Alexander, to the National Executive Committee of the Labour Party. Mr Blair, who has three of the 32 member committee seats in his gift, turned down Mr Brown's third appeal to be appointed to the NEC which plays a central role in the party's election campaigns, finances, membership and annual conference. The third appointment was occupied by Ian McCartney, the party chairman.

Leaders of Britain's five largest trade unions called for the re-admittance of Ken Livingstone by the Labour Party and his adoption as the party's candidate in the London mayoral elections.

4.   The Green Paper, 'Policing, Building Safer Communities Together', outlining the second stage of the government's police reform plans was published. The proposals are part of a wider agenda aimed at the introduction of new methods of accountability for the delivery of local services and encouragement of the disaffected voter to participate in

local elections. Larger regional strategic police forces and 'community advocates' to hold elected police authorities to account were among the proposals. Elections to police authorities and neighbourhood policing panels would take place on the same ballot paper as local elections.

6.   In what turned out to be a one-horse race Michael Howard QC, MP for Folkestone and Hythe, was elected leader of the Conservative Party.

7.   Michael Portillo, Conservative MP for Kensington and Chelsea announced that he would step down as an MP at the next election.

9.   Japan's Liberal Democratic Party won a narrow victory at the general election on a turnout of only 52 per cent. The LDP won 237 of the 480 seats in the lower house, ten seats less than at the 2001 election, but a total of 275 seats with those of their two coalition partners, the New Komeito and the New Conservatives, to enable Prime Minister Junichiro Koizumi to continue in power. The LDP have dominated Japanese politics since 1955.

The Conservative Party leader Michael Howard sacked Theresa May, MP for Maidenhead, as Conservative Party chairwoman.

10.   A trade war was threatened when the World Trade Organization declared that US tariffs on foreign steel, introduced by President Bush in 2002, were illegal. Washington rejected the ruling and the EU urged Washington to lift tariffs or face sanctions on manufactures from 'swing states' where support could be crucial for Mr Bush's re-election campaign.

The new leader of the Conservative Party Michael Howard, the fourth in eight years, announced his 'slim-line' shadow cabinet. In a cull of his predecessor's 26-strong cabinet, Liam Fox and Lord Saatchi became co-chairmen of the party, Oliver Letwin shadow chancellor, David Davis shadow home secretary, Tim Yeo shadow secretary of state for public services, health and education, David Curry shadow secretary of state for local and devolved government affairs, Theresa May shadow secretary of state for environment and transport, Michael Ancram shadow secretary of state for international affairs and shadow foreign secretary, David Willetts shadow secretary of state for works and pensions, David Maclean chief whip, and Lord Strathclyde leader of the opposition in the Lords.

The Lords approved regulations allowing elections to the suspended Northern Ireland assembly to go ahead on November 26.

12.   Fiona Bruce became the first Conservative prospective parliamentary candidate to be selected by an open 'primary' ballot. The 'primary', part of a drive to encourage Conservative constituency associations to select fewer white middle-aged men as candidates, was open to all Warrington South Constituency residents on the electoral register irrespective of party allegiances.

17.   For the third time since March 2003, when the parliament was dissolved following the assassination of Zoran Djindjic, the Serbian electorate failed to elect a president. Fewer than half of the electorate, the minimum level of turnout required to validate the poll, bothered to vote.

        Regional elections in Spain saw the pro-independence Catalan Republican Left double its share of the vote to 16% and thereby become the arbiter of power in the region's parliament between the Socialist party and the Convergence and Union coalition.

19.   Albeit with its majority reduced to 17 the government's plan to establish foundation hospitals was backed by 302 votes to 285 when the House of Commons rejected the Lords amendment to the health and social care (community health and standards) bill which had removed provision for foundation hospitals.

        The US President George Bush arrived in Britain for a four-day state visit amid tight security. However, requests by US security officials to allow US fighter aircraft to patrol London's skies and for the underground system to be closed were refused.

23.   The former Soviet Union foreign minister Edward Shevardnadze who returned to Georgia in 1992 to head the newly independent country, resigned as its president following weeks of mass protests over alleged electoral fraud at the November 2 parliamentary elections.

26.   The Queen delivered Tony Blair's seventh parliamentary programme at the state opening of Parliament. The Queen's Speech promised a bill to 'place universities on a sound financial footing' and the abolition of up-front fees for full-time students, legislation to establish a single tier of appeal against asylum decisions, continuation of the government's

programme of constitutional reform, draft bills on identity cards and a referendum on the adoption of a single currency subject to the government's five economic tests and modernization of the laws on domestic violence.

Voters in Northern Ireland went to the polls in elections to the province's suspended assembly. Ian Paisley's Democratic Unionist Party, which rejects the Good Friday Agreement, emerged as the leading unionist party taking 30 seats, and David Trimble's Ulster Unionist Party 27 seats. Sinn Fein emerged as the leading nationalist party with 24 seats, six more than the SDLP.

27.   Alex Salmond, the Scottish Nationalist Party's Westminster leader added his voice to the furore over the decisive role played by Labour MPs from north of the border in getting the government's plans for foundation hospitals through the Commons. Mr Salmond speaking on the Good Morning Scotland programme said how the SNP hoped to launch a far-wider debate about the 'West Lothian question' to resolve the situation where Scottish MPs vote on England-only laws, but England's MPs cannot vote on matters devolved to Scotland.

President George Bush made a surprise appearance in Iraq to celebrate Thanksgiving Day with US forces.

28.   The Prime Minister Tony Blair launched his 'big conversation', a 77-page consultation document devoted to policy areas in which ideas are presented as options rather than firm government commitments.

DECEMBER

2.   Asked by reporters if the forthcoming Commons vote on student top-up fees would be a vote of confidence and if so, would he resign if he lost, the Prime Minister Tony Blair admitted 'of course my authority is on the line, it always is with issues like this'.

7.   The United Russia party won an emphatic victory at the Russian general elections giving the pro-Putin bloc more than the two-thirds majority in the 450-seat Duma parliament required to make constitutional changes and perhaps, thereby, permit Vladimir Putin a third term as president.

10.   Gordon Brown, the longest serving chancellor since David Lloyd George, in his seventh pre-budget said that the economy had enjoyed its longest peacetime growth since records began in 1870.

The government published a draft euro referendum bill.

Canadian prime minister Jean Chretien retired and was succeeded by his former finance minister, Paul Martin.

12.   The National Audit Office announced findings that suggested the government could save almost £5 billion by managing public spending more effectively.

13.   The Brussels summit on the European constitution collapsed. Leaders abandoned the summit after Spain and Poland refused to accept changes to the system of voting. Both countries were determined not to concede privileges secured at Nice in 2000, which gave them inflated voting powers disproportionate to their populations. Many smaller states were also unhappy about the proposal to reduce the size of the European Commission that would leave some states without representation. Proposed changes included an EU president elected for a two-and-a-half-year term and an EU foreign minister, a new 'mutual defence' clause, and the loss of veto for members in 20 more policy areas including immigration and energy. Britain remains opposed to any concession over its right to veto on foreign policy, tax, social security and rules covering its budget rebate.

13.   The United Nations threatened to withdraw its agencies from Afghanistan if western troops could not halt the violence that saw 15 UN aid workers murdered by resurgent Taliban fighters.

14.   'Ladies and gentlemen, we got him' was how Paul Bremner, senior US administrator in Iraq, announced to the world the capture of Saddam Hussein.

A furore erupted when a 'whistleblower' disclosed the minutes of the main honours committee that vets people for knighthoods and other awards and described Britain's honours system as too secretive and preoccupied with the public relations impact of awards rather than with genuine merit.

Turkish-Cypriot elections seemed to dash any hopes of ending the island's 29-year division when the pro-unification parties failed to win a clear victory over the anti-UN plan parties when rival blocs each took 25 seats in the 50-member parliament.

16.   The National Executive Committee of the Labour Party voted over-whelmingly in favour of the readmission of the London Mayor Ken Livingstone to the party.

17.   Office for National Statistics figures revealed that unemployment had fallen to a 28-year low in the month of November 2003.

18.   The Audit Commission published its annual local authority league table and rated quality in 26 of the 150 councils in England and Wales as excellent, 56 good, 40 fair, 18 weak and 10 poor. Nick Raynsford, the local government minister welcomed the improvement on last year's figures but warned councils to keep down the level of local taxes.

       Jeffrey Donaldson, Ulster Unionist MP for Lagan Valley, an implaca-ble opponent of the Good Friday Agreement, who was elected in 2001 with an 18,432 majority, resigned from his party.

19.   Libya announced its decision to scrap its nuclear and chemical weap-ons programmes and allow completely free inspections by the UN verification team of all its sites.

21.   The Archbishop of Canterbury, Dr Rowan Williams, warned that the detention of terrorists without trial could alienate moderate Muslims.

23.   The Inland Revenue announced that company bosses will be able to hand out a turkey and a bottle of wine to their staff at Christmas, free of tax.

25.   In what was the second assassination attempt in under a fortnight, President Musharraf of Pakistan narrowly missed death when suicide bombers drove cars packed with explosives into his motorcade.

       Beagle 2, the UK's first spacecraft to voyage to another planet, failed to call home.

26.   An earthquake virtually destroyed the Iranian city of Bam, causing massive loss of life.

29.   The Labour peer Lord Puttnam launched a campaign in the House of Lords to block the government's plans for university top-up fees. Lord Puttnam, the Chancellor of Sunderland University, said the plan would lead to a 'market place' for courses and burden students with huge debts.

30.   The extremist Serbian Radical Party, led by Vojislav Seselj, an indicted war criminal, won 27 per cent of the vote in the parliamentary elections to become the country's biggest party. The three main reformist parties that overthrew Slobodan Milosevic took 42 per cent of the vote and 124 of the 250 seats in parliament, just two seats short of a majority.

2. Parliamentary By-elections 2003

There was just one by-election in 2003. It was held in Brent East following the death of Paul Andrew Daisley on 18 June 2003.

1. BRENT EAST 18 September 2003 (Death of Paul Andrew Daisley)

Result

Candidate	Description	Votes
Miss S.L. Teather	Liberal Democrat	8,158
R.J.E. Evans	Labour	7,040
Mrs U.N. Fernandes	Conservative	3,368
T.N. Lynch *	Green	638
B. Butterworth *	Socialist Alliance	361
K.F. Ibrahim *	Public Services Not War	219
W.T. McKenzie *	Independent	197
Miss K. McBride *	Independent	189
H.L. Immanuel *	Independent Labour	188
B.J. Hall *	UK Independence	140
Mrs I.M.J. Cremer *	Socialist Labour	111
N.F. Walsh *	Independent	101
A. Hope *	Official Monster Raving Loony	59
A.A. Barschack *	No description	37
J.J.N. Bardwaj *	No description	35
R.G. Weiss *	www.xat.org	11

Lib Dem gain from Lab: Majority 1,118
*Lost deposit

Turnout and Major Party Vote Shares (%)

	By-election	General Election	Change
Turnout	36.2	51.9	−15.7
Con	16.2	18.2	−2.0
Lab	33.8	63.2	−29.4
Lib Dem	39.1	10.6	+28.5

TABLE 2.1   *Summary of By-election Results in 2001 Parliament*

	Con	Lab	Lib Dem	SNP/PC	Turnout	Change
	Change in share of vote since 2001					
Ipswich	−2.1	−7.9	+7.2	−	40.2	−16.8
Ogmore	−3.6	−10.0	−4.1	+6.8	35.9	−22.3
Brent East	−2.0	−29.4	+28.5	−	36.2	−15.7

3. Public Opinion Polls 2003

TABLE 3.1   *Voting Intentions in Major Polls 2003 (%)*

Fieldwork	Sample Company	Size	Con	Lab	Lib Dem	Other
January						
3–4	YouGov	–	31	38	23	8
3–4	Live Strategy	1006	32	37	25	6
16–17	YouGov	1884	31	37	25	7
17–19	ICM	1002	30	43	21	6
23–27	MORI	1989	31	40	22	7
28–30	YouGov	1949	32	36	24	8
February						
7–8	YouGov	1903	32	37	24	7
7–9	Populus	1004	34	35	25	6
14–16	ICM	1003	31	39	22	8
17–18	YouGov	2357	33	34	26	7
20–21	YouGov	2032	33	35	25	7
25–16	YouGov	–	31	35	26	8
20–25	MORI	1925	29	41	22	8
March						
7–9	Populus	1000	34	34	24	8
14–16	ICM	1002	32	38	24	6
20–24	MORI	970	29	43	21	7
26–27	YouGov	2282	33	40	20	7
April						
10–11	YouGov	–	33	41	18	8
10–12	Populus	1004	29	42	22	7
17–19	ICM	1000	30	42	21	7
22–24	YouGov	2390	32	40	21	7
24–28	MORI	1074	29	43	21	7
May						
2–4	Populus	1000	34	36	22	8
16–18	ICM	1000	29	41	21	9
22–28	MORI	1793	31	39	22	8
28–29	YouGov	–	36	37	20	7
June						
13–15	Populus	1003	33	37	20	10
19–20	YouGov	2024	36	37	20	7
20–22	ICM	1001	34	38	21	7
24–26	YouGov	–	37	35	21	7
26–27	MORI	1007	35	35	19	11

TABLE 3.1 (continued) *Voting Intentions in Major Polls 2003 (%)*

Fieldwork	Sample Company	Size	Con	Lab	Lib Dem	Other
July						
4–6	Populus	1000	34	36	21	9
7–8	MORI	1003	35	38	19	8
18–20	ICM	1001	34	36	22	8
22–24	YouGov	2219	37	34	22	7
17–22	MORI	1940	38	35	21	6
August						
1–3	Populus	1001	32	34	25	9
7–8	YouGov	2071	38	34	21	7
15–17	ICM	1001	32	37	22	9
26–28	YouGov	2365	37	35	20	8
September						
28.8–2.9	MORI	1850	34	36	24	6
4–5	YouGov	–	37	36	18	9
5–6	Populus	1011	34	39	19	8
11–16	MORI	1976	31	40	21	8
19–21	ICM	1002	30	35	28	7
23–25	YouGov	2306	32	31	30	7
24–26	ICM	1002	31	31	31	7
25–26	YouGov	–	33	30	30	7
26–27	NOP	963	29	38	27	6
October						
30.9–2.10	YouGov	2441	33	33	28	6
2–3	YouGov	1971	33	34	26	7
3–5	Populus	1000	31	36	26	7
6–7	Populus	–	31	36	26	7
10–11	YouGov	–	38	33	22	7
16–18	YouGov	–	34	34	25	7
17–19	ICM	1004	33	38	21	8
23–28	MORI	2018	35	38	21	6
November						
30.10–2.11	YouGov	–	34	36	23	7
6	ICM	1007	31	39	22	8
7–8	YouGov	–	34	36	24	6
7–9	Populus	965	31	36	25	8
13–14	YouGov	–	36	39	20	5
14–16	ICM	1002	33	38	21	8
20–25	MORI	1945	35	36	22	7
December						
5–6	YouGov	1779	36	36	23	5
5–7	Populus	1006	33	36	22	9
12–14	ICM	1001	33	38	22	7
11–17	MORI	1913	31	40	22	7
16–17	YouGov	2422	35	40	18	7

Notes: The figures shown for voting intention are the 'headline' figures published by the polling companies concerned. ICM weight their results to produce adjusted figures. MORI, on the other hand, publishes unadjusted figures calculated in the traditional way. YouGov is an internet pollster using three methods of sampling – passive, active and combination. Populus (formerly Live Strategy) subtract the base weight figure for each party from the poll figure for their recalled past vote, and add this sum to that party's actual result at the last election.

TABLE 3.2   *Monthly Averages for Voting Intentions 2003 (%)*

	Con	Lab	Lib Dem		Con	Lab	Lib Dem
January	31	39	23	July	36	36	21
February	32	37	24	August	35	35	22
March	32	39	22	September	32	35	25
April	31	42	21	October	34	35	24
May	33	38	21	November	33	37	22
June	35	36	20	December	34	38	21

Note: These are the simple means of the figures given in Table 3.1.

TABLE 3.3   *Voting Intentions in Scotland 2003 (%)*

	UK Parliament				Scottish Parliament			
	Con	Lab	Lib Dem	SNP	Con	Lab	Lib Dem	SNP
January	12	45	14	24	10	40	13	30
February	14	42	15	25	11	32	16	31
March	12	42	15	25	10	34	14	32
April (beg.)	13	38	17	25	11	31	16	31
April (end)	13	45	13	22	10	38	14	28
May*					15.5	29.3	11.8	20.9
	No poll took place in June							
	No poll took place in July							
August	15	40	14	24	13	31	15	31
September	13	41	14	24	10	33	16	31
October	13	39	18	24	12	32	15	31
November	13	43	18	22	11	35	17	29
December	17	42	12	24	15	35	11	30

Notes: Rows do not total 100 because 'others' are not shown. The figures shown for the Scottish
Parliament are for constituency (not list) voting intention.
Holyrood Elections.
Source: System Three Scotland polls, published monthly in *The Herald* (Glasgow).

TABLE 3.4   *Ratings of Party Leaders 2003 (%)*

	Duncan Smith			Blair			Kennedy		
	Pos	Neg	Net	Pos	Neg	Net	Pos	Neg	Net
January	18	49	−31	33	58	−25	42	20	+22
February	16	53	−37	31	61	−30	42	23	+19
March	21	47	−26	43	48	−5	39	26	+13
April	22	47	−25	47	45	+2	40	26	+14
May	23	44	−21	38	54	−16	38	26	+12
June	21	49	−28	31	61	−30	37	27	+10
July	25	45	−20	32	60	−28	39	26	+13
August	20	47	−27	30	63	−33	38	25	+13
September	19	49	−30	29	64	−35	35	29	+6
October	22	49	−29	31	60	−29	38	24	+14
		Howard							
November	26	17	+9	32	57	−25	40	18	+22
December	22	21	+1	36	55	−19	41	20	+19

Notes: The figures are based on responses to the questions 'Are you satisfied or dissatisfied with the way Mr Blair is doing his job as Prime Minister?' 'Are you satisfied or dissatisfied with the way Mr Duncan Smith/Mr Kennedy is doing his job as Leader of the Conservative/Liberal Democratic Party?' The difference between 100 and the sum of positive and negative responses is the percentage of respondents who replied 'Don't know'.
Source: MORI.

TABLE 3.5   *Best Person for Prime Minister 2003 (%)*

	Blair	Duncan Smith	Kennedy	Don't know
January	33	15	22	31
February	36	12	23	29
March	43	14	15	28
April	42	14	15	28
May	38	19	15	29
June	35	21	18	27
July	31	21	18	30
August	30	19	18	33
September	28	18	21	33
		Howard		
October	29	22	14	34
November	31	27	10	32
December	35	29	13	22

Note: These are answers to the question 'Who would make the best Prime Minister?'
Source: YouGov.

TABLE 3.6   *Satisfaction/Dissatisfaction with Government Record 2003 (%)*

	Satisfied	Dissatisfied	Don't know	Satisfied/ Dissatisfied
January	26	65	9	−39
February	25	67	8	−42
March	35	55	10	−20
April	35	53	12	−18
May	30	60	10	−30
June	25	64	11	−39
July	26	65	9	−39
August	24	67	9	−43
September	27	66	7	−39
October	25	64	11	−39
November	27	63	10	−36
December	29	60	11	−31

Note: These are answers to the question 'Are you satisfied or dissatisfied with the way the government is running the country?'.
Source: MORI.

TABLE 3.7   *Prospective Economic Evaluations 2003 (%)*

	Improve	Stay the same	Get worse	Don't know	Net
January	8	30	54	7	−46
February	8	28	58	6	−50
March	12	29	51	8	−39
April	19	38	37	7	−18
May	14	42	38	6	−24
June	17	40	37	6	−20
July	15	42	37	6	−22
August	13	40	39	8	−26
September	14	43	37	7	−23
October	13	43	38	6	−25
November	14	39	41	6	−27
December	16	42	36	6	−20

Note: These data derive from answers to the question 'Do you think that the general economic condition of the country will improve, stay the same or get worse over the next 12 months?'
Source: MORI Economic Optimism Index.

TABLE 3.8   *The Current Six Most Important Issues Facing Britain 2003 (%)*

	Crime	Defence	Economy	Education	NHS	Race
January	21	64	12	27	35	34
February	20	69	10	27	44	27
March	18	64	13	27	42	26
April	19	26	15	32	49	27
May	25	24	13	30	39	33
June	22	21	10	27	41	29
July	26	24	9	33	43	29
August	24	20	12	33	45	35
September	24	37	14	28	40	29
October	25	21	10	26	40	34
November	29	40	11	27	46	26
December	22	26	12	33	41	29

Note: These data derive from answers to the questions 'What would you say is the most important issue facing Britain today?' 'What do you see as other important issues facing
Britain today?'

Source: MORI Political Monitor.

TABLE 3.9   *Attitudes to a Referendum on the European Single Currency 2003 (%)*

	Vote to join	Vote not to join	Don't know
January	31	62	7
February	24	60	16
March	31	62	7
April	26	61	13
May	29	62	9
June	21	62	16
July	23	60	17
August	25	59	16
September	23	63	14
October	22	63	15
November	20	66	14
December	22	66	12

Note: These data derive from answers to the questions 'If there were to be a referendum, would
you vote to join the European Single Currency (the Euro) or would you vote not to join?'

Source: ICM Single Currency Trends.

TABLE 3.10   *Approval or Disapproval of a Military Attack on Iraq, 2002–2003 (%)*

	Approve	Disapprove	Don't know
23–25 August 2002	33	50	17
13–15 September 2002	36	40	24
20–22 September 2002	37	46	18
27–29 September 2002	33	44	24
4–6 October 2002	32	41	27
14 October 2002	37	42	21
18–20 October 2002	35	40	25
25–27 October 2002	38	40	21
1–3 November 2002	32	41	27
21–22 November 2002	39	40	21
13–15 December 2002	36	44	20
17–19 January 2003	30	47	23
14–16 February 2003	29	52	19
14–16 March 2003	38	44	18
21–23 March 2003	54	30	15
28–30 March 2003	52	34	14
4–6 April 2003	56	29	15
11–13 April 2003	63	23	14

Note: These data derive from the question, 'Do you approve or disapprove of a (the) military
attack on Iraq to remove Saddam Hussein?'
Source: ICM.

TABLE 3.11   *Military Attack on Iraq to Remove Saddam Hussein: Justified or Unjustified?*

	Justified	Unjustified	Don't Know
June 2003	48	40	11
July 2003	51	42	7
September 2003	38	53	9
November 2003	47	41	12
January 2004	53	41	6

Note: These data derive from the question, 'From everything you have seen and heard, do you
think the military attack on Iraq to remove Saddam Hussein was justified or unjustified?'
This question was not asked every month.
Source: ICM.

4. Scottish Parliament and Welsh Assembly Elections 2003

Elections for the Scottish Parliament and Welsh Assembly were held on 1 May 2003. In both cases an additional member system was used, with voters casting one vote for a constituency representative and one for a party list within regions.

TABLE 4.1   *Scottish Parliament Constituency Election Results*

	Votes	%	Seats
Conservative	318,279	16.6	3
Labour	663,585	34.6	46
Liberal Democrats	294,347	15.4	13
SNP	455,742	23.8	9
Scottish Socialist Party	118,764	6.2	–
Independents	44,538	2.3	2
Others	21,339	1.1	–

TABLE 4.2   *Scottish Parliament List Election Results*

	Votes	%	Seats
Conservative	296,229	15.5	15
Labour	561,375	29.3	4
Liberal Democrats	225,774	11.8	4
SNP	399,659	20.9	18
Scottish Green Party	132,138	6.9	7
Scottish Socialist Party	128,026	6.7	6
Independents	33,763	1.8	1
Others	138,187	7.1	1

Source: Electoral Commission, Scottish Elections 2003

TABLE 4.3   *Welsh Assembly Constituency Election Results*

	Votes	%	Seats
Conservative	169,832	19.9	1
Labour	340,515	40.0	30
Liberal Democrats	120,250	14.1	3
Plaid Cymru	180,185	21.2	5
Independents	13,964	1.6	1
Others	26,611	3.1	–

TABLE 4.4   *Welsh Assembly List Election Results*

	Votes	%	Seats
Conservative	162,725	19.2	10
Labour	310,658	36.6	–
Liberal Democrats	108,013	12.7	3
Plaid Cymru	167,653	19.7	7
Welsh Green Party	30,028	3.5	–
UK Independence Party	29,427	3.5	–
Independents	11,008	1.3	–
Others	30,040	3.5	–

Source: Electoral Commission, The National Assembly for Wales Elections 2003

5. Local Elections 2003

On 1 May 2003 there were elections in 340 local authorities across England and Scotland. In England they covered all 36 metropolitan boroughs, together with 40 out of the 46 unitary authorities and 232 out of the 238 shire district councils. In Scotland all 32 local councils had elections coincident with the second cycle of Scottish Parliament contests (see Section 4). In 144 authorities in England the elections followed extensive ward boundary changes.

A summary of the different types of local authority in Britain and a guide to election cycles is as follows.

England

1. *Counties* (34)

   All members are elected every four years. Elections were held in 2001 (on the same day as the general election) and the next round of elections is due in 2005.

2. *Metropolitan Boroughs* (36)

   One third of members are elected annually except in those years when there are county elections. Next elections are due in 2004.

3. *Shire Districts with 'annual' elections* (88*)

   Approximately one third of members are elected annually except in those years when there are county elections. Next elections are due in 2004. *Six authorities did not have elections in 2003 but will, instead, elect half their council in 2004.

4. *Shire Districts with 'all in' elections* (150)

   All members are elected every four years mid-way between county elections. There were elections in 2003 and the next round will be in 2007.

5. *London Boroughs* (32)

   All members are elected in a four-year cycle. Next elections are due in 2006.

6. *Unitary Authorities* (46)

   The election cycle varies across authorities.

7. *Greater London Authority*

   A Mayor and Assembly were elected for the first time in May 2000. Next elections are due in 2004.

Scotland

Unitary Councils (32)

   All members were elected in 2003 (on the same day as the Scottish Parliament elections). The next round will be in 2007.

Wales

Unitary Authorities (22)

All members were elected in 1999 (on the same day as the Welsh National Assembly elections). The next round of elections was put back to 2004 to avoid clashing with the 2003 Assembly contests.

Colin Rallings and Michael Thrasher have supplied the data presented in the following tables. Full details of the 2003 results, including individual ward results and commentary, can be found in their *Local Elections Handbook 2003* (Local Government Chronicle Elections Centre, University of Plymouth), obtainable from LGC Communications, Greater London House, Hampstead Road, London NW1 7EJ.

TABLE 5.1   *Local Election Results 2003*

	Candidates	Seats won	Gains/ Losses	Share of vote
Metropolitan Boroughs (36)				
Turnout 32.1				
Con	785	160	+44	26.0
Lab	833	458	−74	39.9
Lib Dem	701	193	+21	24.7
Other	600	25	+9	9.4
Unitary Authorities (40)				
Turnout 34.6				
Con	1,463	527	−	32.5
Lab	1,303	501	−	27.8
Lib Dem	1,318	488	−	28.0
Other	752	109	−	11.7
Shire Districts (232)				
Turnout 34.3				
Con	6,446	3,607	−	39.4
Lab	4,698	1,526	−	20.7
Lib Dem	4,582	1,796	−	26.0
Other	2,833	1,037	−	13.9
Scottish Councils (32)				
Turnout 49.2				
Con	798	123	+15	15.1
Lab	920	509	−40	32.6
Lib Dem	675	175	+22	14.5
SNP	969	181	−23	24.1
Other	707	234	+26	13.6

Note: Boundary changes can make precise calculations for gains and losses impossible.

TABLE 5.2   *Summary of 2003 Local Election Results (all authorities)*

	Candidates	Seats won	Gains/ Losses	Share of vote
Turnout 35.5				
Con	9,492	4,417	+660	31.5
Lab	7,754	2,994	−880	27.9
Lib Dem	7,276	2,652	+170	24.2
SNP	969	181	−23	3.8
Other	4,893	1,405	+50	12.6

Note: The figures for gains and losses are estimates since boundary changes make precise calculations impossible.

TABLE 5.3   *Quarterly Party Vote Shares in Local Government By-elections 2003 (%)*

	Con	Lab	Lib Dem	Others	Number of wards
Q1	35.0	23.7	35.8	5.5	16
Q2	32.3	28.3	26.0	13.4	28
Q3	30.3	25.2	30.5	14.0	34
Q4	28.4	30.2	29.0	12.4	38

Note: These figures relate to the results of local government by-elections in wards and electoral divisions contested by all three major parties. We have not calculated monthly figures for 2003 owing to the scarcity of three-party by-elections (N=116).

TABLE 5.4   *Seats Won and Lost in Local Government By-elections 2003*

	Con	Lab	Lib Dem	Others
Held	47	32	27	11
Lost	16	23	8	8
Gained	16	7	24	8
Net	−	−16	+16	−